THE
HARBOUR
ISLAND
STORY

Anne & Jim Lawlor

MACMILLAN
CARIBBEAN

Macmillan Education
Between Towns Road, Oxford, OX4 3PP
A division of Macmillan Publishers Limited
Companies and representatives throughout the world

www.macmillan-caribbean.com

ISBN 978-0-333-97051-5

Text © Anne and Jim Lawlor 2008
Design and illustration © Macmillan Publishers Limited 2008

All rights reserved; no part of this publication may be reproduced, stored in a retrieval system, transmitted in any form or by any means, electronic, mechanical, photocopying, recording, or otherwise, without the prior written permission of the publishers.

Design by Mike Brain Graphic Design
Typeset by EXPO Holdings
Cover design by Gary Fielder, Conka

Acknowledgements

The authors and publishers would like to thank the following for permission to reproduce the following photographic material:

Author's own collection, Plates 2, 3, 4, 5, 6, 7, 10, 24, 25, 28, 30, 50, 53, 55, 63, 64, 72, 76, 81, 91; Lester Albury Collection, Plates 36, 41, 42, 43, 44, 45, 46, 47; Paul Albury Collection, Plates 9, 12, 14, 15, 23, 35, 37, 38, 39, 40, 48, 49, 51, 52, 54, 60, 61, 62, 65, 66, 71, 74, 75, 77, 78, 79, 80, 82, 83, 84, 86, 87, 89; Laura Bartenfelder, Valentine's Dive Center, Plates 85, 88, 90, 92, 93, 94, 95;Benjamin, Plate 32; Boston Public Library, Plate 11; Douglas Botting, Plates 16, 17, 18, 19, 20, 21; Department of Archives, Plates 22, 27; William Johnson, Plate 31; David R. MacGregor, Plate 29; Dick Malcolm, Plate 1; Father Irwin Mcsweeney, Plate 56; De Pol/Munro Dreher Lithographs, Plates 8, 34, 67; Public Records Office, London, Plate 13; Harvey Roberts, Plate 59; John Saunders, Plate 33; Peter Strombom, Plates 57, 58; Ivan Ray Tannehill, Plates 68, 70.

Cover: Tripp Harrison Inc. www.trippharrison.com

The publishers have made every effort to trace the copyright holders, but if they have inadvertently overlooked any, they will be pleased to make the necessary arrangements at the first opportunity.

Printed and bound in Malaysia

2012 2011 2010 2009 2008
10 9 8 7 6 5 4 3 2 1

In memory of our father
Paul Albury,
Whose passion for history
lives on in this book

Contents

Acknowledgements vi
List of illustrations vii
List of tables x
Foreword xii

1 The island of the harbour 1
2 The Eleutheran Adventurers found a colony at Segatoo 9
3 Early days 24
4 'Get you on board you dog or I will mix your soul!' 42
5 Brilanders sail to victory 55
6 Dunmore's favourite retreat 69
7 A near run thing 82
8 Slavery to freedom 92
9 The halcyon days 109
10 The ring of the shipwright's hammer 132
11 'Wrack ashore' 154
12 Cast in the foundry 179
13 The fury of nature 203
14 Briland ways 227
15 The enchantment of Harbour Island 248

Appendix 1 An account of the population of the Bahamas in the early years 273
Appendix 2 Harbour Island inhabitants in the 1720s 274
Appendix 3 List of Harbour Island inhabitants in 1731 and 1734 278
Appendix 4 Pirates pardoned by Capt. Vincent Pearce 1717 281
Appendix 5 Harbour Island inhabitants participating in Deveaux' raid 283
Appendix 6 1842 Grant of Land (Commonage) 284
Appendix 7 Early migration of the inhabitants of Harbour Islanders to neighbouring islands 286

Appendix 8	Population of Harbour Island, Eleuthere and New Providence from 1773–1900	289
Appendix 9	Slave registers 1821–1834 Selected Harbour Island slave units	291
Appendix 10	Liberated African apprentices at Harbour Island District	293
Appendix 11	Ships entering and clearing Harbour Island and Eleuthera 1855–1901	295
Appendix 12	Wrecking licence, fees and consort shares	298
Appendix 13	Harbour Island wrecking vessels and crews	300
Appendix 14	House of Assembly Representatives for Harbour Island and Eleuthera	302
Index		304

Acknowledgements

We are greatly indebted to the following for financial support: Joan Albury, Sir Geoffrey Johnstone, the late Noel Roberts, Violet Esfakis, Leandra Esfakis, Sylvia Brown, Bahamas Historical Society, Imperial Order of the Daughters of the Empire, and the Solomon Group.

We acknowledge the moral support from the College of The Bahamas in granting to Anne Lawlor a sabbatical year and a later secondment to the Research Unit. Special thanks to: former Presidents Dr. Keva Bethel and Dr. Leon Higgs; Dr. Joan Vanderpool, Denise Samuels and William Fielding in the Research Unit; Adrilla Wallace Horton and Janet Donnelly former Chairs of the Humanities Division and Dr. Earla Carey-Baines, former Chair of the School of English Studies.

We are thankful for the great help we received from: Laura Smith, staff of Department of Archives, especially Dr. Gail Saunders, Patrice Williams, David Woods and Jolton Johnson, Keith Tinker, Father Irwin McSweeney, Violet Knowles, Jan Hollis, Peter Strombom, Ros Themastopolous, Linda Huber, the late Allan Malcolm, Dick Malcolm, Geraldine Albury, Natasha Shepherd, Whittington Johnson, Howard and Joyce Johnson, Patricia and Trevor Southam, Antonia Canzoneri, Virginia Balance, Lady Anne Johnstone, the late John Saunders, Kendall Butler, Paul Aranah, Ron Lightbourne, June Maura, Danny Albury, Department of Lands and Surveys, Department of Local Government, Norman Plummer at Chesapeake Bay Maritime Museum, Maryland, The Massachusetts Historical Society, Bermuda Archives.

We are grateful to those kind enough to help us with interviews: Damien Gomez, Lilas Imlach, Sydney Albury, Reswell 'Prince' Mather, Jasiel Thompson, Robbie Albury, the late Leroy Johnson, the late John (Jack) Allen Grant, Joseph A. Saunders, the late Joseph (Joe Petty) Mather, Margaret Grant, Ronnie Roberts, the late Blanche Bethel, Atleine Higgs, Sarah Hutchinson, Mary Saunders, Wilson Roberts, Sam Barry, the late Hartman Saunders, Herman Higgs, Lonzo Major, Frank (Curly) Johnson, Norman Higgs, Joy Bishop, Kate Scrimminger, Mrs Duncombe, Gwen Walker, Florrie Major, Bert Sawyer, the late Eugene Higgs, Clement Higgs, Alfred Albury, Bonefish Joe.

We owe a great debt to our local editors: Dr. Gail Saunders (Historical) and Marjorie Downie (English) and to our Harbour Island *research consultants:* Godfrey Kelly and Reswell 'Prince' Mather.

We give great credit to those people who assisted us with photos and maps: Harvey Roberts (Methodist Church), the late Commissioner E. H. McKinney, Lester Albury, Laura Bartenfelder, Valentine's Dive Centre, Harbour Island, Jim Lawlor.

Maps
Dick Malcolm, the late John Saunders, Boston Public Library, Public Records Office, England.

List of illustrations

Fig. 1.   Cockram's Map
Fig. 2.   Harbour's Mouth
Fig. 3.   The bay is one of the most beautiful sheets of water in the Bahamas
Fig. 4.   Houses were built on the bay
Fig. 5.   Pink Sands Beach
Fig. 6.   Ridge with seagrass
Fig. 7.   Coconut groves
Fig. 8.   Pineapple schooner
Fig. 9.   Schooner *Dart*
Fig. 10. Modern yachts at sunset
Fig. 11. Chart of The Bahamas 1694 showing routes of the Spanish galleons
Fig. 12. Eleutheran Adventurers
Fig. 13. Earliest sketch map of Harbour Island 1702
Fig. 14. Map of North Eleuthera
Fig. 15. Preacher's Cave
Fig. 16. Henry Avery
Fig. 17. Pirate flag of Henry Avery
Fig. 18. Pirate flag of Thomas Tew
Fig. 19. Pirate flag of Blackbeard
Fig. 20. Pirate flag of Stede Bonnet
Fig. 21. Pirate flag of Calico Jack Rackham
Fig. 22. Andrew Deveaux
Fig. 23. Dunmore's retreat, known as 'the Residency', on the corner of Gaol Lane and Colebrook Street, was built in 1787 by Governor Dunmore. The building was demolished in 1912 and replaced in 1913 with the present administrator's residence
Fig. 24. The residency of the commissioner/administrator
Fig. 25. The boundaries of the Harbour Island commonages 1840
Fig. 26. Dunmore's Grants 1791
Fig. 27. Lord Dunmore
Fig. 28. Route of the *Midas*

Fig. 29. The schooner *Midas* en route to Bordeaux, a water colour by Philip Browne from the British sloop-of-war *Hermes* which pursued the *Midas*
Fig. 30. Map of Dunmore Town from 1836 onwards
Fig. 31. Map of fruit loading stations
Fig. 32. Bay view circa 1870
Fig. 33. John Saunders' map of the harbour, 1920
Fig. 34. Sugar mill driven by horse
Fig. 35. The *Julia Elizabeth*
Fig. 36. After many voyages to Florida, the *Louise F* ended up as a lumber carrier
Fig. 37. The *Beatrice*
Fig. 38. The *Marie J. Thompson,* the last commercial sailing ship built in Harbour Island
Fig. 39. The *Mary Beatrice*
Fig. 40. William and Lambert Albury
Fig. 41. The craftsmen admiring their handiwork
Fig. 42. Berlin and Harry Albury
Fig. 43. The *Isles of June*
Fig. 44. The *Ena K*
Fig. 45. Tent over boat building area
Fig. 46. The *Betty K*
Fig. 47. The *Lady Dundas*, whose captain, William G. Harris, had captained both previous Harbour Island mailboats, the *Dart* and the *Endion*
Fig. 48. The *Bentley*
Fig. 49. Statue of Sir George Roberts
Fig. 50. Satellite image of the Bahamas
Fig. 51. The Sir George Roberts Library
Fig. 52. The *Gary Roberts*
Fig. 53. Eastern seaboard
Fig. 54. The schooner *Galvanic*
Fig. 55. Location of selected wrecks
Fig. 56. Rev. W.K. Duncombe
Fig. 57. Sarah (Albury) Duncombe
Fig. 58. The Stromboms
Fig. 59. Methodist Church
Fig. 60. Bible Truth Hall
Fig. 61. Anglican Church
Fig. 62. High altar at St. John's Anglican Church
Fig. 63. Roman Catholic Church
Fig. 64. Haitian Church of God

List of illustrations

Fig. 65. William Christopher Barnet Johnson. His bust dominates the entrance to the House of Assembly as a testimony to the importance of religion, education, justice and good government
Fig. 66. George Cole
Fig. 67. Glass Window
Fig. 68. Chart of the track of Great Bahaman Hurricane 1866
Fig. 69. Chart of the track of 1883 Hurricane
Fig. 70. Chart of the track of the 1933 Hurricane
Fig. 71. Cotton Hole
Fig. 72. Repair of Valentine's Dock 2004
Fig. 73. The track of Hurricane Andrew
Fig. 74. Emancipation Day 1890
Fig. 75. Father Richardson's marching band
Fig. 76. *Africa's Hope*
Fig. 77. Hauling net 1939 belonging to Harry Sweeting
Fig. 78. The *Endion*
Fig. 79. Beach picnic
Fig. 80. Cricket team
Fig. 81. Regatta
Fig. 82. Races
Fig. 83. Blasting
Fig. 84. Blasting at sea
Fig. 85. Catch of the day
Fig. 86. Club and marina
Fig. 87. Capt. Howard Brady
Fig. 88. Nurse shark
Fig. 89. Picarron Cove Club
Fig. 90. Deep sea fishing
Fig. 91. *BoHengy*
Fig. 92. Pin cushion
Fig. 93. Eel teeth
Fig. 94. Diving amongst wrecks
Fig. 95. Fish

List of tables

3.1	Population 1721, 1728 and 1731	37
5.1	A comparison of Lt. Wilson's report and the Spanish report on population of settlements	59
8.1	Count by occupation of slaves owned by Harbour Islanders	94
8.2	Size of slave holdings in Harbour Island, Eleuthera and New Providence	95
8.3	Occupational distribution of slave society by age for Harbour Island and New Providence	96
8.4	A comparison of the number of slave children in Harbour Island, Eleuthera and New Providence in the years 1805, 1812 and 1834	99
9.1	Total export of pineapples for the years 1855 and 1864	115
9.2	Export of pineapples from Harbour Island to US in the 1870s	116
9.3	Schooners exporting pineapples from Harbour Island in 1887	116
9.4	Exports of fruit, excluding pineapples, from the Northern Islands 1864	120
10.1	Boats built in Harbour Island, 1796–1843 taken from Customs shipping Register 1826	134
10.2	Harbour Island ships and their builders	138
10.3	Ships built at each port in The Bahamas from 1855–1864	140
11.1	List of wrecks in the Harbour Island/Eleuthera area	156
11.2	Ex-slaves registered as Mariners in 1834	164
11.3	Vessels and men licensed for wrecking 1865–1868	166
11.4	Location of selected wrecks with Harbour Island salvors	168
11.5	Wrecking income and annual earnings in The Bahamas 1856–1872	173
11.6	Wrecked imports and salvage for the colony 1850–1903	176
12.1	Religious Affiliation in the Census of 1943 and 1953 in the N. W. Bahamas	190
12.2	Harbour Island day school: teachers and students' attendance	193
12.3	Private schools in Harbour Island	194
12.4	Enrolment at Harbour Island Methodist Elementary School	195
12.5	Enrolment at the Roman Catholic schools on Harbour Island	195

13.1	Bahamas hurricanes highlighting Harbour Island damage	204
13.2	Free coloured people drowned at the Boag in 1806 hurricane	206
13.3	Houses destroyed at Harbour Island by the 1806 hurricane	207
13.4	The Saffir/Simpson Damage-Potential scale	222
14.1	Growth of Friendly Societies/Lodges in the Harbour Island district	232
15.1	Occupations in Harbour Island adapted from the 1943 census	256
15.2	Harbour Islanders who went on the Contract to the US	258

Foreword

Dr. Gail Saunders

The late Dr. Paul Albury, local historian, would be proud of *The Harbour Island Story*. His intention was to write about his beloved 'Briland', having completed *The Story of The Bahamas* and *The Paradise Island Story* but alas it was not to be. His daughter Anne and son-in-law Jim Lawlor took up the gauntlet.

Integrating some of Dr. Paul Albury's notes, writings and his 'poetic prose', they also conducted extensive additional research among sources available in Nassau, London, Bermuda and the United States.

The result is a well documented, informative and entertaining account of the island which was once second in importance to New Providence within the Bahamian archipelago.

The Harbour Island Story, which is well illustrated, examines the founding of 'Briland', its early days, piracy and the island's part in Deveaux's daring recapture of New Providence. It also decribes Dunmore's and the Loyalists' contribution and vividly recalls privateering and the razing of Royal Island. The authors objectively describe slavery and emancipation and recount the history of a free society including the prosperous days of the 1850s, shipbuilding, wrecking and the experiences of hurricanes. The book concludes with two chapters, 'Briland ways' and 'The Enchantment of Harbour Island'.

New material from official, church, oral and private sources which give fresh insight into most areas is used. An example of this is the excellent detailed account of the laying out of Dunmore Town in 1791 by Lord Dunmore and the expansion of the town between 1836 and 1892.

The entire story is told in a free flowing style and the chapters on shipbuilding, wrecking and hurricanes are particularly enjoyable, incorporating some of Dr. Paul Albury's wonderful stories.

This book adds greatly to our knowledge of Harbour Island specifically and the Bahamas generally and is a significant addition to Bahamian historiography. It is also important as it stands among the few detailed histories of the Bahamas' Family Islands.

The Harbour Island Story is a must for Bahamians, visitors, scholars, students and the general public. In spite of many difficulties, Anne and Jim prevailed and are to be congratulated for completing the book which will serve as the standard text on 'Briland' for many years.

1

The island of the harbour

> The bay is one of the most beautiful sheets of water ever marked by the keel of a yacht, fringed by cocoa-nut groves, and protected from the surges of the ocean by the silver-flashing barrier of the bar.[1]

Harbour Island, so named for its magnificent harbour, lies across a bight on the northeast coast of Eleuthera. Stretching for three miles on a north-south axis across the opening of the bight, this limestone ridge adjoins Jacob, Man and Pierre Islands to the north, to create the 'great Harbour of Harbour Island',[2] almost landlocked except for a few channels. This vast expanse of water on the lee side of the island extends eight miles in length and is on average two miles wide. The harbour not only dominates the geography of the island but it has been inextricably intertwined with the history of the island and its people; at times the harbour has directly shaped and influenced the Harbour Island story.

One of the strengths of the settlement at Harbour Island was observed as early as 1702 in a memorial by Thomas Walker, Judge of High Admiralty Court: 'Harbour Island, on the north side of Eleutheria affords a spacious harbour, and may be made almost impregnable with half the charge as Providence.'[3] Defence and security were of paramount importance at a time when the Spanish and French were mercilessly plundering English settlements on the inhabited islands of Eleuthera and Providence. The landlocked nature of the harbour and the reef-strewn channels between the islands made entry into the harbour a risky business for vessels of any size.

A 1718 manuscript map by John Cockram, a reformed pirate who had undertaken to draft some of the islands for Woodes Rogers, illustrates the inherent difficulties of navigating these waters in the days of sail, and the resulting security that the harbour provided. The barrier reef that lines the windward shores effectively closed out all channels to the north of Harbour Island, and the only navigable entrance was at Harbour's Mouth between the southern end of Harbour Island and Whale Point on Eleuthera. Cockram points out that the breadth of this channel is but a 'musquett or small arm's shott over' and a small fort of fifteen guns, strategically placed on the

Harbour Island shore facing the channel, would mean that no vessel could enter without being sunk.[4]

The Eleutheran and Harbour Island shorelines within the harbour are indented with numerous coves, some deep enough to provide safe anchorages to local fishing and wrecking vessels, drogging and trading vessels and privateer and buccaneer ships throughout the history of the island. At the height of the island's prosperity in the mid-nineteenth century, the harbour played a central role in the lives of the people who lived on Harbour Island and planted pineapple fields on north Eleuthera. The anchorage facing the township was a haven where their vessels rode in safety during the night, and at daybreak the fleet of two hundred boats 'spread its wings to the trade winds and wafted eight hundred men and boys, black and white, to the lovely beach and coconut groves on Eleuthera, two miles away; every night they returned.'[5]

This grand harbour provided a vast expanse of water on which many a Harbour Island youngster learned the art of sailing and navigation to build on their established reputation as first-class seamen, well versed in the laws of the sea. Further, this harbour witnessed the success of the gifted Harbour Island boat builders and proudly baptized many of their finely crafted one, two, three and four-masted schooners as these were launched for the first time into the waters; and of course the wrecking sloops skillfully designed to negotiate the very waters that had bedevilled some unfortunate mariner.

Dunmore Town, the main settlement, nestles in a nook on the harbour side of the island. Among the oldest settlements in the Bahamas, it was named for a former Governor, the Earl of Dunmore (1786–1798), who had a summer residence there. Prior to this, the settlement was simply Harbour Island. Early eighteenth century manuscript maps[6] suggest that the homes were located in the township and plantation houses bordered the town limits to the north and south. The hill running through the centre of the town has created a terraced effect, the homes on the immediate waterfront being just a few feet above sea level; as the elevation increases towards the town centre, the homes lie at different levels on the slope. The early settlers built their homes on whatever land was available in the township and it was not until 1790 that the township of Harbour Island was officially laid out by Governor Dunmore and lots of land granted to the inhabitants.[7]

The harbour shoreline is very rocky and the few beaches in the coves have eroded over time. Sand banks characteristically line the coastline to the north and south ends of the island, and the most striking sand bank immediately north of Dunmore Town is backed by white, sandy, cliff-like banks, very reminiscent of the white cliffs of Dover.[8] Formerly known as Spit Sands and now Girls Bank, it was a popular bathing beach in years past, its peculiar feature being that the tide recedes about half a mile, leaving a clear stretch of unbroken white sand about three quarters of a mile deep and as far as the eye can see. Certain portions of this bank are very compact after the tide has fallen and in the good old days many a horse race was run on this sand track.[9]

In contrast, the eastern shore of the island on the Atlantic coast has been endowed with a wide beach that runs for three miles along the entire length of the island. Referred to as the north beach by locals and Pink Sands by visitors, this stretch of uninterrupted natural beauty is unmatched both in colour and texture of its sand particles – the pulverized coral gives it its distinctive pinkish hue and direct exposure to the Atlantic waves its powdery fineness. The dark brown colour of the Elson reef a quarter of a mile off shore, contrasts with the translucence of the surrounding water and its myriad hints of subtle gradations from green to blue as the depth of the water increases.

At the back of the beach, a ridge built up by sand over the years rises to a considerable elevation in places. This process is clearly evident after a hurricane, when the raging Atlantic seas hurl sand onto the slopes of the sand ridge, creating a drop of ten feet from the base of the ridge to the beach. The ridge has become covered with a coarse wild grass, lilies, bay lavender and sea oats and in recent years a number of residential homes and resorts have been ideally located on its slope.

The prevailing winds, which blow from the southeast, modify the temperature year round and the island, devoid of stagnant pools or swamps, has traditionally been celebrated for its healthy air. People ailing from some fever or infection in Nassau were always sent to Harbour Island to recover their health. A report on the state of the islands in 1722 observed ' Harbour Island is so much courted for her pure, serene and healthful air, that she is proverbially called the Phisitian. When inhabitants of other islands become sick, they go to Harbour Island and are cured within 15 or 20 days.'[10]

Dense vegetation covers the island and is most noticeable in the undeveloped areas of the island to the north and south. Much of this comprises tropical coppice, in which wild fig, tamarind, pigeon plum, sea grapes and mastic are found in abundance. The sandy soil supported the cultivation of root crops such as Indian corn, yams, potatoes and cassava roots in the early eighteenth century, and later on very fine orchards of exotic fruit, including guavas, sugar apples, sapodillas, West Indian cherries, papayas and citrus were cultivated. Most attractive of all are the coconut groves on the northern and eastern shores.

Harbour Island's geographical location in relation to other islands in the Bahamas, specifically Eleuthera, Abaco and New Providence and the North East Providence Channel, has influenced the trade and migration of its native sons and daughters from the time of the earliest settlements. While

Eleuthera is shown in maps as early as the Turin Map of 1523 under the Lucayan name of 'Ziguateo', and 'Ciguateo' on the Descellers Map of 1553,[11] one of the earliest maps to name Harbour Island is the 1720 Moll map of the West Indies. By this time the settlement of 60 families was well enough established so as not to be overlooked by the cartographers of the day. In fact, the English Pilot of 1742 uses Harbour Island as a navigational landmark when plotting a safe route from the continent of America to Providence. It suggests that after heading for the Cow and Bull on Eleuthera, 'steer north west by west for 4 leagues, and you will see an island with several small keys to the Northward, called Harbour Island, with a passage in it at the south end for small vessels, having a fine clear sandy bay, with curious green water.'[12] A later *Bahama Gazette*[13] gives the same directions for all vessels bound to New Providence from the West Indies, America or Europe but recommends this route for the summer only and points out that when abreast of Harbour Island, the Church and the houses on shore are clearly visible. So despite its diminutive one and a half square miles, Harbour Island was well known to the traders and mariners plying the Atlantic waters in the eighteenth century.

Given the proximity of Harbour Island to the mainland of North Eleuthera, it can be no surprise that the lives of the Harbour Island people have been closely linked to those of the Eleutherans, especially those in the settlements of North Eleuthera. Initially the parish of St. John's (1768) included all the settlements on the Eleutheran mainland, and the early missionaries, whose headquarters was in Harbour Island, had the arduous task of visiting all the settlements to baptize, marry and minister to the people. The introduction of St. Patrick's Parish in South Eleuthera in 1795 divided the mainland into North and South Eleuthera, and with the agricultural development of the next century, Governor's Harbour became the commercial centre of South Eleuthera and Harbour Island of North Eleuthera.

The dispensation of justice in the out islands shifted from the missionaries to special magistrates just after emancipation, and Harbour Island became the headquarters for the magistrate whose initial jurisdiction was all Eleuthera, soon after reduced to the North Eleutheran district. The settlements in this circuit included Spanish Wells, Lower Bogue, Upper Bogue, Current, Bluff, Current Island, Gregory Town and Hatchet Bay, the latter two eventually becoming a part of the Governor's Harbour district. Infrastructural needs, law and order and education were the primary concerns of the special magistrates and this was no small task at a time when the district was about to enter a period of great agricultural prosperity and expansion of trade.

The grant of the six thousand acres of commonage land on North Eleuthera to the Harbour Island men who had helped in the recapture of

Nassau from the Spaniards was a more immediate way in which the lives of the Eleutherans and Harbour Island people were intertwined. And when the Loyalist government began granting land in the 1790s, many people from Harbour Island were granted land on mainland Eleuthera, especially around the area that became Gregory Town. The lucrative pineapple industry was the main impetus for the move of a number of Harbour Island families to this area. Before roads connected the settlements on mainland Eleuthera, all pathways from the Eleutheran settlements led to the grand harbour to facilitate the transportation of produce to Harbour Island, which became a port of entry.

The increase in trade in the region had contributed to a fast-growing wrecking industry, which in the Abaco cays was monopolized by the Harbour Island wreckers. For some years, prior to Loyalist settlement, they had been attracted to the perilous waters of the Abaco coastline, which had afforded them many an opportunity to salvage. In addition, Abaco timber was a much sought after commodity for the thriving boat building industry at Harbour Island. In time a number of Harbour Island people married into Loyalist families in Abaco[14] and several families moved from Harbour Island to the Abaco Cays taking with them their superior boat building skills.

The North East Providence Channel, a forty-mile expanse of water that separates the South of Abaco from the North of Eleuthera, provides the entrance passage to New Providence. John Wentworth explained that access to New Providence from the east, west, or south was impossible due to the extensive sand banks and shallow water, navigable only by barques or shallops, and any larger vessels would have to enter New Providence from the northward ocean.[15] Harbour Island's position on the north east coast of Eleuthera and its proximity to this channel meant that Harbour Island was the first inhabited island that vessels passed on their approach to New Providence. And without a doubt, the grand harbour would have offered refuge to many a vessel in distress, whether blown off course, disabled or pursued by the enemy.

Of greater significance, Harbour Island served as a convenient transshipment point between the American colonies and New Providence. As early as 1717, American trading ships out of Boston sailed to Harbour Island to sell provisions to the resident pirates, who 'were frequently coming and going to purchase provisions for the pirate vessels at Providence'.[16] At the height of its agricultural and trading development in the 1850s, American ships which took Eleutheran oranges and pineapples to Baltimore and New York, returned to Harbour Island with cargoes of rice, grits, flour and salt beef, dry goods and ironware, much of which was transshipped to Nassau in the Harbour Island built trading vessels.

Harbour Island is a mere sixty miles to the north east of Nassau and this closeness to the capital has meant that Harbour Island's growth and development has proceeded much faster than that of the more remote family islands. Trade and communication grew in leaps and bounds in the nineteenth century as this community of planters and seamen, shipbuilders and merchants, transported their homegrown fruit and vegetables to the Nassau market. Harbour Island was the first family island to enjoy a scheduled mail boat service from Nassau in 1870, which provided the islanders with provisions, dry goods and correspondence from the capital on a regular basis, an asset not to be taken for granted when such a service has not yet been afforded some of the more southern islands in 2004! On entering the grand harbour, the two-masted mail schooner, the *Dart*, fired a small cannon on the forward deck to announce its arrival.

Infrastructural improvements were expedited by Nassau's proximity to Harbour Island, as all equipment, tools and materials required were only eight hours' sail away. The harbour of the island was made more accessible by the blasting of reef at the northern entrance and the dredging of a channel; the government dock was extended to accommodate larger boats and air travel by sea plane was introduced; the roads from Dunmore Town to Harbour's Mouth were opened and others improved; a radio telegraph station was installed; and a motorized mail boat replaced the Dart. All of these changes took place in the early 1920s and served as a catalyst to propel this small seafaring and agricultural community into a new tourism-based economy. And as such, this one and a half square mile island has become an interesting blend of the old and the new; the rebuilt church, the schoolhouse, the hauling boat and the commonage are reminders of the old world; the marinas, the yachts and the resorts are dimensions of the new world.

The language still reflects some of Harbour Island's old-world traditions; if you should ask an old fisherman where the best place for a good haul is, the answer 'up-a-long' means to the south of the harbour, near Whale Point, and 'down-a-long' means to the north of the harbour, near Jacob's or Man Island. The township itself is quaintly divided into 'up yonder', south of the Anglican Church of St. John's, and 'down yonder', north of that point. And to the initiated, the island of the harbour is better known as 'Briland', a blend of 'harbour' and 'island'.

Memories of Briland
by W.E.Albury (a native son born in 1920)

There are many things 'bout Briland,
That my boyhood days recall;
Of soldier crabs and pigeon plums,
And boys a playing ball.

Sure we played the game of cricket,
And a game of rounders too.
And the team from up past Mission Hill,
Know exactly what to do.

I remember the old shipyard,
Where they build the Ena Kay;
The Isle of June and the Dundas,
And the good old Marie J.

I recall too the Briland fleet,
In the harbour safely moored;
To ride out all the stormy months,
Sure they were all well secured.

The men would go out hauling,
And sometimes they'd take us too;
To go along for the boatride,
Or to supplement the crew.

And when the month of August came,
and the seagrape start to ripe
we'd go along with a ten quart pail,
and eat till we had the gripe.

But of all the mem'ries flowing,
From my mem'ry back of yore;
there is none that seem so vivid,
As the ones of North Side Shore.

The dunes were oh so beautiful,
and the sand so fine and pink;
we boys would ride the breakers in,
when we'd catch them on the brink.

The lilies in the valleys,
and the rushes waving fair;
in the breeze from the Atlantic,
that would rumple up your hair.

I'm going back again some day,
if the time God to me give;
to see once more those scenes of old,
and mem'ries to relive.

Notes
1. S. G. W. Benjamin, *The Atlantic Islands as Resorts of Health and Pleasure,* Harper & Brothers, New York, 1878, p. 29.
2. Cockram's Map, Calendar of State Papers 30, Colonial America, Woodes Rogers to Council of Trades and Plantations, 31 October 1718.
3. CO 5/1312 Part 1, Thomas Walker to Council of Trades and Plantations, 1702.
4. Calendar of State Papers, Colonial America, 30, Woodes Rogers to Council of Trades and Plantations, 31 October 1718.
5. S. G. W. Benjamin, *The Atlantic Islands as Resorts of Health and Pleasure,* Harper Brothers, New York, 1878, p. 29.
6. Calendar of State Papers, Colonial America, 30, Woodes Rogers to Council of Trades and Plantations, 31 October 1718 and CO 5/1312 Part 1, Thomas Walker to Council of Trades and Plantations, 1702.
7. Michael Craton & Gail Saunders, *Islanders in the Stream Vol 1,* University of Georgia Press, 1992, p. 202.
8. *Nassau Guardian*, 31 December 1890.
9. *Nassau Tribune*, 31 August 1921.
10. CSP. 33/127, Charles Carrington of New Providence to the Council of Trade and Plantations, 4 May 1722.
11. Robert A. Curry, *Bahamian Lore,* printed privately at Paris, 1928, Section Lucayan Charts, p. 17.
12. The English Pilot (4th book), London M, DCC, XL11.

13 *Bahamas Gazette*, 11 April 1789.
14 Paul Albury, *The Story of the Bahamas,* MacMillan Education Ltd. 1975, p. 250.
15 CSP, 7/916, John Wentworth to Lt. Governor Thomas Lynch of Jamaica, 23 August 1672.
16 CSP, 29/635, Captain Matthew Musson to Council of Trade and Plantations, 5 July 1717.

2

The Eleutheran Adventurers found a colony at Segatoo

The arrival of the Eleutheran Adventurers in the Bahamas in 1648 broke the human silence prevailing over the islands, since the extinction of the Lucayans. Although uninhabited for more than a century, these islands were not unknown as the waters around them provided key navigational routes for ships plying between Europe and the New World. After the discovery of the Bahama Channel by Ponce de Leon's pilot in 1513, this became the preferred route back to Europe for the Spanish galleons laden with treasure from the Spanish Main and island colonies.[1] It was also used as the return route by the English explorers Hawkins and Drake on their voyages to the West Indies in the sixteenth century. So when the race to trade with and colonize the Americas was entered into by other European nations in the seventeenth century, the Bahama Channel (otherwise known as the Straits of Florida) between the Bahamas and Florida was an established route for homeward-bound vessels.

A contemporary writer remarked that 'the English seamen are little acquainted with these islands although they sail around them yearly'.[2] By this time the English had planted several colonies along the North American Atlantic coast and the circuitous route from England to the colonies took them through the North East Providence Channel and out of the North West Providence Channel to catch the northerly current of the Bahama Channel. The westerlies that blow constantly off the American mainland made a more direct route impossible.

The difficulty of access to the islands due to the many banks, shoals and reefs surrounding them was obviously a deterrent to their exploration or settlement. The lack of mineral resources combined with the problem of access made the archipelago the subject of many unfavourable reports. In this vein De Laet, a Dutch geographer of the time, summarily disposed of the Bahama Islands with this cryptic assessment:

> To the North of Hispaniola and Cuba, between them and the Continent of Florida, lye the many small Lucaick Ilands, so neer

one another, as they make those seas very rough, heady and dangerous: besides this there is nothing worth noting in them…[3]

On the other hand the Spanish with their newly settled colonies to the west and south of the Bahamas were well acquainted with the islands and in their periaguas made frequent trips to the islands in search of sarsaparilla, sassapras, ambergris, hardwoods and dyewoods. George Gardiner, a contemporary of William Sayle, wrote: 'The Spaniards know this place (the Bahamas) well and have a yeerly trade thither… and amongst the Islands are wrecks of divers of their Ships.'[4] Their experience with reclaiming the treasures of Spanish galleons that had met with disaster on some reef in Bahamian waters would further account for their familiarity with the Bahamas before settlement.

Although there is no documented evidence, it is also believed that the English colonizers who had settled Bermuda, eight hundred miles to the north-east of the Bahamas and thirty-six years before the Eleutheran Adventurers, also had more than a passing knowledge of the Bahamian islands and their waters. Whaling and sealing were primary industries in Bermuda and it would seem likely that the seafaring Bermudians might have set their sights to the south-west, a mere five days' sail with a good wind, to explore the Bahamian and Florida coastal waters which abounded with whales, seals and turtle. They regularly visited the islands to procure salt and the occasional sighting of ambergris or wrecks would have been further enticements. Also by the 1640s Bermuda had established trade with the newly settled English colonies on the Atlantic seaboard, and on occasion ships travelling from Bermuda to Virginia or New England were driven to seek refuge in the harbours or inlets of the Bahamas in stormy weather.

So what was the final impetus for resettlement of the Bahama Islands, for so many years uninhabited, for so many years deemed unworthy and lacking in intrinsic value, for so many years perceived as the ugly duckling of new-found territories in the Americas and the Caribbean?

Storm clouds of political and religious controversy, originating in the mother country, had swept across the Atlantic and hung low over the English colony of Bermuda. Puritanism had taken root in Bermuda by the 1640s and the conflict between the royalist majority, supporters of King Charles I and the Anglican Church, and the independent minority, agitators for reforms of Anglican dogma, mirrored the turmoil that had beset England for more than a century. The Bermuda government and church, aware of the schisms tearing England apart and the ensuing chaos and civil war, imposed a systematic programme of repressive measures to encourage conformity to the tenets of the Anglican Church, and Independents who refused to adhere to these tenets were imprisoned.[5]

The bitterness between the Royalist and Independent factions was heightened in 1644, when the Reverends Nathaniel White, Patrick Copeland and William Golding publicly renounced their Anglican orders and organized an Independent church.[6] Thereafter, increased harassment of the Independent Puritans by the Bermuda Government and Church led them to consider leaving the colony. Such was their determination to hold services and preach the gospel as they saw fit, completely free of the forms and tenets of the established church, that the choice of exile over conformity was an easy one.

The Independents were fortunate to have captured the attention of a very influential Bermudian, Captain William Sayle, a former governor and sheriff of the Colony. Sayle was not active in the Puritan movement but his wife had been charged with 'absentinge herselfe from frequenting the ordinances of God'[7] and Sayle was sympathetic to the cause. Since he was in disfavour with the government at the time, he welcomed the chance to throw in his lot with the zealous puritans and lead them to a new land where they would be free to worship as they wished. And the puritans could not have enlisted a more eminently suitable person to lay the groundwork and prepare for their voyage of exile, as Sayle was a natural leader, an experienced trader and an expert navigator.

The intended destination of the Puritan pioneers was first mentioned in a letter from William Reyner to Governor Winthrop of Massachussetts (January 1646):

> Sir we have distrusted what nowe, wherwithe the Lorde hath tried us, have sent two shippes unto the Bohamahs Ilands neare Floridah, to discover some considerable Iland for us to settle upon; hopeinge there to enioye Christe, in the puritye of his ordinances, without this Bermudian Imbitterment.[8]

In this letter Reyner mentioned that two ships had been sent to the Bahamas in the previous year to search for an island that would be suitable for their religious sanctuary. Unfortunately the first had never returned and was presumed shipwrecked, and the second reported that no such island could be found. Reyner also informed Winthrop of a ship that he and Sayle had a half share in a shallop of six tons specially built for the voyage to the Bahamas. And further, 'we have procured a pattent from Parlement, to settle on any of those Ilands, or other in America with such previledges, Immunityes, as hitherto have not bene graunted',[9] a claim that cannot be true since it was not until 1647 that the energetic and enterprising Sayle arrived in London to negotiate on behalf of the Bermudian Puritans.

Sayle could not have chosen a better time to launch his enterprise, as the Puritan-dominated army had confined Charles I, gained control of

Parliament and overcome the Church.[10] Religious freedom was the rally cry throughout England and Sayle had little difficulty gaining financial backing and parliamentary approval for the adventure to the island of freedom.

The Company of Adventurers for the Plantation of the Islands of Eleutheria was formed and comprised mainly merchants and prominent figures in Cromwellian England. While they were staunch puritans, their primary interest was financial gain; of the twenty-six principals, Sayle would be the only Adventurer to go to Eleutheria.

The articles and orders of the Company, drawn up on 9 July 1647, were remarkable for their vision of governance accorded the first English colony in The Bahamas. In one bold stroke of the pen, the Adventurers declared freedom in the three great arenas of human affairs: religion, economics and government. In the matter of religion the articles ordered:

> Whereas experience hath shewed us the great inconveniences that have happened, both in this Kingdom of England and in other places, by a rigid imposing upon all an uniformity and conformity in matters of judgement and practice in the things of Religion, whereby divisions have been made, factions fomented, persecutions induced, and the public peace endangered… It is therefore ordered… That there shall be no names of distinction or reproach, as Independents, Antinomian, Anabaptist, or any other cast upon any such for their difference in judgment, … under the penalty of being accompted… as enemies of the publik peace…[11]

In the matter of economics, a subscription of 100 pounds would be collected from each of the original adventurers, who upon settlement would work the land in common for the first three years, and thereafter be given 300 acres in the settlement and an additional 2,000 acres without. Money from the sale of wrecked goods or ambergris was to be divided between the finder, the public treasury and the original adventurers. The article on government was perhaps the boldest of all in its prescription of a self-governing republic, the first in the New World, comprised of a governor, a governor's council and a senate. The senate had absolute power to appoint justices, distribute public lands, pass laws and manage the public finances. Egbert Smith[12] comments that the Articles and Orders of the Eleutheran Adventurers is one of the most remarkable in the history of democracy as it embodies principles which reflect great idealism and foresight and captures the character of the men who dreamed of freedom in the brave new world in America.

The issue of a patent for the islands was not so clear. There is no doubt that the English Parliament of 1647 would have welcomed the proposed voyage of exile to the Bahamas by the puritans. Perhaps the political chaos prevailing in England at the time explains why the bill of incorporation was not debated and approved in the House of Commons until 1649,[13] two years after Sayle's visit. However no published act or charter for the Puritan colony has ever come to light, despite the reference to a patent by John Bolles and George Gardner.[14] Sayle had left the business of documentation to the Eleutheran Adventurers (merchants in London), some of whom were key figures in the newly established Cromwellian government and he returned to Bermuda on a ship provided by the merchants for the venture, with a few English recruits, some ammunition and other materials required for planting the new colony.

In the spring of 1648 the *William* and a shallop with seventy settlers on board set sail on a south-west course for their land of freedom, newly named Eleutheria (the Greek word for freedom) in the articles and formerly called 'Lucayos' or 'Buhama'. The story of the actual voyage has been handed down to us in the journal of Governor Winthrop of Massachusetts, which appears to be the only existing contemporary account.[15]

The voyage seemed ill-fated from the start. In a cruel twist of irony, matters of religion divided the group in the early days of the voyage. A young man by the name of Captain Butler, who had boarded the ship in England, refused to participate in the puritan services, scorning all forms of worship and invoking the freedom spelt out in the articles. His view was that freedom of religion gave him the right to reject outright all worship but this perspective did not sit well with the zealous puritans from Bermuda. Since freedom of worship was no longer an issue in England, it is likely that the other Englishmen on board supported Butler's position, and by the time the islands of Eleutheria were sighted it was no secret that the pioneering adventurers were divided in two factions deeply entrenched in opposing points of view.

After landing at one of the islands where they intended to settle, Sayle felt that the disharmony created by the two factions did not bode well for the future of the new settlement, so he left Butler and his associates at this site and set sail for another island. As they were about to enter the harbour of the island where they planned to establish the new puritan colony, their ship was wrecked on a reef. They suffered only one loss of life but all their provisions and goods were lost. And so these stout-hearted puritan adventurers, who had given up the security of their Bermuda homeland for their religious convictions, began life anew on this island under extremely hard conditions.

In the absence of Sayle's log book, presumably lost in the shipwreck, a number of pertinent questions arise. What was the course he sailed from Bermuda? Which was the first island sighted? At which island did he leave

Captain Butler and the others? Which island was he heading for when the ship was wrecked? And where did the shipwreck occur? These questions can never be answered conclusively unless some new evidence is uncovered maybe in some heretofore unexamined private collection.

Since the prevailing winds were out of the northeast at the time of year that the *William* departed Bermuda, a steady southwest course was probably easy to hold and the first islands sighted, given the northeast to southwest axis of the archipelago, would have been Abaco or Eleuthera. In order to avoid the fringe reefs and shoals on the windward side of the islands, Sayle's navigational expertise undoubtedly led him on a course through the Northeast New Providence Channel between Abaco and Eleuthera.

The suggestions for the first landfall where Butler and company were left include New Providence, Abaco, Governor's Harbour and Harbour Island. Hallowed tradition supports Governor's Harbour, but access to this mid point on the western coast of Eleuthera would have involved a rather circuitous route through the Providence Channel, turning south off the west of Egg Island and entering the bight of Eleuthera just south of Current Island. Such a lengthy interval between the first sighting of land and the first landfall is somewhat suspect after the five to ten day voyage from Bermuda. Harbour Island is more and more discounted as historical evidence lends support to the idea that it was this island's harbour that Sayle was attempting when the ship was wrecked. New Providence and Abaco are both possibilities given their location, surrounding waters, winds and currents.

John Darrell's description of the islands in 1670 offers yet another possibility, if indeed the Butler group did survive.

> Eleutheria lyeth in 25 and 25 and is the first land that is commonly made before they go to any other… Harbour Island lyeth in a bite of Eleutheria… *and at the east end of Eleutheria is a small island and amongst these three islands and about them is the most and best ambergrease found. There is about 10 families of Bermudians on them…*[16]

Since, unlike the Abacos, there is only one island on the eastern shore of Eleuthera, the island referred to must be what used to be called Savannah Island, now Windermere Island, and its location on the eastern shore of Eleuthera makes it a very logical candidate for the first landfall given the point of departure of the *William* and the second landfall. Early cartographers found it difficult to compensate for the earth's curvature and hence their maps showed the Bahamas lying more east to west than southeast to northwest as shown on the late seventeenth century map where 'Windermere Island' appears on the east end of Eleuthera.[17]

The site of the shipwreck and the first Puritan settlement is less open to conjecture and although Spanish Wells and Gallows Bay on the north Eleutheran coast have both been identified by historians as the location of Sayle's puritan colony, there is increasing historical and archaeological evidence to support the latter.

In a limestone escarpment adjacent to Gallows Bay is located Preacher's Cave. The cave is large and airy with an entrance facing the north and a lofty ceiling with openings through which shafts of sunlight illuminate the interior. At the western end a huge boulder stands with man-made steps hewn out of the solid rock that lead to a flattened area near the top. The late historian Paul Albury remarked, 'It looked for all the world, like a crude pulpit and I was convinced that this, indeed, was the cave where the Puritans had worshipped.'[18]

Although Winthrop's account made no mention of the cave, Richard Richardson, a Bermudian who had visited 'Elethea' in 1657 on a wrecking expedition reported that after quarrelling with some of his associates, he left Sayle's house at Governor's Bay where he was staying 'and went to live in the cave [at Cave Bay] where they did formerly go to service'.[19]

The use of a cave for council or senate meetings was suggested by the testimony of two Eleutheran Adventurers before the Bermuda Council in 1665 when Nathaniel Sayle's claim of a commission from his father William Sayle to govern the pioneer settlement was under investigation:

> William Barnet, sworne, saith, that when hee and Mr. Natha: Sayle were together at Eleutheria, the said Sayle did read a Commission there in the cave concerning the Governing of the people, the which had a brave seal unto it, but whither it came from his Majestie, or the State, he knoweth not.
>
> Peter Sands sworne, saith that hee and Mr. Nathaniell Sayle were at Elutheria together. And there was a paper that hade a Seale at it, the which was published in the Cave, but what was the contents of it he knoweth not.[20]

Given the number of inland caves that exist on Eleutheria, these references alone do not confirm the site. In an 1840 map of the north Eleutheran coast, Paul Albury discovered a small cove to the east of Gallows Bay and behind Hawk's Point called Governor's Bay, most likely in honour of William Sayle, the first governor of the new colony. Governor's Bay was listed as one of the twelve settlements on Eleuthera as late as 1776, but at this time the population was a mere eight people.[21]

The location of the Devil's Backbone, a treacherous run of reef, just fifty yards off the shoreline at Gallows Bay, in conjunction with Preacher's Cave and the now extinct Governor's Bay settlement led Paul Albury to a reconstruction of the route taken by William Sayle in his attempt to enter the harbour at Harbour Island. He suggested that Sayle headed for the break in the reef off Breachy Point and then east into the channel between the reef and the shoreline. The channel between the Devil's Backbone and Gallows Bay is very narrow and with a running sea has always been notoriously difficult to navigate; it was at this point that the *William* struck. And thus, purely by accident, the second landfall was at Governor's Bay.

An archaeological survey of Preacher's Cave also contributed significant support to the historical records. The artifact and feature assemblages from the cave proved both prehistoric and historic activities at the site. The size of the boreholes of pipe stems unearthed in the cave dated historic activities at 1620 to 1680. Two-thirds of the sherd collection was identified as seventeenth century ware. The analysis of human remains exhumed from graves in the cave further confirmed seventeenth century occupation or use of the cave. Outside the cave the large number of pipe stems around fire pits supported its use as a meeting place. Generally the analysis of historical artifacts suggested use of the cave for religious and governmental purposes between the years 1650 to 1700, which was corroborated by the absence of domestic and post seventeenth century artifacts.[22]

In any event it is clear that the Eleutheran Adventurers' first settlement at Governor's Bay was fraught with problems of survival from the start and for the next decade they continued on the margin of existence. Winthrop described their dire straits after the shipwreck, '… they were forced (for divers months) to lie in the open air, and to feed upon such fruits and wild creatures as the island afforded.'[23] They had won their long sought after freedom of worship away from the persecution of the Bermudian Royalists, but they lacked the basic necessities of life. Their noble ambitions with respect to government were superseded by their immediate hardships. How lofty an ideal must have seemed the articles and orders in their struggle to stay alive, how far removed from the reality of their existence.

The execution of Charles I followed by parliament's declaration of England as a commonwealth created a resurgence of royal sentiment in Bermuda in 1649. The Bermudian Royalists rose up in arms acknowledging Charles II as king and threatened imprisonment to anyone who refused to take the oath of allegiance to the king and conform to the laws of church and state. This led to the banishment of Reverend Nathaniel White and his Independent congregation to Sayle's Puritan colony at Governor's Bay.

The arrival of this second group of seventy puritans in Eleuthera, while injecting moral support into the fledgling colony, most likely added to the hardships by straining the already meagre resources. The Bermuda company in London was advised, '...letters from thence (Eleutheria) certifie that the little island they are upon, is a most barren rock, shallow earth, not hopeful to produce food for the inhabitants...'[24] Yet so strong was their faith that they expressed their gratitude to the Lord for 'gathering ourselves together a people indivisable... providing a table for us in the wilderness'.[25] It is clear that in those early years the colony never flourished and the plight of the puritans at Governor's Bay evoked considerable sympathy and goodwill from the neighbouring colonies and England; their moral and material support contributed to the survival of the puritan colony.

In the summer of 1648, Sayle, with eight of the Eleutheran Adventurers, was forced to set off in the shallop to seek help when 'their strength began to fail for lack of food and from exposure'.[26] After nine days' sail they arrived in Virginia where the puritan sympathizers generously provided them with a barque and provisions for the relief of the settlers. When the New England puritans heard about the plight of the colony, a sum of £800 was collected from the churches and was used to purchase provisions and other necessities.[27] The arrival of the ship from Boston with the cargo of much needed supplies in June, 1650, was most timely and no doubt relieved their hardships for a while.

To express their gratitude, the Eleutheran settlers sent ten tons of braziletto to Boston, the proceeds of which went to the initial endowment of Harvard University. Accompanying the gift was a letter of gratitude signed by William Sayle, Robert Ridley and Nathaniel White, the only remaining contemporary document to provide insight into the piety and deep religious faith of our founding fathers. The letter is replete with Biblical references and closes with the affirmation '...that we may express how sensible we are of God's love and tender care of us manifested in yours; and avoid that foul sin of ingratitude so abhorred of God, so hateful to all men.'[28]

President Dunster of Harvard remarked, 'And when the Colony could not relieve us, God hath sent supplies even from poor Cyguotea to enlarge our room.'[29] Remarkable indeed that the donation from a company of exiled and hungry puritans on the island of Eleutheria should make possible the most substantive addition to the college buildings since its inception.

As late as 1656, Cromwell's Council informed the Commander-in-Chief of the English navy in Jamaica 'that about 60 protestant English having been driven from their residence in the Sommers Islands through the violent prosecution of some ill-affected persons there, have gone to Eleutheria, where they have suffered much hardship; he is requested to send a vessel thither to invite them to Jamaica'. Whether or not the invitation to the settlers was made and whether or not any Eleutheran puritans went to Jamaica has not been recorded.

Bermuda provided a regular source of relief. Bermuda's shipping records 1656–1671 listed an average of three vessels per year sailing the Bermuda–Eleuthera route, sometimes heading to the Caribbean first; after 1667, Providence became the Bahamas destination. There were many small vessels like the *Thomas & Marie*, which was fitted out in Bermuda by Edward Atwood in 1663 and sailed to Nevis and then on to Eleuthera with necessary goods and provisions for the settlers sent by their families and friends in Bermuda.[30]

The population of the colony fluctuated and changed composition as many of the original settlers and leaders returned to Bermuda or started life anew in the American colonies, and others banished from Bermuda joined the colony. Much of the migration between Bermuda and Eleuthera was propelled as much by politics in Bermuda as by family and trade connections between the two islands. The largest exodus took place in 1650 when two ships from Sagatea arrived in St. George's Harbour (Bermuda) with 70 people (men, women and children) who 'desired to be received to their former beings and relations, promising obedience to the present government.'[31] The Bermuda Company advised the governor of Bermuda that they had written to Rev. Nathaniel White and other Bahamian settlers inviting 'as many of them as are willing' to Bermuda.[32] By mid-1652, the Puritan party was completely in the ascendant in Bermuda,[33] and all puritans in exile were welcomed back to their former homeland. In 1656, Nathaniel White departed and a year later William Sayle with his family and thirteen passengers returned to Bermuda in the *John*.

Bermuda had started the practice of banishing its socially compromised and criminally minded to the island of Eleuthera; women like Neptuna Downham were banished for committing adultery and Bermudian slaves for conspiring against the English government in 1656. As one of the principals in the 1656 slave uprising, William Force, was a free black, the Bermudian government imposed harsher restrictions on all free men of colour and a proclamation 'that the negroes that are free men and woemen shal be banished from these islands' was issued by the governor. The free blacks 'besought the governor that they might be banished to that island Segatoo rather than the Indies',[34] probably because their free status would be acknowledged in the puritan colony of Eleuthera but not so in the West Indies or the American colonies. The number of free blacks that were banished is difficult to know since blacks, free and enslaved, were excluded from seventeenth century censuses in the British colonies.

While Bermuda never succeeded in expelling all its free black population, the historical significance of this attempt for the Bahamas is that the majority of the early black settlers in Eleuthera were free; this was in sharp contrast to their enslaved status in other colonies at the time. Although William Sayle and other Bermudian merchants and planters owned slaves, the puritan ethic respected and recognized free blacks. One of the articles of the Eleutheran Adventurers guaranteed twenty-five acres of land to all servants upon completing their time of service.[35]

Increasing Spanish raids on Bahamian settlements was another problem that the early settlers had to contend with, and after a 1684 incursion on Eleuthera, a group of nine families took flight to Boston 'having been spoiled by the Spaniards of all they possessed and driven off naked and destitute'.[36] It is interesting to note that they settled in the township of North Yarmouth on Casco Bay, a New England settlement where Puritan sentiment was strong.

The departure of so many of the original adventurers, including the leaders of the expedition, tends to suggest that the struggling colonists at Governor's Bay submitted to the innumerable obstacles and surrendered their noble quest. However, the settlement continued and those remaining managed to eke out an existence, however poor, in the export of seal oil, salt, braziletto, ambergris and salvaged cargo in return for much needed food and farm supplies.

Sayle's return to Bermuda did not signal his abandonment of the colony as he had appointed his son Nathaniel to assume the Governorship and in London had negotiated financial backing for a trading voyage that would benefit the Eleutheran settlers. In 1658, the *William*, Master Thomas Sayle, was commissioned to make a voyage from London to Bermuda and proceed to Eleuthera and the Cariba Islands. The expedition was instructed to collect braziletto, seal oil, ambergris and wrecked goods in the Bahamas and then proceed to Barbados or the Leeward Islands to dispose of its cargo. Rum and sugar from these islands were to be shipped to London while the *William* plied a trade between the Cariba Islands, Eleuthera and the West Indies.[37] The *William's* engagement in this trading route assured the settlers at Governor's Bay of much needed supplies and provided an outlet for any goods they might want to trade.

These early colonists were natural seamen like their Bermudian kinsmen and while turtling, fishing and wrecking over time provided substantive sources of food and trade, they planted just enough corn, potatoes and yacca (cassava) to supply their own needs. Tobacco, needed as legal tender, was the only commodity cultivated on a large enough scale for export and during the 1660s it was being shipped to Bermuda and then on to England. Some tobacco traders in Bermuda had been found mixing the Bahamian-grown tobacco with that grown in Bermuda to avoid paying taxes and in 1670, the Bermuda court ordered 'that all tobaccoes of the growth of Eleuthera, New Providence or any other of the Bahama Islands… whatsoever shall be subject to all laws and orders made.'[38]

While the names of the founding families who persisted and stayed on at Governor's Bay are difficult to retrieve due to the scant records, the names of the leaders who departed are mostly known, a number of geographical features on the North Eleuthera coast having been named for some of them. Ridley's Head, a rocky promontory at the west end of North Eleuthera is named for Robert Ridley, the lay preacher in the group; Hawkes' Point, forming Governor's Bay, is named for Richard Hawkes, a puritan dissident; Houtt Bluff, at the eastern end of North Eleuthera, is named for Thomas Houtt, a deputy governor of the settlement appointed by Nathaniel Sayle; Jeames' man Island to the north of Harbour Island is named for a puritan dissident and wrecker, Capt. Jeames' man (a servant), and Governor's Bay, the site of the first English settlement is named for Governor William Sayle.

The names of some of the pioneer colonists who endured the hardships and remained, are found in various records, and have survived as Bahamian surnames to this day; they are Sands, Barnett, Curtis, Griffin, Davis, Alberry and Sanders. It is difficult to know for sure if these Eleutheran families arrived with the Eleutheran Adventurers or came shortly after; however, their connection with Eleuthera during the colonization period is certain, and to this extent they were founding families.

The spread of settlements from Governor's Bay or the later independent establishment of settlements on the mainland and the offshore cays is not easy to determine, as official records are non-existent for the colonization period, and the records of the proprietary government are entered under Eleuthera and not by settlement. It is not until the missionaries from the Society of Propagation of the Gospel are assigned to Eleuthera in the 1760s, that the names, number and size of the settlements are known. Prior to this, early governors' reports make mention of the three inhabited islands of Eleuthera, Harbour Island and New Providence and it is likely that Eleuthera by the late 1600s included a number of settlements.

The impetus to move to other areas of Eleuthera from Governor's Bay would have been twofold: the need for a protected harbour with good access to the sea and secondly the need for a more protected settlement as the Spanish raids increased in frequency. It should also be kept in mind that Governor's Bay was an accidental landfall and not the intended destination of the Eleutheran Adventurers. The exposed coast of north Eleuthera was not an ideal place for a safe anchorage and when a rage[39] was on, the sheltered Governor's Bay and other such coves could only accommodate small vessels and shallops.

Craton and Saunders suggest that for the first three decades, Governor's Bay remained an important settlement and for the colonists continued as a central point of business and worship, until razed by the Spaniards in 1685.

During these years the colonists increasingly settled the neighbouring smaller islands for security and used the mainland for woodcutting, growing provisions and running hogs. Harbour Island and Spanish Wells were founded before 1670 and by the turn of the century, there were settlers at Cupid's Cay, Current Island, the Bluff and Bogue, the latter two largely settled by the black population.[40]

While this proposed development of settlements on Eleuthera is worthy of consideration, documentation at the turn of the seventeenth century supports an unnamed settlement on the easternmost part of Eleuthera, one at Current on the mainland and one at Harbour Island. The birth of the Spanish Wells settlement on St. George's Cay remains a mystery, and is particularly tantalizing since Spanish Wells has been so frequently proposed as the site of the original settlement.

In 1710, Capt. R.N. Smith of HMS *Enterprise* reported an unnamed settlement on the easternmost part of Eleuthera of about 32 families. He sent a boat ashore and learnt that the frequent raids by the enemy particularly on this part of the island 'had forced the families to abandon their houses and retire to the woods for shelter, where they lay every night to prevent their being surprised by them, having not arms sufficient for their defense.'[41] Later development and population counts suggest that this settlement may have been Savannah Sound, possibly founded by Butler and his group in a move from Windermere Island to the mainland.

Current is the first mainland settlement named in the proceedings of the governor and council in 1725 as the place where Richard Thompson and his family were robbed and plundered by the Spanish pirate Augustin Blanco.

A memorial by Thomas Walker in 1701 describes Harbour Island as 'inhabited by the English' where 'sundry families live now thereon'. Harbour Island is mentioned a number of times for its grand harbour and potential for defence.[42] When John Graves cruised the islands in 1704, just after the Spanish plundered Providence, he reported a population of 60 on Harbour Island and 160 at Eleuthera. There is evidence that Harbour Island was settled before the 1684 raids, and most likely before the proprietary government of 1670.[43]

While 'Spanish well' is mentioned as early as 1658 in a charming account of a wrecking trip by Richard Richardson of Bermuda, it is in the context of the place where they stopped to divide their spoils from a wreck off Jeames' man island, before returning to Sayle's house where they were staying. In Richardson's words, '… And so when we came up we came at Spanish well and there we shared the money…'[44] It is also the striking absence of Spanish Wells in the first census of 1731 and the Eleuthera settlements map of 1776[45] that makes the first settlement difficult to pinpoint. It was not until 1760 that Rev. Robert Carter reported a settlement on Spanish Wells of three or four families.[46] So the theory that Spanish Wells was settled prior to 1670 is not supported in the records. If settled by the early colonists some time after Richardson's wrecking trip, some catastrophe happened; maybe it was ravaged by a hurricane or razed by the Spaniards, and not resettled until 1760.

That the hardships of the Eleutheran settlements continued long after the colonization period, is reflected in the very slow population growth of Eleuthera and Harbour Island over the next century. However, during the 1650s–1680s, England got the upper hand in the European colonial struggle to establish dominance in the region and England's new colonies in Jamaica (1655), New York (1664), New Jersey (1666), Manhatten (1667), South Carolina (1670) and Philadelphia (1682) made the English presence felt in the region. And although the Bahamian settlements and trade were still threatened by the Spanish in Cuba, Hispaniola and Florida, the growing English empire on the Atlantic seaboard of North America provided a source of protection and trade. The settlement of New Providence in 1666 by Bermudians to some extent diverted attention from the first colony in Eleuthera, as Providence became the centre of trade and government. The impact of the new capital on the Eleutheran settlements would not be felt until Royal Government was established in 1718.

Notes

1. Gillian Bain, *The Early History of the Bahama Islands to 1730*, unpublished thesis.
2. George Gardiner, *The General Description of America and the New World*, London 1651, p. 12.
3. Publications of the Colonial Society of Massachusetts Vol. XXXII, 'A Broadside Advertising Eleuthera and the Bahama Islands, London 1647', Boston 1937, p. 78.
4. Gardiner, op. cit., p. 13.
5. Paul Albury, *Story of The Bahamas,* MacMillan Education Ltd, London 1975, p. 40.
6. W. Hubert Miller, 'The Colonization of the Bahamas, 1647–1670', *The William and Mary Quarterly*, 3rd set 11 (January 1945) p. 34.
7. Major General J. H. LeFroy, 'Memorials of the Discovery and Settlement of Bermudas or Somers Isles', *The Bermuda Historical Society*, 1981, p. 632.
8. William Reyner to John Winthrop, Winthrop Papers, Vol. V, 1645–1649, *Mass. Hist. Society 1947*, p. 72.
9. Ibid. p. 73.
10. Miller, op. cit., p. 35.
11. Miller, op cit., p. 34–35.
12. Egbert T. Smith, *Travelogue of the Bahama Islands*, 1950, p. 26.
13. Michael Craton & Gail Saunders, *Islanders in the Stream Vol 1,* University of Georgia Press, 1992, p. 76.
14. Proceedings of the Massachusetts Historical Society, Second Series, Vol. 12, Boston, 1900, p. 5. Gardner, op. cit., p. 12.
15. Ibid, p. 13.
16. Egerton mss. 2395, folio 472, Darrell to Lord Ashley, 13 March 1670/71.
17. Additional MS 5415.g.15, folio 36, An Outline Chart of the Bahama Islands circa 1690. The British Library.

18 Paul Albury, 'Search for the Second Capital', *Journal of the Bahamas Historical Society*, Vol.6, No.1, 1985, p. 20.
19 J.H.Lefroy, *Memorials of the Bermudas*,Vol.II, 1981, p. 112.
20 Ibid, p. 236.
21 SPG Papers, reel 1, Rev. Moss to S.P.G., 20 April, 1777.
22 Robert Carr, Jane S.Day & Sandra Norman, '*Archaeological Investigations at Preacher's Cave, North Eleuthera, Bahamas.' Phase III*, 1993, p. 32–33.
23 James Hosmer ed., Winthrop's Journal 1630–1649, Vol. II, 1946, p. 351.
24 Miller, op.cit, p. 39.
25 A letter from White, Ridley & Sayle to Church Elders in Mass, Dunster's Notebook, 17 May 1650.
26 Miller, op.cit, p. 36.
27 Miller, op.cit., p. 39.
28 A letter from White, Ridley & Sayle to Church Elders in Mass, Dunster's Notebook, 17 May 1650.
29 S.E. Morison, '*The Eleuthera Donation*', Harvard Alumni Bulletin XXXII, 1930, p. 1067.
30 Lefroy Vol 1, op cit., p. 731.
31 LeFroy Vol II, op cit., p. 20.
32 Miller, op.cit., p. 41.
33 LeFroy Vol II, op cit., p. 26.
34 Cyril Outerbridge Packwood, *Chained to the Rock*, Island Press Limited, Bermuda, 1975, p. 175.
35 Robert A. Curry, *Bahamian Lore*, Printed privately at Paris, 1928, p. 36.
36 Sandra Riley, *Homeward Bound*, Island Research, Miami, Florida, 1983, p. 40.
37 LeFroy Vol II, op cit., p. 132.
38 LeFroy Vol II, op cit., p. 322.
39 'Rage', a Bahamian description of towering waves crashing onto the reefs on the windward shore driven by North East winds from the Atlantic.
40 Michael Craton & Gail Saunders, *Islanders in the Stream Vol 1,* University of Georgia Press, 1992, p. 79.
41 CSP 25/421i, Captain R. N. Smith to Council of Trade and Plantations, 12 October 1710.
42 CSP, 19/1042 IX, Thomas Walker to His Majesty, Received January 1702.
43 CSP, 23/277, John Graves to Council of Trade and Plantations, 19 April 1706.
44 Miller, op.cit., p. 42.
45 Michael Craton & Gail Saunders, *Islanders in the Stream Vol 1,* University of Georgia Press, 1992, p. 175.
46 SPG Papers, revised reel 1, Carter to S.P.G. 1760.

3

Early days

That Harbour Island is one of the oldest surviving English settlements in the Colony is undisputed, but the exact year that our founding fathers moved from the Eleutheran mainland to that isle across the harbour is unknown. In a 1701 memorial to His Majesty, Thomas Walker describes the natural security of the island afforded by the landlocked harbour and adds:

> (Harbour Island) is inhabited by the English who claim the liberty of living there by reason their forefathers seated it before the present Lords Proprietors had their charter from Charles ll, and sundry families live now thereon with good store of oranges, limes and pleasant fruits at their doors.[1]

Albury has suggested that once the Eleutheran Adventurers recovered from the setbacks of the shipwreck, it would be but a short while before some of them would move on to the Harbour they were intending, when the *William* struck the reef. By the early 1650s, the island of the harbour, so protected by Mother Nature, attracted a number of the Bermudian colonizers from their exposed settlement on the north Eleutheran coast.[2] And by the turn of the century, a struggling community of sixty inhabitants had conquered the adversities of planting a colony and eked out an existence, however poor, by farming, fishing and trading.

Annexed to Walker's memorial is a 1701 sketch map of Harbour Island, a historical treasure, as it is the oldest surviving map of any of the islands.[3] Remarkable for the precise knowledge it illustrates about the waters off the north-facing Eleutheran coast and in the great harbour, it details with accuracy all the shoals, sand bars and reefs that made the island inaccessible except through the Harbour's Mouth at the southern end of the island, and illustrates the difficulties of maneuvering a course around the shoals and banks within the harbour in a vessel of any size. Undoubtedly, the uninitiated depended on local pilots to lead them to the safe anchorage off the township.

Walker's location of the township of nine houses with one church-like building indicates that the nucleus of the township has remained unchanged throughout its history; the town has always been centred in the leeward nook bounded by Fort Point to the north and Roundhead or Battery Point to the south. The four larger buildings to the north and east of the town were most likely plantation buildings marking the areas that had been planted with corn, peas, yams and potato. The map stands as testimony to a small community of people, most likely from Bermuda, who were well settled on Harbour Island by 1701 and had planted the soil as a source of sustenance. The battery at the southern end of the island commanded the only entrance into the harbour and therefore provided a greater sense of protection from the enemy than other settlements in the colony enjoyed, and in this respect the continuity of this small community was less subject to the disruption of Spanish and French incursions suffered by the others.

The settlement of Providence in 1666 by Bermudians and the establishment of Proprietary Government in 1670 with Charles Town (later Nassau) as the seat of government had little effect on the relatively new settlement of Harbour Island. The trading routes that had been established early on between Bermuda and Eleuthera were extended to include the port at Providence and the dispensation of justice formerly routed through the Bermuda courts of law was now executed in Nassau. The succession of unscrupulous governors appointed by the Lords Proprietors and the constant neglect of the colony's affairs by the proprietors made it easy for the settlers in Harbour Island to ignore the new government and they lived a law unto themselves. Although the structure of the government comprised a council of twelve and an assembly of twenty freemen, no records of the biennial assembly meetings have survived and it is unlikely that Harbour Island had a voice in the government of the day.

The laws governing land grants were of no interest to the people of Harbour Island because their numbers were small and for them occupation of a plot was proof of ownership. The laws that required a licence to cut wood and to search for ambergris, wrecks or whales were disregarded by the inhabitants of Eleuthera and Harbour Island since they had been pursuing these sources of livelihood for years before the proprietors had taken charge; they felt no allegiance to this government and had no inclination to offer them any royalties. Craton and Saunders remarked on this spirit of independence: 'The original settlements on Eleuthera and the offshore cays always remained outside the legal mainstream, relatively content with a society regulated by its heads of households and by custom rather than by formal laws and courts.'[4]

The only seeming attempt by the proprietary governors to make their presence felt in Harbour Island and Eleuthera was Governor Webb's appointment of Matthew Middleton, a Red Sea man, as governor of those islands in 1702 at the time he appointed Read Elding deputy governor of the

Colony.[5] However the records do not indicate that Middleton actively took up the position and the motivation for the appointment is thus open to question.

Constant Spanish and French incursions in this period of early settlement, although not initially directed at Harbour Island, obviously discouraged new settlers and indirectly had an effect on the stability of any settlement in the colony. Some Spanish attacks were retaliatory and resulted from indiscriminate privateering commissions by the proprietary governors against Spanish vessels in times of peace or the salvaging of Spanish wrecks by Bahamian wreckers; others were acts of aggression driven by the belief that the Bahamas was rightly the possession of Spain, not England and they were often committed in times of war.

By 1719, it was recorded that the Spanish had attacked settlements in the colony thirty-four times.[6] In 1684, Juan de Larco led an expedition of two hundred men out of Havana and sacked Charles Town in Providence and then proceeded to North Eleuthera where they laid waste the Governor's Bay settlement. The impact of the attack on the Eleutheran settlement is revealed in a petition by inhabitants of Massachusetts to Governor Andros on behalf of fifty Eleutheran refugees comprising nine families who fled to the township of North Yarmouth in Massachusetts:

> … in July past, arrived at this town of Boston from Eleuthera, one of the Bahama Islands, many families having been spoiled by the Spaniards of all they possessed and driven off naked and destitute… Your petitioners… made application unto the President and Council offering that if the interjacent land might be granted unto us, who have each of us some land upon the place, that we would advance money for their support and supply and settlement on said land…Whereupon we were at the charge of removing about *nine families* of the distressed people and have been at considerable charge in furnishing them with necessaries for their supply and support this winter.[7] (Written: 6 January 1686)

The departure of nine families from Governor's Bay significantly reduced the settlement, as population counts before and after that date suggest that 20–30 families lived in both Eleuthera and Harbour Island at the time. It is also possible that other families from Governor's Bay resettled in other parts of Eleuthera, Harbour Island or New Providence after the attack. Later records show a small settlement at Governor's Bay that continued for at least another hundred years; so the departure of the nine families to Casco Bay did not signal the death of the first English settlement.

A later petition filed in Casco Bay by four members of the Eleutheran refugees reveals the dire circumstances that they had fallen into and most importantly the names of the four petitioners, being of the group of early settlers, the majority of whose names are not known:

> *Nicholas Davis, Nath. Sanders, John Alberry, and Daniell Sanders,* in behalfe of selves, families and the rest of our Company, humbly sheweth your Excellency that whereas we agreed with some gentlemen here, namely,... for the settlement of a plantation about Casco Bay, according to articles drawne upp betweene us, we have performed our part, but inasmuch as these gentlemen have not performed their obligation to us, in which they were bound to supply us that wee might carry on the plantation, we were forced to desert the plantation, because we had not food to subsist there, to our great damage and undoing – for we are now in a farr worse condition than we were before we went thither, not knowing what course to subsist, having worne out our clothes and wasted the little we had. Our humble petition to your Excellency is that we might have relief in the matter; for if we had forfeited our bonds to these gentlemen, as they have forfeited their bonds to us, the law would have been open to them.[8]

The records indicate that these displaced Bahamian inhabitants never found the relief and security that they sought in New England, and eventually returned to the Bahamas. In 1692, Nicholas Davis served as a juryman at the Bulkley trial in New Providence; John Alberry was the captain of the Harbour Island militia for many years; and Daniel Saunders was buried in Harbour Island in 1725.

With the resettlement of Providence by people from Jamaica in 1686 led by Thomas Bridges, Charles Town experienced its most stable period of growth and prosperity since settlement. Unfortunately a succession of uncouth and corrupt governors condoned and actually facilitated the activities of a growing number of pirates who used Nassau as a base and in no time outnumbered the settlers. This provided the Spanish with yet another motivation for their increasing attacks on the Bahamas. The Governor of Havana had complained many times that the inhabitants of the Bahamas, the governor included, were proven pirates, and with the start of the war between England and Spain in 1702, the Spanish plunder of New Providence in 1703 and 1704 was no surprise. Nassau and all its buildings were burnt to the ground and for all practical purposes, proprietary rule came to an abrupt end.

The majority of the 400 inhabitants that had previously lived in Nassau moved to the older settlements in Harbour Island and Eleuthera or newer ones in Exuma and Cat Island. With the demise of the seat of government, the centre of trade shifted to Eleuthera and Exuma and by 1707 Eleuthera was once again the chief place of settlement. With no government in place, the pirates gained a stronghold and Nassau became the 'undisputed centre of worldwide piracy'.[9] The Spanish and French attacks increased and were now directed at Exuma and Eleuthera, the windward settlements on the latter island being totally exposed and frequently subjected to surprise attacks on the unsuspecting inhabitants in the night. Apparently the flat-bottomed Spanish periaguas could carry as many as forty men and in twenty-four hours could be in the Eleuthera waters.

The French involvement in the war also introduced a level of barbarity to the onshore raids, as the French tortured the inhabitants to force them to reveal where their valuables were. Capt. Edward Holmes described how he was on his sloop at Harbour Island with his wife and family when his vessel was fired on and then boarded by one Capt. Martell of a French sloop. Holmes and his wife were tied to a tree in the night, and the next day they tied him to the mast of his sloop, inflicted five hundred blows with a naked cutlass and with lighted matches burnt his fingers to the bone. Having forced him to reveal the hiding place of his valuables, Martell and his crew seized all they possessed, and left Holmes, his wife and child, stripped of their clothes, on a shore some eight leagues from their habitation. Captain Martell was notorious for the cruelties he inflicted on the settlers.[10]

A deposition of Elizabeth Stroude, an inhabitant of Eleuthera, describes the heinous acts perpetrated against the women of Eleuthera and Exuma by French privateers; they were unconscionably beaten and tortured until they divulged the location of their savings; and if they could not be broken, they risked being whipped to death, like the former wife of Governor Trott.[11]

In 1709, several reports claimed that the French and Spanish were in possession of Exuma, Eleuthera and Providence. However, a visit to Eleuthera by Capt. R.N. Smith a year later revealed that there was 'never any French settlement on any of the Bahama islands, they being in possession of the English'; the French and Spanish had so persistently harassed the inhabitants and stalked the woodcutters at Eleuthera and the salt-rakers at Exuma, that these interlopers gave the impression of being proprietors.

When Capt. Smith arrived in Harbour Island, he met Thomas Walker, a former Vice-Admiralty judge in New Providence. Walker explained that he was in possession there, and had been appointed commander-in-chief by the twelve families on the island. He was confident of defending the inhabitants against attacks as he had raised a small battery where he had mounted four guns and some pattereroes.[12] Mr. Walker had been resident in Nassau prior to the Spanish attacks of 1703 and 1704, and had cruised among the islands, finally settling at Harbour Island.

A state of anarchy prevailed during the fourteen years between proprietary and royal government and governors from the neighbouring English colonies complained to the Secretary of State about the Bahamian inhabitants 'who live without face or form of Government, every man doing what's right in his own eyes'.[13] There was growing concern about the pirates obstructing trade and the French or Spanish taking possession of the colony. Certainly it was a time when the colony would not attract new settlers, except pirates, and those already there faced many challenges and hardships.

The small community of settlers at Harbour Island stood firm in their determination to overcome the adversities that beset them, and by the time that Woodes Rogers arrived as the first Royal Governor in 1718, the island boasted a population of sixty families and a militia of eighty.[14] (Appendix 1 – An Account of Population of the Bahamas in the Early Years). Presumably many of these families were formerly from New Providence and others had returned from self-imposed exile now that the crown had taken over civil and military control of the colony.

In contrast to proprietary rule, the administration of Woodes Rogers immediately set out to involve all settled islands in the government, and appointed Richard Thompson Deputy Governor of Harbour Island, and Edward Holmes Deputy Governor of Eleuthera; these men also served on the council of twelve.[15] Rogers further proposed an assembly comprised of representatives from Harbour Island, Eleuthera and New Providence which although not convened until 1729, included four native sons of the island: Seaborn Pinder, John Roberts, John Thompson Senior and John Thompson Junior.[16]

Rogers remarked in his first communication to the Secretary of State that in Harbour Island there were several good men that could be relied on in contrast to Nassau where 'most of them are poor and so addicted to idleness that they'd choose to starve than work'.[17] John Cockram, a former pirate and a resident of Harbour Island, married to Richard Thompson's daughter, became one of Rogers' right-hand men in the suppression of piracy in the region. Cockram, with his superior knowledge of the islands, also draughted maps of the islands for Rogers. Inhabitants of Harbour Island were listed as 'persons fit to supply vacancies' in the assembly: John Cockram, Richard Thompson Jr., William Thompson Sr., William Thompson Jr., John Thompson, John Alberry, Nathaniel Coverly and John Griffin.[18]

The indolence of the Nassau inhabitants versus the industry of the people at Eleuthera and Harbour Island as expressed by one of the copartners, echoed Rogers' sentiments: 'The inhabitants of Eleuthera and Harbour Island being generally industrious, have plenty of all the necessaries of life, having great stores of Indian corn, yams, potatoes and cassava roots. The old inhabitants of Providence have generally been pirates and are neither honest nor industrious, working does not agree with them...'[19] The Eleutherans and Harbour Islanders, while not living a life of luxury, had worked hard to sustain their combined populations of 110 families and establish trade connections with the neighbouring English and foreign colonies.

In the face of renewed threats by a new Spanish governor at Havana to destroy all English settlements in the Bahamas and specifically to surprise Eleuthera and Harbour Island at night, Rogers and later Phenney supported council decisions that improved defence in New Providence but were not in the best interest of the people living at Harbour Island and Eleuthera. For example, at a council meeting in 1720, called to debate whether Harbour Island and Eleuthera 'were important enough to allow people to settle', it was decided that every person able to bear arms in Harbour Island and Eleuthera should come down to New Providence and do militia duty, except ten men to take care of the families on each island, seven old persons on Harbour Island and two to three aged men on Eleuthera.[20] The order in council that no foreign vessel be allowed to go to Harbour Island and Eleuthera to trade, being a discouragement to the inhabitants and traders of Nassau, incited the fury of the Harbour Islanders, and William Thompson on their behalf wrote to council: 'I know not what the Governor and Council means by debarring us of trade without they design to drive us from these islands.'[21] Just as these settlements were about to flourish, the royal government passed laws that were highly prejudicial to their security and trade.

There was some attempt to resist and ignore the royal government. Rogers observed that although he had sent a notice of the Spanish design to Capt. Thompson in Harbour Island and commanded assistance from that island and Eleuthera, no support from either island was offered and the Spanish, true to their promise, invaded Providence. On another occasion Phenney had sent a letter to John Cockram requesting two negroes taken in the pirate sloop, and Cockram explained that he had sold them. The bearer of the letter protested that they were the king's prisoners and Richard Thompson fell into a violent passion, cursing, 'God damn you dog, who made them the King's prisoners – they are our prisoners!' at which Cockram replied, 'O yes sir I must acknowledge them the king's prisoners till condemned, but I will answer selling them, and wish I had 50 of them, I would sell them all.'[22] In a letter of apology to council Mr. Thompson explained that these words were spoken in the 'heat of drink and passion' and acknowledged his error. A sense of defiance is conveyed in Thompson and Cockram's response to Phenney's messenger, perhaps influenced as much by their dislike of government control as by their disrespect for Phenney.

By early 1724, Phenney was fed up with the independent attitude of the inhabitants of Harbour Island and Eleuthera and their unwillingness to recognize the authority of the royal government. He complained to the council that they 'lived in a Manner as if they were under no form of government, often despising the Authority of the present Magistrates and carrying on a clandestine Trade with foreign vessels without regard to officers of this port.'[23] And with the intention of coercing the Harbour Island and Eleuthera people to submit to royal control, council drew up a list of rules and orders to be adhered to by the inhabitants of Eleuthera and Harbour Island. These 'laws' empowered the chief magistrates on the islands to perform or ensure services of worship, to keep records of the inhabitants and registers of vessels and to enforce militia practice; others were trade related and required traders from these settlements to sail to Nassau for a six-month trading permit before leaving the colony; and foreign vessels had to obtain a lawful permit in Nassau to unload at Harbour Island or Eleuthera. To run for government, a candidate was required to own two hundred acres of land and to vote, fifty acres.[24] It is questionable whether all traders from Harbour Island changed their trading practices and complied with the orders; quite clearly the stop at Nassau would have been an inconvenience and would have added at least a day or two to a trading voyage. The requirement of land ownership for eligibility as a candidate or voter would be difficult for the people of Harbour Island and Eleuthera to observe as grants of land were issued only in New Providence during this period.

Sources of trade for the sparsely settled town at Harbour Island in the last quarter of the seventeenth century were derived from the fortuitous pursuits of wrecking, whaling, sealing, turtling and searching for ambergris. The bountiful braziletto across the harbour on Eleuthera would not have escaped their notice as a valuable trading commodity, perhaps the only land-derived item of trade at the time.

Harbour Island was ideally located on the windward coast of North Eleuthera for wrecking; with one hundred miles of Abaco coast line to the north and one hundred miles of Eleuthera coastline to the south, riddled with submerged reef and rock for the entire length, it is no surprise that Harbour Island eventually became a centre of the wrecking trade and the cry of 'Wreck ashore!' a most familiar and welcome alarm. As early as 1708, Oldmixon remarked with mild disapproval:

> As for wrecks, the People of Providence, Harbour Island and Eleuthera, dealt in them as it is said the good men of Sussex do: All that came ashore was Prize, and if a sailor had, by better luck than the rest, got ashore as well as his Wreck, he was not sure of getting off again as well.[25]

It is very likely that many a pioneer home in Harbour Island was furnished with the salvage from wrecks and many a boat fitted out with the same. Salvaged cargoes of rice, flour and sugar often made up for the shortage of provisions that the early inhabitants faced.

Oil from the sperm whales and monk seals was another sought-after commodity and so the hunt for these mammals was begun in Bahamian waters by Bermudians who were skilled in the art of whaling. Richard Stafford on his return to Bermuda from the Bahamas in 1668 reported: '… and there (Bahamas) have been found of this same sort of Whales dead on the Shore, with Sperma all over their Bodies'…[26]; sperma referring to spermacetti, a pearly-white, waxy solid found in the oil of the sperm whale's head and used in the manufacture of candles and later cosmetics. Darrell in 1670 reported that 'the most and best ambergrease' is found amongst the three islands of Eleuthera, Harbour Island and Windemere and that three hundred pounds of a whale cast ashore on Eleuthera had been brought to Bermuda.[27] Ambergris is an opaque, ash-coloured substance, found in the secretion of the sperm whale's intestine and used in the making of perfume. While there are many accounts of whaling voyages to the Bahamas from New England, Jamaica and Bermuda, we do not know if any Harbour Islander ever experienced the sheer delight of standing at the helm of a whaling boat and jubilantly shouting, 'Thar she blows!' on sighting a sperm whale, or even better, of looking into the beady eye of the massive mammal as he struck the first blow of the harpoon.

Because whale hunting was an expensive undertaking requiring large ships and crews, it is likely that the settlers in Harbour Island and Eleuthera rather than actively hunting whales, found whales washed ashore, which they processed for the oil, very much in demand as a fuel and lubricant for the sugar mills of Jamaica and Barbados. It is interesting that the part of Eleuthera that faces the southern end of Harbour Island and borders the Harbour's Mouth channel is called Whale Point. And it is possible that the beaches that line the Eleutheran shore, inside the harbour and behind Whale Point, were the final resting grounds of sperm whales washed ashore by the fury of the Atlantic waves driven by relentless north-eastern winds. Craton and Saunders point out that the ease of capturing the fearless monk seals resulted in their near extinction by the turn of the eighteenth century, in contrast to the difficulty of hunting the whale which ensured its continued existence as a sought-after commodity for centuries.[28]

Turtling was a more reliable means of subsistence for the Harbour Islanders in that the banks on the Eleutheran shore of the harbour were perfect breeding grounds for turtles, and catching them required but two men in a boat with a net or a harpoon. The sounds on the Eleutheran coast of the harbour were reputed for the fine green turtles and hawksbills found there; the former prized for their tasty meat and the latter for their lustrous brown shell. The Spanish from Cuba and Hispaniola had made many turtling voyages to the Bahamas long before the English settled, and turtles remained in high demand as they provided 'an invaluable source of fresh meat for long voyages and for settlements deprived of outside supplies'.[29] Early Bermudian traders recognized their value, one Capt. William James having procured 43,122 pounds of the meat for a trading voyage to Jamaica in 1658. For the early settlers at Harbour Island the turtle served as a vital commodity that could be traded for much needed provisions.

Catesby provides an interesting contemporary account on the manner of taking turtles:

> The inhabitants of the Bahama Islands by often practice are very dexterous in taking them, particularly the Green Turtle. In April they go in little boats to the coast of Cuba, and other neighbouring islands, where in the evening, especially in moonlight nights, they watch the going and returning of the turtle to and from their nests; at which time they turn them on their backs, where they leave them, and proceed on turning all they meet; for they cannot get on their feet again when once turned. Some are so large that it requires three men to turn one of them. The way by which Turtles are most commonly taken at the Bahama Islands is by striking them with a small iron peg of 2" long; this peg is put in a socket at the end of a staff 12' long. Two men usually set out for this work, in a little light boat or canoe; one to row and gently steer the boat while the other stands at the head of it with his striker. The turtle are sometimes discovered by their swimming with their head and back out of the water; but they are oftenest discovered lying at the bottom, a fathom or more deep. If the turtle perceives he is discovered, he starts up to make his escape, the men in the boat pursuing him, endeavour to keep sight of him, which they often lose, and recover again by the turtle putting his nose out of the water to breathe; thus they pursue him, one paddling or rowing, while the other stands steady with his striker; it is sometimes half an hour before he is tired; then he sinks at once to the bottom, which gives them an opportunity of striking him, which is by piercing the shell of the turtle through with the iron peg, which flips out of the socket, but is fastened by a string to the pole. If he is spent and tired by being long pursued, he tamely submits when struck to be taken into the boat or hauled ashore. There are men, who by diving, will get on their backs, and by pressing down their hind part and raising the

forepart of them by force, bring them to the top of the water, while another slips a noose about their necks.[30]

By 1718, the settlement of Harbour Island had grown to sixty families. Using Walker's map as an index of comparison, Cockram's map shows a township that has spread north, south and east, but is still centred in the leeward nook with more buildings on the outskirts of the town. To sustain the increased population, the produce planted not only included the root crops, oranges and lemons of early settlement, but also figs, pomegranates, cotton, indigo and tobacco. These products as well as sugar cane were also produced on plantations on the Eleuthera coast, two miles across the harbour, an attempt on the part of the settlers to move from subsistence farming to farming produce for trade.

At this time, the people of Harbour Island also journeyed to the sounds on the Eleuthera coast, called Little Harbour Island on the Cockram map, to cut timber for building houses and vessels and also for trade. A contemporary visitor to Harbour Island described it as 'very pleasant and fruitful' and observed that most of the families had plantations on Eleuthera which abound in a great variety of timber trees.[31] The industry of the Eleutheran and Harbour Island inhabitants is reflected in Woodes Rogers' 1731 report that these two islands had more acres planted than New Providence, despite the larger population of the latter.

While boat building started as early as 1718 in Nassau, it was not until 1724 and 1725 that two sloops, the *Charlotte* (25 tons) and the *Sarah of New Providence* (18 tons) were built in Eleuthera. Unfortunately it is difficult to extract from the records when the first sloop was built at Harbour Island since 'Bahama' is often indicated as the place where built. However the 30-ton sloop *Richard and John of New Providence*, owned and captained by John Cockram and Richard Thompson and built in Bahama in 1722, and the *Martha of Harbour Island* (7 tons) owned and captained by prominent Harbour Island merchant, James Roberts, and built in Bahama in 1725, were very likely built in Harbour Island. What is interesting is the predominance of Harbour Island inhabitants listed as owners or captains of the Bahamian-built vessels clearing in and out of Nassau in the 1720s: Richard Thompson, John Cockram, Joseph Pearce, James Roberts, George Dorsett, Thomas Cox, John Thompson, Nathaniel Coverley and Thomas Petty.[32]

Generally these trading vessels took turtle and fruit to Carolina and returned with provisions including rice, beef, pork, corn, flour and bread, and hardware such as pitch, tar and shingles. The vessels that traded in Jamaica and Barbados took oil and salt, and returned with rum, sugar and molasses, the Bahamian crew often finding employment in harvesting sugar in Jamaica, and buying Jamaican produce with the money earned. John

Cockram made long trading voyages on which he sailed first to the seaboard colonies in America and procured provisions including European goods, and then sailed on to Barbados to sell or trade them.[33] Governor Pulleine of Bermuda in 1714 had reported to the Council of Trade and Plantations that Cockram, married to the daughter of Richard Thompson, one of the richest inhabitants of Harbour Island, sailed in a sloop between the Bahamas and Curacao laden with brasiletto; Pulleine disapproved because the trade was illegal as the Queen received no duties on the exported brasiletto.[34] However, prior to Royal Government, it is unlikely that duties were collected for imports or exports, given the chaotic state of the country, and all traders subscribed to free trade principles; Cockram was no exception.

Harbour Island's state of defence in 1718 was better than ever before, for there were two small forts, one of eight six-pounders and the other of four nine-pounders, commanding the entrance and the harbour.[35] It is believed that the fort commanding the harbour was strategically located at the southern point of the bay embracing the township formerly known as *Roundhead* and now known simply as *The Point*. This was to protect the settlement against an enemy vessel that might successfully escape the fire of the cannon located at Harbour's Mouth; a very unlikely event, the narrowness of the Harbour's Mouth Channel making it impossible for a vessel to enter at any distance from the southern end of the island. So happily defended by nature was the island, that the inhabitants boasted they could defend themselves against 10,000 men with 4 guns and 20 men.[36] In the face of uninterrupted Spanish attacks since the peace treaty of 1713, the twelve guns at the two forts erased any lingering doubt about their security.

In addition to the forts, the settlement had a militia of eighty men and boys, who were able and prepared to bear arms in 1718. Phenney commissioned officers of the militia companies in Harbour Island, Eleuthera and New Providence. John Alberry was the captain, Seaborn Pinder the lieutenant, and William Thompson the ensign of the Harbour Island Company.[37]

In 1718 Harbour Island seemed poised for a period of sustained growth and development, after struggling to establish itself for so many years. Under the most unfavourable circumstances of corrupt governors, delinquent proprietors, a period of anarchy, pirate occupation and Spanish and French incursions, a handful of tenacious families laid the groundwork for the healthy settlement of sixty families living there when the first Royal Governor arrived. The plantations on Eleuthera provided a reliable source of commodities for trade, and, combined with the more precarious prizes from wrecking, turtling and whaling, the trade outlook was promising. The security provided by the two forts and the militia company was an asset to any settlement in a colony under continual attack. Some resistance by the

Harbour Island people to the new government was not surprising, as they had established a comfortable existence with no outside help.

Woodes Rogers' mission was primarily to rid the colony of pirates and restore commerce, but when he arrived, he recognized that the constant Spanish incursions and plunder of the settlements were a major drawback to the growth of the colony. A number of pirating forays out of Eleuthera on Cuba in 1714 had given the Spanish another reason to raid the Bahamian settlements, and they intensified their attacks especially on the Eleutheran settlements. Initially Woodes Rogers supplied the two forts at Harbour Island with powder and shot, but after the Spanish invasion of Nassau in 1719, Rogers decided that since he had neither manpower nor supplies to defend the settlements on the three inhabited islands of New Providence, Eleuthera and Harbour Island, that the best plan was to concentrate on the defence of Nassau. This of course had a devastating effect on the other settlements.

In 1720 Rogers reported to council, 'All the best men that lived at Eleuthera and Harbour Island are here (New Providence) and I have taken the guns from the fort at Harbour Island and we resolve to defend ourselves here.[38] This was the first of a number of council decisions that broke the momentum of development for the Harbour Island community and shattered their dreams of a stable and healthy community with a prosperous future. The effect of this decision alone reduced the population at Harbour Island by half, after some 70 men and a number of families moved to Nassau, leaving the island defenceless. The settlements on Eleuthera were in a worse position as they were more exposed, not having the natural defence of a landlocked harbour as did Harbour Island.

For the next decade, the Spanish held the Bahamian settlers in Eleuthera and Harbour Island hostage in their own country by their constant presence in Bahamian waters and their relentless attacks on the settlements. The best documented attack occurred in 1725, when the Spanish, led by Augustin Blanco of Baracoa, Cuba landed at Current, Eleuthera, where Richard Thompson Snr. lived with his family. In a hostile manner, the Spanish made Mr. Thompson and his family prisoners by pinioning them, robbed him of all his wealth, and took from him his son, John Thompson, and Boyer Gething, an orphan in his care, all his negroes, household goods and wearing apparel to the value of 3,500 pieces of eight. When Thompson asked Blanco if Spain had declared war against England, Blanco replied that he had a commission 'to take and make prize of all vessels belonging to these islands except the old English vessels for that the Bahamas belonged to Spain'.[39] Blanco further explained that the Governor of Havana obliged him to carry away all the people in the settlements he could take prisoner to build him a fort.

1 Cockram's Map

2 Harbour's Mouth

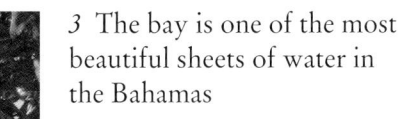

3 The bay is one of the most beautiful sheets of water in the Bahamas

4 Houses were built on the bay

5 Pink Sands Beach

6 Ridge with seagrass

7 Coconut groves

8 Pineapple schooner

9 Schooner *Dart*

10 Modern yachts at sunset

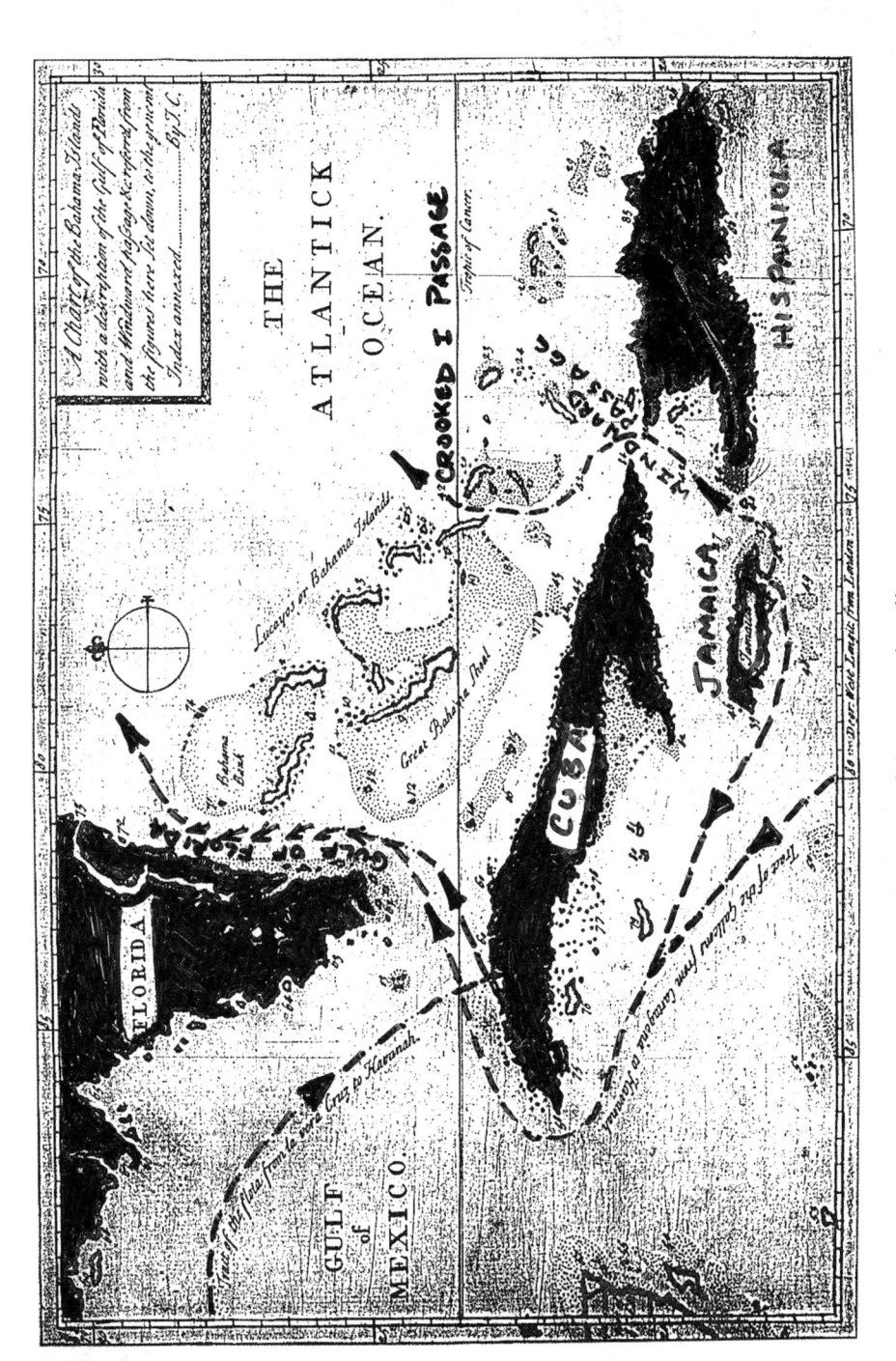

11 Chart of the Bahamas 1694 showing routes of the Spanish galleons

12 Eleutheran Adventurers

13 Earliest sketch map of Harbour Island 1702

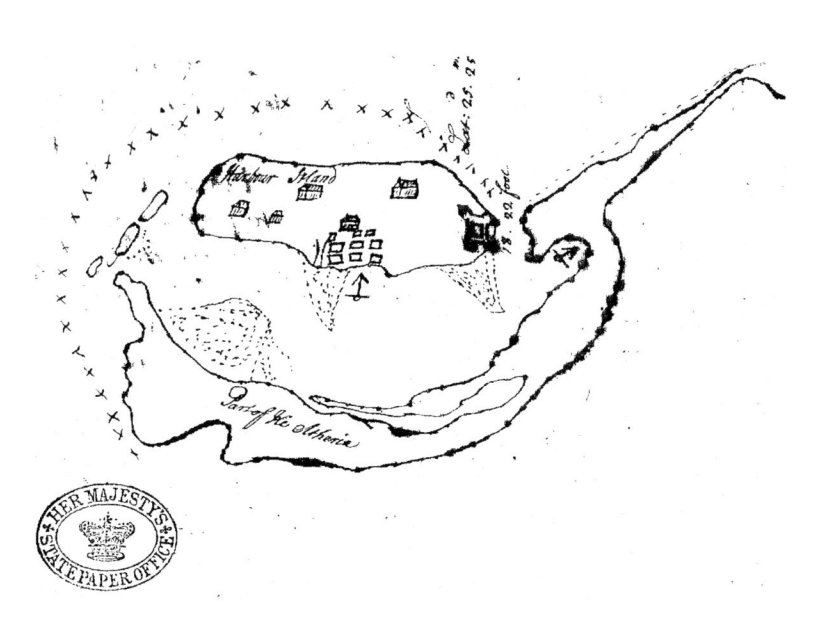

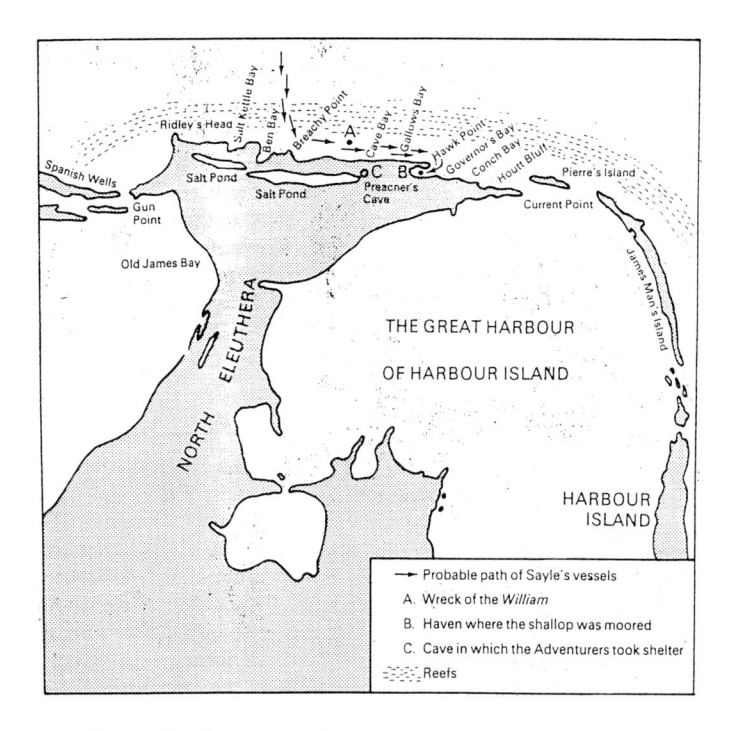

14 Map of North Eleuthera, showing Preacher's Cove, Cave Bay and Governor's Bay

15 Preacher's Cave

16 Henry Avery

17 Pirate flag of Henry Avery

18 Pirate flag of Thomas Tew

19 Pirate flag of Blackbeard

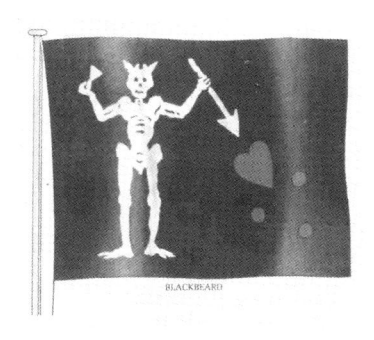

20 Pirate flag of Stede Bonnet

21 Pirate flag of Calico Jack Rackham

In 1727, an order in council commanded that the people of Harbour Island and Eleuthera should come to Providence on vessels sent for that purpose, as Augustin Blanco had promised two months earlier, when at Eleuthera, that he would return to sack all the settlements.[40] This order in essence required that the settlers abandon their homes to seek security from the impending Spanish attack. The order was reissued the following year after the inhabitants of Harbour Island and Eleuthera were 'taken and plundered' by the Spaniards. Although several families are reported to have obeyed the orders, the population counts (see Table 3.1 below) for 1731 strongly indicate that Harbour Island families did not abandon their family homes, while on the other hand, a number of Eleutheran families took advantage of the greater security that Nassau offered. The drastic reduction in the Eleutheran population must have dealt a fatal blow to some of the smaller settlements in Eleuthera at the time.

Table 3.1 further illustrates an overall slow growth rate for the colony between 1721 and 1731 with New Providence showing the highest and most consistent increase of the three settled islands.

With the bias of the Royal Government to settle New Providence, it is likely that the new families arriving from Bermuda and Barbados in the 1720s, and the more than three hundred imported slaves settled in Nassau, while the smaller increase in Harbour Island was from natural growth. This influx of slaves to Nassau and the loss of half the black inhabitants of Harbour Island and Eleuthera between 1728 and 1731, most likely from Spanish raids, also resulted in significant differences in the racial composition of the population. By 1731, Africans or creoles comprised 40 per cent of the New Providence population, 22 per cent of the Eleutheran population and 5 per cent of the Harbour Island population.

The names of some of the Harbour Island families who defied orders to remove themselves to Nassau are left to us in a 1728 list of 'all the men that can bear arms'. At Harbour Island a total of 17 men stood ready to defend

Table 3.1[41] Population 1721, 1728 and 1731

Island	1721 White	Black	Total	1728 White	Black	Total	1731 White	Black	Total
Harbour Island	124	5	129	120	20	140	160	9	169
Eleuthera	150	34	184	200	40	240	73	21	94
New Providence	470	233	703	500	250	750	633	409	1042
Cat Island	12	3	15						
Totals	756	275	1031	820	310	1130	866	439	1305

C.O. 23/1 part 2/103, Governor Phenney to Lords of Council of Trade and Plantations, February 1721.; C.O. 23/2 part.2/7, Governor Phenney to Lords of Council of Trade and Plantations, May 1728; C.O. 23/3/5, Woodes Roger's Report to Board of Trade, February 1731.

their settlement of 140 people: Thomas Curry, John Thompson, Boyer Getheng, John Roberts, Robert Roberts, James Pye, Seaborn Pinder, William Thompson Snr., William Thompson Jnr., Joseph Thompson, James Kimbling, Nathaniel Coverley, William Coverley, William Cash, Joseph Cash, Benjamin Sweeting and William Sweeting.[42] This was a far cry from the militia of 80 men, just ten years before.

A list of Harbour Island inhabitants in the 1720s, compiled from a number of sources, (Appendix 2 – Harbour Island Inhabitants in the 1720s) suggests that some twenty to thirty families stayed in Harbour Island in the 1720s despite Governor Phenney's attempts to centralize all efforts of defence in Nassau. The list is of interest because it shows how well established some families were by the family size and number of families with the same surname. The latter particularly tends to suggest people who had been in Harbour Island for some time and could not simply take up and abandon their families and homes at the behest of government. In the absence of earlier records, it is difficult to trace their ancestry to the founding families, but it is certain that some of them were descendants of the Bermudians and English who first settled the island in the 1650s. Predominant names from the 1720s list are Cash, Curry, Griffin, Pindar, Roberts, Saunders, Sweeting and Thompson.

Of note also in Appendix 2 is the number of children in Harbour Island who were baptized in the 1720s even though there was no resident minister. The people of Harbour Island ensured that when Rev. Thomas Curphey made his annual visit from Nassau, all newborns were baptized into the Christian church. There being no school or church on the island, a house had been set aside for the instruction of the children and the worship of God, and Samuel Flavell, the schoolmaster on the island, read prayers and a sermon every Sunday. Governor Phenney remarked, 'Flavell a sober person, reads the prayer book daily at Harbour Island (North Eleuthera) to interest the children, making it his whole employment with what books he has of his own. I have given him a New Testament and Tillotson's sermons.'[43]

The censuses of 1731 and 1734, taken by Governors Rogers and Fitzwilliam respectively, provide a wealth of information about the composition of the society and the families that lived in it. A comparison of the two shows a general movement of families from New Providence to Eleuthera and Harbour Island, most of them former residents of the islands. The arrival of seven families in Harbour Island by 1734 (see Appendix 3, asterisked names), obviously offset by inhabitants dying or leaving the island, did not affect the overall population. The 1731 census for Harbour Island shows an average family size of five children among 16 nuclear families in contrast to New Providence's average family size of almost three children among 92 nuclear families. Craton and Saunders point out that the incidence of nuclear families and the size of families were predictably higher in Harbour Island and Eleuthera than New Providence, Harbour Island being 'the most tightly knit and insulated of the three'.[44]

The slave population in Harbour Island remained very small and by 1734 was a mere 6 per cent of the total population, the ten slaves belonging to the three long-established Harbour Island families of Benjamin Sweeting Snr., John Thompson and William Thompson. This was in contrast to the larger slave population in Nassau which was distributed in sizeable units of ten plus and 3–9 slaves, or in smaller units of one or two.

After a decade and a half, was the overall impact of royal government on Harbour Island a positive or negative one, and did the early resistance of the Harbour Islanders give way to compliance with and an appreciation of their new administration? Certainly Governors Rogers and Phenney had successfully expelled the pirates, thereby creating an environment more conducive to promoting trade. The task of defending the colony against constant Spanish attacks was indeed much harder and initially led to a decision to order all men and later all families to Nassau from Eleuthera and Harbour Island. The removal of the cannon and powder from the battery was a further blow to their ability to defend themselves, and the embargo against foreign traders unloading at Harbour Island had the potential of crippling their trade. The frustration of the inhabitants with regard to the latter is reflected in the words of William Thompson to council: 'I know not what the Governor and Council means by debarring us of trade without they design to drive us from these islands.'[45] Undoubtedly that thought must have crossed the minds of many who defied the orders of the council and stayed to defend their island home. It was this group of twenty families that held to the dream of their forefathers who had settled the island some eighty years earlier. In effect, the government had done nothing to promote settlement of the island and those who remained had succeeded in developing a healthy but struggling community, with a population somewhat reduced from the 60 families of 1718.

Notes
1. CSP, 19/1042 IX, Thomas Walker to His Majesty, Received January 1702.
2. Paul Albury, unpublished lecture.
3. CO 5/1312 Part 1, Thomas Walker to Council of Trades and Plantations, 1702.
4. Michael Craton & Gail Saunders, *Islanders in the Stream Vol 1,* University of Georgia Press, 1992, p. 91.
5. CSP, 19/180, E Randolph to Council of Trade and Plantations, 19 February 1701.
6. CSP, 31/209, Captain Woodes Rogers to Council of Trade and Plantations, 29 March 1719.
7. Sandra Riley, *Homeward Bound,* Island Research, Miami, Florida, 1983, p. 41.
8. Ibid.
9. Michael Craton & Gail Saunders, *Islanders in the Stream Vol 1,* University of Georgia Press, 1992, p. 103.

10. CSP 24/472 Deposition of Captain Edward Holmes to Council of Trade and Plantations, 20 April 1709; CSP, 24/870, Captain Adrian Wilson to Council of Trade and Plantations, 24 November 1709.
11. CSP, 24/176, Governor Bennett of Bermuda to Council of Trade and Plantations, 29 October 1708; CSP, 24/448, John Crofts to John Graves, 14 April 1709.
12. CSP, 25/421i, Captain R N Smith to Council of Trade and Plantations, 12 October 1710.
13. CSP, 27/651, Lt. Governor Pulleine of Bermuda to Council of Trade and Plantations, 22 April 1714.
14. CSP, 30/737, Captain Woodes Rogers to Council of Trade and Plantations, 31 October 1718.
15. CSP, 30/737, Captain Woodes Rogers to Council of Trade and Plantations, 31 October 1718.
16. Michael Craton, *A History of the Bahamas,* 3 Edition, San Salvador Press, 1986, p. 105.
17. CSP, 30/737, Captain Woodes Rogers to Council of Trade and Plantations, 31 October 1718.
18. Proceedings of the Governor in Council, 14 November 1721, p. 127; CSP, 32/758, Governor Phenney, to Council of Trade and Plantations, 26 December 1721.
19. CSP, 31/545, Mr Buck & Co-Partners to Council of Trades and Plantations, 3 March 1720.
20. Proceedings of the Governor in Council, 19 March 1720, p. 84.
21. Proceedings of the Governor in Council, 10 February 1725, p. 52.
22. Proceedings of the Governor in Council, 18 July 1723, p. 295.
23. Proceedings of the Governor in Council, 13 January 1724, p. 15.
24. Ibid.
25. John Oldmixon, *The History of the Isle of Providence,* The Providence Press, Nassau, 1741, p. 12.
26. LeFroy Vol II, op cit., p. 265.
27. Egerton, 2395, folio 472, Darrell to Ashley March 1671. For discussion of Windemere see Chapter 2, p. 11.
28. Michael Craton & Gail Saunders, *Islanders in the Stream Vol 1,* University of Georgia Press, 1992, p. 89.
29. Ibid, p. 87.
30. Mark Cateby, *The Natural History of Carolina, Florida and the Bahama Islands,* Vol 2, London 1754, Reprint, Savannah, Georgia: Beehive Press, 1974, p. 39.
31. CO 23/13/144, John Barker, Engineer to Lord Carteret, February 1724.
32. CO 23/13/229–267, List of Ships clearing in and out of New Providence, 1721 to 1725.
33. Ibid.
34. CSP, 27/651, Lt. Governor Pulleine, to Council of Trade & Plantations, 22 April 1714.
35. CO 23/1/22b, Woodes Rogers to Secretary of State, Whitehall, 31 October 1718.
36. CO 23/2 part 1/77, Governor Phenney to Lords of Council of Trade and Plantations, 4 May 1722.
37. CO 23/1 part 2/103, Governor Phenney to Lords of Council of Trade and Plantations, February 1721.
38. CSP, 32/47, Captain Woodes Rogers to Council of Trade and Plantations, 20 April 1720.
39. CO 23/12 part 2/41, Declaration of Ridley Pinder and William Addams, 22 April 1725.
40. CO 23/ 2 part 1/133, Governor Phenney to Board of Trade, May 1728; CO 23/14/22, Council Meeting, 14 August 1727.

41 C.O. 23/1 part 2/103, Governor Phenney to Lords of Council of Trade and Plantations, February 1721.; C.O. 23/2 part. 2/7, Governor Phenney to Lords of Council of Trade and Plantations, May 1728; C.O. 23/3/5, Woodes Roger's Report to Board of Trade, February 1731.
42 CO 23/ 2 part 2/14, Governor Phenney to Lords of Council of Trade and Plantations, May 1728.
43 Colbert Williams, *The Methodist Contribution to Education in the Bahamas,* Alan Sutton Publishing Ltd. Gloucester, England, 1982, p. 41.
44 Michael Craton & Gail Saunders, *Islanders in the Stream Vol 1,* University of Georgia Press, 1992, p. 122.
45 Proceedings of the Governor in Council, 10 February 1725, p. 52.

4

'Get you on board you dog or I will mix your soul!'

Benjamin Hornigold, Harbour Island, circa 1716

By 1716, the Bahamas had attracted the greatest number of pirates ever seen in the New World. After governors and merchants in all parts of His Majesty's plantations in America had voiced their concerns about the obstruction of trade with Great Britain caused by the heavy presence of these sea wolves, an order in council was issued:

> … as at this time the pirates have a lodgment with a battery on Harbour Isand, as also that the usual retreat and general receptacle for pirates is at New Providence, her Majesty has given directions for dislodging them…[1]

The existence of these pirate sanctuaries at Harbour Island and Nassau was no mere happenstance; it was a combination of geographical, political and economic factors that led to their growth and development. These infant settlements were the bases from which many pirate sloops hoisted the black flag/Jolly Roger and swooped down on innocent traders, no matter their nationality, in the sea lanes bordering the Bahamas. The pirate ethos prevailed for the first quarter of the eighteenth century, in striking contrast to the Puritan principles that had so inspired the founding fathers of the Eleutheran colony.

It was the English buccaneers out of Jamaica that opened the chapter on the Golden Age of Piracy in the New World. This loose association of pirates and privateers, led by that most infamous of buccaneers, Sir Henry Morgan, sacked the principal towns of the Spanish Empire and conducted patriotic raids on Spanish shipping in the 1660s. The governors in Jamaica gave their stamp of approval to these exploits, by the liberal granting of commissions for a small fee of £20. However by the 1670s, the governors no longer supported hostilities against Spain and when the planters replaced the privateers in the council of Jamaica, Port Royal was no more a safe refuge for the buccaneers.

After the 1680s the buccaneers moved north to the more pirate-friendly colonies of New England, New York and Rhode Island on the eastern seaboard and to New Providence and, later on, Harbour Island.[2] Some chose 'to run at low game' which meant that their cruises and plunder were limited to small trading vessels plying the sea routes between the eastern seaboard ports in North America and the West Indies; others, referred to as the 'Red Sea men', chose 'to run at high game' and pillaged the richly laden Mocha Fleets and the Indian Mogul galleons travelling between ports in the Red Sea, the Persian Gulf and the mainland of India. On their return to the American plantations, they came first to New Providence or South Carolina where they disposed of their ship, and then dispersed into New England, New York and Rhode Island to sell their share of the 'swag' or maybe to fit out again for the Red Sea.[3]

Wherever the source of plunder, pirates were always in need of pirate-friendly governors who would not only permit them to land but would offer them protection from prosecution in return for a share of the loot; sometimes as much as one hundred dollars per crew member.[4] And in the Bahamas there was no shortage of such governors: 'Hardly a proprietary governor escaped censure as a harbourer or encourager of pirates, even if he was not engaged in piratical activity himself.'[5] As early as 1682, Governor Clarke commissioned privateering acts against the Spanish in times of peace[6] and Governor Jones 'highly caressed those pirates that came to Providence' giving them commissions without and against the Council's approval and pardoning and discharging them without trial.[7] The most famous pirate broker was none other than Governor Nicholas Trott who amassed a fortune of £7,000 for permitting Avery and his convoy to land in Nassau after returning from a pirate round in the Indian Ocean. The unscrupulous Governor Trott even charged one of Avery's crew eight chequennes for breaking a drinking glass as they celebrated their newly acquired riches at the Governor's home.[8] Indeed proprietary governors who 'wink'd much at such ill practices [piracy] for filthy Lucre'[9] were a great enticement to pirates in search of a sanctuary.

Another inducement for pirates to settle the Bahamas was the nature of the archipelago with its coastlines of unpredictable 'creeks and shallows, headlands, rocks and reefs-facilities, in short, for lurking, for surprise, for attack, for escape'.[10] The pirates who used Nassau as a base and Harbour Island as an outstation knew all the hidden bays and harbours, invisible to the naked eye; they knew the channels of the Bahamian waters and could outwit any pirate chaser by skillfully maneuvering their smaller vessels around the reef and shoals and into small bays inaccessible to large merchant ships or men-of-war.

The strategic position of the islands at the head of the Caribbean and near the major shipping routes to and from Europe also made the Bahamas an attractive base from which to 'go on the account'. New Providence and Harbour Island were well positioned in relation to these sea lanes connecting the Old World to the New, and the eastern seaboard colonies to the Caribbean. In a matter of hours, pirates in Nassau could hoist their black colours and be cruising the Gulf of Florida (formerly the Bahama Straits), the route used by the Spanish for their homeward-bound voyages; the pirates at the outstation in Harbour Island had an excellent vantage point from atop Look Out Hill, which at 150 feet high, gave them an extensive view of the North East Providence channel, the route used by all vessels going to Nassau and by English merchant ships from England to the American colonies. English and French traders returning from the Caribbean to Europe most often sailed the Windward Passage and then on to the Atlantic Ocean through the Crooked Island or the Caicos passage in the southern Bahamas. All these sea routes ensured the pirates in the Bahamas ample opportunity for plunder.

By the turn of the century, the foundations for the classic era of Bahamian piracy were laid. The pirate ethos was gaining ground, especially in Nassau, and to some extent pirates seemed to command a degree of respect in the community. Lawful citizens were on the decline and in 1697 the governor could not empanel a grand jury without finding a quorum of pirates on it.[11] And like the Jamaica council in earlier years, four members of the council were known pirates; in fact the governor of Eleuthera and Harbour Island, Matthew Middleton, appointed by Governor Nicholas Webb in 1701, was a 'Red Sea Man'.[12]

From afar Governor Blake of Carolina observed 'Hardly a ship comes through the gulf or on our coast but is plundered'[13] and requested one of Her Majesty's frigates to clear the Carolina and Bahamas coasts of pirates. And from close up Governor Haskett remarked on the brigand community at Providence as comprising 'cast out pirates' and in defence of the governors, he contended, 'If a governor will not be governed by them, or at least connive at their practices, they will not suffer him to govern at all.'[14] Meanwhile vessels sailing between the Bahamas and New England ran a great risk of being plundered, no matter their nationality.

An interesting distinction is made at this time in history between 'pirate' and 'privateer'. The pirates, defiant of the laws of society, waged war on and plundered all shipping in armed vessels, earning the sobriquet 'enemies of humanity'. They collectively owned the pirate vessel and had a high regard for individual rights, every pirate participating equally in decisions, regardless of his rank, race and religion and every pirate receiving an equal share of the booty.[15] If caught in their illegal venture, the penalty was death at the gallows. In times of war, the privateers enlisted as crew on a privately owned ship (also called privateer) commissioned by the government to plunder enemy shipping and coastal settlements. The governor sold the owner of the privateering vessel a letter of marque, which was in effect, an official commission to harass and intercept enemy vessels. The privateer crew was under the command of the captain and quartermaster and their position in the crew determined their share of the proceeds from the sale of seized goods. And like the earlier buccaneers, the privateers were well respected for the enemy prizes they captured and were a welcome supplement to the scant naval forces in the region.

In practice, the distinction between pirate and privateer was a fine one; the line between the two often blurred and one became the other. The twelve-year Queen Anne's War (1702–1713) fuelled the pirate momentum in two ways: just as legislation was enacted to suppress piracy, the war provided an irresistible opportunity for the Nassau pirates to pursue and refine their notorious careers under a cloak of legality as privateers; and it further provided a training ground for pirates in times of peace, as unemployed privateers joined 'the Brethren of the Coast' at the close of the war. As the Rev. Cotton Mather in a hanging sermon lamented, 'the privateering stroke so easily degenerates into the piratical'.[16] And often war was not a necessary condition for plunder: when Thomas Petty, a Nassau merchant, was seized in his sloop *Snapper* on a voyage to Jamaica to trade oil, he asked his captor Augustin Blanco of Cuba if war had been declared and Blanco retorted, 'No matter for war, the Spanish have always war with the people of the Bahamas.'[17] The Bahamas were considered the northern cays of Cuba that belonged to the Spanish and Blanco had commissions from the governor of Cuba in times of peace and in times of war.

At the end of the war, the pirate presence in the Bahamas mushroomed rapidly, confirming John Graves' observation of earlier years, '… that the Colony is under very ill Circumstances in Time of Peace, for the War is no sooner ended, but the *West Indies* always swarms with Pyrats…'[18]

This new phase of Bahamian piracy extended from an increasingly popular rendezvous of pirate commanders in Nassau to an outstation or lodgment on Harbour Island and a small group of piratically inclined at Eleuthera. Lieutenant Governor Pulleine of Bermuda wrote in 1714 to the Council of Trade and Plantations:

> … the principal residence are at Providence, Harbour Island and Eleuthera… they have served of late as a retreat for 3 setts of pirates, who committed depredations in a boat with 15/20 men per boat. They have taken from the Spaniards within the last 8 months three score thousand pounds… the names of 2 captains are Cockram and Hornygold both refuged amongst those people.[19]

Cockram operated out of Harbour Island where the pirates raised a battery and kept a guard of fifty men.[20] Hornigold's early connections were with Eleuthera, and he knew Harbour Island and the people well as he was a close associate of Cockram's and visited the place frequently. Their early forays as pirate captains were small scale and targeted Spanish settlements on the northern coast of Cuba and Spanish trading vessels and periaguas, travelling from the missionary stations in Florida to Havana via the Bahamas.

Thomas Walker, as deputy governor in 1715, wrote to the Council of the dire need for a governor in the Bahamas to execute justice on the pirates 'that will be found inhabitants upon Eleuthera and Out Islands'.[21] He described how Daniel Stillwell, formerly of Jamaica and lately resident in Eleuthera, had taken the *Happy Returne*, a small one-sail sloop, to Cuba on pirating voyages. The pirate crew of between three to six persons were largely married men with children, resident in Eleuthera, very probably from the Current area; included in the names were John Kemp, Matthew Lowe, James Bourne, John Cary, John Darville and Zachous Darville. Four 'strangers' also sailed with the Eleutheran pirates: Benjamin Hornigold, Benjamin Linn, Thomas Terrill and Ralph Blankeshire. They piratically seized dry goods, money, negroes and on one occasion a Spanish launch with 11,050 pieces of eight.[22]

It is interesting to note that five of the above Eleutheran pirates would be among the first pirates in the region to take the pardon and forswear their villainous way of life. So that when Vincent Pearse arrived in the Bahamas, a few months before Woodes Rogers, Hornigold, Stillwell, Kemp, Cary and Terrill had accepted King George's pardon for the various treacheries they had perpetrated against the people of Cuba.[23]

So incensed were the Spaniards at the Eleutheran assaults on their vessels and settlements in times of peace that they designed to send a brigantine from Havana to Providence 'to cut off all the people' because they were nothing more than a 'nest of pirates' who had robbed them of large quantities of money.[24] Thomas Walker, who had fitted out a privateer himself for the Cuban coast in the Queen Anne's War, strongly condemned piracy and was determined to take these pirates 'who when they are guilty, do fly into the woods and defend themselves with their arms against the pursuit of justice'.[25] To satisfy the Spaniards of his endeavours to keep the peace between the two nations, Walker first went to Eleuthera and seized Stillwell and Linn, put them in irons and sent them as prisoners to Jamaica and Providence respectively.[26] He then sailed on to Havana to inform the governor of his efforts to quash the robberies of the Eleutheran pirates so that the Spaniards might desist in their plan to cut off all the inhabitants for the treacheries of a few.

As captain of the Harbour Island contingent of pirates, John Cockram was a first-class navigator and his 1718 manuscript map of Harbour Island reflects an accurate knowledge of the coastline and waters, and an eye for geographical detail superior to that of the average seaman. Married to the daughter of the prominent Richard Thompson, Cockram did not fit the popularized stereotype of the pistol-toting, cutlass-brandishing cutthroat pirate but rather fell into the category of 'gentleman adventurer', a distinction proposed by Bacon.[27]

In the thirty-ton merchant sloop, *Richard & John,* Cockram sailed a two-thousand-mile course to Curacao at the southern edge of the Caribbean Sea, where he sold the much sought after braziletto from Eleuthera; a trading voyage started by the Bermudians many years before. The illegality of such voyages, in that the Queen received no dues, did not disturb or deter Cockram, nor was he adverse to plundering and seizing any vessels he met on the way back.[28]

Married into one of the oldest families in Harbour Island, Cockram was well established in the small community of thirty families and the presence of the pirate lodgment, atop Look Out Hill to the north of the township, was of mutual benefit to the pirates and the inhabitants. From the lofty hill, on a clear day, a sail could be espied for miles out to sea, giving the pirates good time to prepare for their voyage of plunder. With a steady prevailing wind, a fast one-sail sloop could even get to Nassau in time to apprise the pirate captains there of the sighted vessel, and they were always fitted out and ready to go on the account.

The inhabitants welcomed the pirate presence at Harbour Island as it added a measure of security to the island against the constant incursions by the Spanish; the battery, which the pirates raised to the north of the township, was a strategic complement to Walker's battery at the southern end of the island. By this time the Spaniards from Cuba knew the Eleuthera coastline well; the Current settlement and the East End settlement had survived countless depredations and the Spaniards realized that despite the natural security afforded Harbour Island by its landlocked harbour, their shallow-bottom periaguas were able to maneuver around the reefs, shoals and sandbars and they could therefore enter the harbour through the channels to the north, a route which vessels of any draft could not use. Thus in the absence of a government to protect them from the harsh reality of their Spanish foes, the Harbour Island people had little choice but to embrace the pirates.

Thomas Walker criticized the Eleutheran and Harbour Island people for their acts of piracy and for harbouring and provisioning pirates and fitting out their vessels. Indeed Harbour Island had become an entrepot for pirate provisions, and trading ships from the American colonies brought a range of merchandise and sold it to the pirates in Harbour Island, who in turn sailed to Nassau and sold it to the more than one thousand pirates based there by 1717. A Capt. Musson who had made his way to Harbour Island after being shipwrecked, reported two ninety-ton trading ships from Boston, selling provisions to the pirates at Harbour Island.[29]

Cockram was a close associate of Benjamin Hornigold and it was not uncommon for one to visit the other, especially during the time that Hornigold was resident in Eleuthera. On one of these occasions, while anchored off the township of Harbour Island, Hornigold's surgeon had attempted to escape from Hornigold's command, having been pressed into the pirate captain's service for his medical expertise and in spite of having a great disdain for the piratical way of life. So as to delay his return to the ship one evening, Howell offered to mix some medicine for Hornigold, to which the captain, by now very suspicious of Howell's real intent, thundered, 'Get you on board You Dog or I will mix your soul!'[30] Howell failed to persuade the inhabitants of Harbour Island, in particular one of Richard Thompson's daughters, to assist in his escape lest Hornigold should burn or destroy their houses, 'the whole place being in such fear of Hornigold, that no inhabitant durst speak against or contradict any order of said Hornigold'.[31]

Most histories of Bahamian piracy have focused on the colourful and terrifying Blackbeard and the raw courage and unchecked brutality he showed in his acts of plunder; but in fact Blackbeard's life as a pirate captain was relatively short-lived. It was his tutor, Benjamin Hornigold, who played a more central role in pirate activity, gaining great notoriety among the governors in the region. Many pirates served their apprenticeship under the fierce and formidable Hornigold; the Bahamian waters and neighbouring sea lanes being their training ground, and Hornigold, 'the dean of the school'.[32] No one was held in higher esteem by the Brethren of the Coast than this master pirate and it was nothing less than a privilege for any pirate captain to consort with him. Hornigold claimed that all the Bahamian pirates were under his protection; when Stillwell was thrown into irons by Thomas Walker for plundering the Cuban coast, Hornigold threatened to burn his [Walker's] house and shoot his father.[33]

While the main target of Hornigold's attacks was Spanish vessels taken off the coast of Cuba and Florida, he had no compunction about attacking English vessels from the American colonies, Jamaica or Bermuda. On one occasion, Hornigold escorted a convoy of six pirate ships to the Crooked Island passage, a favourite lurking place for both the pirates and the Spanish, as it was frequently travelled by the English on their return voyage to the American colonies and England; four of the pirate ships captained by Hornigold, Bellamy, Napping and possibly Blackbeard, hove to the windward and two captained by LaBouche and Stede Bonnet, to the leeward, where they awaited their prey. Before the week was out, a fleet of three English vessels, the *Union,* the *Dover* and the *Boston Galley,* laden with merchandise from Jamaica, appeared on the horizon. The pirates weighed anchor, hoisted the Jolly Roger and attacked and robbed the vessels.[34] The idea of convoy as a measure of protection against these ruthless pirates failed miserably.

However Hornigold was not the epitome of a cutthroat pirate: unlike many Bahamian pirates, who engaged in savage treatment of their captured enemies, Hornigold was humane with his captives and they regarded him with admiration. In the words of Governor Woodes Rogers, 'in the acts of piracy he committed, most people spoke well of his generosity'.[35] He had once returned a stolen sloop to its owner in Jamaica after seizing a Spanish sloop off Florida for his own use. Without a doubt, he was a very able and daring pirate and his close connections to Harbour Island and Eleuthera were a blessing to both inhabitants and pirates.

It is interesting to note that during the heyday of Bahamian piracy, 1714–1718, the indefatigable Spanish pirate, Augustin Blanco, was compelled to desist in his land and sea attacks on the Bahamas, and for the first time in many years, the Eleutherans were free of the anxiety of a surprise attack from Cuba, and were no longer forced to sleep in the woods for safety.

Occasionally, pirates from Nassau would stop at Eleuthera or Harbour Island on their way out on a cruise, and seize a vessel or provisions needed for their voyage. Charles Vane and Calico Jack Rackam visited the Eleutheran settlements frequently for this purpose. On a voyage to Hispaniola, the villainous Vane plundered the inhabitants of as many fresh provisions as his sloop could carry, including hogs, goats, sheep and fowl[36] and on another occasion seized the sloop *Lark* anchored off Harbour Island.[37] And Rackam, better known for his affairs of the heart, once stole seven or eight fishing boats off Harbour Island, along with their nets and other tackle.[38] Compared to the depredations committed by the Spanish, the losses from these pirate forays were small.

The contrast between the pirate headquarters in Nassau and the outstation in Harbour Island was striking. Led by a group of notorious commanders including Edward Teach, Charles Vane, Thomas Barrow, Charles Bellamy, Henry Jennings and Thomas Burgess, the pirate population grew unchecked in Nassau, and by 1717, one thousand pirates outnumbered the legitimate inhabitants, many of whom had left Nassau to escape the newly established pirate rule. Pearse described the Nassau pirates as 'young resolute wicked fellows'[39] and the forty burnt-out carcasses of trading vessels along the harbour shore affirmed their wickedness. Riotous revelry was the order of the day and the pirates indulged in nonstop drinking, dancing, singing and carousing until their money was spent or another cruise was in the offing. Nassau was no town of permanent homes with industrious dwellers; the transient and fast-changing pirate population had turned it into a shantytown of improvized tents and palm-leaf shelters. Perhaps they realized their sojourn was but for a short while.

The pirate lodgment at Harbour Island to the north of the island was removed from the township, and the physical separation ensured that the pirates were not automatically an integral part of the old community of Puritan descendants. Cockram's marriage into a well-established Harbour Island family suggests that the old inhabitants did not ostracize the pirates but nor did they have to tolerate their drunken and licentious lifestyle; given the absence of punch houses in the town, all their merry making and celebrations probably took place at the lodgment, out of sight of the townsfolk. The pirate population of fifty was but a fraction of the legitimate settlers that had grown to sixty families by 1718,[40] and as such the pirates could not rule this pioneer settlement, nor could they impose their pirate ethos on a prevailing Puritan ethic.

Long before the Crown put together a plan to dismantle the pirate bases at New Providence and Harbour Island, the Governors in Jamaica, Bermuda and the American colonies issued commissions to privateers to seize all pirate vessels and take the pirates prisoners, as their constant depredations had brought all lawful commerce to the verge of ruin. This measure alone had little effect on the growing number of pirates in the region but it might explain an eyewitness account of a curious incident that took place in Harbour Island in December1719, a year and a half after Governor Woodes Rogers' arrival. The day that Commander William Martindale anchored his sloop in the harbour at Harbour Island, there arrived two American privateer sloops. One was commissioned from Rhode Island with a crew of thirty-eight men, and the other commissioned from New York with a crew of forty-two. Two days later, fifty men from the privateers took up arms, charged into the township, and tried to set the houses on fire. Many Harbour Islanders were wounded in the encounter, but they managed to drive the privateers away by retreating to the garrison and firing at them. The motivation for the attack is unclear. Perhaps they did not know that Woodes Rogers had dislodged the pirates, who had refused to take the pardon, or perhaps some pardoned pirates had resumed their former lifestyle, and the attack on the township was a reprisal.[41]

The deliverance of the Bahamas from the control of the pirates was long in coming, but finally the Crown resumed control of the islands and orchestrated a foolproof plan to eliminate the pirates. It included a proclamation of pardon, increased naval patrols, the appointment of a governor, rewards for captured pirates and their trial and execution.

Ironically enough, Benjamin Hornigold and John Cockram were to play a central role in the successful execution of the plan.

A preliminary step was to convey the news of the royal pardon to the pirates, and Governors Heywood in Jamaica and Bennett in Bermuda were instructed to send vessels to the Bahamas with the news that King George would pardon all pirates for their unspeakable atrocities and barbarities at sea, if they would forswear their piratical way of life before 5 September 1718. Governor Heywood reported a positive response in that his vessels had met with Hornigold and one or two of his consorts who were resolved 'to welcome Tydings of an Act of Grace from his Majesty King George which wee embrace and return his Majesty our hearty thanks for the same'.[42] On the other hand Governor Bennett's envoy was not well received at Nassau, where he was fired on but managed to read the proclamation to 300 pirates and persuade only five pirates, including the notorious Henry Jennings, to surrender and return to Bermuda to receive the pardon.[43]

Some months before Woodes Rogers' arrival, the governor of New York sent Capt. Vincent Pearse, naval commander of the sixth-rate *Phoenix* to the Bahamas to further negotiate the pardon on behalf of King George.[44] Pearse's visit was very successful as one hundred and fourteen pirates, followed by an additional ninety, accepted certificates of surrender and sailed off to their respective governments to receive the pardon. In a communication to the Lords Commissioners of the Admiralty, Pearse records the names of the Bahamian pirates who surrendered, (see Appendix 4)[45] an invaluable document as so little is known about the pirate crews. In addition to Hornigold and the Eleutheran pirates, Capt. John Cockram, Capt. Josiah Burgess, Capt. Francis Lesley and Capt. Thomas Nichols 'struck their pirate colours' and surrendered. It is interesting to note that within three months, twenty of the pardoned pirates, one being Charles Vane, hoisted their black colours and set off on the account again, and by the time Woodes Rogers arrived, that number had probably doubled. More than sixty of the pardoned pirates returned to Nassau, Eleuthera or Harbour Island to settle and engage in legal pursuits.

The appointment of Woodes Rogers 'to drive the pirates from their lodgment at Harbour Island and Providence'[46] was well-considered. As a former privateer, commissioned to attack French and Spanish ships in the Queen Anne's War, he had proved himself a courageous and capable commander, capturing some twenty vessels with plunder valued at £800,000. He understood the pirate mentality and possibly empathized with their circumstances, but he was unswerving in his determination to execute the royal mandate. As he headed into the Northeast Providence Channel on board the *Delicia*, a former East Indiaman, in convoy with one sloop, the *Buck* and one transport, the *Willing Mind*, he must have wondered what kind of reception awaited him in the colony. He dropped anchor off the south point of Royal Island where he had planned to meet HMS *Milford*, HMS *Rose* and the sloop *Shark,* on pirate patrol in the region; in convoy they would make the final approach into Nassau.[47]

Roger's anxieties about the pirates' welcome were somewhat quelled when several inhabitants from Harbour Island sailed out to welcome their new governor. They conveyed the good news that there were over a thousand pirates in New Providence, some of whom had already received the pardon, and others who were prepared to accept the King's pardon on his arrival.[48]

The convoy proceeded to Nassau and, on landing, Woodes Rogers was saluted by six pardoned captains led by Benjamin Hornigold and three hundred inhabitants, who readily surrendered to the new governor. The only resistance came from the defiant Charles Vane, who had resumed his life of piracy and terrorized the shipping between the eastern seaboard colonies and England. The day after Rogers' arrival, Vane hoisted his pirate colours, fired a gun to show his contempt for the new government, and made his escape out of the eastern entrance to the harbour. The *Buck* followed in hot pursuit but could not outsail the cunning pirate. Vane and several other pirates threatened to repossess Providence in a short time.

Governor Rogers realized that some of the principal pirates who held to the pardon would be most effective in proclaiming the amnesty and apprehending the unrepentant. So he immediately commissioned Hornigold and Cockram to pursue the notorious Vane to Green Turtle Cay, where he had taken two vessels he had seized off the Carolina coast.[49] Vane outwitted his pursuers once again but Hornigold and Cockram captured Nicholas Woodall, a pardoned pirate sailing with Vane. Governor Rogers' position was considerably strengthened by the assistance of the former pirate captains, and in a letter to Whitehall he acknowledged, 'Capt. Hornygold having proved honest and disobliged his old friends by seizing their vessels, it divides the people here and makes me stronger than I expected.'[50] After Hornigold and Cockram's successful apprehension of Capt. Augur and his crew of thirteen at Exuma, Governor Rogers, impressed by their sincerity and support, commented, 'I am glad of this new proof Capt. Hornigold has given the world to wipe off the infamous name he has hitherto been known by…'[51]

Governor Woodes Rogers had successfully dislodged the pirates from the Bahamas and the pirate bases at New Providence and Harbour Island were no more – the final bastion of the English pirates in the New World had been dismantled. And it is important to recognize the crucial role played by the two former pirate captains from Eleuthera and Harbour Island, because without the help of Hornigold and Cockram, Rogers' task would have been more difficult. However, pirate activity did not cease in the region and by 1720, some 15–25 pirate ships with 1,500–2,000 pirates continued to intercept merchant vessels in the Caribbean and North American waters.[52] Increased naval patrols and fewer dishonest governors would eventually eliminate the pirates entirely; by 1724, most pirates were Spanish.

Only months after his arrival, Woodes Rogers recognized that the pirates were not so big a problem as the Spaniards and he requested a man-of-war for defence and 'provided pilots at Harbour Island so ye ships of war may go there on their way hither'.[53] It seemed that the removal of the pirates from the Bahamas had led to a resumption of endless Spanish incursions on the Bahamian settlements. The Spaniards were as opposed to the new English government in the colony as the pirates, but for another reason: they believed that they owned the islands. No one could know in the 1720s, that the frequent depredations by the Spaniards on Bahamian vessels and settlements under the pretense of having commissions from the governors of Havana, Baracoa and other parts of Cuba would continue, almost without cease, until 1782 when they finally captured and occupied Nassau for one year.

Notes

1. United Service Journal III, 1834, p. 217.
2. Neville Williams, *Captains Courageous*, Barrie & Rockcliff, London, 1961, p. 132.
3. CSP, 14/519, Report of Governor Nicholson, Virginia, 14 June 1695.
4. Neville Williams, *Captains Courageous*, Barrie & Rockcliff, London, 1961, pp. 134–5.
5. Michael Craton & Gail Saunders, *Islanders in the Stream Vol 1*, University of Georgia Press, 1992, p. 104.
6. CSP, 10/284, Sir Thomas Lynch to Lords of Trade and Plantations, 29 August 1682.
7. John Oldmixon, *The History of the Isle of Providence*, The Providence Press, Nassau, 1741, p. 14.
8. CSP, 15/260-63, Report of Governor Goddard of Bermuda, 18 December 1696.
9. CSP, 23/277, John Graves to Council of Trade and Plantations, 19 April 1706.
10. Zoe C Durrell, *The innocent island – Abaco in the Bahamas*, Durrell Publications. Distributed by Stephen Greene Press. Brattleboro, Vermont. 1972, p. 21.
11. Neville Williams, *Captains Courageous*, Barrie & Rockcliff, London, 1961, p. 149.
12. CSP, 18/211, E. Randolph to Council of Trade & Plantations, 11 March 1700; CSP, 19/180, E. Randolph to Council of Trade & Plantations 19 Febrary 1701.
13. CSP, 18/52, Governpr Blake, Carolina to Earl of Jersey, 10 June 1700.
14. CSP, 20/720, Governor Haskett to Council of Trades & Plantations, 9 July 1702.
15. http://www.radio4all.org/anarchy/pirates.htm.
16. Douglas Botting, *The Pirates,*Time-Life Books Inc., Alexandria, Virginia, 1975, p. 25.
17. CO 23/1 part 3/112, Thomas Petty to Governor Phenney, 15 April 1725.
18. CSP, 23/277, John Graves to Council of Trade and Plantations, 19 April 1706, p. 6.
19. CSP, 27/651, Lt. Gov. Pulleine of Bermuda to Council of Trade & Plantations, 22 April 1714.
20. CSP, 29/596, Council of Trade and Plantations to Mr Secretary Addison, 31 May 1717.
21. CO 5/1265/1-E (#2)/26, and CSP 28/276, Thomas Walker to Council of Trade & Plantations, 14 March 1714/15.

22 CSP, 29/240i, Deposition of John Vickers, 3 July 1716.
23 ADM 1/2782, Captain Vincen Pearse to Lords of the Admiralty, 3 June 1718, Public Records Office.
24 CSP, 28/459, John Graves to Council of Trade and Plantations, 15 June 1715.
25 CO 5/1265 1-e folio29, Thomas Walker to Council of Trade and Plantations, 1721.
26 Proceedings of Governor in Council, 10 December, 1721, p. 142.
27 Edgar Mayhew Bacon, *Note on Nassau,* Grand Central Printers, New York, 1926, p. 20.
28 CSP, 27/651, Lt. Governor Pulleine, to Council of Trade & Plantations, 22 April 1714.
29 CSP, 29/635, Captain Matthew Musson to Council of Trade & Plantations, July 1717.
30 Proceedings of Governor in Council, 23 December 1721, p. 189.
31 Ibid.
32 Robert E. Lee, *Blackbeard the Pirate,* John F. Blais, Publisher, Winston-Salem, NC, 1974, p. 11.
33 Sandra Riley, *Homeward Bound,* Island Research, Miami, Florida, 1983, p. 55.
34 ADM 1/1597/3, Captain Bartholmew Candler to Lords of the Admiralty, 19 July 1717; ADM 51/4394/3 Journal of Captain Bartholmew Candler, 26 July 1717.
35 CSP, 30/807 Governor Woodes Rogers to Secretary Craggs, December 1718.
36 Captain Charles Johnson, *A General History of the robberies and murders of the most notorious Pirates,* George Routledge & Sons, London, 1926, p. 122.
37 Ibid, page 105 and ADM 1/2782, Captain Vicent Pearse to Lords of the Admiralty, 3 June 1718, PRO.
38 Captain Charles Johnson, p. 119.
39 ADM 1/2782, Captain Vicent Pearse to Lords of the Admiralty, 3 June 1718, PRO.
40 CO 23/13/20, Woodes Rogers to James Craggs Secretary of State, Dec 1718.
41 CSP, 31/492ii, Governor Bennett of Bermuda to Mr Popple, 24 December 1719.
42 CO 137/12/5i, Peter Heywood to Lords Commissioners for Trade and Plantations, 7 February 1718.
43 Michael Craton, *A History of the Bahamas,* Third Edition, San Salvador Press, Canada, 1986, p. 93.
44 ADM 1/2782, Captain Vicent Pearse to Lords of the Admiralty, 4 February 1718, PRO.
45 ADM 1/2782, Captain Vicent Pearse to Lords of the Admiralty, 3 June 1718, PRO.
46 CSP, 30/64, Mr. Secretary Addison to Council of Trade & Plantations, 3 September 1717.
47 ADM 51/801, Captain Thomas Whitney's Log, 24 June 1718. PRO.
48 Michael Craton, *A History of the Bahamas,* Third Edition, San Salvador Press, Canada, 1986, p. 95; Botting, p. 140; Bacon p. 26.
49 Captain Charles Johnson, p. 114.
50 CO 23/13/20, Woodes Rogers to James Craggs Secretary of State, Dec 1718.
51 Ibid.
52 David Cordingly, *Under the Black Flag,* Harcourt Brace & Company, 1995, p. 202.
53 CO 23/13/29, Woodes Rogers to Secretary James Craggs, December 1718.

5

Brilanders sail to victory

It was on 12 April 1783, that a flotilla of six small transports and two armed vessels convoyed by two privateers, the 26-gun *Perseverance,* Commander Capt. Thomas Dow, and the 16-gun *Whitby Warrior,* Commander Capt. Daniel Wheeler, anchored in the lee of Salt Cay, just outside the eastern entrance to Nassau harbour. This expedition, originally out of St. Augustine's, was led by the young and daring Colonel Andrew Deveaux, a Loyalist refugee from Carolina, recently domiciled in St. Augustine. Their mission was to wrest the Bahamas from the hands of the Spanish by reclaiming Nassau, which had been under the Spanish rule of Governor Don Antonio Claraco y Sanz for almost a year. As the engagements of the following five days played out between the invading English force and the defending Spanish garrison, the differences in military traditions were highlighted: Deveaux was trained in the guerilla battles of the Carolinas where the only rule was not to lose and Claraco was from a more European military background where a common code of conduct and procedure was practiced among professional armies and officers.[1]

Deveaux's expedition was a private venture and the men enlisted in St. Augustine included American Loyalists, Bahamian refugees and privateers. The Bahamian refugees who had fled to St. Augustine after the Spanish occupation of Nassau were an invaluable asset because they not only provided much needed intelligence about the journey and the layout of Spanish defence in Nassau but they assisted in the recruitment of some 120 Harbour Island and 50 Eleutheran men and secured the loan of 50 fishing boats from Harbour Island. The readiness with which 'almost every man capable of bearing arms' in Harbour Island joined the enterprise, was a sure measure of the indomitable fighting spirit and patriotism of the small island community.[2] The addition of 170 men more than doubled the total force and was a welcome relief to Deveaux, who had already recognized that while his sea force was adequate, his land force was not. The 50 fishing boats would play an important part in Deveaux's ingenious strategy to free the Bahamas from its foreign rule.

Unbeknown to Deveaux, the timing of the enterprise was in his favour. A few days prior to his arrival, Governor Claraco received the news that peace had been declared and New Providence was to revert to English control in exchange for Florida; as a result Claraco relaxed his defensive measures and put the garrison on low-level alert.[3] And even when the unusual boating activity at the eastern entrance of the harbour was brought to his attention, he misread the purpose of their presence and believed that some smuggling activity was taking place. He did not entertain the idea of an invading force because his informants in St. Augustine had told him that any British attack on New Providence would be a 'major expedition of one to two thousand troops escorted by large ships of the line'.[4] It was an amazing irony that after having put so much effort into improving Fort Montague and Fort Nassau and building a citadel, the *Casa Fuerte,* around the governor's house, in readiness for the much anticipated attack, that Governor Claraco should look the enemy straight in the face and not even recognize him. He could not have been more unprepared. While Claraco sent out land and sea patrols to the east of the island to search for contraband activity, Deveaux reviewed the final details of his two-pronged attack on Fort Montague for the following day.

Deveaux based his plan of attack on the knowledge that even after the addition of the volunteers from Harbour Island and Eleuthera, his total force of 300 was less than half of the 600–700 soldiers garrisoned in Nassau; in addition, 70 of his land troops had no muskets.[5] As a near contemporary reflected, 'The conquest of a fortified island by so disproportionate a body of men could only be effected by consummate ingenuity and address.'[6] And indeed Deveaux realized that he had to make the Spanish believe that the invading troops were significant in number and posed a serious threat.

At daybreak on 14 April, Deveaux launched a simultaneous sea and land attack on Fort Montague. Under the command of Major Archibald Taylor, a group of privateers from the *Whitby Warrior* and the *Perseverance* were instructed to take the three Spanish galleys anchored off Fort Montague. Deveaux led the land force of 150 men, primarily comprising of Harbour Island militia, to take the fort and the Spanish soldiers garrisoned there.[7] Deveaux's use of the Harbour Island fishing boats reflected his military genius. Even though the seaward sentry spotted the fishing boats approaching the fort, no alarm was sounded because it was not until the boats pulled up alongside the galleys that they realized they were full of men. The true intention of all the boating activity was then revealed, too late for any organized resistance. Two of the three galleys were taken by Taylor and the privateers, and the third abandoned by its crew.

To deceive the Spanish about his strength, Deveaux used an age-old artifice,[8] landing troops at a point just east of the fort (probably Dick's Point). He organized a steady stream of fishing boats busily rowing back and forth between the vessels and the landing point, and from the fort it seemed as if boatloads of reinforcements were landing, when in fact the same people taken ashore, returned to the mother vessel crouched down and hidden behind the gunwales, and then sat up for a return journey to shore, thus giving the impression of many more troops than they actually had.[9] By the time Deveaux and his troops arrived at Fort Montague, the officer in charge had beaten a hasty retreat, but not before lighting a fuse to blow up the fort. Fortunately Deveaux captured two Spanish soldiers, one of whom was persuaded to cut the fuse to save his life. The fall of Fort Montague to the invading force had been unexpectedly easy and they then turned their attention to Nassau.

By this time the confused Claraco realized he was dealing with an invasion and not a smuggling enterprise, and in an effort to buy time and delay any further advance, he showed Deveaux copies of the letter from Havana proclaiming peace, but the colonel dismissed the report as 'trifling'.[10] Deveaux described his 'formidable force' to Claraco in an attempt to force his surrender, and they finally agreed to a truce. A dividing line between the two forces was marked by a fig tree on the White Grounds, half way between Fort Montague and Nassau and a guard of twenty-five men from both sides was identified to ensure that no one crossed the line.[11] However, Deveaux was not interested in a long cessation of hostilities; the brief respite had effectively prevented a counter attack to Fort Montague and given him time to plan his next strategy, but it was important to complete his siege of Nassau before an American force arrived or peace was officially confirmed.

On 15 April, while Claraco waited for Deveaux at an arranged meeting place to exchange copies of the truce, the skilled strategist was busy deploying his band of Harbour Island and Eleutheran novice soldiers and veteran Loyalists to two adjacent hills, Society Hill (later the site of Fort Fincastle) and probably Mount Fitzwilliam, just south of the city. The hills overlooked the township and Fort Nassau and the even higher *Casa Fuerte*, the elevation giving his troops a commanding field of fire.[12] Deveaux used men of straw on the hills to make his numbers look greater, and the careful spread of his men between the White Grounds and the hills gave him a clear advantage. By this time the Nassau residents who had been unaccepting of the Spanish occupation had joined the ranks of the invading force, and victory seemed close at hand.

Exhausted and fearful of a direct attack on the citadel, Claraco made a final desperate bid to end the siege, and at daybreak the next day, the Spaniards bombarded Society Hill with a fierce and unrelenting cannonade. In response to this, Robert Rumer, a former resident of the Bahamas and chief planner of the campaign, along with a party of free blacks and slaves from Harbour Island, laboriously dragged seven cannon up the hill and mounted them in embrasures cut out of solid rock.[13] A volley of fire at point blank range was directed at *La Casa Fuerte*.[14] This courageous action by some of the Harbour Island volunteers forced Claraco to surrender, and Deveaux hoisted English colours on Society Hill, where four years later Lord Dunmore built Fort Fincastle. Deveaux's guerrilla tactics had easily outmaneuvered the more traditional strategy of the Spanish governor.

Although almost a year had passed, it must have seemed to Claraco but a short time before that the overwhelming joint Hispano-American invasion under the command of Don Juan Manuel de Cagigal, Capt. General and Commander-in-Chief over Cuba, had descended on the township of Nassau. As many times as Nassau and Eleuthera had been raided, plundered and sacked by the Spaniards from Cuba, never had a force of this magnitude threatened Bahamian sovereignty. Governor Maxwell's 585 soldiers and militia, augmented by 800 armed sailors in a dozen corsair vessels[15] were no match against the superior force of an armada comprising Cagigal's 45 transport ships and 2,500 soldiers escorted by the American 40-gun flagship, *South Carolina*, with 500 men, 8 smaller warships of the South Carolina Navy and 12 transports.[16] The invasion force exceeded 5,000 men, crew included. Governor Maxwell had no choice but to capitulate and the colony fell to the Spanish without resistance.

The factor that drove this invasion against the Bahamas, was the very successful fleet of Bahamian privateers which in the context of the American Revolutionary War was demolishing the trade between the American rebels and the Caribbean, specifically Cuba. In the four and a half years of war prior to 1782, the Bahamian Vice-Admiralty Court had condemned 172 ships seized by Bahamian privateers: 137 American, 14 Spanish, 24 French and 1 Dutch.[17] So great was the number of American prisoners that Nassau could not 'keep or victual them' and many were set free at the closest American port.[18] To capture the Bahamas was to eradicate the threat that the Bahamas posed to their trade, so at a time when Britain's fortunes were on the wane and her power greatly diminished, the combined forces of Spaniards and Americans seized the moment.

Calgago had guaranteed a minimal disruption of life and confiscation limited to public property and private weapons of war, if Maxwell struck the British colours without delay.[19] And indeed the surrender agreement negotiated and penned by Maxwell, could not have been more generous and favourable to the interests of the Bahamian residents under foreign rule. Any person wishing to leave had eighteen months to close out his affairs. For those remaining under Spanish rule, the agreement promised continued ownership of land, houses and vessels, and freedom of worship. The islands were to continue under English law and customs, all Bahamian officials retaining their positions even in the colony's council, and British courts remaining open.[20] Except for a Spanish governor, and a foreign flag and garrison, life for the Bahamian residents in Nassau would go on as before the occupation; or such was the intention of the terms of surrender.

The inhabitants of Harbour Island and Eleuthera, removed by twenty leagues of sea from the new foreign rule, were even less affected. Samuel Higgs continued as the magistrate in Harbour Island and Samuel Higgs, John Miller, Ridley Pinder and Robert Bell as the representatives for Harbour Island in the House of Assembly. It was likely that Harbour Island residents never even saw a Spaniard unless on a visit to the capital. An inventory of correspondence kept by the Spanish government indicated communication between the local officials on the out island settlements and the new government, and on at least one occasion an official visit by the local magistrate of Harbour Island to the Spaniards in Nassau.[21]

The Spanish occupation had brought to an end the prosperous times enjoyed by the Bahamian privateers during the Revolutionary War. In addition, a high tax imposed on American imports and a restriction on trade with British colonies ushered in a period of very restricted trading and economic depression under the new Spanish regime.[22] It is unlikely that the Harbour Island merchants paid much attention to these new trade laws, and contraband trade soon replaced the lucrative privateering. A report two years later claimed, '... we are credibly informed foreign vessels trade to and from the Out Islands particularly Turks, Harbour Island, Eleuthera and Abaco and illegally supply the inhabitants with the produce of other countries and carry off cotton, dyewoods and other produce to foreign ports, free of any restraint of duties and custom house fees, while fair traders pay all'.[23] Out of the immediate purview of the new Spanish governor and in the face of scarce provisions from a declining trade, some Harbour Island merchants would have yielded to the temptation of contraband.

Harbour Island also realized an increase in population as a result of the Spanish occupation. A contrast in population counts for 1782 before and after the occupation shows a dramatic decline in the New Providence inhabitants of 1,000 and a significant increase in Harbour Island and Eleuthera of roughly 100 and 150 respectively.[24]

While the decrease for New Providence may in part be due to privateers who were not in port, it is likely that a number of Nassau residents left to

Table 5.1 A comparison of Lt. Wilson's report and the Spanish report on population of settlements

Settlement	Inhabs before conquest	Inhabs after conquest
Harbour Island	500	611
Eleuthera	450	602
New Providence	2,750	1,755

seek refuge in Harbour Island and Eleuthera, especially those with family connections in the out island settlements, while others fled to St. Augustine, the last English refuge on the American continent. These refugees no doubt aroused the sympathy of their out island compatriots for the sufferings of their Nassau brothers under the Spanish yoke. While initially the wealthy mercantile class had shown no reluctance to work and trade with their country's enemy, there were many who simply could not afford to leave or whose meager life savings were tied up in property in Nassau, making it difficult to escape their foreign master.

The Spaniards had not realized the extent of corsair activity among the Bahamian merchants and the resulting difficulty of staunching the life blood of the economy. They invoked draconian measures against the owners of vessels that continued to privateer, confiscating property and money owed to them, and imprisoning some at Fort Nassau and others in Morro Castle in Havana. While the local population had accepted the confiscation of military goods and armaments from privateer owners and merchants as part of the surrender agreement, they saw imprisonment and the confiscation of money and property as flagrant violations of the terms of capitulation. It is interesting to note that John Miller and a later Harbour Island representative Alexander Roxbourgh, having lost respectively $14,500 and $4,500 worth of military stores seized by the Spanish, refused to post the 300,000 peso bond with the Havana treasury and ended up in a Cuban jail to await their trial.[25]

Heavy wartime demands on the Cuban public treasury meant that Governor Claraco received no funds to underwrite the cost of the government and the garrison, and as a result the confiscated money and property of the Bahamian privateers was used to finance the occupation. The ongoing extortion of money by the Spanish authorities, on occasion wrongfully confiscated by association, led to heightened tensions between the two groups; and the earlier Bahamian complacence or passive tolerance of their foreign rulers changed to a mindset 'ripe for action against the conquerors'.[26]

The Bahamians made known the injustices perpetrated against them by their Spanish captors to the British authorities in the nearby British colonies and appealed for their assistance but without success. Finally, Robert Rumer and several other Bahamian exiles in St. Augustine, after failing to enlist the help of Governor Tonyn in their campaign against the Spaniards, found the ideal person to command the assault and recapture Nassau. A former South Carolina militia officer, Andrew Deveaux had recently arrived in St. Augustine with other Loyalist refugees from Charleston and he welcomed the opportunity to lead such an expedition and 'strike a blow for the empire'.[27]

Deveaux's mere 24 years belied his military experience gained as an ardent loyalist in the Revolutionary War. His ability and determination in the British ranks had won him two commissions, one as captain commandment of the Royal Foresters, a loyalist regiment of provincials, and the second as major of the Granville County Loyalist Militia. The bitter battles he fought in Carolina as a member of the militia had taught him some valuable lessons in warfare strategy and forged his early reputation as a skilled commander. And in addition to his experience, his bold and daring nature coupled with his enthusiasm for the undertaking convinced Robert Rumer that he had found the right person to lead the recapture of Nassau. In a spirit of renewed optimism for the success of their mission, the two gentlemen set about planning the voyage and the coup.

As the invasion fleet left St. Augustine on 1 April 1783, on a course for Hole-in-the-Wall, Abaco, the appointed rendezvous, there could be no doubt that the motivation driving this campaign was as much captured booty as the honourable objective 'to restore the inhabitants to the blessings of a free government'.[28] Apart from the impressive privateer escorts of the *Perseverance* and *Whitby Warrior* and their crews, the force comprised veteran Loyalists, many destitute in exile, and a number of Bahamian privateers operating out of St. Augustine since the occupation. This latter group included Richard Sweeting, Jeremiah Tinker, John Petty and William Lyford, who as veteran privateers provided Deveaux with good advice about the voyage. Robert Rumer had also persuaded his close associate and friend Sam Higgs from Harbour Island to join the expedition.

After additional forces that had planned to meet at Hole-in-the-Wall failed to show up, Deveaux realized that the success of the recruitment exercise at Harbour Island and Eleuthera was more critical than ever. He held a council of war, and it was the Bahamian contingent that he relied on most heavily to inform his strategy over the next few days. The privateers advised him where best to post guard ships in the sea-lanes to and from Nassau so as to capture any vessels that might carry intelligence about the imminent siege. And Robert Rumer and Samuel Higgs discussed how they might best persuade the people in Harbour Island and North Eleuthera to join the enterprise. Perhaps the idea of rewards of land was considered.

The next day, they sailed across the northeast providence channel and anchored off the township of Harbour Island. Roderick McKenzie was dispatched to Eleuthera and Deveaux, Rumer and of course Higgs recruited in Harbour Island. Higgs, as captain of the Harbour Island militia, and Rumer, well known among the people, easily won their support. In a 1786 letter, Harbour Island inhabitants affirmed '… had it not been for the entire confidence we placed in Mr. Robert Rumer whom we had known for sometime before, and who was generally esteemed amongst us; his prudent, spirited and good conduct determined the inhabitants almost to a man to accompany him...'[29] As the popular historian from Harbour Island Paul Albury boasts of his forebears 'almost every male who was fit to fire a gun' joined Deveaux's campaign.[30]

The breakdown of the male population for 1782 was Harbour Island, 97 whites, 2 mulattoes and 80 blacks and Eleuthera, 102 whites, 25 mulattoes and 23 blacks.[31] This would suggest that the 120 recruits from Harbour Island and 50 from Eleuthera came from all three racial groups with whites predominating. Because this was not an official military operation but rather a private expedition, there were no official lists of participants and the 1786 memorial for Rumer, signed by 71 of the Harbour Island volunteers, is the only surviving document to identify some of the group.[32] The following family names were well represented by the volunteers: Roberts, Saunders, Currey, Russell, Albray, Sawyer and Cleare.[33] (See Appendix 5.)

From Harbour Island, the flotilla sailed almost due west and anchored off Egg Island, the last stop before the final approach to New Providence. Deveaux and his troops spent several days here liaising with key people in the capital and soliciting precise details about the layout of the forts and the garrison so that he could formulate a foolproof plan of attack. He also used this time to train and arm the new recruits, some of whom were taking up arms for the first time, while others were seasoned privateer crews. Deveaux's advantage with these men was that many were very familiar with the layout of Nassau, some having come to Harbour Island and Eleuthera after the Spanish occupation, and once they were informed of the plan, they could be charged with leading the land attack.

The siege lasted for five days and on 18 April 1783, after 11 months and 10 days of Spanish rule, Claraco surrendered and the Bahamas was restored to British rule. After the capitulation, the 700 Spanish soldiers were dismayed and embarrassed when they came face to face with the victors and saw this disparate, non-uniformed band of 220 men, some without muskets, who had so valiantly taken back Nassau against considerable odds. 'The Spanish troops, in laying down their arms, ... could not refrain from expressing the utmost mortification and confusion as they surveyed their conquerors, not only so inferior in point of numbers, but ludicrous in their dress and military appearance.'[34] It was no doubt the cunning artifice of Colonel Deveaux that convinced the Spaniards of the 'formidable foe', but the campaign could not have been won without the reinforcement of the old inhabitants of Harbour Island and Eleuthera.

Of interest in the contemporary accounts of the recapture of Nassau, especially that by Deveaux himself, was the glaring omission of Robert Rumer, and his role in initiating the plan and spearheading the recruitment. Several memorials were written by the participants in the expedition to attest to Robert Rumer's bravery and dedicated service to the success of the campaign. The Harbour Island contingent testified that 'our success on that important occasion was greatly owing to his (Rumer's) well planned form of operations and spirited exertions in carrying it into execution'.[35] And in his own account of the events, Rumer charged Deveaux with taking all the credit for himself for the recapture 'which had he been left to himself would have never been effected'.[36]

The irony of the recapture was in its occurrence nine days after the deadline of the Treaty of Versailles for ending all hostilities and the resulting restoration of the Bahamas to Britain, thereby preempting the necessity of the raid. The question at the heart of the matter was whether or not Deveaux knew that hostilities were to end on 9 April. Historians have suggested that if Deveaux did not know before he left St. Augustine, then he certainly would have by the time he was at Salt Cay where Nassau residents were in constant communication with him. Claraco had made no secret of the news proclaiming peace as he set in motion a low alert status at the garrison, two days before Deveaux's arrival.[37] And in his own defence, Claraco claimed that Deveaux proceeded with hostilities despite receiving copies of the letter with the news of peace, thus forcing him into the awkward predicament of fighting for a colony in peacetime that was no longer Spanish.[38] On the other hand Deveaux's claim that he did not know peace was concluded prior to the recapture is supported in depositions from the privateer captains Dow and Wheeler. They both maintain that it was not until 21 April when a Capt. Kelly arrived from St. Thomas and Tortola, that they received the news.[39]

The contentious issue of the timing of the strike against the Spanish Bahamas is perhaps explained by the fact that Deveaux, the owners of the privateers and other principals had invested considerable funds and time in the venture. It was in essence a privateering voyage and how the colony was returned to British authorities mattered greatly: 'military conquest meant fame and booty, while a peaceful transition of authority meant nothing to Deveaux's soldiers of war'.[40] And for this reason Deveaux had to press ahead with the invasion so the privateers and veteran loyalists would see returns on their investment.

In addition to the cannon and galleys seized at Fort Montagu, Claraco surrendered '4 batteries with about 70 pieces of cannon and 4 large galleys (brigs and snows)' and all government property, a handsome booty if it could be sold.[41] However when Dow and Wheeler realized the recapture had taken place in peace-time, they renounced all rights and claims to the booty and wanted to be disassociated from the entire event.[42] A letter to Deveaux from grateful Nassau residents reveals the final outcome in their expressed regret 'that the Expedition had not been undertaken some weeks sooner as you then might have been reimbursed for your own expenses and might have had the pleasure of bestowing due rewards on your deserving officers and men'.[43] And meanwhile, the former Spanish governor urged immediate restitution of all seized and surrendered goods to the Spaniards, since the recapture was 'out of time, having been made at a period of profound peace'.[44] It is certain that the motivation that drove the Bahamian refugees and the Harbour Island and Eleutheran recruits was more honourable, and the timing of the siege should not diminish their courageous and heroic efforts to reclaim their country and end the foreign rule. The volunteers from the out islands comprised 75 per cent of the landing force, their gallant advance on Nassau forcing the Spaniards to give up all defence and retreat to the *Casa Fuerte,* and the 50 Harbour Island fishing boats, facilitating Deveaux's ingenious stratagem. There is a ring of truth in the words of the Harbour Island participants, '… and we may without vanity assert that had it not been for the Reinforcement which we made, the Expedition in all probability would have proved not only fruitless, but a defeat would have been attended with the most fatal consequences'.[45]

In time, Deveaux and many of the veteran loyalists were granted generous tracts of land by Lord Dunmore for their part in the campaign.[46] The recruits from Eleuthera and Harbour Island enjoyed the rights to commonage, a system of land cultivation from sixteenth century England, where land adjacent to a town or parish was planted by the inhabitants as a common farm. Some five commonages totaling 14,619 acres were given to the Eleutherans and Harbour Island patriots on the mainland: 560 acres at Savannah Sound, 3,879 acres at Tarpum Bay, 3,000 acres at Rock Sound, 1,180 acres on north west Eleuthera for the Spanish Wells people and 6,000 acres on north east Eleuthera for the Harbour Islanders.[47] It is interesting that the Tarpum Bay commonage was the only one listed in the Dunmore land grants, and this may explain the different figures variously quoted for the acreage of land in the other commonages. Despite the absence of regular titles, commoners, generations removed from Dunmore's time, knew that the commonages were a gift from Lord Dunmore and asserted their right to the commonage by occupation.[48]

The start of the Harbour Island commonage on Eleuthera predates the others, as the inhabitants of Harbour Island had planted the Eleutheran shoreline across the harbour from the early 1700s, as indicated in Cockrem's map.[49] These early settlers had very likely brought the idea of commonage from Bermuda, well known for its division into parishes, each with its own commonage. And thus the gift of 6000 acres on the northeast Eleutheran coast essentially extended the boundaries of the strip of land that the Harbour Island people had been farming for many years, and further endorsed their right to that land.

The attempts by outsiders to obtain commonage land drove the Harbour Island commoners to petition in 1810 that the lands they held in common not be granted to individuals. Government's recognition of the commoners' right to the land was underscored in its response: 'As the inhabitants of Harbour Island and their forefathers have, for upwards of a century, used as a common and cultivated in patches the land on the Eleutheran shore, opposite that island, it is ordered that no grant be issued for land on the Eleutheran shore, opposite Harbour Island, but that the same be reserved for the inhabitants of that island in general, and that they be permitted to use and enjoy the same as heretofore.'[50] This decision was based not on written records of a grant, but on tradition of occupation by the Harbour Island people. Despite the uncertainty of the tenure, it protected the land from sale and guaranteed the continued and undisturbed use of the land by the commoners. And the idea prevailed that the commonage was the exclusive rights of 'old inhabitants of all colours' resident in Harbour Island.

Agricultural development in Eleuthera led to an influx of individuals from other islands and settlements, many of whom settled in Harbour Island and started planting the commonage. The increase in population made it more and more difficult to identify that group of old inhabitants whose forefathers had sailed to victory, giving them exclusive rights to the commonage. The Harbour Island commoners realized that they needed a better right than that of a reserved occupancy and for $1,000 they secured a grant of the commonage in 1842. This grant is a landmark piece of legislation, because for the first time it defines the commonage in terms of its tenants and boundaries.

The grant was issued by Queen Victoria to some 324 heads of family from Harbour Island, including descendants of the old inhabitants who fought with Deveaux and a number of new residents.[51] (See Appendix 6.) While folklore continued to link all commoners with the Deveaux campaign, the 1842 legislation granted commonage to all residing in Harbour Island at the time. These grantees and their heirs were given the commonage 'in perpetuity' and no portion of the commonage could be sold. The boundaries of the commonage (see map), as stated in the grant, are the harbour of Harbour Island and the vertical from Bottom Harbour to Cotton Hole on its eastern border, the sea to the south, land reserved for the use of Current, Bluff and Spanish Wells inhabitants on the west, and the sea and the harbour of Harbour Island to the north. A recent g.p.s. measurement calculates the area of the commonage at 9,000 acres, instead of the earlier estimate of 6,000 but a good portion is ponds, sounds and marshes.[52]

The commonages generally faced increasing problems of encroachment as new settlements sprang up and available farm land declined in the nineteenth century. In addition, after emancipation, many former slaves remained on commonage land, which they continued to farm as a means of survival. Rights to the various commonages became highly contentious and difficult to resolve, and government in 1896 passed a quieting act 'to provide for the more beneficial use of lands held in common'.[53] This Act required a register of commoners to be kept by the commissioner and outlined general rules, the commoners in each commonage being authorized to formulate rules to secure the full and beneficial use of the land for all registered commoners. Of most significance was the entitlement of every person residing in a settlement adjacent to a commonage and farming the commonage at the time of the Act to become a registered commoner.[54]

The Harbour Island Commonage Development Association was struck to oversee the affairs of the commonage in North Eleuthera. This committee has mainly been involved with the vetting of applications from persons who wish to become registered commoners and the fair use of the commonage by the farmers as stipulated by their rules. In order to be registered as a commoner, one must be a direct descendant of an original grantee or an earlier registered commoner; Harbour Island people have used affidavits to prove their right of entitlement. A registered commoner can only have access to the land, if he has been domiciled in Harbour Island for a minimum of six months prior to his application to the committee. And the committee has been steadfast in its requirement that those allotted a portion of the commonage must cultivate it. However commercial enterprises have increasingly taken up land space without committee approval and government has built an airport, well fields and most recently a garbage dump on commonage land.

The initiative, taken by the Association in 1999, to form the first development cooperative in the Bahamas, was enthusiastically welcomed by the Harbour Island commoners. Monies raised from the sale of shares would go into capitalizing agricultural-related businesses on the commonage by the cooperative or in joint venture with the commoners.[55] In addition, the cooperative would oversee the running of the commonage and ensure enforcement of agreements entered into for the use of the land. It is interesting to note that Governor Haynes-Smith had strongly recommended such a cooperative for better control of the commonages over a hundred years before.[56]

No matter that time and legislation have distanced the Harbour Island commonage from those courageous Harbour Island men, who fought valiantly to take their country back from foreign rule; no matter that the fleet of 200 sail spreading 'its wings to the tradewind' and 'wafting eight hundred men and boys, black and white' to the commonage is an era of bygone days[57]; every Harbour Islander, young and old clings with pride to the tradition that the commonage was granted by Dunmore to their ancestors, for services rendered when they sailed to victory in 1783.

Notes
1. James A. Lewis, *The Final Campaign of the American Revolution; Rise and Fall of the Spanish Bahamas* (University of South Carolina Press, 1991) p. 76.
2. Lewis pp. 64–65.
3. Lewis p. 66.
4. Lewis p. 68.
5. CO 23/26/105b. Andrew Deveaux to Sir Guy Carleton dated 6 June 1783.
6. Daniel McKinnen, *A Tour through the British West Indies, 1804* (R. Taylor, Black Horse Court, London). p. 250.
7. Thelma Peterson Peters, *The American Loyalists and the Plantation Period in the Bahama Islands*, (University of Florida, 1960) p. 20; Lewis p. 75.
8. David Cordingly, *Under the Black Flag*, (Harcourt Brace & Company) p. 49. Sir Henry Morgan used the same stratagem against the Spanish at Maracaibo hoodwinking them into thinking he was going to make a land attack whereas he made an assault from the sea.
9. McKinnen, p. 250; The Private Collection of P.W.D. Armbrister, *Manuscript: Historical Notes*.
10. Lewis p. 77.
11. Lewis p. 77.
12. Bahamas Handbook 1977, *The Colonel from Carolina* (Etienne Dupuch Jr Publications, Bahamas), p. 24; Lewis 78.
13. Lydia Austin Parrish, *Records of Some Southern Loyalists*, (A collection of Manuscripts of some Loyalists, most of whom migrated to the Bahamas, typed by Maxfield Parrish 1953) located at Widener Library, Harvard University and on microfilm at Nassau Public Archives, p. 225; Sandra Riley, *Homeward Bound: A History of the Bahama Islands up to 1850* (Island Research, Florida 1985) p. 133.
14. Lewis p. 79.
15. Michael Craton and Gail Saunders, Islanders in the Stream: *A History of the Bahamas*. Vol 1, (Athens, University of Georgia Press, 1992), p. 168.
16. Eric Beerman, *The Last Battle of the American Revolution: Yorktown. No, The Bahamas!* (The Americas, West Bethseda MD, July 1988) p. 85).
17. Beerman p. 83; Lewis footnote p. 48, 49.
18. Michael Craton, *A History of the Bahamas*, (San Salvador Press 1962), p. 143.
19. Lewis p. 29.
20. Lewis p. 46.
21. Lewis p.121 (note 12).
22. Lewis p. 48.
23. CO 23/26/160, Report of American Loyalists, date not given but late 1784 or early 1785.
24. Lt John Wilson's report on the Bahama Islands 1783, located in the Boston Public Library. CO 23/26/86, Extract Don Antonio Claraco to Governor Maxwell late 1783.
25. Lewis p. 49.
26. Lewis p. 55.
27. Paul Albury, *The Story of the Bahamas*, (MacMillan Caribbean 1975), p. 104.
28. CO 23/26/105½ Correspondence Carleton/Deveaux of September 1783 transmitted by Thomas Roker 22 February 1785.
29. CO 23/26/224/25 Memorial of 71 Harbour Island participants in the recapture of Nassau 25 April 1786.
30. Albury, p. 106.

31 Lt John Wilson's report on the Bahama Islands 1783, located in the Boston Public Library. See Appendix 8.
32 See Appendix 5.
33 CO 23/26/224 Memorial of 71 Harbour Island participants in the recapture of Nassau 25 April 1786.
34 McKinnen p. 252.
35 CO 23/26/224 Memorial of 71 Harbour Island participants in the recapture of Nassau 25 April 1786.
36 CO 23/15/163 Robert Rumer to Lord Sydney 11 March 1784.
37 Lewis p. 67.
38 CO 23/26/86, Extract Don Antonio Claraco to Governor Maxwell late 1783.
39 CO 23/26/40–42 Depositions of Thomas Dow and Daniel Wheeler 21 May 1783.
40 Lewis p. 76.
41 CO 23/26/105½ Correspondence Carleton/Deveaux of September 1783, transmitted by Thomas Roker 22 February 1785.
42 CO 23/26/40–42 Depositions of Thomas Dow and Daniel Wheeler 21 May 1783.
43 Parrish p. 226.
44 CO 23/26/86, Extract Don Antonio Claraco to Governor Maxwell late 1783.
45 CO 23/26/224 Memorial of 71 Harbour Island participants in the recapture of Nassau 25 April 1786.
46 Land Grants were as follows:
Isaac Baillou – 500 acres Blue Hills, 20 acres New Providence
John Buckley – 220 Long Island (Buckleys named after him)
Andrew Deveaux – 780 & 390 acres Cat Island, 220 acres Long Island, 420 acres New Providence
Seth Doud – 200 acres Cat Island, A lot on New Providence.
Samuel Higgs – 300 acres Eleuthera
George Holiday – A lot on New Providence
Alexander Lorrimer – 940 acres Cat Island
William Lyford – 592 & 292 acres Cat Island, 448 acres New Providence (Lyford Cay)
Simon Martingale – A lot New Providence
John Morris – 300 & 240 acres Long Island
Robert Rumer – 1200 acres Rum Cay, 100 acres Long Island, 60 & 60 acres Rose I
Richard Sweeting – 460 acres Exuma, A lot New Providence,
Archibald Taylor – 100 & 120 acres Long Island, 300 acres Watlings Island.
47 CO23/243/350 Report by Governor Haynes Smith 6 May1896.
48 CO 23/93/367 Report of Stipiendry Magistrate Thomas Winder 8 June 1835; CO 23/107/314 Burnside's Report 28 December 1840.
49 Cockram's map.
50 CO 23/108/108½ Sir Francis Cockburn's dispatch of 22 April 1840.
51 See Appendix 6.
52 Interview with Damien Gomez ; CO 23/107/312 Burnside's Report 28 December 1840.
53 The Statute Law of The Bahamas Vol IV, p. 1855.
54 The Statute Law of The Bahamas Vol IV, section 3, p. 1855.
55 Nassau Tribune, 26 May 1999.
56 CO 23/243/350 Report by Governor Haynes Smith 6 May1896.
57 S.G.W. Benjamin, *The Atlantic Islands*, (Harper and Brothers, New York 1878) p. 29.

6

Dunmore's favourite retreat

The winds of the American Revolutionary War swept hard and fast across the thirteen American colonies lobbying for independence from Britain, and their force extended beyond the shores of the American continent. Indeed they ushered in momentous changes in the long-standing relationship between the Bahamas and the American eastern seaboard colonies, whose puritan settlers had suffered the same hardships as the Eleutheran Adventurers, faced the same adversities as pioneer settlers, and fought the same enemy as English colonies. The friendship between the two sister colonies went back uninterrupted to 1649, when the New England colonists so generously gave to the destitute pioneers. Kinship connections were established from as early as 1684 between the two, as Bahamian refugees, in the wake of Spanish attacks, fled to the northern colonies. Steady trade had further enhanced the relationship between the Bahamas and the American colonies. The outbreak of the revolutionary war brought an abrupt change to this long-standing relationship forged over one hundred and thirty years and for the first time in its history, the Bahamian colonists became the enemy of those American colonists fighting for independence. From the rebels' point of view, a strike against the Bahamas was in effect a strike against Britain.

The closing of the American ports at the opening of the war dealt a serious blow to the flourishing trade with Charleston and St. Augustine, where Bahamian merchants sold pineapples, lemons, limes, oranges, turtle and wood and brought back much needed provisions such as flour, rice, grains, livestock and lumber.[1] The wartime scourges of provision scarcity and inflation were somewhat delayed by a licence allowing Bahamian merchants free and open intercourse with the rebels for the first two years. The 1776 authorization for privateering by the American congress was further cause for alarm among Bahamian merchants, should the American privateers destroy what little trade remained.

While Nassau suffered the indignity of two attacks by rebel privateers[2] and the inhabitants were reduced to 'little above a starving condition'[3], the Harbour Islanders were not so adversely affected. Rev. Richard Moss, the first Anglican minister at Harbour Island, complained that '…we are so unhappy here to have our harbour made into a place of trade for the Americans… Their ships are always lying in this harbour'.[4] While the merchants at Harbour Island welcomed the exchange of much needed American provisions for Eleutheran salt and locally grown fruit and vegetables, they were intimidated by the rough behaviour of the rebel privateers.[5]

On one occasion, rebel captains, after hearing Moss preach a sermon and pray for the health of the King of England, were much enraged by the homage paid to King George. They went to Moss' house at night and abducted him to their vessel with the intention of taking him prisoner to America. Several Harbour Island people intervened on Moss' behalf and rescued him from the hands of the American rebels.[6]

Bahamian loyalty to the crown was questioned more than once in the early days of the war and many were charged with being rebel sympathizers. While undoubtedly some Bahamians joined the rebel cause, the majority of them were indifferent to the outcome of the War, and their continued trade with the rebels was driven more by self-interest than ideological persuasion. If some behaved equivocally, it was more from the difficulty of striking a balance between sovereign fealty and family ties on the main land than support for the rebels.

The entry of France and then Spain into the American Revolutionary War, in support of the rebel colonies, awakened the Bahamian people from their state of passive ambivalence and catapulted them into action. Nassau was revived as a formidable privateering base from which Bahamian privateers effectively crippled the trade between the rebel colonies and the Caribbean by the capture of a large number of American vessels.[7] The Vice-Admiralty Court register lists[8] a number of names with Harbour Island connections as captains of the privateers: George Dorsett, George Johnson, Henry Johnson, William Johnson, John Petty, John Pinder, John Sweeting, Richard Sweeting, Benjamin Watkins, Robert Bell and Robert Henzell, the last two being representatives for Harbour Island in the House of Assembly for 1780 and 1784 respectively.

Many Out Island people had resorted to smuggling to offset the very serious decline in trade as a result of the privateering war being waged in Bahamian waters. Once Nassau was distracted with the Spanish occupation, smuggling became an easy way to overcome the acute shortages faced by the Out Island people. One of Lt. Governor James Powell's first requests in 1785, was for a shallow-draft vessel to cruise about the islands, particularly Turks Island, Harbour Island, Eleuthera and Abaco 'where most of this vile traffic, so injurious to the fair Trader and his Majesty's Revenue is carried on with impunity…'[9] He reported that goods smuggled into these out islands, most often in American bottoms, were auctioned by noon in Nassau, and the departing vessels took with them salt, woods and later cotton, none of which was officially cleared out or accounted for in customs duties.

The Versailles Treaty of 1783 ended the Revolutionary War and recognized the new United States of America. In addition, the Bahamas was officially restored to Great Britain and Florida ceded to Spain. This latter agreement triggered the start of the Loyalist migration from Florida to the Bahamas. Over the following three years, more than 5,000 Loyalists and their slaves, who had retreated behind British lines in East Florida, poured into the Bahamas to begin life anew. At the same time, some 1,000 Loyalists sailed from New York to Abaco. This influx had the staggering effect of doubling the population of 4,002, raising the black population from one-half to two-thirds of the total and increasing the inhabited islands from 7 to 12. It was a watershed event in the history of Bahamian affairs where a new merchant planter economy was superimposed on the old largely seafaring economy, laying the foundation for agricultural development in the nineteenth century.

The interface between the old and new inhabitants played out differently on the islands, some of which were inhabited exclusively by the Loyalist refugees, others of which were inhabited by the old inhabitants and yet others by both old and new. The Loyalist planters and their slaves in the southern plantation islands were far removed from the older settlements and posed no threat to the status quo. Eleuthera and Harbour Island, the second and third most populated islands at the time, were not settled in the early years by the Loyalists, and thus the old inhabitants there felt no sense of intrusion and could better avail themselves of the opportunities created by the Loyalist presence in Nassau. However the situation was volatile in Nassau, where the new inhabitants outnumbered the old inhabitants by the year 1788, and the better-educated and wealthier planters and merchants from America tried to wrest the government from the old guard of wreckers, privateers, fishermen and woodcutters.

Adam Christie, a Loyalist and later a council member, referred to the two 'violent and indecent factions, with which no honest man could at all times act…'[11] and Governor Maxwell described the Loyalists in Nassau as '…the most tormenting, Dissatisfied people on earth…'[12] The Loyalist William Wylly, a barrister-at-law, was very critical of the 'perversion of public justice prevailing' and assailed the council members as destitute bankrupts and habitual drunkards of the lowest description'.[13] The political rivalry between the two groups was intense and pitted the resourcefulness and tenacity of the old inhabitants against the ambition and determination of the new.

A missionary at Harbour Island, Rev. Thomas Robertson, sided with the old inhabitants in a 1791 report to the Society for the Propagation of the Gospel:

> I make no doubt that the society well knows the Bahamas has long been disturbed with political disputes between old and new inhabitants. I live upon a small sequestered island at a distance from them, and when I happen to go to New Providence, I endeavour to be on good terms with them all yet in my humble opinion I think the Governor and Council act humanely in protecting the old inhabitants who are all very poor ignorant people from the oppression of the new who effect to despise them.[14]

Harbour Island and Eleuthera were fortunate not to be among the islands initially settled by the Loyalists, as the old inhabitants there, especially from the settlements predating Nassau, might have protested more vociferously than the Nassau inhabitants. Although the populations of these two islands had grown slowly, the majority of inhabitants were inextricably tied to the soil that their forefathers had settled over a century before. Their sense of ownership was deep rooted, even though they had no official grants of land, and any large influx of refugees to their shores would have met strong resistance.

Prior to the Loyalist arrival, Rev. Moss described the settlement of Harbour Island as 'a tight and orderly community of sixty families, living mainly a maritime life, building their own ships, and growing subsistence crops and raking salt on the nearby mainland of Eleuthera'.[15] Some of the mariners with more substantial vessels undertook longer voyages to the Gulf of Florida to turtle and fish, to the Abaco mainland to cut wood or to the Abaco Cays to wreck. Their wooden houses were simple in structure using shipbuilding skills, the windows were wood-shuttered and the roofs cedar-shingled or palm-thatched. It is likely that the settlement expanded along the harbour shoreline so that the mariners could keep an eye on their fifty-vessel sailing fleet. The only public buildings were a church/school house, built in 1764, on the corner of Bay and Church Streets, and St. John's Anglican Church, built in 1768. The seaside settlement was probably reminiscent of a New England fishing village.

The reconstituted assembly of 1784 reduced the number of seats for the islands of New Providence, Harbour Island and Eleuthera, until then the only islands represented in the House, from 24 to 14 members, and the islands of Cat, Andros, Long, Abaco and Exuma were represented for the first time by 11 members, 9 of whom were staunch Loyalists. Representation for Harbour Island and Eleuthera was reduced from 4 to 3 members, and this had little effect on their voice in the assembly since their populations were just over 600 in 1782. Samuel Higgs, Thomas Johnson and Robert Thompson Henzell were good representatives for Harbour Island since Higgs and Johnson were native sons of the soil and lived in Harbour Island, and Henzell most likely was connected to the Harbour Island Thompsons. The requirement in later years that representatives be resident in Nassau would change the effectiveness of family island representation in the House of Assembly.

Perhaps the single most important change that came about as a result of the Loyalist influx into the Bahamas was the purchase of the Bahamian land from the Lord Proprietors in 1787. Since 1718, the royal governors controlled the military and civil government but the monopoly of land allocation and the collection of quit rents remained the prerogative of the Lords Proprietors. Governor Fitzwilliam in 1733 had argued that new settlers would only be attracted to the infant colony if the Crown purchased the right of the soil and the governor thereby empowered to grant lands.[16] Fifty years later, Governor Shirley's 1773 analysis of tenures confirmed that land titles were limited to town lots in Nassau and tracts on New Providence, Rose and Hog Island; out island people had never received land grants, and apart from 2 or 3 families who held land by warrants of survey, they had no title to their land but that of possession.[17] So the purchase of the Bahamian land by the Crown, largely motivated by the arrival of the Loyalists, was a blessing for old and new inhabitants alike.

Although Harbour Island was not directly affected by the arrival of Loyalists to her shores during the massive exodus from East Florida, Governor Dunmore's attraction to and sustained interest in the island and the eventual interconnections between the Harbour Islanders and the Abaco Loyalists meant certain changes for Harbour Island, most of which were positive.

The controversial governor was not long in his new position, before he realized the value of Harbour Island as a necessary retreat from the political imbroglio that gripped Nassau. Furthermore, Dunmore had entered the foray by refusing to dissolve the illegally constituted assembly, thereby fixing himself firmly in the old inhabitant camp. The old settlement on Harbour Island, free of politically zealous Loyalists, was an ideal sanctuary and by 1787 he had built himself a summer residence on the hill overlooking the harbour (Fig. 29).

Dunmore's attention to Harbour Island must have been a welcome change to the previous governors who dismissed the settlement as being unworthy of consideration. Governor Shirley had described it as 'a small and barren spot inhabited principally because of its healthy situation and its vicinity to the island of Eleuthera...'[18] Dunmore on the other hand was impressed by the Harbour Island people and remarked, 'I could not but view with peculiar pleasure, the early and persevering industry of the inhabitants of Harbour Island to improve their town and country'.[19] And in one of his reports he described the Harbour Island people as '... a remarkable tall, stout, healthy set of people as any I've seen in any country'.[20]

While Governor Shirley did not mention Harbour Island in his list of islands with harbours, the security-conscious Dunmore observed that the harbour at Harbour Island was the best adapted of all he had seen for sloops of war or privateers to lay, in the event of a war with the French, Spaniards or Americans, 'as from the hill they can discover vessels at considerable distances, and if they want to pursue them can easily go in the ocean'.[21] It was not long before he built a fortification on Barracks Hill and posted a guard, most likely at the same site as the pirates' lookout seventy years before.

He then turned his attention to the laying out of the town, named Dunmore Town in his honour, and the granting of lots to the inhabitants. In 1788, Dunmore had sent Messrs. Sterling, O'Halloran, Dumaresque and Josiah Tattnall, the Surveyor General, to Harbour Island. These gentlemen were charged with the responsibility of assessing land claims and counterclaims, surveying the land for division into lots with appropriate roads, and processing the applications for grants. Since Harbour Island was an old settlement, the grants were no more than official proof of ownership of the land, by people who had lived on and cultivated the land for more than a century.

On 5 October 1790, front lots in the newly laid out Dunmore Town were granted to Governor Dunmore and upwards of 130 others.[22] The back lots of the township continued to be held by title of occupancy.[23] A.T. Bethell provides us with the names of ninety of the original grantees but The Church of Latter Day Saints provides a complete list, mostly old inhabitants, and the number of the lot granted. The predominant names of Albury, Cash, Cleare, Curry, Johnson, Roberts, Russell, Saunders, Sweeting and Thompson were established Harbour Island families, listed in the 1731 census. Also included were five Loyalists who became prominent in Dunmore's council and probably lived intermittently at Harbour Island: Philip Dumaresque, Josiah Tatnall, William Jones, Moses Franks and Adam Christie, the latter two eventually becoming outspoken critics of Dunmore. Free mulattoes and free blacks were also among the original grantees: Thomas Lightbourn, Samuel Patrick, William Simms, Rebecca Sweeting and Florence Thompson.

Governor Dunmore was further immortalized in the naming of Dunmore Street, the main street through the town, parallel to Bay Street, and Murray Street named for the governor's family surname. The names of other main streets reflected loyalty to the Crown, adding to the old-world colonial charm of the township. King Street, Crown Street, Prince's Street, Clarence, Duke, York and Pitt Streets honoured the Old Empire.

The initial meeting between the old inhabitants of Harbour Island and the new inhabitants of Maxwell Town and Carleton on the Abaco mainland, probably took place as early as 1783, soon after the Loyalists from New York had arrived in Abaco to start life anew. The Eleutheran and Harbour Island people had cut timber and fished for turtle, ambergris and wrecks in the Abacos for over 125 years and considered the island their home away from home.[24] The plantations reported by Lewis prior to the Loyalist arrival were possibly planted by Harbour Islanders to feed the crews on their wrecking or woodcutting expeditions.

When Philip Dumaresque, one of the Abaco Loyalists from New York, wrote, 'the earlier inhabitants of the island did not welcome us with cordiality'[25] and that Maxwell had appointed him a magistrate '...to keep me from being insulted by the Abaco blackguards...'[26] the Harbour Island fishermen and woodcutters were implicated. Undoubtedly the arrival of more than one thousand Loyalists to this heretofore unsettled island was somewhat disconcerting to the old inhabitants of Harbour Island.

The widespread failure of the cotton harvest in 1788 triggered an exodus from Abaco and the southern plantation islands. Many planters returned to Georgia and others went to Caicos, Long Island and South Eleuthera. A population increase for Harbour Island between 1788 to 1790 strongly suggests that many Abaco Loyalists might have settled there as well. By 1789, Dunmore reported some ten families and slaves remaining on Abaco, largely those lacking the capital of the planter-merchant elite and having no choice but to adjust to the only practical economy of the Bahamas, one directly or indirectly tied to the sea.[27] Several of the remaining Loyalist families in Abaco sought refuge in Harbour Island from the constant harassment by French privateers off Abaco. And by 1796, Martin Weatherford, John Cornish, John Cooke, David Melone, Ephram Melone, Wyannie Melone, Jacob Adams, Anne Ferguson and John Harris were comfortably settled in the newly laid out Dunmore Town.[28]

The integration of these Loyalists into Harbour Island society was harmonious and without the acrimony prevailing in Nassau. Craton and Saunders pointed out that the Loyalists from Abaco were very different from the aristocratic planter-merchant class in Nassau and they 'found more affinities with the old inhabitants of Harbour Island and Eleuthera than with Nassauvians or the planters of the southern islands'.[29] Indeed many of the Abaco Loyalists married into the old established families of Harbour Island, and the proprietors' names listed in the later slave registers for Abaco are remarkably identical to those for Harbour Island.[30] The offspring of the first generation Loyalists continued to marry into the Harbour Island families and eventually only a few of the original Abaco Loyalist names survived: namely Cornish, Adams, Cooke, Harris, Malone, Weatherford and Archer. (See Appendix 7.)

The Harbour Island inhabitants availed themselves of the new opportunities arising from the dramatic increase in the colony's population. The demand for food and building supplies was greater than ever before in the history of the country, and more and more people turned to cultivation of the soil. A number of Harbour Island people bought land at the Cove (later Gregory Town) on Eleuthera and started cultivating plantations of vegetables and fruit for the Nassau market.[31] The grants of land ranged between from 120 to 400 acres, and their purchase represented the first attempts of the Harbour Island people to move beyond subsistence farming and cultivate crops for export. In the 1790s a fleet of twenty-three sloops and schooners from Harbour Island plied the waters between Harbour Island and Nassau with the freshly grown produce.[32]

Several Harbour Island men were engaged in the increasingly profitable timber cutting on Abaco, the timber being much in demand for the building of houses and boats. Loyalist land owners had given permission to the Harbour Island woodcutters to cut cedars and other woods on their lands at Great and Little Abaco,[33] which boasted red cedar large enough to build a vessel of 350 tons. This steady source of employment was disrupted in 1797 when the French privateers captured the Harbour Island vessels and occupied the Abaco coast, creating a scarcity of timber.[34]

The reopening of the land office in 1802, after a 12-year moratorium on the granting of land, gave rise to a repopulation of Abaco, especially the offshore cays, by the Loyalists who had settled in Harbour Island and possibly by Harbour Island wreckers wanting to establish a base on the cays.[35] The devastation and loss of homes suffered by the Harbour Island people in the 1806 hurricane might have been a further incentive for those with Abaco connections to migrate to the cays to the north. Over the first two decades of the nineteenth century, a steady trickle of people moved from Harbour Island and Spanish Wells to the Abaco cays and for the first time, Green Turtle Cay, Man of War, Hope Town, Great Guana Cay and Cherokee Sound were permanently settled. The first children born on the cays were from intermarriages between Abaco Loyalists and Harbour Island old inhabitants, which ensured close social and trading connections between the cays and Harbour Island, and initially baptisms and marriages of these children frequently took place in Harbour Island.

Green Turtle Cay, like Harbour Island, was a racially integrated settlement with the black population living on the periphery of the townships. Early settlers on Green Turtle Cay were Curry, Kemp, Lowe, Albury and Saunders. Hope Town and Man-of-War were predominantly white settlements, similar to Spanish Wells, and the slaves of these nearly all-white settlements lived on the mainland. The early settlers on these cays were more of a mix between old and new: Malone, Adams, Russell, Tedder, Albury and Roberts in Hope Town and Archer, Albury and Weatherford on Man-of-War. Whether the racially segregated living was a result of rigid master-slave relationships or the lack of available land on the cays is not clear. It would necessarily be reinforced later in 1838, especially on the smaller cays, when the land given to the freed slaves was by necessity frequently located on the mainland.

It is befitting to have a closer look at the controversial loyalist governor, John Murray, 4th Earl of Dunmore, so beloved by the old inhabitants of Harbour Island and Eleuthera and so besmirched by the Loyalists in Nassau. Historians have profiled him in a very negative light, readily exposing his unarguable defects but ignoring the contributions he made during his 9-year tenure as Governor of the Bahamas. In addition, the good he achieved for the colony has been overshadowed by his notoriety as a despotic governor, because his arch opponents in the Loyalist faction, William Whylly, Adam Christie and Moses Franks were most prolific in their written criticisms of him which no doubt contributed to his eventual recall in 1796.

Dunmore's abuse of power was seen in his suspension of the justice system, his packing the House of Assembly and his alleged duplicity in the granting of land. The level of self-interest pervading his land grants exposed his lack of integrity and before long he unashamedly owned land in Andros, Long Island, Abaco, Eleuthera, Harbour Island and New Providence along with two sumptuous houses on New Providence and the substantive summer retreat in Harbour Island. It was no wonder that so many of his actions came under fire as he made one of his sons a representative for Eleuthera and the other an agent for Turks, and then committed the ultimate act of nepotism by appointing his son Lieutenant Governor without approval from London. These were all unquestionably indefensible actions that brought a dimension of corruption to his government.

On the other hand, Dunmore's institution of a tribunal to examine the claims of freedom of slaves was seen as a ploy to acquire more slaves for himself and an attempt to rankle the Loyalists whose wealth and status were based on slaves. However Dunmore's partiality to slaves was demonstrated during the Revolutionary War, when as Governor of Virginia he offered freedom to all slaves in Virginia and North Carolina who bore arms in His Majesty's troops. From Dunmore's point of view the tribunal was to ensure that the promise of freedom was honoured and more immediately to quell the malaise among the Abaco slaves. In a letter to Lord Sydney, his sympathy for the slaves was clear when he explained that the recent unrest among the slave population was occasioned by the whites 'who had detained several of these poor unhappy People under various pretences in a State of Slavery' and were sending out posses to round up blacks whom they suspected of being slaves.[36]

Dunmore was seen to be headstrong and extravagant when he continued to build another fort on Society Hill and batteries at Winton, Hog Island and Potter's Cay, after England had complained bitterly about the excessive cost of Fort Charlotte, and instructed him to suspend all work except in the case of a 'sudden and unforeseen emergency'.[37] And Dunmore was further charged with disobeying His Majesty's instructions to desist in the granting of land. Dunmore explained that on the first count, he had no objective other than the defence of the colony and that the only land granted after the moratorium was what was being processed at the time of his receiving instructions. The infrequency of boats from England and the arrival of dispatches from the home office some 8–11 months after they were sent also contributed to the significant delay between an instruction and the governor's response to it. In his own defence, he asserted, 'My conduct where blamable is due to local difficulties rather than a willful adherence to my own judgment or plans.'[38]

Had Dunmore obeyed the home office's decree that provisions not be imported in foreign vessels and had he not issued a proclamation allowing American vessels to bring in corn, grain, pulse, flour, bread, rice and salted provisions, Bahamians would have faced acute shortages. Although he contravened the trade laws, he acted in the best interest of the inhabitants. English laws enacted three thousand miles away were often not beneficial to the colonies. And to this extent, a resourceful and innovative governor who was not afraid to step outside the legal boundaries was an indisputable asset.

Dunmore's relationship with the people of Harbour Island was not always without rancour. His appropriation of land on the ancient burial ground, which he fenced in for use as pastureland and cultivation for his slaves, upset the parishioners. When Rev. Gordon, on the advice of the council, pulled down a part of the wall to assert the right of the parish, Dunmore's overseer ran up threatening to shoot the first man who should throw down another stone.[39] Another problem for the church was Dunmore's purchase of the deceased Rev. Robertson's house, which was on land not yet granted but designated for a glebe.

Perhaps Dunmore's most inglorious hour on this little island was an unfortunate encounter with a 55-year-old planter, John Cleare, in which Dunmore displayed a virulent outburst of temper, most unbecoming of his position. In Cleare's written deposition he explained that while he was in conversation with Samuel Higgs, Governor Dunmore approached and asked Higgs, 'Is this the old rascal...?' When Higgs answered in the affirmative, Dunmore viciously attacked Cleare and beat him with a stick over the head, without provocation.[40] Whatever the motive, Dunmore exposed a dark side of his nature, just weeks before his recall.

These minor wrangles did not diminish the respect and admiration that the Harbour Island people felt for the governor. His frequent visits to his retreat in Harbour Island had given the people many opportunities to see his more caring and human attributes. On one occasion, he pleaded the case of the poor inhabitants of Harbour Island and Eleuthera, requesting that they be exempted from charges for warrants of survey and land grants like the Loyalist refugees.[41] Although the request was denied, his empathy for the 'poor industrious set of people' and the old inhabitants on Harbour Island won him their trust and affection. On another occasion when the attorney general, Moses Franks, condemned wrecking as a 'repugnant' business and criticized Dunmore for giving out wrecking papers exempting vessels so engaged from customs duties, Dunmore argued the case for the oldest industry in the Bahamas. He pointed out that the wrecking business had saved many lives and much valuable property, and had been the lifeblood of many Bahamians for generations.[42] He disregarded Franks' objection and continued to grant wrecking licences and papers. The welfare of the people was a priority of the governor and he rarely followed advice or sometimes even instructions that were not in the best interest of the inhabitants.

The power that Dunmore wielded over the people at Harbour Island was implied when Rev. Philip Dixon pointed out that there was no point complaining to the Harbour Island inhabitants about Dunmore's refusal to rent his residence to him 'so abjectly devoted are most people to him'.[43] And on a more critical note, Adam Christie, in a letter to Dunmore's successor, explained how easily Dunmore packed the assembly:

> At Harbour Island and Eleuthera whose inhabitants are ignorant indigent Fishermen and Woodcutters, Lord D. can put in what Members he pleases, and I understand he is now about to visit them for the purpose of managing the Election ... His retaining his property at Harbour Island, is a proof that he wishes to retain his influence there, and his influence never did any good anywhere.[44]

In a rather dispassionate letter to Dunmore on the eve of his departure, the inhabitants of New Providence thanked him for the fortifications and public works. For many people in Nassau, especially the Loyalist faction, his recall was long overdue. In contrast the Harbour Island inhabitants with a greater sense of gratitude and a deeper sense of affection expressed their 'painful feelings at his unexpected departure' and recognized the great strides the colony had made in agricultural and commercial development. 'This island (Harbour Island) has experienced your excellency's generous and friendly attention, not only by the laudable example which you have shewn us of improving our town and island, but of your excellency's invariable goodwill and kindness to the people at large and your distinguished humanity to the poor.'[45] The Eleutherans went one step further in praise of Dunmore and dated the prosperity of the Bahamas back to Dunmore's arrival 'for the commerce and internal improvements have since then surpassed all former times'.[46] Dr. Paul Albury noted, of the controversial governor who laid out the town on Harbour Island: '…today history looks at him more kindly and the town which perpetuates his name is proud of its association with John Murray, 4th Earl of Dunmore'.[47]

Notes

1. CO 23/22/59 – 72, Report of Governor Shirley to Earl of Dartmouth, 1773.
2. Hopkins and Rathbourn.
3. Sandra Riley, p. 98.
4. United Society for the Propagation of the Gospel, Reel 1, Moss to Society 20 April 1777.
5. Craton and Saunders, Vol 1, p. 168.
6. USPG Reel 1, Moss to Society 20 April 1777.
7. See Chapter 5, p. 47.
8. CO 23/ 25/46–47, Prizes condemned by the Prize Court, 1778–1782.
9. Sandra Riley, p. 164.
10. Craton and Saunders, Vol 1, chapter 12, note 1, p. 421; Report, 1784, 7, Wilson Papers, Boston Public Library.
11. Thelma Peters, *The American Loyalists and the Plantation Period in the Bahama Islands,* University of Florida 1960, p. 98.
12. Craton and Saunders, Vol 1, p. 179.
13. Lydia Austin Parrish, *Records of Some Southern Loyalists,* (A collection of Manuscripts of some Loyalists, most of whom migrated to the Bahamas, typed by Maxfield Parrish 1953) located at Widener Library, Harvard University and on microfilm at Nassau Public Archives, p. 36/44.
14. USPG Reel 1, Thomas Robertson to Society 6 October 1791.
15. Craton and Saunders, Vol 1, p. 174.
16. CSP 40/57, Petition of Governor Fitxwilliam to the King, 23 February 1733.
17. Craton and Saunders, Vol 1, p. 165.
18. CO 23//22/59 Governor Shirley's report to Earl of Dartmouth, 1773.
19. CO 23/35/25; Dunmore to Harbour Island inhabitants, 19 October 1796.
20. CO 23/30/240 Dunmore's Report, 1 September 1790.
21. Ibid.
22. CO 23/34/5–7 A list of Lots of Land granted by His Excellency Lord Dunmore… from the 18 June 1790 and 31 May 1794. This list gives the grant of the lots at Dunmore Town as 5 October 1790, whereas CO 23 33/112b dates the Dunmore Town Grants as 5 October 1791.
23. CO 23/34/361, Stephen Haven to Rev. Gordon dated 19 May 1796.
24. Sandra Riley, p. 158.

25 Sandra Riley, p. 136.
26 Sandra Riley, p. 158; Gardiner, Whipple and Allen Family Papers vol. II 49, MHS.
27 CO 23/30/238 Lord Dunmore's Report 1 September 1790; Peters p. 55.
28 These names do not appear on the 1791 Grants of Dunmore Town yet appear on the list of Harbour Islanders welcoming Governor Forbes 1796, CO 23/35/173. The Melones and Jacob Adams eventually returned to Abaco.
29 Craton and Saunders, Vol 1, p. 182.
30 Sandra Riley, p. 275.
31 Lands and Surveys map of Eleuthera, Sheet 2 dated 26 August 1966 in conjunction with the Land Grants in the various CO 23 files listed below.

Name	Acres	Reference	Date	
Higgs, Henrietta	52	Co 23/74/35	1820/Oct	from HI
Saunders, Benjamin	200	Co 23/30/301	1789/3rd/Dec	from HI
Typuse, Andrew	40	Co 23/28/54	1788/7th/Feb	Loyalist
Ranger, John		Co 23/30/301	1789/3rd/Dec	from HI
Curry, Joseph	220	Co 23/29/45	1788/27th/Oct	from HI
Sweeting, Samuel	260	Co 23/29/39	1788/2nd/Oct	from HI
Nix, John	100	Co 23/30/223	1789/12th/Dec	also HI
Parkes, George C	160	Co 23/30/219	1789/8th/July	from HI
Sears, Richard	156	Co 23/33/117	1791/26th/Feb	from HI
Johnston, Samuel	400	Co 23/30/306	1790/20th/Jan	from HI
Johnston, Samuel Jr	120	Co 23/30/310	1790/6th/May	from HI
Johnson, Samuel	120	Co 23/33/118	1791/26th/Feb	from HI
Mullin, Patrick	260	Co 23/30/218	1789/8th/Jul	Loyalist
Higgs, Samuel	300	Co 23/29/38	1788/2nd/Oct	from HI
Kemp, Benjamin	260	Co 23/29/39	1788/2nd/Oct	from HI
Kemp, Martha	260	Co 23/33/117	1791/11th/Jan	from HI
DuBois, Isaac	200	Co 23/29/45	1788/27th/Oct	Loyalist
Dubois, Isaac	500	Co 23/30/222	1789/25th/Dec	

32 Shipping Notices in the *Bahama Gazettes* of 1790 through 1794.
33 *Bahama Gazette* 4 November 1794; Sandra Riley, p. 185.
34 CO 23/35/149, Governor Forbes to England, 28 February 1797.
35 Sandra Riley, pp. 193–196.
36 Craton and Saunders, Vol 1, p. 200.
37 CO 23/34/96, Whithall to Dunmore, January 1796.
38 CO 23/36/20, Forbes to Duke of Portland, May 1797.
39 CO 23/34/359, Wm Morrice, Secretary USPG to J.King, 2 November 1796.
40 CO 23/34/365, John Clear to Adam Chrystie, 28 June 1796.
41 CO 23/29/3, Dunmore to Lord Sydney, 1789.
42 CO 23/33/125, Moses Franks to London 1795; Sandra Riley p.187.
43 CO 23/33/134b Dunmore to Rev Dixon, 1794.
44 Peters page102; Parrish p. 208.
45 *Bahama Gazette* 5 October 1796.
46 *Bahama Gazette* 1 November 1796.
47 Bahamas Handbook, 1967–68, Etienne Dupuch Publications, p. 26.

7

A near run thing

> Harbour Island is so happy to all others in the Bahamas and so much courted for her pure, serene and healthful air. Proverbially called the Phisitian. Natives or inhabitants of other islands in great sickness but strength enough to get to Harbour Island, it is scarce in memory they have failed to recover a good state of health in 15 or 20 days.

This 1722 report was early recognition of the healing powers of the Harbour Island air, and increasingly over the eighteenth century, Harbour Island became a reputed health resort.[1] And after Governor Halkett built wooden barracks to accommodate 50 men on Barracks Hill in 1803, sick troops were constantly sent to 'the most healthy island in the Bahamas' to recover their health.[2] Halkett excused his erecting the barracks without the necessary prior approval as a matter of urgency: the barracks would save the lives of many troops, especially those newly arrived in the Bahamas.

It was fashionable among high society in Nassau to escape the fevers that raged through the garrison in the summertime. It was to this end that Governor Cameron went to Royal Island with his family one summer, while the fever inflicted a high mortality rate among the 99th Regiment stationed in Nassau.[3] And William Whylly with his family spent the summer at Harbour Island in 1803, during which time 50 dying men from the 7th Regiment of the Royal Fusiliers were sent to Harbour Island. With the help of Whylly's horse, the more sickly were transported to the newly built barracks, and all except one, were restored to good health. When they were sent back to Nassau at the end of the year in 'perfect health', many contracted yellow fever and died three days later.[4] Although Harbour Island and New Providence are little different in latitude or rainfall, the contrast between the constant good health of troops in Harbour Island and the high mortality rate among troops in Nassau was a matter of geology. Harbour Island consists of lofty ridges of deep loose sand at the base of which is porous stone, so that the rains sink as fast as they fall, and so completely are they absorbed, that not a gallon of stagnant water is to be found, throughout the year, on any part of the island. On the other hand, New Providence is flat and abounds in swamps, salinas and fresh-water ponds, the substratum of which is solid rock, through which rainfall escapes very sparingly. The combination of a sultry and moist atmosphere, as exists in New Providence, was medically proven to produce bilious or yellow fevers.[5]

And thus it was no surprise when Governor Dowdeswell, troubled with a feverish complaint, was advised to pass some time at Harbour Island, for the benefit of the change in the air.[6] The high recovery rate of those staying at the barracks quickly justified their expense, and in time Harbour Island became widely celebrated for its salubrity, despite the age-old association of tropical climes with unhealthiness.[7] After the initial use of the barracks as a clinic for fevered troops from Nassau, it eventually became an official military outpost where soldiers were posted in times of war as an advance guard or when the barracks were overcrowded in Nassau. In 1806, a detachment of the 99th Regiment stationed in Nassau, consisting of 2 officers, 3 sergeants, 1 drummer and 47 rank and file were sent on command to Harbour Island.[8] These troops were resident in the barracks which were blown down in the 1806 hurricane, the worst ever in the history of the island, and presumably they played a major part in rebuilding the barracks, the church and 160 homes, extensively damaged by the hurricane.[9]

Although the soldiers lived on Barracks Hill, outside and to the north of the township, they fraternized with the locals and engaged in community work when off garrison duty. Their presence at the military post brought an added measure of security to the island and they generally enjoyed the respect and affection of the community. Letters from the Harbour Island inhabitants to the captains of regiments about to leave, typically expressed regret about the imminent departure of the troops, commended their peaceful and orderly conduct and thanked them for their public service. Capt. William Major of His Majesty's 2nd West Indian Regiment was praised 'for the works of public utility' especially the erection of a telegraphical flag post and the necessary appendages 'which has made our island assume a respectable appearance'.[10]

Capt. John Smith of the 2nd European Garrison Company, stationed at the barracks for two years, reflected nostalgically on their stay at Harbour Island. He remarked that 'the mild, inoffensive and peaceable disposition of the people' was endearing to him and the soldiers, and they would forever remember the tranquil days spent there.[11] Apparently, the War of 1812 had not directly affected the Harbour Island community up to the time of the regiment's departure, and they therefore were not called to combat duty while posted there.

The United States' declaration of war against England signalled the start of the War of 1812, also known as the 2nd War of American Independence. This was the American response to the continued impressment of American sailors into the service of the Royal Navy[12] (to offset deserters from HM's navy) and the illegal British blockade of French ports in Europe, a major obstruction to the profitable trade between the New England merchants and France.[13] While the War of 1812 had a number of dimensions and played out in a range of domains, privateering was central to the maritime warfare between the young United States and England. Since the US Navy was no match against the superior Royal Navy, the United States Congress encouraged privateering whereby skilled American seamen in fast American merchant vessels inflicted serious damage on British shipping. For the colony of the Bahamas it was but an extension of the maritime warfare waged for the previous twelve years against the French and the Spanish, an offshoot of the Napoleonic Wars, the only difference being the enemy 'whose habits, customs and manner so nearly resemble our own [Bahamian]'.[14]

The 36-year-old United States was seen as a 'pugnacious upstart'[15] and Governor Cameron condemned the war as an act of unprovoked hostility.[16] The news of the war aroused angry indignation and resentment among Bahamians, especially the Loyalists, who had not too long before been persecuted by the rebels and forced into exile. For the old inhabitants, the spectre of the losses suffered from the American and Spanish incursions during the Revolutionary War still loomed large in their memory, and they did not take their new foe lightly.

In contrast to the Revolutionary War, the Bahamas was in a much better state of defence at the outbreak of the War of 1812, in large part due to the fastidious attention to defense of Governor Dunmore. In addition, militia acts from Dunmore's days ensured that militia companies were formed on the out islands, and with the help of the Loyalists, most of whom had good military experience from active service in the revolutionary war, the local militia became stronger and better trained and disciplined. By 1812, in addition to the militia companies in New Providence, there were an artillery and battalion company at Crooked Island, a militia company at Exuma and Long Island, and three companies at Harbour Island, from a population of 1250.[17] The names of the officers at Harbour Island were as follows:

	1st Company	*2nd Company*	*3rd Company*
Captain	William Mather	Robert Kelly	James Curry
Lieutenant	Thomas Roberts	John Roberts	John Thompson
Ensign	Joseph Albury	John Harris	Samuel Kemp

PWD Ambrister noted that with the exception of Harbour Island, militia officers were typically from Loyalist families. In Harbour Island the officers were mainly old inhabitants who most likely drew on the expertise of the regiments stationed at the barracks.

Colonel Andrew Deveaux who recaptured Nassau from the Spaniards in 1783.

22 Andrew Deveaux

23 Dunmore's retreat, known as 'the Residency', on the corner of Gaol Lane and Colebrook Street, was built in 1787 by Governor Dunmore. The building was demolished in 1912 and replaced in 1913 with the present administrator's residence

24 The residency of the commissioner/administrator

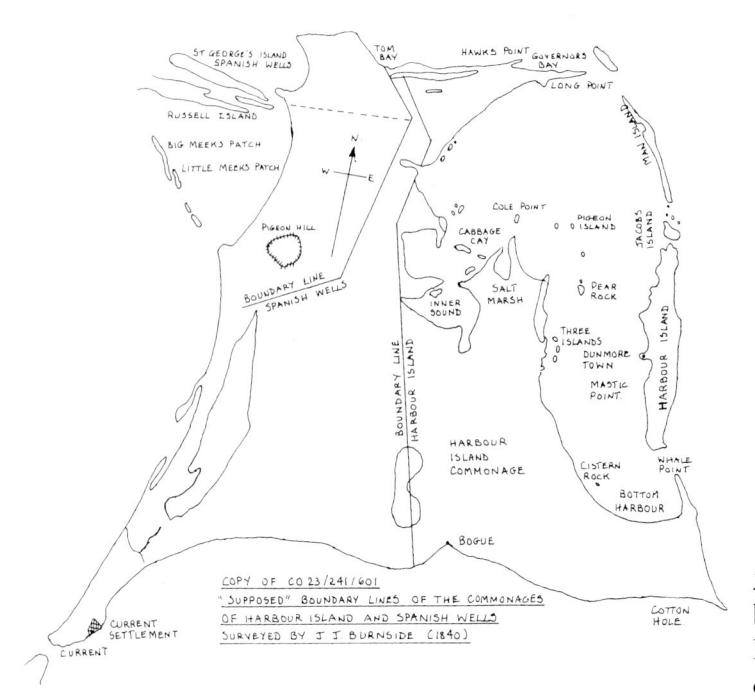

25 The boundaries of the Harbour Island commonages 1840

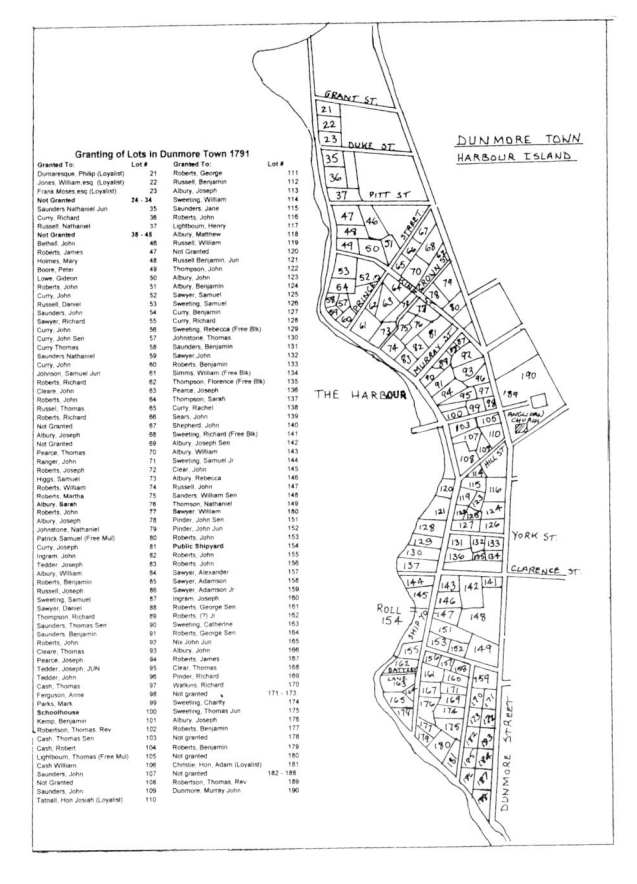

26 Dunmore's Grants 1791

27 Lord Dunmore

28 Route of *Midas*

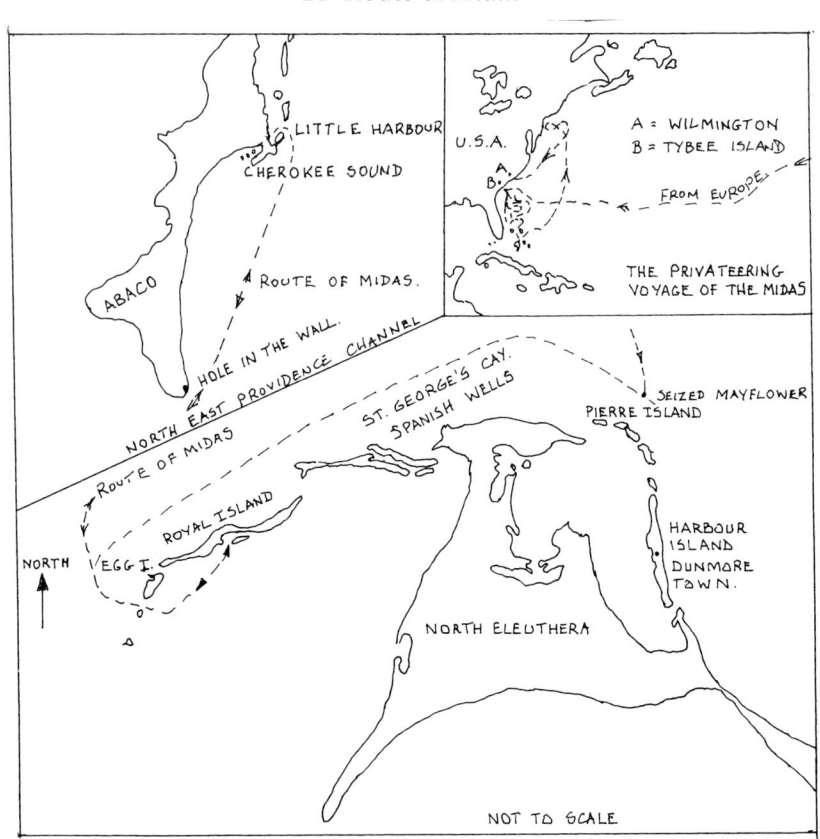

29 The schooner *Midas* en route to Bordeaux, a water colour by Philip Browne from the British sloop-of-war *Hermes* which pursued the *Midas* (courtesy David R. MacGregor)

30 Map of Dunmore Town from 1836 onwards

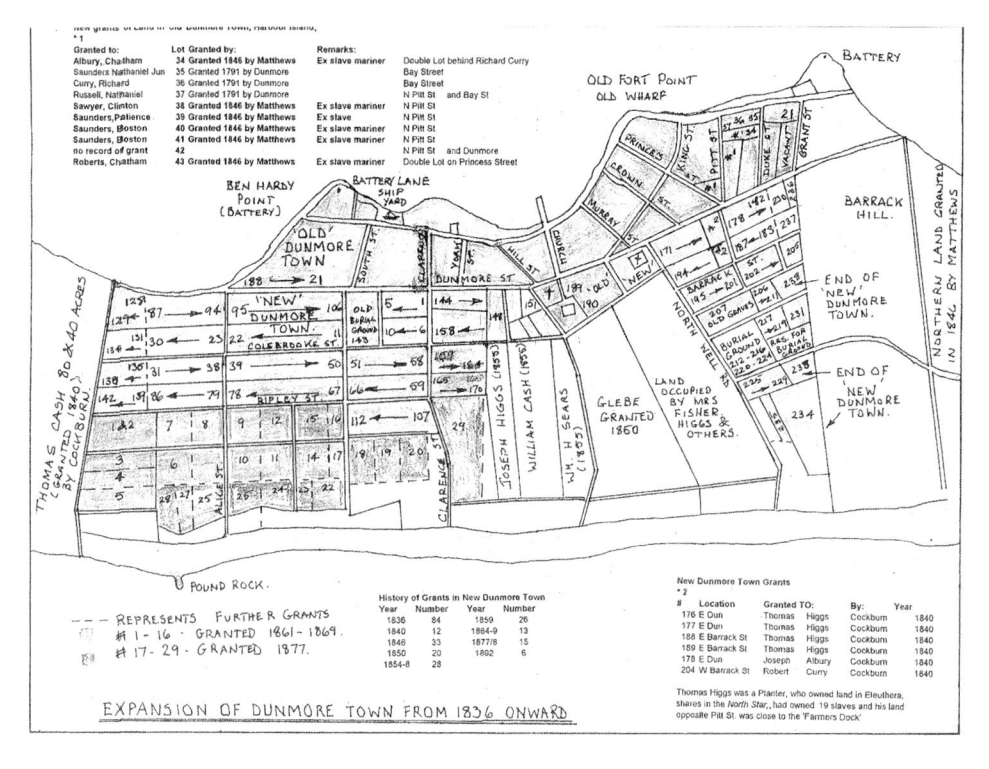

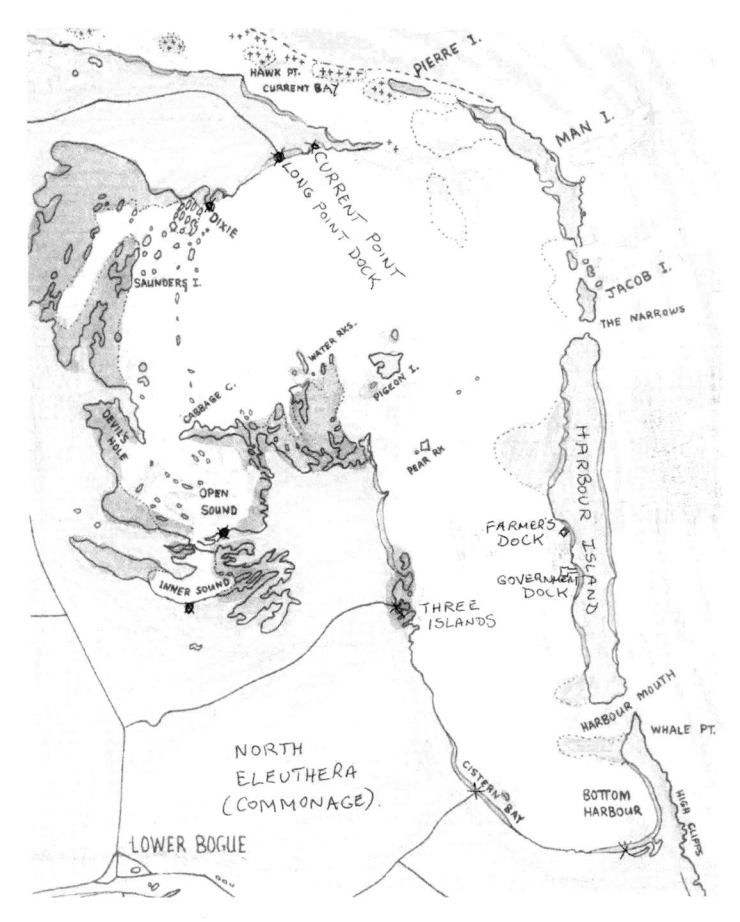

31 Map of fruit loading stations

32 Bay view circa 1870

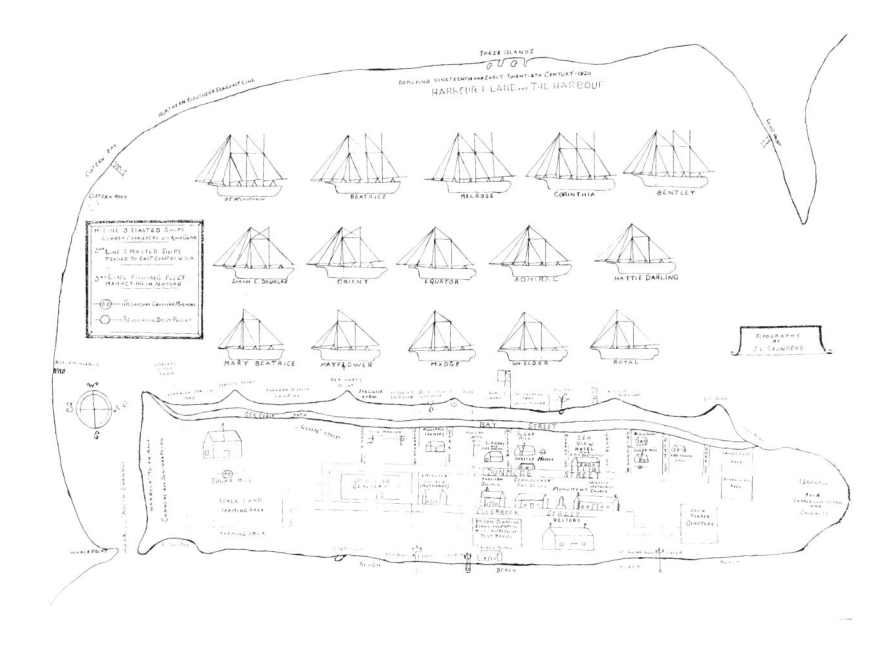

33 John Saunders' map of the harbour, 1920

34 Sugar mill driven by horse (Drehes)

35 The *Julia Elizabeth*

36 After many voyages to Florida, the *Louise F* ended up as a lumber carrier

37 The *Beatrice*

38 The *Marie J. Thompson*, the last commercial sailing ship built in Harbour Island

39 The *Mary Beatrice*

40 William and Lambert Albury

The stage for the sea battles between the American and Bahamian privateers was the all-important Northeast Providence Channel, also known as the Hole-in-the-Wall Passage. The entrance to the channel is bounded to the north by South Abaco, and to the south by North Eleuthera and its offshore cays of Spanish Wells, Royal Island, Egg Island and Harbour Island. This channel was the gateway into the Bahamas from the Atlantic and in times of peace, packets from Falmouth to Charleston would travel through the Northeast Providence Channel, pass through the Berry Island Passage and then into the Gulf of Florida. Nor was it far removed from the sea-lane used by vessels going from the eastern seaboard ports to the Caribbean. And in wartime, control of the channel meant control of the trade.

At the beginning of the War of 1812, it had been customary for one or two British cruisers or Bahamian private vessels of war to be stationed in the Northeast Providence Channel to intercept the American trade with Cuba. And indeed more than half of the 503 vessels condemned in the Vice-Admiralty Court in Nassau from 1805, were seized between the years 1812–1814.[18] The Bahamian privateers seemed to be holding their own while the strength of the Royal Navy was fully engaged in the final throes of the Napoleonic Wars on the other side of the Atlantic.

However after Napoleon's defeat at Waterloo, the British moved their fleet and troops across the Atlantic, and an effective blockade of American ports along the Chesapeake coast by the British forced thousands of unemployed seamen and former merchant vessels to join the fast-growing fleet of American privateers. This drastically changed the momentum of the war and it was not long before the American cruisers replaced the Bahamian/British privateers in the Northeast Providence Channel. The *Bahama Gazette* reported the change as follows:

> But now amongst the sundry and manifold changes of the world, that system is altered, and the American cruizers now take their stations there to intercept our trade (Bahamian), especially that from Europe. Nay so daringly it is done that they venture within sight of this island (New Providence), capture our island traders and with all the sangfroid imaginable, declare their intentions of going ashore to the settlements most adjacent to the cruizing ground, to pillage and set fire to the houses.[19]

As early as July 1814, American cruisers had stationed themselves in the Northeast Providence Channel to intercept the British trade to and from the Bahamas and between St. Augustine and the English colonies in the Caribbean. Additionally, American privateers in the channel posed a constant threat to internal droghing and trade between the islands especially New Providence, Eleuthera, Harbour Island and Abaco. At least six 'stout privateers' fitted out of the southern ports of America were reported cruising in Bahamian waters.[20] And therefore the arrival in September, 1814, of the 76-foot schooner *Midas,* armed with 12 carriage guns and a 42-man crew, under the command of Capt. Alexander Thompson, was not surprising, but was occasion for alarm.[21]

Commissioned at Baltimore and refitted out at Savannah, the *Midas* belonged to a class of very successful privateers, superior in speed and maneuverability, and later dubbed Baltimore clippers.[22] Her tall masts and tremendous spread of sail made her an awesome sight to behold under sail and in open water she could overhaul a Bahamian vessel with great facility. Closer to shore the smaller Bahamian sloop or schooner was able to navigate banks and waters too shallow for the *Midas*' draft, and escape into hidden bays and inlets, unknown to the American seamen and often inaccessible.

The arrival of the sloop *Sally* in Nassau on 13 September brought news that confirmed the worst suspicions of Bahamians about the purpose of the *Midas*' visit to the Bahamas. On board the *Sally* were three crewmen off Mr. Cleare's sloop, the *Mayflower,* which had been seized by the *Midas* at Pear Rock, just as she was about to enter the harbour of Harbour Island, with a load of cedars from Abaco. Capt. Thompson had stopped the *Sally* off Royal Island later that day and put on board the crew from the *Mayflower,* keeping the Harbour Island sloop to facilitate his plan. While the crew was extremely relieved not to have been detained and spoke highly of Capt. Thompson's good treatment of them,[23] they explained that two black crew members of the *Mayflower* had been kept by Capt. Thompson as pilots and his intention was to arm the sloop and send her into Royal Island to pillage and burn the houses there.[24]

A sense of helplessness prevailed as there was not one armed schooner in port to send in defence of the threatened settlements. By this stage in the war, a number of Bahamian privateers, including the *Dash,* the *Francis,* the *Mary* & *Caledonia an*d many other sloops and schooners had been captured by the faster American privateers[25] and those remaining were out on cruises. In fact it was Capt. Thompson on the *Midas,* who had captured the *Dash* with three American prizes off Tybee Lighthouse, at the mouth of the Savannah River, in the early summer.[26] The *Bahama Gazette* lamented the vulnerability of the islands to the assaults of the privateer:

> There is nothing therefore to prevent them (privateers), if they should be so inclined, to pillaging and setting fire to all the houses on Royal Island and Harbour Island; at Spanish Wells they may also do the same, nay more, they might even venture off our

harbour (New Providence), and with menacing impunity do us an injury...[27]

The absence of Royal Navy ships or vessels over the previous month was perhaps a result of the assumption that the British blockade of the American coast afforded ample protection to the Bahamas, but this was not the case. The irony was that by the time the alarm was raised in Nassau, Capt. Thompson had already committed his treacherous act.

On the morning of 12 September 1814, the *Midas* anchored off Royal Island and Capt. Thompson ordered two carronades and 21 armed men, under the command of his first officer Mr. Dickinson, transferred to the *Mayflower*.[28] They cast off from the privateer and headed into the harbour where the *Mayflower* dropped anchor and two boats full of armed men landed on a plantation owned by Mr. Benjamin Barnett. They drove the inhabitants away, plundered the premises of specie amounting to 733 doubloons or $11,728 dollars and set fire to all the buildings, including the stone kitchens, on Mr. Barnett's property and a neighbouring plantation belonging to Mr. John Albury, formerly of Harbour Island.[29]

An eyewitness account provided by Benjamin Barnett's daughter revealed the cruel barbarity of the event. When she and about 20 children returned from the woods where they had taken refuge and remained for two days without food, they found the entire settlement burnt to the ground. The marauders were impervious to the earnest entreaties of a venerable old man of 70, named Richardson, to save some place of shelter for his family, out of compassion for their 'poor old age'. And at the height of their violent rampage they declared that had Mr. Barnett been there, they would have cut off his head and burnt his body with the house. The *Bahama Gazette* reported a total of 27 houses fired,[30] while Capt. Thompson's logs recorded three 'dwelling houses' and 14 'negro hutts'.[31] The most horrible and indecent act committed was when they broke open the vault containing Mrs. Barnett's remains in search of money. The *Bahama Gazette* sums up the avaricious nature of these men when it states: 'Not even the remains of the dead were held sacred by this rapacious banditti'.[32]

And worse still, the news that Capt. Thompson had every intention of continuing his predatory warfare in the Northeast Providence Channel, was cause for further alarm. It was reported that Capt. Thompson was awaiting the arrival of another American privateer upon which he intended to land at Harbour Island. After all, the prospects for booty there with a population of 1,252[33] were much greater than at the fledgling settlement on Spanish Wells. According to one informant, Capt. Thompson had considered burning the settlement at Spanish Wells but the 'insignificance' of the settlement saved it from being targeted by the privateers. The difficulty of approach to Spanish Wells surrounded by shallow water and the existence of a battery were further deterrents and the privateers turned their attention to Harbour Island.[34]

For the next two weeks, Capt. Thompson, in the *Midas,* continued to enforce his blockade of the Channel, as he cruised along the north coast of Eleuthera between Egg Island to the west and Harbour Island to the east. During this time he lay off the northern entrance to Harbour Island for much of the time, his presence being a serious deterrent to trade and a constant reminder of their predicament. During this time, he seized and burnt the schooner *Stinger* belonging to Mrs. Higgs of Harbour Island, and detained the crew on the *Midas*.[35] And days later he gave chase to the *Nellie,* a sloop that traded between Abaco and Harbour Island. The sloop was fortunate enough to make her escape into the harbour of Harbour Island before the *Midas* caught up with her.[36]

There is no doubt that Capt. Thompson coerced the crew of the *Mayflower* and *Stinger* to divulge critical information about the approach into the harbour and the fortifications of Harbour Island, and presumably they would act as pilots when the attack took place. What intelligence was passed on to Capt. Thompson or the accuracy of it is unknown, but the truth was, although the possibility of a privateer landing at Harbour Island had been a concern for some time, the settlement at Dunmore Town was in a weak state of defence at the time. No troops had resided at the barracks since the departure of Capt. John Smith and the 2nd European Garrison Company in March, and although they had three militia companies, they lacked arms and ordinance with which to defend themselves against a privateer landing. The *Bahama Gazette* reported the dire circumstances of Harbour Island:

> Harbour Island is defenceless and its people are poor, at least, those that are not poor one way, are poor another, and if that privateer should form the cruel determination to take and burn it, we should have to lease another Poor House…[37]

Even though the dangers to which the Harbour Island people were exposed in their persons and properties were well known to the governor by 15 September, a week would pass before an armed vessel became available to transport a detachment of troops to the island. Fortunately for Harbour Island, the American privateer, for which Capt. Thompson waited, had not yet arrived, and therefore delayed the landing.

On 22 September, the armed schooner *Swift* left for Harbour Island with a company of His Majesty's 2nd West India Regiment, under the command of Capt. Major.[38] Her arrival in Harbour Island was timely, as the following day, the *Midas* appeared off Harbour Island, fired a gun and hoisted American colours. The *Swift* and the troops prepared to receive an invading force, but no landing was attempted by the enemy.[39]

After the arrival of the troops, the earlier anxieties of the Harbour Island people about their defenceless state were replaced by untempered bravado. A call for volunteers to go out and attack the American cruiser was made and reportedly one man had offered his services. And a defiant warning reflected the sentiment of the people at Harbour island: 'Perhaps these insolent Yankees may yet pay dear for their temerity, by infesting the shore of these peaceful islanders; for should they ever approach it to a distance within the throw of a staff and grains, their lives are sure to be the forfeit.'[40]

As it turned out, the only landing that Capt. Thompson made after the Royal Island attack was at Little Harbour, Abaco, where he filled all the water casks, landed the crew of the *Stinger* and set the *Mayflower* adrift.[41] He cruised east of the Abacos for a week, captured and burnt a British schooner and boarded three other vessels, which he could not legitimately seize.[42] Whether he came to repent the burning of Royal Island and realized that he had gone too far, or, tired of waiting for another American privateer for reinforcement, he gave up his blockade of the Northeast Providence Channel and his plan to pillage and plunder Harbour Island. The Harbour Island fishermen and traders must have breathed a sigh of relief at the *Midas'* departure.

At the close of the war, President Madison revoked the *Midas'* commission and Capt. Alexander Thompson was deposed from his command of the privateer for exceeding his commission in the illegal raids against the settlements at Royal Island. Secretary of State, James Munroe admonished Capt. Thompson and explained that '… severe measure of retribution is for the Government alone to prescribe the manner…'.[43] In his defence, Capt. Thompson penned a six-verse song, which explained his attack on Royal Island as an act of retaliation against the British raids on the United States ports, and in particular against the British take-over of Washington DC and the burning of the Capitol and other public buildings by Admiral George Cockburn.[44] The first and third verses defiantly justify the burning of Royal Island:

To lend a hand in time of need	Determined to avenge the Cause
When Britain she did burn	With freedoms sons combined
Our Town in every Part with speed	I thought I would support the Laws
By noted George Cockburn	And pay him in his Kind.[45]

Whatever drove Capt. Thompson to such flagrant outrages in his command of the *Midas* in the War of 1812, for the inhabitants of Royal Island, the firing of the settlements dealt a mortal blow to their survival. As a viable settlement it was never again to rise from the ashes. For the inhabitants of Spanish Wells, their 'insignificance' was a blessing; their small numbers made them unprofitable for plunder. And for the inhabitants of Harbour Island, it was a 'near run thing'.[46]

Notes

1. C023 2 part I/77, Carrington to Council of Trade & Plantations, 1722. CSP 33/127, 4 May 1722.
2. CO 23/43/139, March 1803, Gov. Halkett to Secretary of State.
3. CO 23//50/115, 13 Dec 1806, Report of Gov. Cameron.
4. Journal of Council in Assembly 1805–1810 page 191, 28 Sept 1810.
5. *Royal Gazette*, 11 Oct 1805, letter to editor; ibid Journal of Council.
6. CO 23/39/1, 9 Sept 1799, Gov Dowdswell to Duke of Portland.
7. CO 23/46/125, Sept 1804, Dyer to Secretary of State.
8. CO 23//51/38$\frac{1}{2}$, 12 Feb 1807, Comm. Major to Gov. Cameron.
9. CO 23/50/50, 8 Oct 1806, Gov. Cameron to My Lord.
10. *Royal Gazette*, 11 Feb 1815, p. 3.
11. *Royal Gazette*, 19 March 1814, p. 3.
12. www.odu.edu.impressment, p. 1.
13. *Royal Gazette* 15 April 1813 p. 3.
14. Sandra Riley, page 198; CO 23/59/84, President Vesey Munnings to the Council 5 Nov 1812.
15. Paul Albury, unpublished Lecture *The Bahamas and the War of 1812*, East Rotary 5 October 1984.
16. PWD Armbrister, unpublished *History of the Bahamas*.
17. Ibid.
18. Craton, p. 167.
19. *Bahama Gazette*, 15 Sept 1814, p. 3.
20. CO 23/61/99, Gov. Cameron's Report September 1814.
21. Ellen K. Plummer, *Midas goes to War*, The Weather Gauge, Fall 1993, p. 8.
22. Ibid, p. 8.
23. *Royal Gazette*, 14 Sept 1814, p. 3.
24. *Bahama Gazette*, 15 Sept 1814, p. 3.
25. CO 23/61/99, Gov. Cameron's Report September 1814.
26. Edgar Stanton Maclay, *A History of American Privateers*, Burt Franklin Publishers, 1898, p. 437.
27. *Bahama Gazette*, 15 Sept 1814, p. 3.
28. Ellen K. Plummer, p. 13.
29. *Bahama Gazette*, 25 Sept 1814, p. 3
30. *Bahama Gazette*, 22 Sept 1814, p. 3.
31. Ellen K. Plummer, p. 13.
32. *Bahama Gazette*, 25 Sept 1814, p. 3
33. CO 23/59/37 Population Report of 16 July 1812.
34. *Bahama Gazette*, 18 Sept 1814, p. 3.
35. *Bahama Gazette*, 22 Sept 1814, p. 3.
36. *Bahama Gazette*, 18 Sept 1814, p. 3.
37. *Bahama Gazette*, 25 Sept 1814, p. 3.
38. *Royal Gazette*, 28 Sept 1814, p. 3.
39. *Bahama Gazette*, 6 Oct 1814, p. 3.
40. Ibid.
41. *Royal Gazette*, 5 Oct 1814, page 3; Ellen K. Plummer, p. 14.

42 Ellen K. Plummer, p. 14.
43 Ellen K. Plummer, p. 15.
44 Ellen K. Plummer, p. 14.
45 Ibid.
46 Paul Albury, unpublished lecture *The Bahamas and the War of 1812*, East Rotary 5 October 1984, p. 12.

8

Slavery to freedom

While the plantation economies on the American mainland and the Caribbean island nations required extensive importation of African slaves on a regular basis throughout the seventeenth and eighteenth centuries the largely maritime economy of the Bahamas did not depend so heavily on imported labour. Although some African slaves were introduced to the colony to plant indigo, tobacco, coffee and subsistence crops from the beginning of settlement, their numbers were relatively small. And the absence of a major staple crop for export meant that the labour regime for the Bahamian slave was not as rigorous or intensive as that of his African compatriots in the rice and cotton fields of the American south or the sugar plantations of the West Indies. Even after the American Loyalists introduced cotton plantations on the southern islands, the isolation and rural setting of these plantations resulted in a less rigid division between master and slave, and the short-lived success of the cotton fields brought greater freedom to those slaves whose owners departed the colony or moved to Nassau. In terms of labour intensiveness, perhaps the Bahamian experience closest to that of the Caribbean or the plantations of the American south was the work of the slave gangs who raked salt in the salt ponds at Turks and Caicos, Acklins and Ragged Island.

As Howard Johnson observed, though similar in its experience of colonialism and slavery, the Bahamas represented a divergent pattern of social and economic development in the larger context of the British West Indies.[1] The Bahamas never attained the status of a true plantation economy and the slave society that evolved was significantly different; the slower growth rate, the longer dominance of the white Bahamians, the smaller slave holdings, the occupational distribution, the smaller percentage of Africans and the faster rate of manumissions all made the life of the Bahamian slaves quite distinct from that of other parts of the Caribbean and the American south.

And further, the unique history of each island within the Bahamian archipelago, particularly the economic base and settlement patterns, resulted in widely differing conditions for the slaves from one settlement to the next. The older and predominantly white settlements of Harbour Island, Eleuthera and Abaco engaged in a maritime economy and some subsistence farming. The mariner slaves, as crewmen and captains on the locally built sloops and schooners, went fishing and turtling in the sounds and waters of The Bahamas or the Florida Straits; they went wrecking off the reef-strewn coast of Eleuthera and Abaco or they sailed to the Abaco and later the Andros mainland to cut wood, much needed for their islands' boat-building industry.

The southern agricultural islands, settled by the Loyalists for cotton cultivation, were predominantly black settlements, and the majority of Loyalist slaves cultivated cotton on the task system, a method of labour management which allowed slaves to cultivate their own provision grounds, once finished the tasks assigned to them by their owners.[2] The collapse of the cotton industry sharply reduced the demand for slave labour on these islands, allowing the slaves greater autonomy than existed elsewhere in the British West Indies. The Bahamian case demonstrates 'that slavery and freedom were not polar opposites',[3] and that the majority of slaves in the Bahamas did not suffer the brutal regimes of those working the monoculture plantations.

Prior to the arrival of the Loyalists, the importation of African slaves into the Bahamas was sporadic, and never involved the large-scale influx of West African slaves that occurred in the plantation islands. And while there is evidence of direct importation from the Guinea Coast in 1721,[4] the majority of Bahamian slaves came indirectly from the southern mainland colonies, the British West Indies or as prisoners off seized Spanish and French prizes. Due to the absence of records, little is known about their country of origin in Africa and it is believed that most of the slaves in the early years were Creoles, that is, born in the Bahamas.

Of the three principal inhabited islands, the increase in slaves in New Providence from 409 to 1,800 between the years 1731 and 1773 was significant compared to that of Harbour Island from 9 to 90 and Eleuthera from 21 to 237. This contrast reflected the introduction of small plantations on New Providence where, by 1731 there were 8 units of more than 10 slaves working cotton, sugar and indigo or large-scale provisions,[5] whereas Eleuthera and Harbour Island inhabitants were engaged primarily in maritime pursuits. During this period, New Providence shifted from a predominantly white (60.7 per cent) to a predominantly black (63.7 per cent) population, while the Harbour Island and Eleutheran population remained predominantly white, 82 per cent and 68 per cent respectively. By 1773, 84.6 per cent of the total black population lived in New Providence. (See Appendix 8.)

The population of the old settlements on Harbour Island and Eleuthera was unchanged by the Loyalist influx of some 1,600 whites and 5,700 slaves which doubled the colony's population and raised the proportion of slaves and other blacks from one-half to three-quarters of the whole.[6] It was not until the first decade of the nineteenth century that the slave population of Harbour Island and Eleuthera increased dramatically as the people of these islands shifted to more extensive farming to supply the increased demands of the Nassau market and to export fruit and vegetables to the southern American colonies. It is likely that these new arrivals were from the failed cotton plantations in the southern Bahamas, and their effect was to double the slave population in Harbour Island and to triple that in Eleuthera. It was during this period that the slave population in Eleuthera surpassed the white and represented 60 per cent of the total, whereas in Harbour Island the white population would outnumber the black well into the 1860s, some two hundred years after settlement. (See Appendix 8.) Thus the relationship between masters and slaves in Harbour Island was very different from that in other islands. The biracial settlement in Green Turtle Cay off Abaco, probably came closest to the Harbour Island demography; the two being in between the exclusively black settlements of the southern islands and the exclusively white offshore cays of Eleuthera and Abaco.[7]

The triennial slave registers from 1821–1834 provide an excellent insight into the slave society at Harbour Island; they provide a lens through which we can see the social and economic conditions that shaped the Harbour Island slaves' existence before and after emancipation. On the eve of emancipation the records showed for Harbour Island some 511 slaves listed in units of varying sizes belonging to 104 mostly old established families. It must be noted though, that the numbers given in various records of the time are confusing. The total of 511 does not include those slaves belonging to Harbour Island owners and living mainly in Eleuthera, but also those residing in Abaco and New Providence and the complete count of slaves with Harbour Island owners may be as high as 622 (See Table 8.2). In 1834,

Table 8.1 Count by occupation of slaves owned by Harbour Islanders computed from slave registers of 1834

Occupation	@ HI.	@ El	@ Abaco	@ NP	Total
Domestics	187	12	5	15	219
Field Labourers	70	61	4	0	135
Mariner	104*	1	1	0	106
Carpenter/ Mech	2 C+ 1 M	0	1	0	4
Washer	0	0	0	1	1
Nil (children)	147	7	0	3	157
Total	511	81	11	19	622**

* 14 seized by customs before 1834
** Additionally: 7 slaves were manumitted, 23 forfeited, 8 sold, 8 willed before 1834

Table 8.2 Size of slave holdings in Harbour Island, Eleuthera and New Providence (Extracted and modified from Gail Saunders, *Slavery in The Bahamas*, p. 95)

Island	1–5	6–10	11–20	21–30	31–40	41–50	51–100	101–150
Harbour Island	66	28	10				1*	
Eleuthera	89	37	24	3	4	1	2	1
New Providence	306	81	30	10	4	1		

*Added to table from slave register returns are Christopher Fisher's 62 slaves, willed to and divided among his daughters some time after 1831. (Slave Register 1831 & 1834.)

Stipendiary Magistrate Winder reported a total of 938 apprentices in the Harbour Island District,[8] including The Cove, where a good number of liberated Africans lived.

These numbers alone indicate that the average size of a slave unit in Harbour Island was relatively small. Table 8.2 of slave holdings highlights the difference in size compared to slave units in New Providence and Eleuthera.

Apart from the sizeable 62-slave unit owned by the wealthy Capt. Christopher Fisher, a landowner and merchant of Harbour Island, the largest units in Harbour Island were of 11–20 slaves, and it is interesting to note that most of these slaveholders were widows: Patience Cleare had a unit of 14, Margaret Curry 11, Jane Higgs 17, Jane Johnson 12, Mary Roberts 10, Sarah Roberts 14 and Martha Sweeting 13. The majority of units in Harbour Island were 1–5, likewise in Eleuthera and New Providence. The difference was the spread of larger units for New Providence and especially Eleuthera, reflecting the larger acreages under cultivation. According to Craton and Saunders, a modest labour force on a true plantation was between 31–50 slaves,[9] so the majority of units throughout the colony were more like small farms.

Small slave units encouraged more frequent interaction between the owners and slaves, which deepened the levels of understanding between the two cultures and heightened the mutual respect one for the other. Gail Saunders remarked that the owners of smaller units were less threatened by revolt and tended to treat the slaves less rigidly.[10] George Kerr, Speaker of the House of Assembly, reported that an average slave unit contained 3–12 slaves, working side by side and being taken home by their master for a meal.[11]

Although Gail Saunders argues for evidence of family structure based on an analysis of the slave register returns,[12] the case is not so clear for Harbour Island. In the majority of Harbour Island units, adult women (possibly mothers), children and older slaves comprise the unit, and it is probable that adults from different slaveholdings set up common nuclear-type households. However, some slave units in Harbour Island do strongly suggest a family structure of mother, father and children, while others, comprising adult male slaves only, are working units of planters or mariners. (See Appendix 9 for a sample of slaveholdings in Harbour Island.)

The breakdown of the occupational distribution among the slaves also offers some insight into the social conditions that prevailed in Bahamian slave societies, especially with regard to the nature of the work and the relationship between the owner and his slaves. Table 8.3 below suggests a high level of domestication among the slaves working in New Providence and Harbour Island. If we look at the total slave population engaged in some type of work, more than half of those slaves in both Harbour Island and New Providence were employed as domestics, two-thirds being under the age of 24. The similarity between the two islands ends here. The balance of Harbour Island's working slaves are evenly distributed between 24 per cent mariners and 24.3 per cent field slaves, the former being on average older than the latter. Whereas for New Providence with a more diversified occupational structure,[13] mariners represent 14.8 per cent and field hands 15.8 per cent of the working slave population. This was in marked contrast to the agricultural islands where, for example, in Eleuthera and Cat Island, 55.57 per cent and 59.73 per cent of the slaves respectively were field hands.[14] And in the plantation colony of Jamaica 66 per cent of the slaves laboured in the sugar fields.[15]

Whittington Johnson observed that the relative percentage of domestic slaves was higher in the Bahamas than in any other British colony, the domestic to field slave ratio being 1:2 in the Bahamas and 1:6 in the plantation colonies.[16] However in Harbour Island the domestic to field slave ratio was

Table 8.3 1834 Occupational distribution of slave society by age for Harbour Island and New Providence (Modified from tables in Gail Saunders, *Slavery in the Bahamas, 1648–1838*, pp. 125 and 127)

Age > Occuptn	0–10	11–15	16–24	25–29	30–39	40–49	50–59	60+	Total	%	% total work
Harbour Island											
Nil	149								149	29.16	
Domest.	48	36	47	10	21	14	8	2	186	36.4	51.3
Field	16	18	6	9	11	17	6	5	88	17.22	24.3
Mariner	1	20	32	11	5	11	5	2	87	17.03	24.0
Trade					1			1	0.20	0.3	
New Providence											
Nil	418	1			1	2		21	443	19.69	
Domest.	218	207	225	87	124	104	69	38	1072	47.64	59.3
Field	14	16	45	18	58	39	48	49	287	12.76	15.8
Mariner	6	18	105	37	45	38	13	6	268	11.91	14.8
Trade	0	12	41	14	35	28	10	16	156	6.93	8.6

2:1, the inverse of the colony's average. This statistic in itself argues for a less rigorous regime among the majority of the Harbour Island slaves. Wylly's 1815 account, somewhat Panglossian in perspective, claimed that domestic slaves in The Bahamas had as easy and comfortable a life as any free domestics elsewhere.[17]

While the slave register returns neatly classify each adult slave by occupation, it is important to realize that with the varieties of the season and 'casualty', the nature of the Bahamian slaves' occupation changed.[18] A report to Chalmers describes the division of labour on a weekly basis for the slave owners and slaves of Harbour Island:

> At the north end of Eleuthera, there are a very considerable number of small plantations – or rather farms. The proprietors of these, do not live on them, but for the sake of health and the convenience of fishing, they nearly all reside in a little barren but wholesome island called Harbour Island …the owners being half of their time employed in fishing and turtling, they work on their farms seldom more than 2 or 3 days a week, taking their negroes along with them backward and forward. Few indeed of these poor people own more than a negro or two, which therefore necessarily accompany them in all their avocations…[19]

This close working relationship between master and slave lasted throughout the slavery period. The domestics and field slaves were under the constant supervision of their owners and together they worked to eke out a living from the commonage granted to them by Lord Dunmore. While the domestics spent the days working in the humble dwellings of their owners and helping with the daily tasks in the household, the field slaves were divided between stock raising on the common to the east of the township and the cultivation of fruits and vegetables to the south and the north of the township, but mainly on the commonage across the harbour on the Eleutheran mainland. The distance between master and slave in the city did not obtain in Harbour Island, as for the most part both master and slave lived at the same social and economic level.

An 1829 report to Chalmers describes the lot of the field slave:

> Every field slave has his ground of capital affording the best mart for the several articles that may thus constitute his pecuniary interest, not a drogher or plantation boat arrives at Nassau but is filled with these little traders. They leave from their master's service, bringing with them for sale their own several ventures of poultry and provisions.[20]

The 1797 Consolidated Slave Act had mandated that slaves be allocated provision grounds to raise their own food, and the Harbour Island slave owners assigned grounds on the commonage to their slaves. In this way, the ambitious slaves had the opportunity to operate as small producers and traders, which gave them some little independence from their masters, long before emancipation. It is interesting to note that of the 320 grantees of commonage land in 1842, at least 103 were former slaves. (See Appendix 7).

It was indeed the mariner slaves who enjoyed the most practical freedom. The slaves in Harbour Island had the advantage of learning navigation from men whose reputation on the sea was undisputed and established over by long tradition. And so it was no surprise that the crews on the wrecking, droghing, turtling and fishing boats from Harbour Island were in great measure composed of skilled mariner slaves. 'Our black seamen are equal to any in the world', wrote Wylly. He further explained that the mariner slaves were generally allowed a certain proportion of the profits from each voyage and there was no difference between their treatment and that of the white crew.[21]

Whittington Johnson's claim that conditions for the Bahamian slave were 'less demanding and degrading' than elsewhere in the British West Indies is well supported by the working conditions of most slaves at Harbour Island. However a less rigorous labour regime did not always guarantee the master's good treatment of the slaves. While a growing cadre of historians supports the idea that slaves in the Bahamas were treated less severely than their counterparts elsewhere, there was always the exception.[22] And such was the case in Harbour Island despite the relatively easy working conditions and the closeness between master and slave.

The case of a female slave at Harbour Island, May Barnett, who had been brutally beaten with a cow-skin about the back, shoulders, bosom and face, by her master, Richard Barnett, was brought to the courts by the Harbour Island magistrate William Smith. He denounced Barnett's cruel conduct and testified that the female slave had been excessively flogged and the wounds crawled with all manner of maggots and vermin.

In defence of the accused, the courts heard that May was an abusive woman of bad character, was very disobedient and quick-tempered, and liked liquor. In defence of the victim Mr. Barnett was alleged to be of cruel and wicked mind with a malicious disposition, having done the same the year before. Judge Sandilands in his summation urged the jury to find the defendant guilty, but after an entire night's deliberation, the jury delivered a verdict of not guilty.[23]

This incident occurred under Sir James Smyth's governorship, when there seemed to be an increase in the cruel punishment of slaves, in reaction to Smyth's determination to outlaw the practice of flogging female slaves.

Smyth was unremitting in his efforts to do away with cruelty to slaves, which did not sit well with the slaveholders and stirred a refractory spirit among the slaves. It was ironic that in a country where cruelty toward slaves was said to be virtually non-existent, such cases should increase in the years prior to emancipation, when legislation had become more focused than ever before on protecting the slaves and ensuring their civil rights.

The benefits of a favourable climate and a high-protein diet and the absence of harsh working conditions and endemic diseases (such as malaria or yaws), all combined to make the slave population in the Bahamas healthy.[24] The inadequate diet and labour-intensive work of the slaves in the British West Indies led to high mortality rates and a demographically unhealthy slave society. With regard to food intake, slaves of Jamaica and Barbados received approximately 500 calories daily from the food consumed in contrast to Bahamian slaves who as a result of the 1797 Consolidated Slave Act were entitled to approximately 3,275 calories.[25] Healthy slaves meant higher fertility rates.

By 1810, the fertility of Out Island slaves was rapidly increasing, and a comparison between the 1805 and 1810 data confirmed that slaves in Harbour Island and Eleuthera were healthier in this regard than those in Nassau or any other Out Island[26] (See Table 8.4.) The slave societies in these two Out Islands had achieved the necessary balance between the sexes in the childbearing age range, so that their numbers were rapidly growing by natural increase.

The rate of increase of children born to slave families was much higher for Harbour Island than for Eleuthera or New Providence between the years 1805 and 1834, and by 1834 more than half of the slave population of Harbour Island were under the age of 15. There was no commensurate increase in the overall slave population for Harbour Island in this period, because of the movement of planters and their slaves from Harbour Island to the Cove, Royal Island, Current Island and Spanish Wells to cultivate small plantations.

Table 8.4 A comparison of the number of slave children in Harbour Island, Eleuthera and New Providence in the years 1805, 1812 and 1834[27]

Settlement	1805 – under 12 nu. / % slave pop	1812 – under 12 nu. / % slave pop	1834 – under 15 nu. / % slave pop
Harbour Island	97 (35.66)	222 (41.18)	288 (56.36)
Eleuthera	408 (38.09)	404 (36.79)	625 (47.94)**
New Providence	887 (29.11)	1288 (38.92)*	913 (40.57)

* The New Providence statistic is under 15 for the year 1810
** The figures and percentage calculated for Eleuthera represent the common average for the Agricultural Islands

In 1824, Bahamian lawmakers passed the first of a trilogy of acts comprising the amelioration reforms, the purpose of which was to improve the lives of the slaves and to protect their rights. The statute, encouraging slave owners to provide religious instruction to their slaves and to baptize them, echoed the first slave laws in Governor Phenney's time, and the later 1797 Consolidated Slave Act. The earliest records of slave baptisms in Harbour Island are provided by the first resident minister in 1768, Rev. Richard Moss. He reported that 37 out of a total of 110 slaves, roughly 33 per cent, were baptized.[28] Thereafter, the baptism of slaves in Harbour Island took place sporadically, and between 1797 and 1834 a total of 295 slaves were baptized.[29] The spiritual state of the slave society was much improved as the eve of emancipation approached. It is interesting to note that although many of the slaves were given anglicized names such as John, Mary etc, some retained African names: Sewiza, Cloe, Tembo and Mehalia; others were of a patriotic nature: Chatham, Prince Devon and London; many were Biblical: Rachel, Ishmael, Israel, Esther and Leah.

In Harbour Island, the Methodist missionaries had preached about the morality of marriage since 1813, and Rev. John Rutledge confessed, 'Marriage sounds very harsh in the ears of most slave owners, this difficulty will wear away as the Gospel swells.'[30] Slave owners had traditionally opposed slave marriages because it made the transfer of slaves from one island to another more complicated, and many believed that to concede to marriage between slaves was to concede to their freedom at the same time. However by 1823, Rev. W. Wilson reported slaves were marrying in Harbour Island.[31]

Included in the 1824 Act was a statute mandating the recognition and encouragement of marriages among slaves and between slaves and free blacks in the Colony. The New Slave Code of 1826 added restrictions to the slaves' right to marry, such as the consent of the owner and the stipulation that the slaves' duties to his master came before his marital duties.[32] Only a few marriages between slaves took place in Harbour Island in the wake of the new legislation. Rev. Thomas Pugh highlighted the barriers that the Methodist missionary in Harbour Island faced:

> There appears to be an almost insuperable barrier in the way of our own usefulness among the black and coloured people, particularly in the out settlements, where there is no clergyman – they cannot possibly go to town to get married because they have no money. Many of them lately made application to me with tears to perform that ceremony, their owners have also given consent, but I cannot do it under the existing laws of the Bahamas. I have sent a petition to his Excellency the Governor, for a licence but have not received one.[33]

In 1835, former slaves in Harbour Island took advantage of their new status as free people and asserted their rights to a legal marriage. The register of marriages for Harbour Island shows that of the 113 marriages that took place for that year, 77 were between former slaves.[34] Based on Table 8.2, it would appear that most of the former slaves of marriageable age were married the year after emancipation. This strongly suggests that the slave family in Harbour Island was a stable nuclear unit and two-parent household. It supports Craton's evidence for a high incidence of stable family units among the Bahamian slave society and refutes the widely-held notion of fragmented and dysfunctional slave units.[35] And it further explains the excellent demographic health and high birth rate of slave society in Harbour Island.

A staunch abolitionist, Sir James Carmichael Smyth had been sent out as Governor of the Bahamas to enforce the slavery reform laws, and he met considerable resistance, led by the Bahamas House of Assembly, to the amelioration efforts. Several islands, including Current, Eleuthera, Abaco and Harbour Island, sent in petitions asking for the removal of Sir James Smyth for his 'maladministration' of the colony. The petition from Eleuthera charged that the governor no longer had the respect of the inhabitants because of his 'mild laws for the government of the slaves', who were now turbulent and discontented.[36] And the Harbour Island petitioners threatened to ignore the amelioration measures until Smyth was recalled.[37] Whether the petition was driven by political intrigue or genuine protest is difficult to verify.

The missionary from Harbour Island reported that 1 August 1834, passed 'without the least excitement whatever, or disposition toward it',[38] and with the exception of a disturbance at Exuma, the momentous occasion, marking the end of slavery, passed peaceably throughout the colony.[39] However, a week before emancipation, an outrage was committed against the mission property in Harbour Island by four white youths. In the dead of night they entered the mission yard and violently rang the chapel bell, tore down the posts holding the bell, seriously damaged the mission house, and then proceeded through the streets of the settlement 'committing various acts of lust and lobbing the property of one of our leaders into the sea'.[40] Possibly this was no more than the drunken rebellion of four youngsters, but the timing and innuendoes of the report suggest it was a malicious attack against the Methodists, much resented for their supreme efforts to raise the condition of the slaves.

Special Magistrates were appointed from England to the Out Islands to oversee the smooth transition from slavery to the apprenticeship system and to ensure that the new arrangements put in place in the settlements were to the mutual benefit of both apprentice and employer.[41] Governor

Colebrooke advised, 'The magistrate should consider himself specially commissioned as the friend, advocate, protector and guardian of the ignorant and unprotected apprentice, and should at all time be his adviser.'[42] One of the most important tasks for them was to put land into the hands of the emancipated classes to afford them more practical freedom. For the Special Magistrate assigned to Harbour Island and Eleuthera, Thomas Ripley Winder, this was no small task, as many families were old inhabitants and land tenure in many cases was not clear. Although the 1824 Melioration Act had granted slaves the right to own property, the price of land was so high that it was out of reach of the poorest classes, and no slaves bought property on Harbour Island prior to emancipation.

The laying out of Dunmore Town and the granting of land in 1791 by Lord Dunmore resulted in a largely segregated residential spread of the township: 127 whites, mostly old inhabitants, had properties with modest wooden houses near the bay or on the hill overlooking it, and six free blacks and mulattoes were granted properties on Dunmore Street, on the periphery of the town.[43] As the slave population increased, they built small wooden cabins raised from platforms made of rock on the unoccupied back lots of the town; the cabins so raised to allow poultry to roost underneath. Further back to the east of the township, the poorer slaves lived in huts constructed entirely of palmetto thatching, not high enough for grown-ups to stand in.[44]

Winder was very sympathetic to the dilemma of the apprentices under his charge. During his circuit through the district, demands were constantly made to him by the poorer classes for small allotments of land for cultivation, in particular by former slave mariners.[45] In Dunmore Town, many former slaves wanted to buy the property they had lived on for years at the back of the town, but were too poor to afford it. Winder commiserated, 'I will become a freeholder myself so I can vote in the next election, and if necessary purchase a number of lots to reserve for the apprentices, who from the grinding system presented by some employers are kept poor…'.[46] And in a later report he criticized the Abaco, Eleuthera and Harbour Island employers for their indigence, illiteracy and inability to look after their apprentices in contrast to the plantation islands (Southern Bahamas), where the apprentices were well cared for.[47]

The inhabitants of Harbour Island in 1835 petitioned Governor Colebrooke to survey and lay out in regular allotments 'grounds to the north-east and north north-east of Dunmore Town and all other unoccupied grounds'.[48] The following year, in order to facilitate the request, Colebrooke declared the said grounds crown land.[49] Winder later reported that several new streets and upward of 200 allotments for buildings and gardens were laid out at the back of the town, some of which were put up for sale.

Eighty-four lots, 60 foot front by 150 foot depth, were readily disposed of at upset prices to the poorer classes, including former slaves and apprentices recently manumitted, some of whom were asked to remove themselves from the crowded part of the town.[50]

The map of the expansion of Dunmore Town from 1836 onwards illustrates how the Old Dunmore Township (purple coded) was extended to accommodate the increasing demands for land. The new expansion (green coded), mentioned by Winder, included 238 allotments, which were divided into two major areas: the larger 'up yonder' section of 170 lots and the 'down yonder' section of 68 lots (#171–238).[51] It is interesting to note that the new streets, Colebrooke and Ripley in the 'up yonder' expansion, were named for the current Governor and the special magistrate Thomas Winder, 'Ripley' being his middle name; and the 'down yonder' streets Grant and Nesbitt, respectively named for the former Governor Lewis Grant and the Colonial Secretary C. R. Nesbitt. Later expansions are coded blue and red. Of further interest is the nucleus of former mariner slaves, who in 1846 were granted lots to the north of old Dunmore Town in the Pitt Street area. This suggests that the mariner slaves may have been better off than their counterparts in the field, since lots in the old township were not cheap.

Governor Colebrooke encouraged employers to adopt the custom developed in the late slavery period of allowing the apprentices to work for three full days for themselves on the provision grounds allocated to them in lieu of provisions and clothing.[52] This option appealed to the Eleutheran and Harbour Island employers, most of whom were too poor to provide weekly rations to their apprentices as stipulated by law. It was this trend that led to increasing demands for provision grounds at the commonage on Eleuthera, and caused great confusion about who had the rights to the commonage. A petition from the inhabitants of Harbour Island led to the 1842 grant of the commonage to all the residents in Harbour Island, a total of 324 heads of household.[53] Given the small size of Harbour Island, it was fortunate that the commonage was available for use as provision grounds, and further that the grant was extended to former slaves and other inhabitants whose forebears had not sailed to victory with Deveaux. (See Appendix 7.)

On 1 August 1838, full freedom was granted to all the apprentices in the colony and Rev. Thomas Lofthouse from Harbour Island reported a special watch-night service had been held for the apprentices on the eve of Emancipation Day and that both employers and apprentices were looking forward to the end of the apprenticeship system, the former 'as anxious as the coloured people'. About the celebrations, Lofthouse wrote:

> … the 1 Aug. passed off… among the coloured people in a manner highly creditable to themselves and satisfactory to all who had the

pleasure to witness their orderly upright and religious proceedings as well as the joy and gladness they manifested on that memorable and never to be forgotten day.[54]

Donald McGregor, Winder's successor, remarked on the friendly relations between the former apprentices and their masters in Harbour Island,[55] and the missionary from Eleuthera reported that many black and white people dined together on 1 August.[56] So whatever misgivings the Eleutheran and Harbour Island people had about amelioration and emancipation, when the day of complete freedom arrived, both black and white embraced their new circumstances. By emancipation the majority of apprentices were engaged in provision and subsistence farming and stockraising,[57] and in fact, many apprentices, content with relations since abolition, wished to continue in the service of their former employers, so for them the change in circumstances was not dramatic.[58]

In addition to the former slaves, approximately 60 liberated Africans, in the employ of Harbour Island people, also ended their apprenticeship on 1 August, 1838. This was but a small proportion of the 4,851 Africans freed in the colony between the years 1811–1838, from slavers en route to Cuba, either wrecked or intercepted by British men-of-war in Bahamian waters.[59] The liberated Africans came to Harbour Island by one of two ways. Some of the larger planters like Christopher Fisher and Benjamin Curry brought one or two Africans to Harbour Island, either directly from a wreck or after they were landed in Nassau, to serve as apprentices on their plantations.[60] And the majority of the liberated Africans comprised a group that had been saved by Harbour Island wreckers, after a Portuguese slaver carrying more than 350 slaves, struck a reef off Harbour Island.

McGregor remarked on the courage of the Harbour Island wreckers for undertaking the rescue mission in the face of a severe storm and praised their humane and Christian attitude when they stripped themselves of some of their clothing to cover the naked Africans. Unfortunately a large number of the adult males on board drowned because they were fettered to prevent any resistance, and some 52 very young Africans, ranging in age from 8–17 years, were taken into Harbour Island. Thirty-eight were distributed to employers in Dunmore Town, nine went to Current, three to Bluff and one to Cove. (See Appendix 10.) The majority of them were employed as domestics in the various settlements and smaller numbers were employed as mariners and field labourers, while James Kelly employed one as a carpenter.[61] Although on the social hierarchy, liberated Africans ranked above slaves, it is unlikely that they received preferential treatment by the poor Eleutheran and Harbour Island employers; rather they worked alongside the former slaves and the poor whites in their struggle to survive.

While the missionaries painted a picture of cordial relationships between former slaves and their employers at emancipation, the same records indicated racial discord beneath the quiescent surface. The residential segregation in Harbour Island was but a physical manifestation of a growing prejudice against the blacks. It was ironic that the Methodist missionaries whose principal aims were to educate and instruct the blacks in the Christian religion, should find themselves at the centre of intense racial prejudice, where classes at the Wesleyan Sunday School and pews in the Wesley Chapel were racially segregated.[62] Initially Harbour Island whites were willing to forego an education for their children, rather than have them mix with black children,[63] but by 1835, 'the distinction of colour has been set aside', reported the missionary's wife with regard to the school.[64] However the segregation of the chapel and assignment of the pews continued as a bone of contention between the races for years, licking the flames of a growing racial intolerance in Dunmore Town. One missionary lamented 'the collision with caste…The two races are almost two distinct churches, worshipping under the same roof. Strange to say the colours can associate for everything else but that of religious edification. White and black cannot meet at the same hour'.[65] Despite their close working association that continued throughout the nineteenth century, the blacks and whites in Dunmore Town were socially and residentially segregated.

Governor Gregory confirmed that Abaco and Harbour Island were the two Out Islands that adhered to this racial prejudice 'with extraordinary tenacity', and a missionary warned that the party feeling against the whites was so intense that on the slightest provocation, violence could break out.[66] One such outburst occurred in 1860 when a group of blacks interrupted the first cricket match played by some whites, who had leased acreage for a cricket pitch. The protest occurred due to the exclusivity of the match and the fact that it was an area traditionally used for truck farming by the blacks. Although the protestors successfully brought the match to an early end, they were fined and some opted for a jail sentence, so incensed were they.[67]

And in 1885, there was a most notorious incident involving five Harbour Island men, who dared to test their right to enter the Methodist chapel through the door that traditionally had been used by the whites. These men were old-time residents of the island and had helped to rebuild the church, and so it came to pass that Israel and John D. Lowe, David Tynes, William A. Johnson and Joseph Whylly courageously challenged the segregationist practices of Wesley. When they defiantly entered the church through the 'wrong' door, the service was immediately discontinued until they had been removed. The next day they were prosecuted for brawling and fined £1 each. Unfortunately it had little immediate effect on the discrimination practices of the church.[68]

Even the two-masted schooner *Dart,* the first scheduled mailboat from Nassau to Harbour Island was segregated, and the blacks could not enter the cabin. The evidence of colour prejudice in Harbour Island in the second half of the nineteenth century supports David Lowenthal's claim that emancipation increased the racial divide. However, the distance between the blacks and whites in Harbour Island was not as wide as in Nassau where colour separated the races in housing, education, occupation and social intercourse. The growing maritime and farming industries in Harbour Island meant that blacks and whites continued to work together despite the social and residential segregation. And in the larger context, the racial situation in the colony was not as harsh as in the southern States of America with its inflexible colour line, but on the other hand it did not conform to the West Indian norm; it lacked the exclusiveness of the former and the equality of the latter.[69]

The conditions of slavery and emancipation were different from island to island. Although emancipation coincided with an economic downturn for the colony generally, for Harbour Island and Eleuthera it triggered a spirit of industry and optimism among the former slaves. It was in great part due to their efforts that the groundwork was laid to propel Harbour Island and Eleuthera to the most prosperous times ever experienced in their history. With the extensive and successful cultivation of ground provisions and fruit, particularly the pineapple, Eleuthera gained its reputation as the breadbasket of the colony; with its increase of shipping and trade as a port of entry, Harbour Island gained its reputation as the second city of the Bahamas.

Notes

1. Howard Johnson, *The Bahamas in Slavery and Freedom,* Ian Randall Publishers Ltd. 1991, vi.
2. Ibid, 17.
3. Ibid. vii.
4. CO 23/12 part 2, 81 Governor Phenney to Council of Trade & Plantations, 20 April 1727.
5. Howard Johnson, *The Bahamas from Slavery to Servitude,* University Press of Florida, 1996, p. 15.
6. Michael Craton & Gail Saunders, *Islanders in the Stream, vol 1,* University of Georgia Press, 1992, p. 179.
7. Spanish Wells off the northeast tip of Eleuthera has traditionally been an all white settlement and still is today. Cherokee Sound, Hope Town, Man-O'-War and Great Guana Cay are off the windward coast of Abaco.
8. CO 23/94/159, Report of Stipendiary Magistrate Winder, 31 July 1834.
9. Craton & Saunders, *Islanders in the Stream, vol. 1,* p. 278.
10. Gail Saunders, *Slavery in The Bahamas 1648–1838,* The Nassau Guardian, 1985, p. 94.
11. CO 23/72/32 Report of George Kerr, Speaker of the House of Assembly, 7 February 1823.
12. Gail Saunders, *Bahamian Society after Emancipation,* Ian Randle Publishers, 1994, p. 46.

13 Salt, Driver/Overseer, Nurse/Midwife, Sundry and Unknown are minor occupations in New Providence only and do not appear for Harbour Island.
14 Saunders, *Slavery in The Bahamas 1648–1838*, p. 122.
15 Craton & Saunders, *Islanders in The Stream, vol. l*, p. 284.
16 Whittington B. Johnson, *Race Relations in the Bahamas 1784–1834*, The University of Arkansas Press, 2000, p. 28.
17 Craton & Saunders, *Islanders in the Stream, vol 1*, p. 259.
18 Saunders, *Slavery in The Bahamas 1648–1838*, p. 121.
19 George Chalmers Papers 1796–1817, Letters from the committee of correspondence, 2 May 1816, p. 133.
20 Ibid., 2 Feb. 1829, p. 188.
21 W. Johnson, *Race Relations in the Bahamas 1784–1834*, p. 33.
22 Ibid., p. 109.
23 C.O.23/89/34, Nesbitt's Report on the court proceedings, 2 August 1833.
24 Saunders, *Slavery in The Bahamas 1648–1838*, p. 68.
25 W. Johnson, *Race Relations in the Bahamas 1784–1834*, p. 28.
26 Craton & Saunders, *Islanders in the Stream, vol. l*, p. 263.
27 Slave Statistics, 1805: CO 23/48/144; 1810/12: CO 23/54/37; 1834: Saunders, *Slavery in The Bahamas 1648–1838*, 125, 127, p. 128.
28 SPG Reel 1, Richard Moss to SPG, 24 January 1769.
29 Register of Baptisms, Parish of St. John's, Harbour Island 1808–1877, Dept. of Archives, Nassau.
30 Wesleyan MMS (London) Archive, W.I. Correspondence General, 1817–1819, Box 113, 1818, Box 2, 66/3. John Rutledge to Rev. George Marsden, 4 May 1818.
31 Ibid., Box 4, Box 118, 1823, 200/187, W. Wilson to MMS, 29 Nov. 1823.
32 Craton & Saunders, *Islanders in the Stream, vol. l*, p. 230.
33 MMS, Box 8, Box 127, 352/8, 1828, Thomas Pugh to MMS, 2 August 1828.
34 Register of Marriages, Parish of St. John's, Harbour Island, 1835.
35 Saunders, *Slavery in The Bahamas 1648–1838*, p. 112.
36 C.O. 23/87/186, Petition from Samuel Knowles & 113 others, Eleuthera.
37 C.O. 23/86/237, Petition from John Saunders & 135 others, Harbour Island, May, 1832.
38 MMS, Box 11, Box 135, 506/25, C. Penny, Harbour Island, 28 Aug. 1834.
39 Craton & Saunders, *Islanders in the Stream*, l:393.
40 MMS, Box 11, Box 135, 506/25, C. Penny, Harbour Island, 28 Aug. 1834.
41 James Martin Wright, *History of The Bahama Islands, with a Special Study of The Abolition of Slavery in The Colony*, The Macmillan Co., 1905, p. 507.
42 C.O. 23/94/164, W.M.G. Colebrooke, 18 Sept. 1835.
43 http://marina.fortunecity.com/reach/244/gen/hi 1-10.jpg, LDS Film 12, D22.3421.
44 Nassau Quarterly Mission Papers ll, 1886, Bishop Churton's report on visit to Harbour Island; Craton & Saunders, *Islanders in the Stream*, ll: p. 147.
45 Votes of the House of Assembly, 1836, Reports of Special Magistrates, Thomas Winder.
46 C.O. 23/96/231, Report by Thomas Winder, March, 1836.
47 C.O. 23/96/225, Report by Thomas Winder, 11 March, 1836.
48 C.O. 23/94/460, Petition to Governor Colebrooke, 24 Nov. 1835.
49 C.O. 23/97/480, Government Notice, W.M.G. Colebrooke, 15 Nov. 1836
50 Votes of The House of Assembly, Reports of Special Magistrates, 1836.
51 Department of Lands and Surveys, 1936 map of Harbour Island grants.
52 Craton & Saunders, *Islanders in the Stream*, ll: 13.
53 Record Book I.4, 209–223, Registrar General's Office.
54 MMS, Box 27, Box 217, 1300/19, T. Lofthouse, Harbour Island, 9 August 1838.
55 Ibid.

56 Saunders, *Slavery in The Bahamas 1648–1838*, 212; James Eacott, Eleuthera to M.M.S., 2 August 1838.
57 Gail Saunders, 'Health of Bahamian Slave in 1834', Journal of The Bahamas Historical Society, ll:l, p. 12, October, 1980.
58 Wright, *History of The Bahama Islands, with a Special Study of The Abolition of Slavery in The Colony*, p. 528.
59 Howard Johnson, 1996, p. 55.
60 Returns of African Apprentices 1811–1838 from the C.O. 23 series of records.
61 C.O.23/100/233, Major Donald McGregor, 11 November 1837; C.O. 23/109/45, D. McGregor, 1838.
62 MMS, Box 5, Box 122, 226/82 & 94, R. Moore from Harbour Island, May 1825; MMS, Box 27 Box 218, 1320/3, J.Blackwell from Harbour Island, 24 Feb., 1846.
63 C.O. 23/135/123, Governor John Gregory, 15 May 1850.
64 MMS, Box 11, Box 136, 514/56, Maria Penny from Harbour Island, 14 Feb.,1835.
65 MMS. Box 29, Box 219, 1352/24, J. Hartwell from Harbour Island, 25 August 1853.
66 C.O. 23/135/123, Gov. John Gregory, 15 May 1850; MMS, Box 29, Box 221, 1406/23, J. Jordan from Harbour Island, 26 July 1872.
67 Craton & Saunders, *Islanders in the Stream*, ll: 149.
68 L.D. Powles, *Land of the Pink Pearl*, 1888, pp. 111–112.
69 Saunders, *Bahamian Society After Emancipation*, p. 2 & p. 79; David Lowenthal, *West Indian Societies,* New York, 1972, p. 67.

9

The halcyon days

> The inhabitants gain a livelihood cultivating pineapples on Eleuthera. A fleet of two hundred boats is owned in the settlement. Every morning at sunrise this little fleet spreads its wings to the trade-wind, and wafts eight hundred men and boys, black and white, to the lovely beach and cocoa-nut groves on Eleuthera, two miles away; every night they return.[1]

It was the granting of the commonage on North Eleuthera to 323 heads of family in Harbour Island in 1842, which set the stage for a growth spurt in agriculture, unprecedented in the history of the island. While many mariner sons of Harbour Island left the sea to plant more extensively, it was but a momentary departure, as they sailed in the skillfully built Harbour Island sloops engaged in the transportation of produce to Nassau and the United States mainland in the third quarter of the century. This combination of locally crafted sloops and commercial production of fruit and vegetables on the mainland propelled Harbour Island to its zenith in trade and production. It was a time of stability, it was a time of peace and prosperity; these were halcyon days.

Harbour Island's prominence, as a shipping port and agricultural centre did not happen overnight. From the early 1718 Cockram map, extensive plantations are shown on the Eleuthera coast, forming the western boundary of the magnificent harbour, and being part of the acreage later known as the commonage.[2] And Harbour Island itself was declared a fine island for oranges, lemons, pomgranetts, figs, cotton, tobacco and indigo. A 1724 report by John Barker described Harbour Island as 'pleasant' and 'fruitful' with 20–30 families most of whom had plantations on Eleuthera.[3] Woodes Rogers observed that there was more land planted on Harbour Island and Eleuthera than New Providence,[4] and Shirley's 1769 report reckoned a mere 1000 acres planted at New Providence and the same at Eleuthera.[5] So while Bahamians remained chiefly employed in cutting wood and timber for export in exchange for provisions, there was a small contingent of planters who cultivated fruit and vegetables for the local market and foreign trade.

As Harbour Island was the largest settlement in Eleuthera in terms of population, it is reasonable to suspect that Harbour Island contributed significantly to the fruit exports, which were general and not island specific for the period. Nassau being the chief port of entry into the colony, legal trade entailed smaller vessels of 8–30 tons, bringing the native produce from Eleuthera to New Providence to be transshipped in larger vessels of 40–70 tons to colonies in America, particularly South Carolina.[6] New Providence's trade depended on Out Island produce, consisting of limes, oranges, pineapples and turtle, which they bartered for provisions such as flour, corn, beef, pork and wine with Nassau merchants or American trading vessels.[7]

At the close of the eighteenth century, Harbour Island's local trade was thriving with the increased Loyalist population in Nassau, but certain events in the first quarter of the nineteenth century brought Nassau's trade with the American colonies to a standstill, adversely affecting the local trade from the Out Islands. Firstly, a cross-fire of trade embargoes between the American and British governments created a serious shortage of provisions in the Bahamas and virtually shut down the principal foreign market that absorbed Bahamian fruit and vegetables. Secondly, when Key West transferred from Spanish to American hands in 1821, the United States banned foreigners from wrecking, fishing and turtling off the Florida coast, further reducing another important dimension of Bahamian trade. The dire circumstances of the Bahamian traders and inhabitants were a far cry from the promising opportunities of the 1790s. Some relief was provided by supplies such as Indian corn from Cuba, but some traders turned to smuggling, and some wreckers and fishermen migrated to Key West.

William Dowson, a Methodist missionary, described the Harbour Island inhabitants as being 'in a wretched plight, since the sudden stop that has been put on commerce to the United States has aggravated the distress which will no doubt increase as more of the ports continue shut. The people here have scarcely any Indian or other corn and flour must be purchased at an exorbitant cost'.[8] Dowson also avowed that some people in Harbour Island had refused intercourse with the American smugglers, but since the penalty for smuggling among the Methodists was ejection from the society, the missionary might be the last person to be informed about the local smugglers.[9] And a later missionary further defended the honour of the Harbour Island people claiming that when American smugglers came to trade with the people for their fruit, they would rather let it rot on the trees and their families 'want bread' than to deal 'in unaccustomed goods'.[10] While undoubtedly Harbour Island had its share of law-abiding citizens, the ethics question would not be big in the minds of the growing number of wreckers among the Harbour Island mariners.

A Methodist missionary in 1826 reported that the captain and owner of a schooner in Harbour Island had been detected smuggling and was fined by the local authorities. And to make matters worse, a few of the Methodist merchants were found to have retailed what the captain had unlawfully imported and were expelled from the society.[11] And there were likely many more similar occurrences that went unrecorded. A Royal Gazette story[12] urged that the smuggling trade with Abaco, Harbour Island and the northern part of Eleuthera be put down because of its adverse effects on revenue at a time when the country was in considerable debt. And finally an 1824 map of the Bahamas[13] provides evidence of extensive smuggling along the coast of all the windward islands.

The American government attempted to encourage seafaring people who made a living in the Gulf of Florida by fishing, turtling and wrecking to emigrate to the Florida coast; they were particularly interested in Bahamian immigrants whose knowledge of the shoals off the Keys and the Bahama banks off the coast of Florida and Cuba made them very suitable candidates.[14] The newly established Vice Admiralty Court in Key West must have been an added incentive to the Bahamian wreckers but it was not until the 1830s that a large number of Abaconians arrived in Key West after extensive failure of their vegetation[15] and a smaller number of Harbour Island inhabitants in search of better opportunities. An 1841 memorial referred to the considerable portion of inhabitants of Abaco and Harbour Island who migrated to Key West with their families and became residents of the neighbouring keys for wrecking, turtling, fishing and boat-building.[16] Among the early immigrants to Key West from Abaco and Harbour Island were: William Curry, Samuel Kemp, John Braman, Benjamin Albury, John Lowe Jnr., Albert Saunders, Richard Curry, Richard Roberts, and Benjamin Curry.[17]

The outbreak of cholera in the Bahamas in 1852 drove a second group of emigrants from the North Eleuthera area to Key West.[18] Some 40–50 persons hastily left Spanish Wells for Key West from fear of cholera, and so great was the panic at Dunmore Town that many persons 'very imprudently embarked in their vessels with their families'.[19]

Had these early migrating Harbour Island families been able to look into a crystal ball and see the glory and opulence of the halcyon days to come, they might not have left so readily. By 1830, the restrictions on trade between the American and British colonies were revoked,[20] and the spirit of industry and trade, so evident in the 1790s, was rekindled in Dunmore Town.

An 1835 petition from the inhabitants of Harbour Island expressed their dreams for the future:

> … many of your petitioners within the last few years have been engaged in shipbuilding to an extent hitherto unknown in this

island in hopes at no distant period to have become the principal shippers of the fruit produce in the neighbouring islands in their own vessels, and to have improved not only their own circumstances, by the investment of their small capitals in that way, but also that of the whole population of the island…[21]

And the petitioners went on to ask that a customs house officer be appointed at Harbour Island to eliminate the inconvenience of fruit traders having to clear in and out of Nassau and to prevent the trade from being monopolized by foreigners.

By 1837, Harbour Island was established as a port of entry, and this new facility had an almost an immediate effect on the economy. Magistrate Thomas Winder observed the increasing 'spirit of enterprise' in the fast-growing settlement of 1,400 people. They built two-masted fruit schooners, suitable for the export of their own produce from the Eleutheran mainland. This included bananas, oranges, limes, melons, pineapples – and a range of wrecked goods. And in addition, it afforded American traders visiting Eleuthera in search of fruit cargoes, the opportunity to trade directly with the fruit-growing district.[22]

Since there were no roads connecting the settlements on North Eleuthera at the time, Bluff, Current and Current Island often hired schooners from Harbour Island to transport their produce to the American market.[23] As the cultivation of fruit was extended on the commonage, an intricate network of locally owned sloops was engaged in the daily business of collecting the produce at well-known landing sites on the Eleuthera coast. From Bottom Harbour, Cistern Rock, Three Islands, the Sounds, Long Point, Dixie and Current Point they transported the goods across the harbour to Harbour Island where the local or American schooners loaded the fruit for the American colonies. (See map of loading stations.)

The earliest record of pineapple cultivation in the Bahamas is 1697,[24] and although a native fruit of the West Indies,[25] the pineapple was most likely introduced by the early settlers, whose native Bermuda cultivated the succulent bromeliad. Considered a luxury import fruit in Stuart England, the rapid development of the pineapple on the Eleutheran mainland coincided with a sharply increased demand for tropical commodities by the industrialized countries of the North Atlantic in the second half of the nineteenth century.[26] From the 1850s, Eleuthera became known as 'the great pine-garden' of the Bahamas, and its large tracts of richly fertile red earth bore pineapples and sustained the pineapple industry, which became the number one industry of the colony in 1882.[27]

The Bahama red loam is found in the deep pockets of the honeycombed rocks on the leeward shoreline slopes of Eleuthera. The hilltops surrounding

Bluff have the highest percentage of the organic minerals that give the soil its peculiar fitness for the growth of fruit. And numerous patches of the red soil in The Crosskill Hills near Gregory Town, The Red Bay slopes, and a strip that starts behind Tarpum Bay, widens at Savanna Sound and stretches to Governor's Harbour, have been highly successful in the cultivation of 'pines'. A sliver of this valuable redland stretches eastwards of Ridley Head into the Commonages of Spanish Wells and Harbour Island. (See map 'Red Soil of Eleuthera'.[28])

Many of the colonial governors criticized the primitive 'slash and burn' cultivation methods used by the pineapple growers. The farmer traditionally cleared the land by burning the bush but leaving the roots in the soil. He then planted the pineapple suckers, sometimes 20,000 to an acre and used little or no fertilizer. The plant took eighteen months to produce the first apples, which were picked 'in the tree' for the English market and 'close to the fruit' for the local and American markets or for preserving. The trees were self-propagating but the pines grew progressively smaller each season until after four or five years they fell below economic size and the land had to be left fallow for fifteen to twenty years. The planter then moved to virgin acreage to start anew.[29]

Governor Gregory's report remarked on the profitability of the pineapple trade but pointed out its precarious nature in that an entire pineapple estate could be instantly destroyed by too much wind or rain, a drought, a bush fire or even worse a hurricane. And secondly the pine was a delicate and perishable fruit that had to be picked at exactly the right time, for if harvested too soon, it had a bland flavour and if too ripe it was very susceptible to the rigours of the transatlantic voyage. And so it was crucial that as soon as the fruit was harvested, a schooner be on the spot to take them off.[30] And it was in this last respect that Harbour Island had a significant advantage over all the settlements in North Eleuthera cultivating fruit.

Although pineapple cultivation as a commercial enterprise had started in the more central and southern settlements of Eleuthera, namely Governor's Harbour, Tarpum Bay and Rock Sound a century before,[31] they were not blessed with a sheltered deep-water harbour and a local fleet of schooners. Additionally, the prevailing winds from the south made it difficult for schooners to anchor off and load the fruit on the lee of the island. And so it fell to the planters of North Eleuthera to capitalize on their proximity to the island across the harbour and its fleet of sloops and schooners.

The opening of Harbour Island as a warehouse port in 1867 was another step in its rise to a bustling commercial centre.[32] This made it possible to store and transship goods between the American colonies and Eleuthera and Nassau. The inhabitants of North Eleuthera depended to a certain extent on supplies from Harbour Island and almost the whole export trade consisted of produce from Eleuthera.[33] The warehouse facility enhanced the trade potential of the small island and the earning power of the fourteen storekeepers, who had petitioned for the warehouse port.

From 1835, records show a steady growth in pineapple exports from Eleuthera and Harbour Island. While the southern settlements of Eleuthera initially exported both to England and the United States, Harbour Island trade was directly to the American ports of Boston, Baltimore, New York and Philadelphia. Table 9.1 shows the prominence of the Harbour Island pineapple trade in comparison with other pineapple exporting islands. In 1855, Harbour Island exported just over three times as many pineapples as Eleuthera and 62 per cent of the total pine export. And in 1864, Harbour Island exported over twice as many as Eleuthera and 48 per cent of the total. Harbour Island was without question the principal exporter of pines to the United States.

By the mid-1860s, the lucrative returns of the pineapple exports persuaded more people to plant in North Eleuthera. After the boom of blockade running, many investors turned their attention to the pineapple industry and tracts of land in the pine- growing islands were bought to extend pineapple cultivation.[35] Former wreckers of Harbour Island were reported to 'have all gone for pine cultivation'[36] and the comparison of the 1861 and 1871 census[37] reveals a decrease in the number of mariners from 305 to 187 and an increase in planters from 91 to 260. By 1874 the *Guardian*[38] reported numerous pinefields in North Eleuthera and by 1878, the resident justice of the Harbour Island district remarked that 'the soil had never been so extensively tilled'.[39]

A northeaster forced Henry Bleby, a Wesleyan missionary, to abandon his vessel at Spanish Wells and walk across 'rugged, rocky, thorny footpaths of North Eleuthera and through numerous pineapple fields to Current Point'.[40] A contemporary description of the same pine fields portrays their aesthetic beauty: 'A pine field when the pines are ripe looks as if it were on fire, the scarlet of the spiked leaves forming a flame colour with the vivid orange yellow of the fruit.'[41]

The pineapple exports peaked in Harbour Island in 1872 with a record total of 119,100 dozen pineapples to New York and Baltimore, (see Table 9.2) representing a quarter of the national exports. Throughout the 1870s, Harbour Island's pineapple exports remained substantive, but total exports fell by 38 per cent as a result of high import duties in the US, delays of shipments due to unfavourable weather and a fire in 1876 that destroyed several of the fields of the principal cultivators at Current Point and Dixie.[42]

Harbour Island's location made it the first port of entry that any trading schooner coming through the Northeast Providence Channel could enter.

Table 9.1 Total export of pineapples for the years 1855 and 1864[34]

Years >	1855				1864			
Export to Amount > Islands:	Great Britain		United States		Great Britain		United States	
	Quantity Dozens	Value pounds	Quantity Dozens	Value pounds	Quantity Dozens	Value pounds	Quantity Dozens	Value pounds
Nassau, NP	9,500	1,979	7,600	767	53,000	7,037	78,240	6,860
Harbour I.	–	–	36,500	3,357	–	–	100,775	9,526
Eleuthera	6,969	1,436	4,982	4,284	8,500	1,479	39,700	3,699
Abaco	–	–	9,568	1,125	–	–	10,511	1,204
Total	16,469	3,415	58,560	9,533	61,500	8,516	229,226	21,299

Table 9.2 Export of Pineapples from Harbour Island to US in the 1870s[43]

Year	Quant/Value	New York	Baltimore	Philadelphia	Boston	Total
1872	Quantity/doz	97,400	21,700			119,100
	Value/pounds	8,504	2,369			10,910
1874	Quantity/doz	83,000	7,500	3,500		94,000
	Value/pounds	7,850	750	350		8,953
1876	Quantity/doz	54,800	4,000	6,000	9,000	74,800
	Value/pounds	4,579	333	523	675	6,115

It therefore served as an important intermediate stop for schooners travelling on to Nassau and it was also the port at which many schooners coming from the United States mainland traded directly.[44] Therefore it should be no surprise that at the height of the halcyon days as many as 40 to 65 sailing vessels cleared in and out on trading voyages in any one year. In the early 1860s, the majority of the trading vessels entering and clearing out of Harbour Island were British, most likely Bahamian owned, and a small number were foreign vessels, the majority being American. But when the Harbour Island mariners started cultivating in the 1870s, the majority of traders were American. It is interesting to note that the peak of commercial activity in Harbour Island was twenty years ahead of the peak for Eleuthera. And it was Gregory Town, Hatchet Bay, Governor's Harbour and south Eleuthera settlements that carried the pineapple trade of the Bahamas into the twentieth century. (See Appendix 11.)

Table 9.3 shows the details of the shipping entering and clearing out of Harbour Island in the pineapple season of 1887. Although by this time, cultivation on the commonage had declined, a rebirth in pineapple cultivation was taking place at Bluff with the introduction of new fertilizers, and the

Table 9.3 Schooners exporting pineapples from Harbour Island in 1887[45]

Date sailed	Bound for:	Schooner	Captain	Pineapples
30 April 1887	Baltimore	*Judy J McPherson*		2,000 doz
7 May 1887	Baltimore	*Alice Hodges*	J Beauchamp	4,500 doz
17 May 1887	Baltimore	*William Layton*	C Flowers	4,000 doz
18 May 1887	Baltimore	*Gertrude*	J T Albury	3,000 doz
18 May 1887	Baltimore	*William Henry*		4,500 doz
26 May 1887	Baltimore	*David Caril*	E T Somers	5,000 doz
27 May 1887	Baltimore	*Alberta*	O S Young	7,800 doz
4 June 1887	Baltimore	*William O Flowers*		8,000 doz
17 June 1887	Baltimore	*Lilian W. Owinge*	J Allison	5,000 doz
17 June 1887	Baltimore	*Alice Hodges*	J Beauchamp	5,000 doz
6 July 1887	Baltimore	*Early Bird*	L Wilson	4,500 doz
27 July 1887	St. Augustine	*Manatee*	J W Zellen	7,000 doz
			TOTAL	60,300 doz

20 August 1887 *Edwin Janet* sailed for Abaco to take cargo of pineapples to Baltimore

export total of 60,300 dozen from Harbour Island was not much reduced from that of the late 1870s. Baltimore imported exclusively from the Bahamas by this time, and the Harbour Island district provided 20 per cent of the pines imported by Baltimore for its pineapple canning industry for the year 1887.

Of equal importance with foreign trade to Harbour Island's commercial prosperity, was the very busy coastwise trade. Harbour Island was ideally located at 'one end of the most active axis of interinsular trade'[46] and as the halcyon days faded and foreign trade declined, the warehouse port continued to attract an increasing number of local traders, carrying fruit to Nassau and provisions back to Harbour Island for distribution to the neighbouring settlements. As many as 218 Bahamian sloops entered and cleared coastwise upholding Harbour Island's reputation as a thriving commercial port.[47]

It was during the halcyon era that Harbour Island established itself as the unofficial capital of Eleuthera and recaptured its status as the second town of the Bahamas, lost during the Loyalist preoccupation with cotton cultivation. In 1871, its population rose to 2,172, the highest ever in the history of the island. This growth reflected the diversity of a strong economy fuelled by agriculture, boat building, wrecking, fishing and trade. In 1849, The *Nassau Guardian* reported that within the previous seven years Dunmore Town had considerably improved and about 100 houses had been built, many of stone.[48] From as early as 1854, it was reported that money was so plentiful at Harbour Island that the people were obliged to come to Nassau to purchase iron chests.[49] In his response to the devastation wreaked on Harbour Island by the 1866 hurricane, Burnside remarked that 'this is the largest and most opulent settlement after Nassau, whose population is very well able to bear their own losses and help one another'.[50] And Rev. F. B. Matthews commented on the island's general air of commercial prosperity and contentment.[51]

Harbour Island had grown into a bustling seaport, its commodious harbour crowded with the home fleet of 200 sloops and schooners. The two wharves and ship building stocks were alive with the daily activities of stevedores and seamen who obtained their supplies from ships' chandlers, warehouses and numerous small stores along the front street. At night the men slaked their thirst at the five taverns throughout the town. On the slopes of the ridge that runs the length of the town, were a mixture of the simple old Puritan houses and the newer and grander two-story buildings of the new merchant class. On the crown of the ridge stood the resident justice's residence and the old Anglican Church overlooking both the harbour and the Atlantic Ocean. And the Wesleyan chapel was the largest in the Bahamas. Governor Rawson observed that not even in the cathedral was seen on Sundays a greater number or a more expensive display of dresses, chiefly silks.[52]

John Blackwell, a Methodist missionary, reported in 1846 widespread poverty among black and white families in Harbour Island but for eight families who were prominent mercantile traders in the rapidly growing pineapple industry.[53] Many of these were established old Harbour Island families, whose forefathers had fought in the Deveaux recapture of Nassau and included Samuel Higgs, Joseph Higgs, Robert Higgs, Thomas Johnson, John Roberts and J. H. Cleare. Other prominent land and boat owners and leaders in church and civic functions were Thomas Cash, W. H. Sears and W. H. Smith.[54] By the 1880s more inhabitants bearing the same family names shared in the prosperity of the halcyon era and were 'fairly well to do'.[55] And by 1896, Capt. R. H. Ranger, Henry W. F. Sturrup and William A. Cash had joined the ranks of wealthy cultivators and traders in pineapples.[56]

In contrast to the rich mercantile traders, there was extreme poverty among the former slaves and white labourers throughout the nineteenth and into the twentieth century. The fact that most of these poorer classes in Harbour Island had access to land on the commonage after emancipation did not save them from the insidious truck-and-credit system. The peasant farmer did not have the resources of the land and boat-owning merchants, who could ride out the problems of the pineapple trade such as drought, delays in sailing, market fluctuations and hurricanes. And in addition, the poorer planters needed a means of acquiring pineapple slips for planting and transportation to carry their produce across the harbour to the Harbour Island merchants. Generally they opened accounts with the storekeepers in Harbour Island who advanced not only the seeds or slips for planting, but food and clothing to carry them through the eighteen months between planting of the slips and harvesting. The planters then paid for these advances with the fruits of their labour, and whether the year was good or bad, the closing of the account seldom left anything but the smallest margin in favour of the debtor.[57]

Truck and credit as a system of labour management was open to all kinds of abuse by the merchant class. Governor Robinson wrote about the distress of the poor planters in Harbour Island when advances were withheld:

> … it has been customary for the storekeepers, who are chiefly Wesleyans, to advance provisions on the next year's crop, but it is reported to me they have refused to do so as the poor people did not at the last election vote for their candidates, but for those for what was styled the government party…[58]

Even those planters who worked a plot on plantation estates owned by wealthy proprietors, to whom they were required to give one-third of their harvest and sell the remainder, were obliged to take truck instead of cash payments. The resident justices of the Harbour Island District constantly reported dissatisfaction between the owners of pine fields and employees with regard to labour and its payment.[59] Although the direct traders paid the Harbour Island merchants in gold from the USA, this money did not circulate among the poorer classes.[60] Very often the planters got low prices for their pineapples, or received goods that were overpriced, of no use to them and poor in quality. Before the following pineapple season, to avoid starvation, they mortgaged their crops again in return for an advance,[61] and thus the cycle of debt continued. The greatest indictment of this practice was pronounced by Governor Haynes Smith: ' …industry and labour in the Colony are enclosed in the bonds of the Truck System which eats into the vitals of all labour in the Colony and destroys all enterprise and energy'.[62]

In 1875, Governor Robinson, at the prospect of a bleak pineapple season, advised the principal pineapple growers of Eleuthera to divert the industry of the colony into 'more profitable and less precarious channels than pineapples'.[63] And although pineapples were very much the principal article of export in the third quarter of the nineteenth century from Harbour Island, the planters did cultivate other fruit for export as Table 9.4 below shows.

As far as fruit export revenue went, Harbour Island was way ahead of Nassau and Eleuthera and earning 72 per cent of the total revenue. Oranges shipped to the US were in the millions for the three islands, and Harbour Island exported 65 per cent of the total. It is interesting to note the high premium on pineapples (see Table 9.1) compared to oranges where 100,775 dozen pineapples (1.2 million) exported from Harbour Island earned L9,526 and 1,137 million oranges earned L1,467. Of the three fruit-producing islands, Harbour Island was the most productive and had the greatest range of fruit.

In the late 1870s, the planters at Harbour Island and North Eleuthera expended their energies in extending their existing cultivations of coconuts, oranges and bananas, and in response to the urge for diversification, they introduced sugar canes, tomatoes and potatoes as export crops. The most progressive step was the introduction of sugar mills and the manufacture of sugar, syrup and molasses, and canning factories for the preservation of pineapples and other fruits.

The sugar factories of Dunmore Town Sugar Company and Roberts and Johnson of Harbour Island were opened in 1876. In its first year, the former company made and sold more than enough sugar and molasses to pay for its operational costs and the new Victor mills, imported from the US. In addition, they planted some 20,000 to 30,000 canes, the deep, fertile, black soil at the southern end of Harbour Island producing canes nine feet

Table 9.4 Exports of fruits, excluding pineapples, from the Northern Islands 1864[64]

Description	Island > To	Unit	Nassau, NP Qty	Value L	Harbour Isl. Qty	Value L	Eleuthera Qty	Value L-s	Total Qty	Value L-s
Oranges	GB	Millions	8	14	0	0	0	0	8	14–00
Oranges	USA	Millions	370	473	1,137	1,467	250	313–0	1,758	2,253–01
Grapefruit	USA		7,000	5	2,400	3	0	0	9,400	8–00
Lemons/limes	USA	Barrels	0	0	56	24	1	0–6	57	24–06
Cocoanuts	USA		1,500	5	58,400	199	0	0	59,900	204–00
Sappodillas	USA		0	0	3,000	3	0	0	3,000	3–00
Melons	USA		300	6	600	10	50	0–10	950	16–10
Bananas	USA	Bunch	200	10	8,150	455	20	2–0	8,370	467–00
Tamarinds	GB	Barrels	1	1	0	0	0	0	1	1–00
Total				514		2,161		314–16		2,990–16

high.[65] This initial success raised the interest and expectations of the people in the development of cane as an export commodity.

By 1880, there were nine sugar mills in the Harbour Island District: five in Harbour Island owned by Messrs. Harris and Company, Capt. W. Sweeting, J.W. Albury, A. Kelly and Joseph H. Roberts, one at Man Island owned by Mr. Roberts, one at Egg Island owned by Messrs. Roberts and Johnson, one at Royal Island owned by Mr. John Baldwin and one being erected at Spanish Wells.[66] Other islands such as Eleuthera, Abaco, Bimini and Exuma also attempted to diversify into sugar production.[67] It was not long before the Harbour Island entrepreneurs realized that although the quality of the sugar, syrup and molasses was first class, they could be imported at a cheaper rate from the US By 1885 several manufacturers had disposed of their mills, and those still grinding cane converted it to syrup for home consumption.[68] This syrup production continued intermittently over the years; in 1905 two horse-powered mills produced 5,000 gallons of syrup;[69] in 1914 four sugar mills produced 4,000 gallons[70] and in 1919 the last mill in operation produced 650 gallons.[71] Later attempts to revive the sugar industry were short-lived.

Two years after the first pineapple preserving company was formed in Nassau, Benjamin Harris of Harbour Island established the Harbour Island Preserving Company and opened a canning factory in 1878. Lady Brassey described the simple process of tinning the fruit.

> The 'apples' are first stripped of all their leaves; then they are swiftly peeled; stalk and eyes are dexterously removed; and the best fruit are thrown whole into the coppers full of hot syrup, where they are boiled ten times. They are put singly in tins, which are after-wards hermetically sealed. Those of the second quality are cut into slices and treated in the same manner. The third quality is cut into squares, the fourth is merely scraped; but all are cooked in syrup and packed in tins decorated with attractive pictures'.[72]

It was a very proud moment for Harris when his first full shipment of preserved pineapples was loaded on the Harbour Island-built schooner *Pioneer* for Baltimore, consisting of 1,506 cases of 2 dozen each 2 pound jars, 16 cases of 2 dozen each 3 pound cans, 198 cases of half-gallon cans and 99 cases of 2 quart cans.[73] By 1882, Harris was also canning tomatoes at the factory.[74]

Joseph S. Johnson, a Nassau resident from Harbour Island, was the largest preserver of pineapples and other fruits in the Colony. As the pineapple industry was revived by the introduction of fertilizer in the 1880s and the Bahamian industry was edged out of the US market by competition from Cuba and Florida and rising US tariffs, more preserving companies opened in the colony to absorb the large quantities of pines not disposed of. In 1884, Johnson opened a preserving factory in Dunmore Town,[75] which was in full operation during the pine season and by 1889 exported 3,510 cases.[76] When Hawaii was annexed to the US in 1898 and Hawaii's canned pineapples entered the US duty free,[77] the fruit-preserving industry in the colony met the same fate as the sugar factories; by 1908 the canned pineapple industry was in sharp decline and by 1914 exports ceased.[78]

Another ephemeral industry at Dunmore Town was manila, also called hemp or sisal. By pressing the leaves of the sisal plant, a valuable fibre was extracted that was used for the manufacture of cordage. Governor Shea vigorously promoted sisal cultivation as a way in which to diversify. In 1888, 10,000 suckers planted on new ground increased the existing cultivation on Harbour Island.[79] The next year the total sisal plants for the island was 80,000 to 100,000[80] and 17 bales of $1\frac{1}{2}$ tons of fibre were shipped from the district to Nassau for the English market.[81] Sisal fields were also planted on the commonage, several outlying settlements of North Eleuthera, such as Bluff, and other islands. By 1890 the stock of sisal plants had jumped dramatically; Harbour Island planters had cultivated 296,550 plants, New Providence 560,000 and Abaco 357,320.[82] Planters at Harbour Island engaged in the new industry wrote to Governor Shea: 'We are pleased to note the recent sisal industry is favourably progressing, the plants having met with a quick and profitable sale.'[83]

The two-step process of preparation of the leaves and extraction of the fibre, described by Governor Shea, was simple but laborious. The leaves were split to expose the internal part and after they were soaked in salt water for about seven days, the pulp was then readily separated from the fibre by passing the whole substance through the hands.[84] In 1891, J.S. Johnson established a factory at Dunmore Town for extracting the fibre from the hemp leaves by use of a steam-powered scutching machine.[85] The lack of machinery to press the leaves was a setback to the initial success of the industry. In 1892, only 43 bales were cleaned and the remainder of the leaves sold for cleaning at three shillings per million pounds.[86] Ever resourceful, the planters concentrated on nurseries and shipped large quantities of young sisal plants to Andros and other islands, making a considerable sum of L10,000 for the year 1894.[87] By 1895, it was reported that Johnson's Factory had been at work but 1500 tons of sisal had been lost, as there was no means of preparing it.[88] The following year, Resident Justice Armbrister reported sisal cultivation had come to an end.[89] But a few brave souls soldiered on and as late as 1924, advanced market prices for sisal encouraged cultivation at Hatchet Bay, Gregory Town and Harbour Island,[90] where a rope-making facility was situated adjacent to the 'Up Yonder Shipyard'.

Other short-lived industries engaged in by Harbour Island merchants reflected their ingenuity and adaptability to changing markets. Facing a shortage of provisions, especially fresh meat, some Harbour Islanders returned to raising livestock, once a very important industry. Returns in the 1900s showed stocks of horses, horned cattle, sheep, goats, pigs and poultry.[91] Pineapple-preserving companies at Nassau, Harbour Island and Eleuthera, also preserved tomatoes, guavas, bananas and wild grapes.[92] They even experimented with a shipment of preserved conchs, which never attracted a market.[93] Harbour Island fishermen from as early as 1838 sporadically exported sponges gathered in the sound across the harbour and in 1937 the Harbour Island Sponge Planting Association attempted to put the industry on a firmer footing by planting 50,000 wool and velvet sponge cuttings in the harbour. Although they grew rapidly, they did not escape the widespread blight of 1938.[94] The boldest example of new enterprise was Mr. Gilbert Kelly's 3,000 pounds of various kinds of fish, cured, dried and packed for export to Havana.[95]

In 1896, Governor Shea, ever ready to promote improvements in agriculture, brought out two experts from Kew Gardens, England, to advise the planters. At the Temperance Hall on Harbour Island, Dr. Morris spoke to the growers about tomatoes, potatoes, onions, oranges, grapefruit, egg plant and pineapples, which were always grown for subsistence and exported if the crop exceeded local demand. He advised that tomatoes and potatoes were best suited for cultivation at Harbour Island.[96] Some of the inhabitants heeded this advice and these two crops generated intermittent small amounts of revenue for the next quarter of a century. Others turned their attention once again to oranges. There were no large orchards but the foundation was laid for a citrus industry.[97] By the 1920s, the market value of citrus fruit had soared and there were 2,441 orange and 1,771 lime and sour orange trees at the north end of Harbour Island called 'the Narrows'.[98] Other planters leased three-acre lots of Crown Land at the southern end of the island and planted 40 pounds of onion seeds and 10 acres of Irish potatoes.[99]

Harbour Island, in conjunction with the other fruit and vegetable growing settlements of the District, namely Spanish Wells, Bluff and Current, contributed more produce to the local market in Nassau than any other district in the Colony. Actual export figures were obscured for a number of reasons. A certain amount of the District's produce, carried weekly by some fifteen local boats to agents in Nassau, was subsumed under the Nassau exports. Secondly, with direct trade to the United States, false bills of lading were often used, as in the case of the three schooners that left Harbour Island showing 258,000 oranges, when in fact they carried 620,000 oranges besides bananas, coconuts and other fruits.[100] However commissioners' reports provide some indication of the range and quantity of the District's exports. For example, Commissioner Ambrister's 1914 Report listed the following items: 80 tons of onions, 40,000 coconuts, 600 tons of sweet potatoes, the most valuable crop for the year, 30,000 dozen pineapples, 75 tons of sisal fibre and 30,000 hats from Spanish Wells and Current.[101]

Many of the north Eleutheran people continued to farm for the local and United States eastern seaboard markets into the first quarter of the twentieth century, but many Harbour Islanders, whose fathers had given up seafaring occupations for the 'golden' pineapple of the halcyon days, returned to the sea. By 1896, Harbour Island was once again a chiefly seafaring town where a great number of owners, captains and crews of seagoing vessels lived.[102] The increasingly versatile boat-building industry at Harbour Island provided a home fleet that promoted domestic fishing and foreign trade. The resident justice observed that more ships were built for foreign trade and owned at Harbour Island than at any other port in the colony; 35 men were employed in supplying the local market with fish, 103 sailed on foreign voyages and 72 on coasting voyages.[103] This represented most of the male population, with boys as young as 12 years shipping before the mast.

Harbour Island fishermen used one-mast open sloops or dinghies as small as ten feet to supply fish for the local market. Using hand-lines, traps made of palmetto leaves or nets of sisal, these hardy seamen did not have to go far, as the wide expanse of harbour at their doorstep was replete with conchs and many species of shallow-water small-scaled fish. They knew the best shoals and channels for good fishing, and were well versed in the best tides and phases of the moon. They followed the seasons, welcoming the arrival of the crab season, the loggerhead season and the most anticipated season of all, when it became every fisherman's dream to cast his net on that elusive school of 2,000 passing jacks.

The fishermen out of Harbour Island who supplied fresh fish to the Nassau market set sail on two-masted sloops called smack boats. The best known of the Harbour Island fleet were *Mary Beatrice, Mayflower, Madge, William Elder* and *Royal*, all, interestingly enough, captained by an Albury. These 20–30 foot boats carried a crew of 6–8 men and had large open wells for the storage of live fish. They left Harbour Island for six weeks at a time, fishing at Six Shillings, Booby Rocks and the many shoals and cays on the way to New Providence, where they sold their fresh fish at the Nassau Market. They then made several more fishing voyages, using Nassau as a base for a faster turn-around, and returned home with provisions and the balance of their earnings. After a short time at home, they sailed again.[104] In 1907 there were a mere four to five fishing smacks in the Harbour Island District and by 1912, the smack fleet grew to 38 and employed 190 men.[105]

The halcyon days

And the shipbuilders were busy building more. By 1922, Spanish Wells took the lead in smack fishing as many Harbour Island mariners had been lured into the more lucrative mercantile trade.[106]

Of great pride to Harbour Island was its home-crafted fleet of two and three-masted schooners often chartered by merchants in fruit-growing settlements and agents in Nassau. The two-masters, *William H. Albury, The Admiral, Hattie Darling, Julia Dean* and *Fearless,* plied the waters between Harbour Island, Nassau and Miami, carrying fruit and passengers to Miami and returning with lumber, shingles, dynamite, gasoline and passengers.[107] The three-masters, *P.J. McLaughlin, Bentley, Beatrice, Melrose* and *Corinthia* were lumber carriers, the latter three custom built in Harbour Island for the lumber trade. They carried lumber from the Gulf ports or Abaco to Cuba, took on brown sugar to New Orleans, Pensacola or Tampa and returned to Harbour Island with white sugar and supplies.[108] Commissioners Johnson and McKinney often remarked on the large sums of money circulated on Harbour Island from this mercantile trade, ordinary mariners bringing home an average of $100.00 per month.[109]

A fine example of an industrious mariner, who rose to be a prominent and prosperous sea captain in the mercantile business, was Capt. R. H. Ranger of Harbour Island. At the tender age of 12, he shipped before the mast on the New York-bound schooner *Equator,* owned by W. F. Albury. He soon took command of the vessel and spent twelve years sailing to New York, Charleston and Savannah, carrying pineapples in summer, oranges in winter and returning with lumber and other freight. Capt. James W. Culmer from Tarpum Bay, who was to become one of the wealthiest men in the Bahamas, hired Ranger to command, first, the *Sarah E. Douglas* then the *Hattie Darling,* shipping fruit and engaging in a general trading business. In 1880, Ranger was proud to command the newly built *Mabel Darling,* of which he was three-quarter owner, Culmer being the other quarter-owner. For many more years he engaged in taking pines to America, returning with lumber and goods.[110]

The Harbour Island mariners who sailed on the lumber schooners were the most highly regarded of all the sailors. There was a degree of glamour and adventure in 'going foreign' as they called it, and their earnings were greater than those of the domestic fishermen and local traders. Their wives and girlfriends looked forward to the return of their handsomely dressed men and their gifts of gold twenty-dollar pieces, doubloons, silk stockings and sweet perfumes. However, they faced more risks and hardships than most mariners, and their voyages took them away from home for ten-month periods.[111]

It was the custom for the crew of the *Beatrice* to sign up for the voyage after the hurricane season, and on 15 October, weather permitting, they set sail. For the following ten months they made ten trips between Mobile,

New Orleans or Wilson City, Abaco to the northern Cuban ports of Porta Padre, Neuviotas, Nippy Bay or Mantanzas, carrying long-leaf yellow pine for Cuba's fast-growing sugar industry. The loading of the lumber in Wilson City was a backbreaking exercise that the crew performed; in the gulf ports stevedoring crews spared them this ordeal. The unloading in Cuba had its own challenges: passing the planks one by one out of a dark, sweltering hold with temperatures above a hundred degrees Fahrenheit, feet blistered from pitch boiling out of seams, and hands and arms torn by yellow pine splinters. There was never a moment of respite; as soon as the *Beatrice* was loaded she put to sea, and as soon as she was unloaded she put to sea, and at sea they swabbed, cleaned, chipped, caulked, painted, sewed canvas, spliced rope and pumped the bilge. As Paul Albury commented, 'The crew had to be able-bodied men. No place at all for the sick or the weak'.[112] The first sighting of the Anglican church spire at Dunmore Town on their return in August of the following year must have filled their hearts with great joy.

Throughout the first quarter of the twentieth century, the lumber trade brought great prosperity to Harbour Island, especially during the war years when the freight rates were high. However, by 1925, Harbour Island owned only two vessels, the *Dart* and the *Julia Elizabeth*, some having been sold to Nassau merchants and others wrecked,[113] and all legal foreign trade came to an end.

The illegal liquor trade during Prohibition was clouded in secrecy, so word-of-mouth anecdotes in the Lucerne Hotel, Nassau, the rendezvous of the rum-runners, may or may not be historically accurate. A near-contemporary writer observed, 'The vessel masters from Harbour Island were "out front" with schooner and fast motor boats puncturing the Coast Guard Line, criss-crossing the Gulf Stream with their keels, running the stuff to shore'.[114] Official reports of the period 1919 to 1933 are silent on bootlegging so it is quite difficult to assess the Harbour Island involvement. We do know that Harbour Island men made up the crew of the *Alma R*, captained by William Thompson of Abaco, which made several bootlegging trips to New York, before the Feds caught up with them.[115] In 1927, the schooners *Julia Elizabeth* and the *Dart* were used solely as lighters between Nassau and Gun Cay, Bimini,[116] where the liquor barges anchored as floating hotels for the retailing of booze. Harbour Island was very prosperous during this period and it is uncertain whether all the revenue was from legal foreign trade.

Although Dunmore Town was 'the foremost settlement outside of Nassau', and there was much wealth there, many members of the labouring class emigrated in pursuit of a better life. The population of Harbour Island dropped from 2,172 in 1871 to 793 in 1931[117] as three waves of migrants gravitated to Key West, Miami and New Providence. The declining pineapple industry, severe weather conditions and the bondage of the truck system forced many labourers and several unemployed ships' carpenters to Key West, where 'not only a high rate of wages is paid, but the people get paid in cash'.[118] A further attraction was the opportunity for employment of their children at the cigar factories. By 1892, 8,000 of 25,000 inhabitants at Key West were Bahamian,[119] and an alteration in US immigration laws slowed down the migration but it continued into the 1900s.[120]

While the migration to Key West was generally permanent, the building of the city of Miami in 1905–1906 and the establishment of the citrus industry in Florida gave rise to 'livelihood migration', which was largely a temporary exodus. Between 1910–1920 the migration from the Bahamas to Miami and Florida intensified, much of it facilitated by the Harbour Island-owned two-masted schooners. In 1913, for example, of the ten ships carrying passengers between Nassau and Miami, 7 were Harbour Island schooners: *William H Albury, Louise F, Sarah E. Douglas, Admiral, Hattie Darling, Julia Elizabeth* and *Fearless*.[121] Although it is difficult to know how many emigrants from Harbour Island joined the exodus to Miami, by 1919 the depopulation was considerable. The commissioner bemoaned the loss of the more 'energetic and ambitious people who are dissatisfied to remain in the same old rut and have more chance to advance successfully in the rapidly developing city of Miami'.[122] The immediate effect of the manpower shortage was offset by the large remittances sent by emigrants to their families.[123]

In the 1920s the US passed laws that curtailed the flow of immigrants from the Bahamas, and labourers from the Out Islands who had formerly gone to Florida in the season, then went to Nassau, which was enjoying prosperity from bootlegging, tourism and land and construction booms. At the end of the nineteenth century, the Out Islands were home to three-quarters of the colony's 47,565 inhabitants, and by the middle of the twentieth century more than half of the 84,841 people lived in the capital. The population at Harbour Island dropped to one-third of its burgeoning population in the Halcyon years.

By 1915, Governor Allardyce after visiting Harbour Island remarked, 'The glory of Harbour Island as a busy shipping port and the centre of an agricultural district has in a measure departed'.[124] Any revival of agriculture was doomed to failure by labour shortages due to migration, the general disinclination of the remaining workforce to accept illegal truck, the competition of cheaper fruit from Cuba and America[125] and the preference of tourists for American produce. In agriculture, Harbour Island was not productive and faced 'the wilderness years'. As many able men and women left home and carved out a new life elsewhere, a few families in Dunmore Town held on to what they knew best – building ships.

Notes

1. *Harper's New Monthly Magazine*, No. CCXCIV, Vol. XLIX, 1874, 771; S.G.W. Benjamin, *The Atlantic Islands as Resorts of Health and Pleasure,* New York, Harper Brothers Publishers, 1878, p. 771.
2. CSP, vol.30 (1717–1718), 737, Woodes Rogers to Council of Trade and Plantations, 31 October 1718.
3. CO 23/13/160, John Barker to Lord Carteret, February 1724.
4. CO 23/3/23, Woodes Rogers to Council of Trades and Plantations, 1731.
5. CO 23/8/8, Thomas Shirley to to Council of Trades and Plantations, 1769.
6. CO 23/5/163, James Scott to Board of Trade, 1752.
7. CO 23/1/17 part 3, Governor Phenney to Council of Trade and Plantations, 1723.
8. MMS, Box #6, Box 123 – 1824 -1826, WI, Sheet 294/280, Dowson to Society, 15 December 1826.
9. MMS, Box #6, Box 122 – 1824 -1826, WI, Sheet 277/132, Dowson to Society, 18 May 1826.
10. MMS, Box #8, Box 127 – 1823 –1829, WI, Sheet 381/77, T Pugh to Society, 21 August 1829.
11. MMS, Box #6, Box 123 – 1824 -1826, WI, Sheet 290/251, J Horne to Society, 2 November 1826.
12. *Royal Gazette*, 16 July 1825.
13. CO 23/73/104, Earl of Bathurst to Governor Lewis Grant, 13 August 1824.
14. CO 23/73/103, Earl of Bathurst to Governor Lewis Grant, 13 August 1824.
15. MMS, Box #12, Box 138 – 1836–1839, WI, Sheet 582/110, Samuel Simons to Society, 2 May 1837.
16. CO 23/110/352, Memorial of John Provost Baldwin, 27 April 1841.
17. Browne, Jefferson B, *Key West: The Old and New,* University of Florida Press, Gainesville, 1973, p. 12 and Curry, William Harley, *Kinfolks,* Clefan Publishing, Portland Oregon, 1934, p. 1681.
18. *Nassau Guardian*, 23 October 1852.
19. *Nassau Guardian*, 22 December 1852.
20. Ragatz, Lowell Joseph, *The British Caribbean 1763–1833,* Octagon Books, New York, 1971, p. 354.
21. CO 23/94/187, Petition of Harbour Islanders to Governor Colebrook, 10 October 1835.
22. CO 23/99/232, Report of Resident Justice Winder to C R Nesbitt, 15 April 1837.
23. *Nassau Guardian*, November 14 1857.
24. CO 23/12/46, Memorial of John Graves, 31 March 1697.
25. Lefroy, Lt. Gen. Sir J. H. *Memorials of Bermuda Vol. 1,* Bermuda Historical Society, 1981, p. 55 & p. 136.
26. Johnson, Howard, *The Bahamas in Slavery and Freedom,* Ian Randle Publishers, Kingston, Jamaica, 1991, p. 63.
27. Hawkins, Richard, *The Baltimore Canning Industry and the Bahamian Pineapple Trade,* in *The Maryland Historian,* Vol. 26, #2, Fall/Winter 1995, p. 11.
28. Shattuck, George B, editor, *The Bahama Islands,* The Geographical Society of Baltimore, MacMillan Co. New York, 1905, Plate xxix, following p. 168.
29. Powles, L. D., *Land of the Pink Pearl,* Sampson Low, Marston, Searle & Rivington, London 1888, p. 222.
30. CO23/135/115$\frac{1}{2}$, Governor Gregory's Report, 15 May 1850.
31. *Nassau Guardian*, Report of the Agricultural Society, 6 January 1866.
32. CO 23/189/226, Minutes of the Executive Council, 22 April 1867.
33. CO 23/185/74, Governor's Report on Blue Book 1865.
34. Governor Rawson's Report for the year 1864, p. 43.
35. CO 23/202/474, Governor Walker to Lord Granville, 30 November 1870.
36. CO 23/197/36, Governor Walker's Report on the Blue Book of 1868.

The halcyon days 129

37 Census Reports in Blue Books of 1861 and 1871.
38 *Nassau Guardian,* 15 August 1874.
39 Resident Justice, Solomon's Report in Votes of the House of Assembly, 1879.
40 MMS, Box #29, Box 221, Box 1874, Bahamas, Sheet 1414/8, H Bleby to Society, 27 Jan 1874.
41 *Harper's New Monthly Magazine,* No. CCXCIV, Vol. XLIX, 1874, 771; S.G.W. Benjamin, *The Atlantic Islands as Resorts of Health and Pleasure,* New York, Harper Brothers Publishers, 1878, p. 771.
42 *Nassau Guardian,* 22 April 1876.
43 Compiled from *Nassau Guardians* of 20 July 1872, 15 August 1874 and 19 August 1876.
44 Craton and Saunders, *Islanders in the Stream, Vol 2,* University of Georgia Press, 1998, p. 147.
45 *Nassau Guardian,* 20 August 1887.
46 Craton and Saunders, *Islanders in the Stream, Vol 2,* University of Georgia Press, 1998, p. 147
47 Resident Justice, J C O'Halloran's Reports, Votes of the house of Assembley, 1894.
48 *Nassau Guardian,* 3 November 1849.
49 *Nassau Guardian,* 4 March 1854.
50 CO 23./185/436, Burnside's Report to Governor Rawson, 1866.
51 Nassau Quarterly Missionary Papers, June 1887, p. 6.
52 Governor Rawson's Report for the year 1864, p. 83.
53 MMS, Box #27, Box 218 – 1846, WI, Sheet 1320/3, J Blackwell to Society, 24 February 1846.
54 Department of Lands and Surveys, Book 2, Grants 1846 and Department of Archives, Boat Building in the Customs Shipping Registers of the 1830s and 1840s.
55 Powles, L D, *Land of the Pink Pearl,* Sampson Low, Marston, Searle & Rivington, London 1888, p. 204.
56 Reilly, William Benedict, *The Bahamas,* The Monthly Illustrator, Vol XIII, #4, November 1896, The Bahamas Edition, p. 41–45.
57 CO 23/225/20, Governor Blake's Report, 12 August 1884.
58 CO 23/214/322, Governor Robinson to Lord Carnavon, 2 September 1875.
59 Resident Justice J. S. Solomon's Report in Votes of the House of Assembly, 1890.
60 Ibid., p. 1883.
61 Powles, L. D. *Land of the Pink Pearl,* Sampson Low, Marston, Searle & Rivington, London 1888, 97.
62 Johnson, Howard, *The Bahamas in Slavery and Freedom,* Ian Randle Publishers, Kingston, Jamaica, 1991, p. 166.
63 CO 23/214/131, Governor Robinson to Lord Carnavon, 24 June, 1875.
64 Governor Rawson's Report for the year 1864, p. 83.
65 C.O. 23/217/13, Governor Robinson's Report, 5 January, 1877.
66 *Nassau Guardian,* 21 January, 1880.
67 Blue Book 1878.
68 Resident Justice J. S. Solomon's Report in Votes of the House of Assembly, 1885.
69 *Nassau Guardian,* Letter to the editor, 3 January 1906.
70 Commissioner P. W. D. Ambrister's Report in Votes of the House of Assembly, 1914.
71 Commissioner Dewees Johnson's Report in Votes of the House of Assembly, 1920.
72 Brassey, Lady, *The Trades, The Tropics and the Roaring Forties,* London, 1885, p. 342.

73. *Nassau Guardian,* 21 August, 1878.
74. *Nassau Guardian,* 11 February, 1882.
75. *Nassau Guardian,* 28 June 1884.
76. Resident Justice J. S. Solomon's Report in Votes of the House of Assembly, 1889.
77. Hawkins, Richard, *The Baltimore Canning Industry and the Bahamian Pineapple Trade*, in The Maryland Historian, Vol. 26, #2, Fall/Winter 1995, p. 7.
78. Hawkins, Richard, *The Baltimore Canning Industry and the Bahamian Pineapple Trade*, in The Maryland Historian, Vol. 26, #2, Fall/Winter 1995, p. 14.
79. *Nassau Guardian,* 22 February, 1888.
80. Resident Justice J. S. Solomon's Report in Votes of the House of Assembly, 1889.
81. Resident Justice J. S. Solomon's Report in Votes of the House of Assembly, 1890.
82. *Nassau Guardian*, 11 January, 1890.
83. C.O.23/232/288, Harbour Islanders address to Governor Shea, May 1890.
84. CO 23/239/111, Report of the Visit of Governor Shea, 24 April 1894.
85. *Nassau Guardian,* 4 March 1891.
86. Resident Justice, J. C. O'Halloran's Reports, Votes of the House of Assembly, 1892.
87. CO 23/239/111, Report of the Visit of Governor Shea, 24 April 1894.
88. Resident Justice, J. C. O'Halloran's Reports, Votes of the House of Assembly, 1895.
89. Resident Justice, P. W. D. Ambrister's Report, Votes of House of Assembly, 1896.
90. Resident Justice, E. H. McKinney's Report, Votes of the House of Assembly, 1925.
91. Blue Books 1909–1920 & C.O.23/678/44, Report on the development of agriculture in the Bahamas, E.A. McCallan, May, 1939.
92. Blue Book 1878.
93. Blue Book 1881.
94. Commissioner W. P. Roberts' Report, Votes of House of Assembly, 1938 & *Nassau Guardian,* 29 December 1938.
95. *Nassau Guardian,* 29 July 1876.
96. CO 23/245/355 Report of Dr Morris of Kew Gardens, 8 February 1896.
97. Resident Justice, P.W.D. Ambrister's Report, Votes of House of Assembly, 1896.
98. Commissioner E. H. McKinney's Report, Votes of House of Assembly, 1925.
99. Commissioner E. H. McKinney's Report, Votes of House of Assembly, 1923.
100. *Nassau Guardian,* Letter to the editor, 3 January 1906.
101. Commissioner P. W. D. Ambrister's Report, Vote of House of Assembly, 1914.
102. *Monthly Illustrator*, Vol XIII, #4, November 1896, The Bahamas Edition.
103. Resident Justice, P. W. D. Ambrister's Report, Votes of House of Assembly, 1896.
104. Interview with Mr. Leroy Johnson, Harbour Island, August, 2001.
105. Resident Justice Francis Armstrong's Report, Votes of House of Assembly, 1908 & Commissioner P. W. D. Ambrister's Report, Votes of House of Assembly, 1913.
106. Commissioner Dewees Johnson's Report, Votes of House of Assembly, 1918.
107. *Nassau Guardian,* Shipping News, 28 January 1913.
108. Blue Book 1918–1919.
109. Commissioner Dewees Johnson's Report, Votes of House of Assembly, 1919.
110. *Monthly Illustrator*, Vol XIII, #4, November 1896, The Bahamas Edition.
111. Albury, Paul, 'The Beatrice – The History of a Ship', unpublished lecture 1970.
112. Ibid.
113. Commissioner Dewees Johnson's Report, Votes of House of Assembly, 1926.
114. Major H. MacLachlan Bell, *Isles of June,* Robert M. McBride & Company, NY, 1934, p. 87.
115. Thompson, Leonard Maurice, *I wanted wings,* Decatur, Ill. White Sound Press, 1995, p. 9.
116. Commissioner Dewees Johnson's Report, Votes of House of Assembly, 1929.

117 Blue Books 1871 & 1931.
118 Powles, L. D. *Land of the Pink Pearl,* Sampson Low, Marston, Searle & Rivington, London 1888, p. 205.
119 Wells, Sharon, *Roots of Key West Emigres,* Historic Key West Presentation, Key West Board, Fla, 1982.
120 Resident Justice, J. C. O'Halloran's Reports, Votes of the House of Assembly, 1892.
121 *The Tribune,* 4 July 1914.
122 Commissioner Dewees Johnson's Report, Votes of House of Assembly, 1920.
123 Johnson, Howard, *Bahamian Labour Migration to Florida in Late Nineteenth and Early Twentieth Centuries,* International Migration Review, vol 22, 1988, p. 101.
124 CO 23/276/75, Governor Allardyce to A. Bonar Law, 21 August 1915.
125 CO 23/678/44, Report on the Development of Agriculture in the Bahamas, E. A. McCallan, May 1939.

10

The ring of the shipwright's hammer

In the years before the Second World War, the young fishermen of Harbour Island could tell you 'The *Equator* is a good fishing drop'. And looking through a water glass, one could see a conglomerate of rotting planks and frames that had once been a proud ship. The *Equator* was a handsome vessel, a clipper-built schooner with a 66-foot keel, launched in Harbour Island in 1857.[1] In the Great Bahama Hurricane of 1866, the *Equator* capsized at her mooring, dug her spars into the harbour mud and broke them off. When the wind and sea subsided, an inspection crew went out to assess the havoc. There she was floating bottom up – and holding on to her keel, with all claws dug in, still alive, was the ship's cat. The cat has been dead many years but its ordeal still evokes sympathy for its plight, admiration for its endurance and a respect for the tenacity for how desperately it clung to life.

The *Equator* carried fruit to New York for many years and assisted in many salving adventures in the heyday of wrecking. In the severe weather of February 1904, she was blown off course while entering the Harbour Island harbour and the *Mabel Darling*, in similar difficulties, accidentally collided with her stem (bow) and she ended on a sandbank, severely damaged. As was customary with ships no longer able to sail, she was burnt to the water line and the remains of her hulk towed out and sunk – to become a home for the fish. Now there is nothing to see and her grave is overgrown with sea grass. She is gone completely. Gone too are the men who owned her and the proud artisans who built and rigged her. The sailors who took her out on the ocean and the wives who waited for her return have long since departed for another world.

The story of the *Equator* and her cat can serve as an allegory for the history of shipbuilding in Harbour Island.

Just as seafaring was in the blood, so shipbuilding was inherited from the Bermudian forebears of the inhabitants of Harbour Island:

> Upon the 19 June 1610, Sir George Sommers imbarked himself at James towne in a small barge of thirtie tonne or therabout, that he built at the Barmudas: wherin he labored from morning unto night as duelie as any workman doth labour for wages, and built her all

41 The craftsmen admiring their handiwork

42 Berlin and Harry Albury

43 The *Isles of June*

44 The *Ena K*

45 Tent over boat building area

46 The *Betty K*

47 The *Lady Dundas*, whose captain, William G. Harris, had captained both previous Harbour Island mailboats, the *Dart* and the *Endion*

48 The Bentley

49 Statue of Sir George Roberts

50 Satellite image of the Bahamas

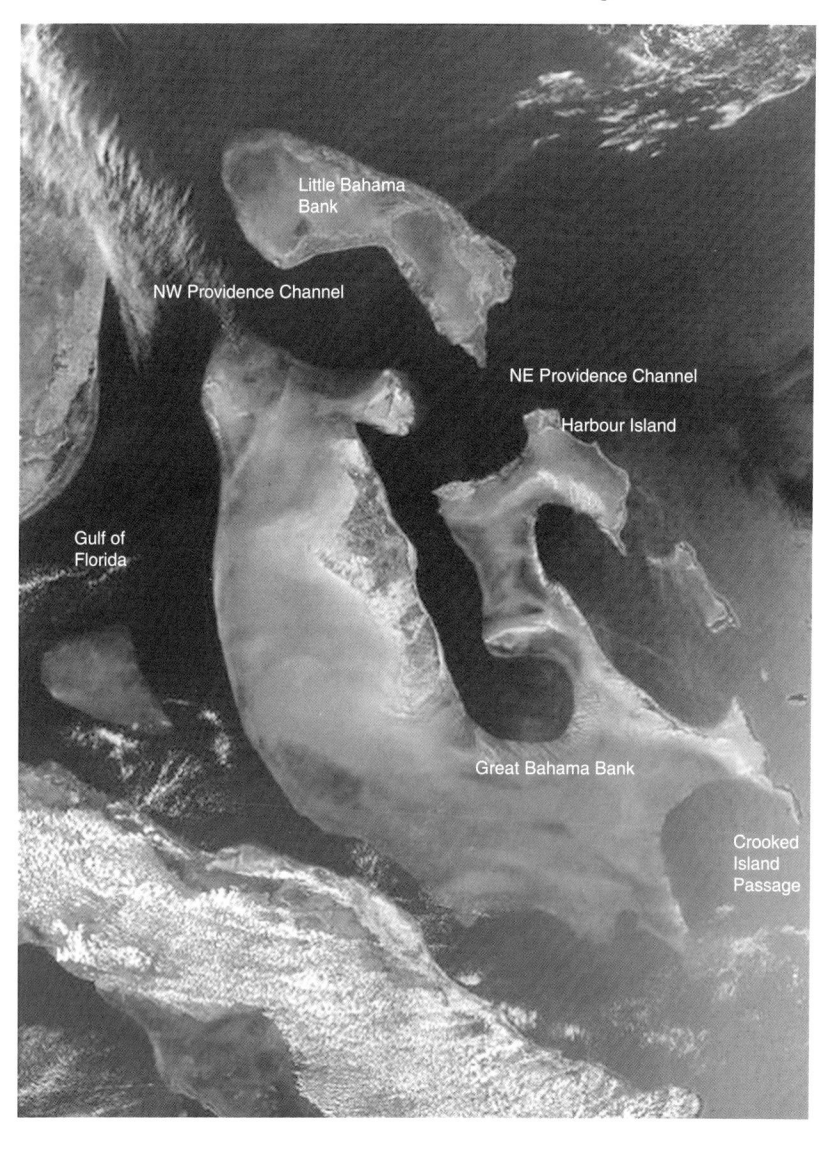

51 The Sir George Roberts Library

52 The *Gary Roberts*

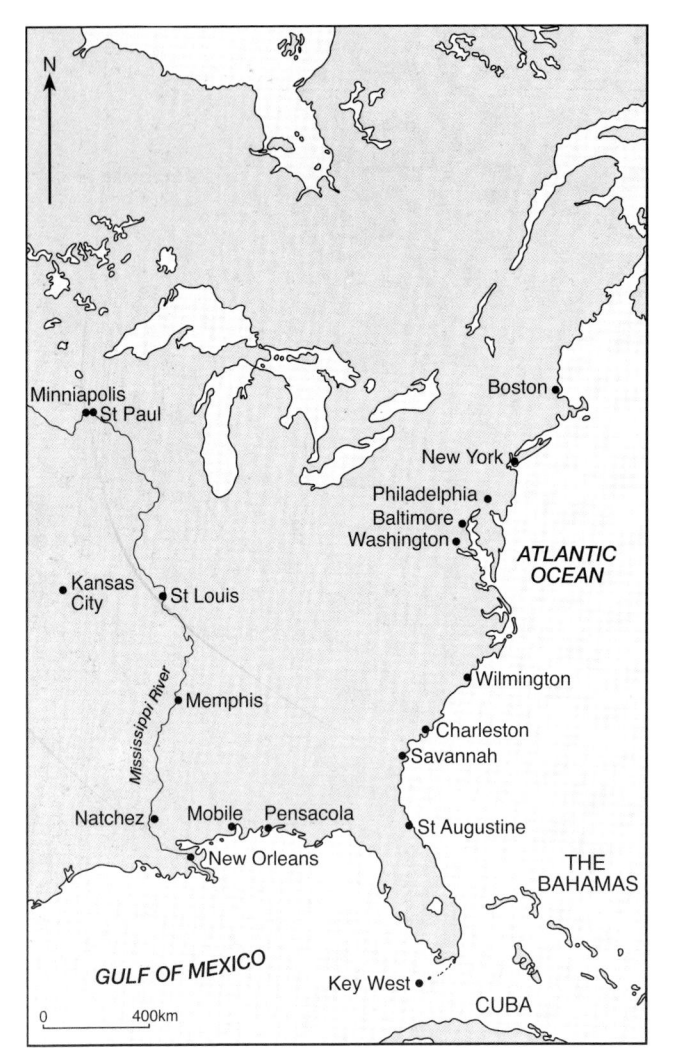

53 Eastern seaboard, the Northern Bahamas, the Gulf of Mexico and the Mississippi River

54 The schooner *Galvanic*

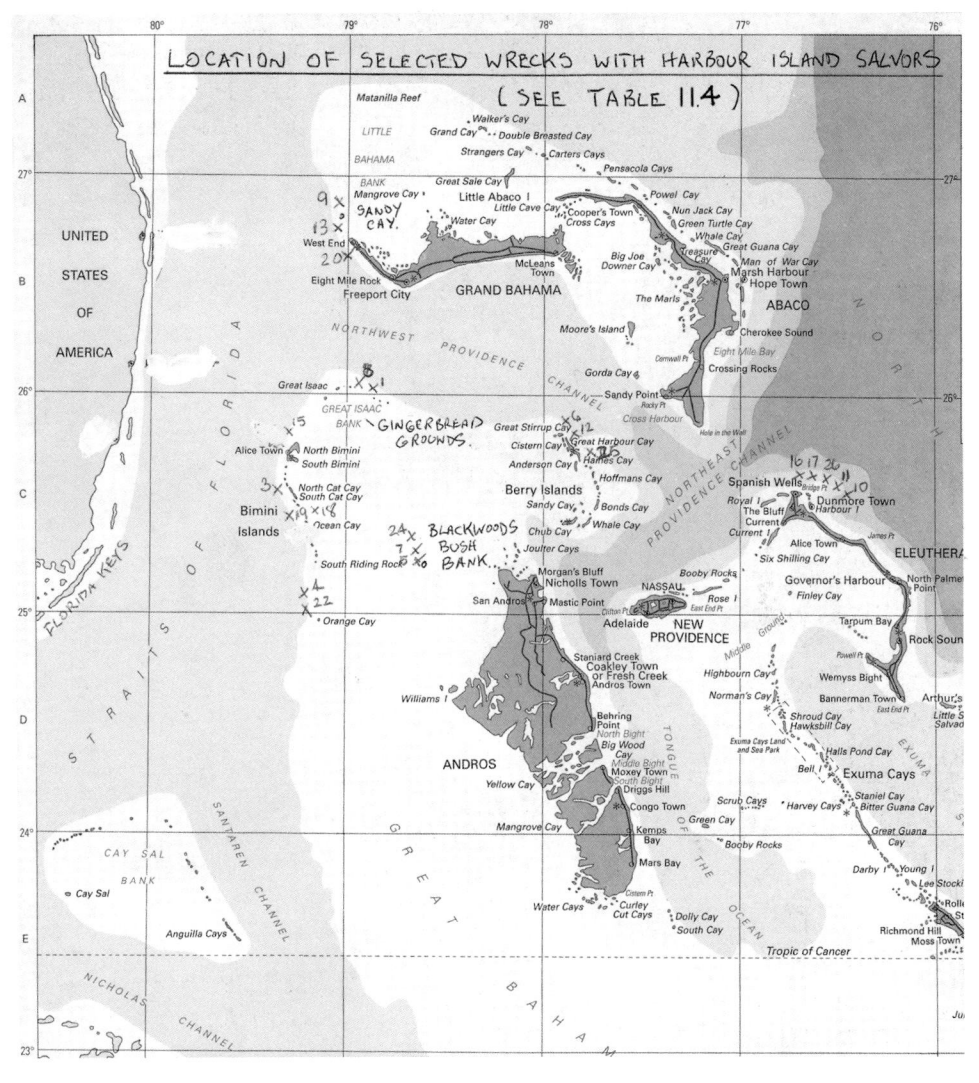

55 Location of selected wrecks

56 Rev. W.K. Duncombe

57 Sarah (Albury) Duncombe

58 The Stromboms

with cedar, with little or no yron work at all: having in her only one boult which was in the kilson.²

William Reyner and William Sayle each had a half share in a shallop of six tons specially built for the voyage to the Bahamas³ and at least one of the Eleutheran Adventurers, Lewis Middleton, followed the trade of boatwright.⁴ And from those humble beginnings, the sound of the shipwright's hammer rang the livelong day throughout the Bahama Islands for three centuries, signalling the construction of new additions to the sailing fleet. Most prominent in the early years and most enduring were the boat builders of Harbour Island, who custom-built boats for the type of trade dominant at that period.

Building a vessel is an altogether different exercise to building a house. The house carpenter depends on his straight edge and square plumb line. But in the construction of a ship nothing is straight, square or plumb. It is all a matter of bends, curves, angles and bevels. Furthermore, a ship has to float and be strong enough to withstand being heeled over and tossed about by gale-force winds and mountainous waves. Thus, ships' carpentry requires a superior training and skill. It used to be said in the Bahamas that if you wanted a good house built, get ships' carpenters to build it.

Longfellow's poem about the building of New England sailing ships can equally be applied to the early Harbour Island vessels that would have been built to be versatile – small, light and maneuverable but capable of carrying wrecked goods, turtle and fruit:

> *Built for freight and yet for speed,*
> *A beautiful and gallant craft;*
> *Broad in the beam,*
> *that the stress of the blast*
> *Pressing down upon sail and mast,*
> *Might not the sharp bows overwhelm;*
> *Broad in the beam, but sloping aft*
> *With graceful curve and slow degrees,*
> *That she might be docile to the helm,*
> *And that the currents of passing seas,*
> *Closing behind, with mighty force,*
> *Might aid and not impede her course.*⁵

Governor Montford Browne's 1775 picture of the Bahamas is of a people ranging from island to island stripping them of their valuable timber for export to the French and Dutch Islands. This excellent timber could have been used to build frigates of 18–26 guns.

134 *The Harbour Island Story*

Table 10.1 Boats built in Harbour Island, 1796–1843 taken from Customs Shipping Register 1826.

Reg #	Boat Name	Launch /Built	Burthen tons	Length feet	Masts	Builder	Captain	Subscribing Owner/from
65	Eagle	1796	19.25	33	1	Unknown	Benjamin Lowe*	Benjamin Lowe/HI*
21	William & John	1811	16.1	32	1	Unknown	Winer Bethel*	Jane Francis Higgs/HI*
4	Spinzvell	1812	20.3	41	1	Unknown	Jacob Johnson*	William Henry Sears, William Cash/HI*
8	Whipper	1812	32	41	1	Unknown	John Curry*	Joseph Saunders, Benjamin Lowe/HI*
60	Venus	1814	24.5	36	1	Unknown	Alex Mason*	John Pinder*
40	Sisters	1817	18.9	33	1	Unknown	John Thomas Rea*	John Thomas Rea*
18	Maria	1820	19.5	35	1	Unknown	James Roberts*	Henry Roberts, Prince Coleman/HI*
Non	Morning Light	1820	Built in Eleuthera			Unknown	Jacob Johnson*	John Henry, Thomas, Mary E, Rebecca Johnson/HI*
9	French Delight	1821	35.6	41	1	Unknown	William Cash*	Thompson Saunders, Anthony Eneas/HI*
Non	Eliza Ann	1825	Built in Cove, Eleuthera			Thomas Cash	Richard Sweeting*	Richard Sweeting/El, Benjamin Lowe/HI*
Non	Mullet	1825	8.3	25	1	Thomas Evan Hall	Thomas Evan Hall	Thomas Evan Hall
21	Babamian	1827	23.7	54	2	Samuel Johnson	Samuel Johnson	John Saunders/NP, Samuel Johnson/HI
13	Emma	1827	28.9	60	2	Christopher Fisher		Christopher Fisher
34	Liberty	1827	23.7	41	1	Joseph Hart	Henry Johnson	Henry Johnson, Gus Johnson/HI
21	Superior	1827	96.4	61	2	Joseph Higgs	Samuel Higgs	Samuel, Joseph, Jeremiah Higgs, Anthony Eneas/HI
3	Builder's Son	1829	28.5	40	1	Benjamin Harris	Joseph W Ingraham	Joseph W, Joseph Ingraham, Benjamin Harris/HI
6	Lilly	1829	107.3	64	2	Samuel Johnson	William Johnson	Samuel Johnson, Henry Johnson/HI
17	Union	1829	35.5	42	1	T & J Higgs	T & J Higgs	Thomas & Jeremiah Higgs/HI
12	Willing Mind	1829	15.8	33	1	William Cash	William Cash	William Cash, Anthony Eneas/HI
23	Ann	1830	21	33	1	Unknown	Richard Sweeting	Richard Sweeting
12	Blossom	1830	97.6	63	2	Joseph Higgs	Henry Johnson	Samuel, Jeremiah, Henrietta Higgs, Anthony Eneas/HI
19	Seaborn	1830	13.5	31	1	Unknown	William Jarvis	Alexander Mason/NP
26	Mary Ann	1831	21.5	35	1	Unknown	James Roberts	James, Henry Roberts, Prince Coleman/HI
13	Active	1832	35.9	47	1	Samuel Johnson	William Johnson	Samuel Johnson
22	Nimble	1832	92.2	60	2	William Holbert		Richard Sweeting
23	Johnson's Plan	1833	17.1	33	1	George Johnson	George Johnson	George Johnson
15	Olive	1833	19.5	36	1	John Albury	Richard Albury	John Albury/HI, William Durham/The Cove
19	First of August	1834	21.8	34	1	Unknown	David Ingraham	Benjamin Harris, William Harris/HI

The ring of the shipwright's hammer

	Ship	Year	Length	Beam	Masts	Captain	Owners
9	*Vesper*	1834	49.2	47	1	Joseph Higgs	Henry Johnson	Joseph Higgs, Samuel Higgs/HI
9	*Martha Jane*	1835	28	38	1	James Palmer	Thomas Johnson	Thomas, Samuel Johnson, William Albury/HI
15	*Rover*	1835	54.6	51	1	William Clear	William Johnson	William, Thomas, John Clear/HI
30	*Dunmore*	1836	44.7	64	2	Benjamin Harris	William Prudden	Anthony Eneas, Thomas Cash/HI
6	*North Star*	1836	30.2	48	2	James Palmer	James Roberts	James Roberts, Thomas Higgs
20	*Rebecca*	1836	53	52	2	Samuel Johnson	William Johnson	Samuel Johnson, William Johnson/HI
64	*Splendid*	1836	19.1	42	1	James Roberts	William Bethel	Richard Higgs Curry
14	*Esther Ann*	1837	Built at Green Turtle Cay				Richard Sweeting	James, Benjamin, Henry Roberts, Prince Coleman/HI
17	*Isabella*	1837	37.2	53	2	William Sweeting	John Thompson	Thomas Cash
11	*Leo*	1837	35	52	2	Thomas Cox	Thomas Johnson	Henry Johnson, John Albury/HI
15	*Superior*	1837	22.9	51	2	Joseph Curry	Joseph Curry	Joseph Curry, John Lowe/HI
43	*Dandy*	1838	36.2	50	2	Samuel Roberts	William Johnson	Jn, Jos Roberts, Wm, Saml Johnson, Wm, Sarah Petty/HI
	Trio	1838	34.8	51	2	Joseph Higgs	Benjamin Sweeting	Joseph Higgs, Samuel Higgs/HI
5	*Manchester*	1839	50.1	57	2	James Kelly	William Cleare	James Kelly, John Cleare, Thomas Cleare/HI
15	*Racer*	1839	37.1	57	2	Jeremiah Higgs	John Saunders	Jeremiah Higgs, John Saunders/HI
3	*Brittania*	1840	28.7	55	2	James Miller Kelly	Henry Kelly	James M Kelly, Henry Kelly, Robert Kelly/HI
4	*Corine*	1840	38.6	59	2	Thomas Johnson	Joseph H Johnson	Samuel, Joseph Henry, Johnson, Wm Thomas Albury/HI
5	*J.S.*	1840	35.8	55	2	Joseph Higgs	Glinton Higgs	Joseph Higgs, Samuel Higgs/HI
6	*Magnet*	1840	33.1	58	2	Unknown	William Johnson	James Roberts, Samuel Johnson/HI
	Tellfair	1840	Built in Abaco			Unknown	John Thompson	John Thompson, Anthony Eneas/HI
15	*Wesleyan*	1840	22.3	35	1	Thomas Dorsett	William Albury	William Albury, Richard Higgs Curry/HI
15	*Louisa Ann*	1841	22.2	43	1	John Albury	Robert Tedder	John Albury/HI, William Durham/El
Non	*Morning Star*	1841	67.6	72	2	Unknown	William Prudden	Thomas Cash/HI
21	*Union*	1841	20.2	41	1	James Roberts	John Bethel	James Roberts, Frederick Sweeting/HI
Non	*Urania*	1841	57.4	68	2	Benjamin Harris	Benjamin Harris	Benjamin Harris, Samuel, Thomas Fred Johnson/HI
10	*Arthusa*	1842	37	59	2	Joseph Roberts	?	Anthony Eneas
11	*Champion*	1842	41.6	60	2	William Johnson	William Johnson	William, Thomas, Robert, John Henry Johnson/HI
Non	*Tweed*	1843	50.7	64	2	Wm John Turton	Richard Albury	Wm, Jn, Cleare, Wm, Elijah Petty, Jos, Trudy Roberts,
	Tweed						owners continued>	Wm, Saml Johnson/HI

*: Captains and Owners would be of a date later than 1826 and not at the time the ship was built.

> There are seldom less than 12–14 vessels on the stocks and a very beautiful ship was launched here some days ago, equal if not superior to many of our frigates. There are 70 sail, which are generally employed in wrecking or the running of goods (except in the fruit season when they carry turtle, pineapples, lemons, oranges and limes to different parts of America and the West Indies but the most valuable cargo is braziletto, cedar and mahogoney planks, mastic, gum elemi, Eleuthera bark, lignum vitae to Great Britain and they bring back provisions from America or Britain and rum, molasses and sugar from West Indies).[6]

At that same time, Harbour Island was described as 'a tight and orderly community of 438 inhabitants, living mainly a maritime life, building their own boats, growing subsistence crops and raking salt on Eleuthera'.[7] And surely most of the 50 fishing boats that assisted in the Deveaux raid would have been built in Harbour Island, using the large hardwood trees that covered the Commonage on Eleuthera across the harbour.

The early eighteenth century saw the gradual emergence from piracy to legalized privateering. Former pirate Capt. John Cockram in the Harbour Island schooner *Richard and John,* mixed privateering voyages on behalf of Governor Woodes Rogers from Curacao to Hispaniola carrying timber. In 1792, at the end of a century dominated by privateering, the Harbour Island people built a privateering sloop, *The Primrose*, of 58 foot length, 18 foot breadth and 74 tons burthen. The 'Letter of Marque' read:

> In pursuance of an Act passed in the Twenty-fifth Year of the Reign of King George the Third, entitled, an Act to further Increase and Encouragement of Shipping and Navigation: *William Rose, William Slater and Benjamin Lord Junior... together with John Ferguson, Senior of New Providence, Merchant are sole owners... whereof John Symons is at present Master...* to distress and annoy the Spaniards by making capture of their ships and destroying their commerce... the said sloop... having on board Ten Carriage Guns, carrying shot of 3 to 4 lbs weight... with small Arms and Ammunition, and manned with 40 men.[8]

Another interesting feature was the Articles of Agreement in which one half of the nett proceeds went to the owners and the other half to be divided between the Captain and crew. Punishments for cowardice, and disobedience were to be loss of part of their share; compensation of 100 pounds was payable if an arm, leg or eye was lost.[9]

In 1768, New Providence was the only port visited by foreign vessels; hence produce of other islands was brought there together with wrecked goods.[10] In 1785, trade with America was carried on by smuggling goods into the islands and thence to Nassau by small craft. These goods were then sold by auction at noon.[11] In 1797, the principal employment of the inhabitants of Harbour Island was cutting timber on the island of Abaco and carrying it to New Providence in their small vessels,[12] making several voyages per season. The loss of many Harbour Island small vessels to the French enemy led to a scarcity of timber in Nassau and the need to build new ships.

Considering normal wear and tear and rot, the profusion of reefs throughout the Bahamas, the paucity of navigational aids, the calamitous effects of hurricanes and enemy privateers – the average life of Bahamian vessels could not be much more than 20 years, although many Harbour Island-built boats lasted much longer. As trade expanded every generation of shipwrights was called upon to build and rebuild the fleet and until recent times shipbuilding constituted an important sector of the economy.

We have the names of many early Harbour Island ships but no record of their size and where they were built. The Customs Shipping Register,[13] which began in 1826, is a valuable record of shipbuilding in the Bahamas and because it recorded the re-registry of ships when they changed owners we have records of a few boats built as far back as 1796 as shown in Table 10.1. The early vessels at Harbour Island were 'built of the best materials' as the 1805 advertisement for the sale of the smack, *Good Intent,* stated.[14]

The Harbour Island-built one-masted sloops, the *Venus* (Capt. Barnet), the *Spinwell* (Capt. Albury) and the *Eagle,* (Capt. Johnson) were 3 of the 8 vessels on hand to save the cargo of the American Schooner *Vixen* sailing from Philadelphia to Havana but was cast away on Fish Cay, Abaco, in October 1815. Advertised for sale the next day were 400 pieces of white Russian sheeting, flour, beef, butter, lard, spermacetti, tallow candles, soap, hats, potatoes, apples and the hull of the *Vixen* as she lay on Fish Cay.[15] But the Harbour Island shipwright's also built sturdy ocean-going two-masted schooners. After the failure of cotton, when the Loyalists began to leave the Bahamas, the Harbour Island-built *James,* owned by Henry and James Woods, in 1803, carried 70 slaves from Exuma to Wilmington[16] and later that same year 120 slaves to St. Augustine.[17]

With the resumption of trade to America in 1827 and the subsequent reduction of illegal trade, Harbour Island merchants redoubled their efforts to provide more ships. The one-masted sloops were supplemented by the two-masted schooners, *Bahamian, Emma, Superior, Lilly, Blossom* and *Nimble,* to carry fruit from Eleuthera to America, lumber from Abaco and wrecked goods from the vicinity of Hole-in-the-Wall, Abaco and the

Table 10.2 Harbour Island ships and their builders

Shipbuilder	Ships built:				
Thomas Cash	*Eleuthera*				
Thomas Evans Hall	*Mullet*				
Samuel Johnson	*Bahamian*	*Lilly*			
Christopher Fisher	*Emma*				
Joseph Hart	*Liberty*				
Joseph Higgs	*Superior*	*Blossom*	*Vesper*		
Benjamin Harris	*Builder's Son*	*Dunmore*	*Urania*		
Thomas & Jeremiah Higgs	*Union*				
Wiliam Cash	*Willing Mind*				
William Holbert	*Nimble*	*Constance*	*Humming Bird*		
Geroge Johnson	*Johnson's Plan*		*Eureka*		
John Albury	*Olive*	*Louisa Ann*			
James Palmer	*Martha Jane*	*North Star*			
William Cleare	*Rover*	*Eliza & Susan*	*Active*	*Rebecca*	
James Roberts	*Splendid*	*Union (2)*			
William Sweeting	*Isabella*				
Thomas Cox	*Leo*	*Corine*		*Trio*	*J S*
Joseph Curry	*Superior*			*William H Cleare*	*Defiance*
Samuel Roberts	*Dandy*				
James Miller Kelly	*Manchester*	*Brittania*	*George B Mather*		
Jeremiah Higgs	*Racer*				
Thomas Dorsett	*Wesleyan*				
Joseph Roberts	*Arethusa*				
William Johnson	*Champion*	*Ellen*			
Wm Jn Turton Roberts	*Tweed*				
James Henry Albury	*Ellen*				
John T Albury	*Sainte Marie*	*Equator*		*Margaret*	
William Dorrel	*Hornet*	*Melrose*	*Lady Shea*		
John Cleare	*Mary Jane*				
Ezekial Sweeting	*Olivia*				

The ring of the shipwright's hammer

Thomas Johnson	J H Johnson			
Thomas Wm Johnson	Good Will			
Ethelbert Johnson	Dimisherre			
Frederick Sawyer	Exchange			
John Sawyer	Rover (2)	Julia Elizabeth	Edwin Janet	Duit
James N Roberts	The Graceful			
Henry BoHengy Sawyer	Dorothy S	At Last	Lola	
James W Roberts aka }	Pioneer	Hattie Darling	Mabel Darling	Kate Sturrup
Sonny Jenks Roberts }	Orient	Blanche	Beatrice	Louise F
Charles P Johnson	Nautilus			
Eddy Jinx Roberts	Corinthia	Marie J Thompson	Isles of June	
Harry Albury	Eula J	Rosebud May	Dobell	Charm
T Berlin Albury	Ena K	Patricia K	Hickory III	Betty K
Earl & Gerald Johnson	Gary R	Noel Roberts	William Sayle	Captain Roberts
Victor Cleare	Saint Mary of Stafford	Arawak	Passing Jack	Samana
				Lady Dundas
				Liberty
				Dairy Maid

Table 10.3 Ships built at each port in the Bahamas from 1855–1864

Port	1855 No.	1855 Tons	1856 No.	1856 Tons	1857 No.	1857 Tons	1858 No.	1858 Tons	1859 No.	1859 Tons	1860 No.	1860 Tons	1861 No.	1861 Tons	1862 No.	1862 Tons	1863 No.	1863 Tons	1864 No.	1864 Tons	TOTAL No.	TOTAL Tons
Nassau	5	278	3	94	5	175	4	162	4	62	5	111	8	94	12	82	8	122	5	137	59	1217
Harbour I	5	177	4	218	6	308	4	259	3	80	0	0	3	173	0	0	0	0	1	12	26	1227
Abaco	14	382	13	379	10	428	6	251	6	167	8	110	14	188	17	185	13	99	7	44	108	2233
Andros	5	103	2	56	0	0	1	17	1	14	1	11	1	120	0	0	2	15	0	0	13	228
Berry I	2	99	0	0	1	21	0	0	0	0	0	0	0	0	0	0	0	0	1	23	4	143
Long Cay	2	53	0	0	0	0	0	0	2	83	0	0	0	0	0	0	2	17	0	0	6	153
Acklins	0	0	1	10	0	0	0	0	0	0	0	0	0	0	1	18	0	0	0	0	2	28
Eleuthera	0	0	0	0	1	48	1	21	2	105	0	0	0	0	1	9	0	0	0	0	5	183
San Salv.	0	0	0	0	0	0	1	17	0	0	0	0	0	0	0	0	0	0	0	0	1	17
Bimini	0	0	0	0	0	0	0	0	0	0	1	30	0	0	1	5	0	0	0	0	2	35
G Bahama	0	0	0	0	0	0	0	0	1	23	0	0	0	0	0	0	1	9	0	0	2	32
Inagua	0	0	0	0	0	0	0	0	0	0	0	0	0	0	1	5	1	14	2	17	4	36
Rum Cay	0	0	0	0	0	0	0	0	0	0	0	0	1	11	0	0	0	0	0	0	1	11
Long I	0	0	0	0	0	0	0	0	0	0	0	0	0	0	0	0	1	16	0	0	1	16
TOTAL	33	1092	23	757	23	980	17	727	19	534	15	262	26	467	34	315	28	292	16	133	234	5559

Bahama Bank to Nassau. Just before the designation of port of entry was granted in 1837, larger ocean-going, two-masted schooners – *Dunmore, North Star, Rebecca* and *Splendid* – were built. And as Table 10.1 shows, 16 more two-masted schooners but only 4 one-masted sloops were added to the Harbour Island fleet by 1843.

Almost all the boats in those early days were owned by families such as the Higgs, Johnson, Cleare and Roberts family and quite often there was a clear division of labour within the family. A few members were planters, a son or a slave was a sea captain and one member a skilled boat builder. But gradually, there emerged some shipwrights that were renowned for their skill and were in demand the emerging merchant elite, as business expanded. Table 10.2 shows that Samuel Johnson, Joseph Hart, Joseph Higgs and Benjamin Harris were called upon when a fine ship was needed. William Holbert, married to Jane Roberts of Harbour Island, built two schooners and two sloops before being granted, in 1837, Lot #1, the shipyard, at Spanish Wells.

Many Harbour Island shipbuilders migrated taking their boat building prowess to Abaco, New Providence and Key West, and as Table 10.3 shows, Abaco outstripped both Nassau and Harbour Island as a boat building centre. But during the decade 1855–64, the 26 sloops and schooners launched at Harbour Island averaged 47 tons, while those built elsewhere in the Bahamas less than half that size and later even larger ships were built at Harbour Island for the citrus, pineapple and lumber industries.[18] And, of course, many of these were purposely built for wrecking:

> Wrecking Schooners are built at Nassau, Abaco and Harbour Island. These vessels are 5–100 tons (costing £15 per ton) made from native woods that are durable and strong.[19]

It became quite commonplace for Harbour Island captains to sail their home-built ships to many ports of the US. The fruit trade to New York was a sea road well travelled by the *Corine*, the *Dandy*, the *Ventrosa*, the *Eliza & Catherine*, the *J. H. Johnson*, the *Equator* and the *William H. Cleare*, which also sailed to Savannah, the *Baltic* to Charleston and the *Rebecca* to Mobile. These trips were not without incident and some of these ships had interesting histories.

The two-masted, 68 foot long schooner, the *William H. Cleare*, built by Benjamin Harris, seemed to lead a precarious existence. During the era of blockade running, when officials of the American North were suspicious that Bahamian vessels were assisting the Southern cause, Capt. J. H. Bethel arrived in New York with a cargo of pineapples from Eleuthera and cleared the Custom House with a cargo of merchandise. As the *William H. Cleare* was leaving port a Revenue Cutter came alongside. The commander boarded the *William H. Cleare* and was not satisfied with the ship's papers and clearance. The Customs Officer cursed at Bethel in the presence of his young daughter Isabel. Another steamer came alongside damaging the *William H. Cleare* and the coastguards performed a more rigorous search, breaking open the cargo, searching trunks and opening packages and private personal letters addressed to inhabitants of Harbour Island, commenting on them and laughing.[20] Eventually, the ship was allowed to sail back home to Briland. A few weeks later as Capt. Petty of the schooner *Ellen* was lying becalmed one day's sail from New York, the US ship *Mercedita* altered her course deliberately and bore down on her and cut her amidships. The *Ellen* sank immediately.[21] It is not known whether Bethel's demand for an apology for the insult to a British citizen, redress for the delay and compensation of at least $500 was granted, but the owners of the *Ellen* accepted three-quarters of the compensation asked for, plus costs from the US Government.

In 1869, a group of exiled Cubans in New York took part in a conspiracy to mount a revolution in Cuba. The Nassau firm of Tunnel and Loinez, Colonial Agents, bought or hired several Harbour Island-built wrecking schooners to assist in the carrying of Cuban soldiers, arms, flags, and uniforms, which were transshipped from New York through Nassau or one of the nearby islands to Cuba. The Cubans were regularly housed at Waterloo at a house called 'The Barn' and embarked from the Montagu shore. The *Galvanic,* the *Sarah Ellen,* the *Tweed* and the *William H. Cleare* carried Cuban insurgents, while the *Tryphena,* the *Violin,* the *Exceed* and the *Dandy* assisted by acting as coal lighters to the *Cespedes,* renamed the *Lilian,* at Atholl Island or the Fleming Channel. After many protests by the Spanish Consul, the judgment against the owners of the *Lillian* and *William H. Cleare* was a fine of 60 pounds each.[22]

The granting of the warehouse port to Harbour Island, the peak pineapple exports and the success in wrecking kept the boat builders busy and the *Pioneer,* the *Edwin Janet* and the *Julia Elizabeth* were launched. But by 1876, the tide turned and the *Nassau Guardian* reported on the 'depressed state of trade at Nassau and Harbour Island, where the people were hoarding capital rather than investing it in an unremunerative credit business and hard times was the general complaint'. At Harbour Island:

> … the once busy bay which echoed with the sound of hammer and mallet in shipbuilding, is now quiet and the artisans sit on their haunches, and chat over the coming crops, drought, tonsillitis – which is prevalent, poison fish and future prospects.[23]

The depression in Harbour Island did not last long as the planters bought land to cultivate sugar and ships were needed again for the produce of three sugar mills and a pineapple-canning factory. Soon, the ship's carpenters were busy and the sound of their hammers echoed up and down the harbour again.

Training for the exacting work of shipbuilding was entirely by the apprenticeship system. As a rule, a boy of 14 or 15, just out of school, would be taken on as apprentice by his father or some other relative. And if he was sufficiently talented, in five to ten years he would become a competent shipwright entitled to full pay. Of course, some never advanced beyond the stage of second-rate competency and these were called jacklegs. Others, with little or no training or talent became carpenters' assistants, or were employed in the rough sawing of hardwood timber, caulking and pitching, and in the cutting of galvanized rod iron into bolts.

Two of Harbour Island's greatest shipbuilders emerged in the last quarter of the nineteenth century. Thomas W. Johnson, built the two-masted schooners, the 72 foot *Good Will*, the 76 foot *Edwin Janet*, the 73 foot *Julia Elizabeth* and the 36 foot sloop *Duit*. Surely though, the most prolific shipbuilder in Bahamian history must be James W. Roberts, known as Sonny Jenks Roberts, who was instrumental in building at least nine of Harbour Island's finest ships. His son William Edward 'Eddie Jinx' Roberts worked along with him and went on to become as respected a shipwright as his father. Early in the twentieth century, Eddie Jinx had competition from Harry and T. Berlin Albury, the sons of John T. Albury, and Earle and Gerald Johnson. Another respected boat builder was Henry 'BoHengy' Sawyer, who built the 40 foot yacht *Dorothy*, a 40 foot smack *At Last* and a 40 foot workboat *Lola*. Mention must also be made of Brilander Victor Cleare who built the *Saint Mary of Stafford* before moving to Hatchet Bay to build the power boats, *Arawak*, *Samana* and *Passing Jack* for Austin Levy. These men loved their trade and were highly skilled.

The October 1878 launching of the 64 foot schooner *Hattie Darling*, built by Sonny Jenks, started a new frenzy of boat building in Harbour Island. Her sister ship, the 77 foot *Mabel Darling*, followed in 1880, reflecting the fine workmanship of Sonny Jenks, who followed with another new vessel, the 100 foot *Mary Culmer*, launched 1884. The names of these vessels reflected the names of the daughters of Harbour Island Representative J. S. Darling and James W. Culmer, a business partner of R. H. Ranger.

No one has ever described the launching of a ship more beautifully than Longfellow:

> *Then the Master*
> *With a gesture of command*
> *Waved his hand;*
> *And at the word,*

Loud and sudden there was heard,
All around them and below,
The sound of hammers, blow on blow,
Knocking away the shores and spurs.
And see! She stirs!
She starts, she moves, she seems to feel
The thrill of life along her keel,
And, spurning with her foot the ground,
'With one exulting, joyous bound
She leaps into the ocean's arms![24]

At Harbour Island, it must be said that many of the larger schooners had difficulties when rolling down the stocks – a problem that eventually restricted the size of vessels built in Harbour Island. At this same time several small vessels were built for sponging and fishing, which gave steady employment to ships' carpenters, but by 1885, work was again scarce and many ships' carpenters migrated to Key West for steady employment and higher wages.[25]

Another surge in the shipbuilding industry saw several small vessels launched and five smacks fitted for fishing.[26] A new shipbuilder, Charles P. Johnson, was given his first contract in 1891 to build the 50 foot schooner *Nautilus* for G. R. George to be employed in the sponge industry. The schooner was well built with the best materials and with extensive cabin accommodation for the comfort of passengers.[27] The new trend seemed to cater to the well being of passengers as Sonny Jenks built another 79 foot schooner, the *Orient,* launched 1892, with four comfortable state rooms. The versatility of Sonny Jenks, assisted by Eddie Jinx, was demonstrated in his last boat, the *Louise F,* launched in 1910. She was built and specially fitted for passenger traffic between Nassau, Miami and Key West and could boast superior cabin accommodations, spacious, airy and private staterooms, and an excellent dining salon. After many voyages to Florida the *Louise F* ended up as a lumber carrier.

As the nineteenth century closed, the seafaring town of Harbour Island had a booming shipbuilding industry that provided both for local and foreign trade. The twentieth century opened well as Sonny Jenks built the schooner *Blanche,* launched in 1902 by Blanche, wife of Lorenzo Brice of Brice and Ranger, to carry pineapples from Governor's Harbour to New York. But the violent weather of the next two years caused Harbour Island some serious setbacks. In 1903, the schooner *Orient* encountered a hurricane on her voyage out of Baltimore and although the crew was rescued, the ship was dismasted and abandoned. The *Equator* was lost in February 1904; in May, 62 open plantation (working) boats sank at their moorings during a rainstorm[28] and tragedy again struck in October of the same year.

The three-masted schooner *Melrose*, built by John T. Albury and captained by Charles J. Kelly, sailed from Jacksonville with a cargo of lumber when the wind increased from 60 to 90 mph. Capt. Kelly and his crew of seven struggled hard to sail the ship in terrible conditions and two of the crew were washed overboard but managed to climb back. Then the sea threw the schooner off beam ends and the mastheads struck the water and she slowly fell over, the passengers climbing over the rails onto the side of the vessel, where they remained for three hours with the waves breaking over their heads. The foremast, three top masts and the jib boom broke away and the ship turned and faced the sea. The mizzenmasts went out of her and a passenger, Mrs. Weller, was crushed to death and her husband's arm broken. All hands and passengers moved forward and remained there from Saturday night until Monday morning. The Captain ordered the anchors to be let go for safety but five hours later they were all washed off and at the mercy of the waves. Five people reached the shore but the remaining passengers and four of the crew were drowned. The survivors buried themselves in the sand to keep warm and the next day the Captain and three crew members walked to Hobe Sound and a rescue party came and took them to Palm Beach. The lumber on board was insured but the ship wasn't.[29]

With the opening of the lumber camp, Wilson City, Abaco, businessmen connected with Harbour Island felt that they should build a 'lumber dragger', a class of ship built specifically for the lumber trade. In a number of conversations with Dr. Paul Albury, Capt. Victor Cleare recalled the building of this ship, the *Beatrice*, which was launched at Harbour Island in 1908.

The *Beatrice* had a number of owners as was customary with large vessels. Equal shares were owned by: Sonny Jenks Roberts, who was to build the ship; his son Eddie Jinx Roberts, the second building boss; another son, Capt. Lafayette Roberts, who was to sail it; Robert Ranger, L. G. Brice and William Ranger of Brice and Ranger, the Nassau agents; Bruce Cleare, the father of Victor Cleare; Mr. Monell of New York, who was to be the American agent. Insurance was either unwanted or unavailable and the risk of loss was so great that an individual thought it preferable to own shares in a number of vessels rather than stake everything in a single craft.

The Master or Boss carpenter had an awesome responsibility throughout. In consultation with the other owners the dimensions of the vessel were decided. She was to be a three-masted schooner of 360 tons capable of carrying 350,000 board feet of lumber. Overall length would be about 132 feet and the beam about 35 feet. The cost was estimated at $16,000. A scale half-model was then made by the Master to reflect these statistics. And from the scale model a full bill of materials was drawn up. It should be pointed out that many small vessels were built without the aid of a half model or anything else: in those cases an eye for design and experience was the only guide. On the other hand a few of the large vessels were built from drawings or blue-prints – a more sophisticated method than the use of half models.

All the material for the *Beatrice* with the exception of that obtained from local wrecks had to be imported. The yellow pine for keel and keelson, beams, planking, ceiling and decking was brought from an American port on a schooner too large to enter the harbour. It was necessary to throw it overboard and raft it down the harbour to the shipyard site. Messrs. Linsey and Woodside were the agents at Fresh Creek, Andros, who were responsible for providing the required hardwood. Guided by moulds, which were sent to them, they selected the Madeira and horseflesh trees to be felled. Some pieces were extremely heavy. Those to be used for the stem and main stern post were thirty feet long and had to square 12" × 12". Having a weight of seven pounds per board foot each of these two logs weighed four tons or more. Moving the timber to the coast where it could be loaded onto sloops was a Herculean task. This had to be done in the rainy season when wet ground and swollen creeks made dragging easier. It was a community project with men, women and children hauling on strips of wild fig tree bark, which were secured to the logs.

Back in the shipyard at Harbour Island one man was detailed to prepare the bolts, which would be used to rivet the pieces of timber together to form a frame. These were made by cutting galvanized iron rods into appropriate lengths and heading them at one end. Shipbuilders were required to be parsimonious and back in the nineteenth century it was not uncommon to fire a hard, dry hulk and save the bolts for new construction. All day long the saws whined as timber and planking was cut to size. It must be remembered that the saws used were hand saws as there was no electricity at Harbour Island then. Finishing was done with wood-block planes. These were clumsy tools, which, unlike the iron-block planes, which succeeded them, had to be disassembled for every adjustment of the cutting blade.

The walls of the hull of the *Beatrice*, as with those of other large vessels, comprised three strata. In the centre was the hardwood framing, eight inches thick; on the outside the planking, four inches thick; and on the inside, the ceiling, three inches thick. The strength of the vessel depended largely on binding these stratums inseparably together. To achieve this, treenails, or tunnels as they were commonly called, were employed. Holes were bored clean through plank, timber and ceiling and these tunnels (tight-fitting octagonal pegs of wood) were driven through. Finally, the tunnels were split at each end and wedged. Thousands of these inch-and-a-quarter-diameter holes had to be bored through eight inches of hardwood and seven inches of yellow pine. The tool used was a lip-ring auger and it took four twists of the handle to make one complete turn. For the sake of economy the Boss considered it best to have this done on a work-pay basis. The rate was a half-penny per hole and a good man could bore a hundred in a day. The men, all on day pay, worked from 6:00 a.m. to 5:00 p.m., six days a week; with an hour for breakfast and an hour for lunch. Every day they earned a princely sum: a Boss Carpenter – 6 shillings; a Competent Carpenter – 4 shillings; jacklegs – 3 shillings; others – 2 shillings 6 pence.

It took a year to build the hull of the *Beatrice* and she was launched on 17 April 1908. The launching, which began early in the morning, was itself an anxious business for the cradle jammed in the slipway. The *Vim* was up from Nassau, the first motor vessel to enter Harbour Island harbour. With her tugging away, with hundreds of townspeople hauling on blocks and tackle and with the aid of jackscrews and bumping beams, she was finally got into the water before dark. During the process, Mr. John T. Albury got his arm caught between a bumping beam and the cradle, and the elbow was mashed as flat as a shilling.

Alongside a rigged schooner in the harbour the spars were hoisted into place. This too was a gigantic undertaking for the spars were very heavy pieces of wood large in diameter and of great length. It was a revelation to hear that in all Captain Victor's life as a shipwright and sea captain, he had never known of a vessel's spar to be made from squared new lumber. They all came from wrecks. The *Marie J. Thompson*, a four-master, was built by Eddie Jinx Roberts, the son of Sonny Jenks. Her spars and booms were about the same size as those of the *Beatrice* and they were supplied by the same wrecking agents as were those of the *Beatrice*. Not only spars and booms, but much other material came from wrecks.

Fully rigged at last and seaworthy, the *Beatrice* was brought to Nassau for registration. This being completed she sailed for Wilson City, Abaco, under Capt. Lafayette Roberts to begin her life's work as a lumber dragger. She was joined in 1913 by the 90 foot, three-masted schooner *Corinthia*, built by Eddie Jinx Roberts and owned by Thaddeus George Johnson, Earl Johnson, Bruce Cleare, and A. Bates Curry. Despite a depression at the start of the First World War, the lumber schooners were very profitable. But the attraction of the growing City of Miami drew mariners and carpenters away, and by 1920, Harbour Island was said to be depopulated of energetic and ambitious people.[30]

Like the great escapologist Harry Houdini, shipbuilding in Harbour Island made another remarkable recovery. Thursday 18 August 1921 was a Gala Day in Harbour Island as a large assemblage of people witnessed the launching of the largest ship ever to slide down a Bahamian runway. Three excursion boats from Nassau, small motor craft with trailers from Spanish Wells and many other boats from adjacent settlements and Nassau, brought visitors to see Lady Cordeaux, the Governor's wife, name the *Marie J. Thompson,* after the daughter of the owner Norberg Thompson of Key West. In a clear voice, she praised the skill of the builder Eddie Jinx Roberts, who over the previous three years had laboured on at 8 shillings a day, through stoppages due to lack of finance and labour strikes for higher wages. At 210 foot long, with 4 masts, 700 ton burthen and capable of carrying 650,000 feet of lumber, she presented great difficulty in launching. After several attempts over 3 days, at last she was pulled down by the *Priscilla* and hundreds of straining men. The accommodation on the *Marie J. Thompson* included a stateroom, 2 berths and a chart room in the Captain's quarters; 2 staterooms, a dining hall and a social hall for passengers; 3 staterooms for the first and second mates and the cook; and a pantry. This was the last commercial sailing ship built in Harbour Island.

The final years of Harbour Island sailing ships reads somewhat like a Shakespearean tragedy. The two-masted *Mary Beatrice,* built in Harbour Island in 1882, started life as a fishing smack but during the bootlegging era turned to the more lucrative trade of smuggling Chinese labourers at $500 each, from Cuba into New York. American and British authorities took 8 months to unravel the mystery of the blood-stained ship, the *Mary Beatrice,* which floated into the New York Harbour from Rum Row with 15 Chinese aboard. The Chinese claimed that unknown assailants had attacked and killed five Chinese and two young crew members, William and Lambert Albury. After months of investigation, detectives thought that the unknown captain of the vessel had asked the Chinese for another $250 each and deserted the ship when they refused to pay it; the Chinese were then thought to have slain the two young Harbour Island men out of revenge. The mystery was never solved.

The Harbour Island-built two-masted schooner *Admiral,* owned by Thomas Sweeting, made hundreds of profitable trips, fishing and hauling cargo between Nassau and South Florida for 40 years. Anchored in Miami Harbour, awaiting rehabilitation, for many months, she carried with her the marks of countless battles with the churning seas. A number of tugs tried to move her but she could not be moved. Early in a June morning of 1925, the aged vessel sank in the mud of Miami Harbour. At sunset she was a dirty, rugged and stalwart ship; by dawn she was junk.[31]

The *Beatrice* made her last voyage in 1926, and on the return trip from Cuba, she was wrecked on a dark and stormy night near Green Cay. On hearing the news, old Mr. Ranger of Brice & Ranger shed tears. But he might have cried for more than that – not only was the *Beatrice* gone – but an entire era of foreign-going Bahamian sailing vessels was on its deathbed too.[32]

The *Marie J. Thompson* lasted five years sailing, under Capt. Borden, between Key West, British Honduras and England with a cargo of mahogany.

Her captain found that she sailed sluggishly on her last trip from England and finding her bottom was covered in moss, took her to Jamaica, which was the only dry dock able to cater to her length. Halfway up the slip, the chocks gave way and when equipment was brought to float her, the bottom broke and she ended upside down. The Bahamian registration of the *Marie J. Thompson* closed on 23 September 1927. When news of her demise reached Harbour Island many people cried like babies – all that wealth and money gone.[33]

Although the days of the large commercial sailing ships had ended, Harbour Island shipbuilders still produced fine workboats, smacks and wind-propelled dinghies. Carpenters had steady employment over the next few years repairing numerous other vessels. The few fine craftsmen left proved to be the most versatile in the island's shipbuilding history.

In October 1921, the sailing ship *Endion* was bought in New York, refitted and converted to a power vessel, in Harbour Island, to accommodate passengers. The following year Henry 'BoHengy' Sawyer built the first 5-horsepower motor boat in Harbour Island. For the Agricultural Exhibition and Regatta of 1923, T. Berlin and Harry Albury built a very much admired row boat and showed a collection of builder's models of vessels built in Harbour Island, which included the model of the *Marie J. Thompson*.[34] In that same year the Albury brothers, under contract to the Board of Pilotage, built a barge to assist the Dredger *Lucayan*, in the deepening of Nassau Harbour. Winston Churchill, the war-time Prime Minister of England, remembered the *Lucayan*, which inspired him to use the same design on the *Mulberry*, the class of landing craft that helped the Allies storm the beaches of Normandy on D-Day.[35]

Not to be outdone, Eddie Jinx built a large glass-bottom boat for the Bahamas Hotel Company and a 60 foot power boat, the *Ara*, with a Fairbank-Morse engine, to be used for towing by Nassau Pilot, Willard Brown. The *Ara* was a double-ender, the stern shaped the same as the stem, which was made of one piece of horseflesh from across the harbour on the Sound, Eleuthera. The man who found the horseflesh was rewarded with the princely sum of 4 shillings. The tug boat *Ara* was used by Capt. Willard and his son, Capt. Freddie Brown for many years. Harry Albury countered with the 50 foot MV, *Eula J*, with seating accommodation for 20 passengers, suitable for short cruises in the winter season.[36]

The year 1924 was a very busy one as tourism took off after the building of the British Colonial Hotel. T. Berlin Albury built a motor boat with a Palmer engine for Mr. Smith of Andros to be used for the Nassau Winter Season. At the same time his brother Harry built a sloop for a planter at Spanish Wells to supply vegetables to the growing tourist trade in Nassau. The Winter Season in Nassau provided excitement in the form of yacht races and two 26 foot yachts were built in Harbour Island by Eddie Jinx; one built for Mr. Crawford and the other for liquor merchant, Bruce Kilroy Thompson.

In 1925, Eddie Jinx built the 100 foot schooner *Isles of June,* with a motor auxiliary, to be used for carrying lumber from Jacksonville to Nassau for the Kelly Lumber Yard. Berlin Albury followed up the next year with the 110 foot *Ena K* schooner rigged with a 120 horsepower Fairbanks-Morse engine, which was installed at Symonette's Shipyard, Nassau. The *Ena K* was to be used for carrying hardware and passengers on the Nassau to Miami run. T. Berlin Albury continued over the next several years to build fishing smacks and small motor boats for Spanish Wells. But just as boat building looked as if it was dying out again, Allan H. Kelly commissioned a large barge for use as a liquor warehouse at Gun Cay. Allan H. Kelly added to his fleet in 1930 with the launching by his daughter Patricia of the 87 foot *Patricia K,* built by T. Berlin Albury.

The early 1930s saw a slow shipbuilding period with but eight motor boats built at Harbour Island for the tourist season in Nassau and one fishing smack. In 1932, a yacht was built called the *Saint Mary of Stafford* by Victor Cleare for the Anglican Bishop of Nassau; and another vessel was built for the conveyance of liquor.

The visit of a famous yachtsman to the prestigious boatbuilding island of Harbour Island describes the state of boat building in 1936:

> The industry seemed to me at Harbour Island to consist of a few boatbuilders with hand tools working under primitive conditions.

He found no boatyards or modern tools; men just only men building under the trees on the beach and all timber had to be imported from the United States at 20 per cent duty.[37]

Even under these conditions, the Albury brothers received a contract, in 1937, for an auxiliary schooner for the Adirondack Florida School at Cocoanut Grove. Mrs. Dorothy Albury launched the 65 foot *Hickory III*, a schooner rigged with fore and main topmasts; the mainsail, foresail and 2 jibs gave a sail area of over 2,000 square feet. The ship, which had an auxiliary engine, was designed by Mr. Lawrence Huntington, a top United States sailing ship designer, who at that time resided in Harbour Island.[38]

The largest vessel ever to have been built in Abaco was the *Abaco Bahamas*. In the hurricane of 1932, she broke away from her deep-sea moorings at Parrots Cay and drifted to Murphy Town, 5 miles away and sank. Abaco's loss was Harbour Island's gain as T. Berlin Albury, a shrewd man for a bargain, bought the *Abaco Bahamas,* took her to Harbour Island, dismantled her, using serviceable material to renovate the *Isles of June* and build the new freight boat *Betty K,* for Kelly's Lumber Yard.[39] The 1938 launching of the *Betty K,* named for the daughter of C. J. Trevor Kelly, was a grand affair, with many locals from Harbour Island and her neighbouring settlements and many distinguished visitors from Nassau, some of whom had flown down in the newly-formed Bahamas Airways plane.[40] Another launch in that year was an impressive 12 foot sailboat designed and built by 13-year-old Carlisle, son of Harry Albury.

Just a few months before the sombre days of the Second World War, flags flew and the Harbour Island town band played as Lady Dundas, the Governor's wife, broke a bottle of champagne over the bow of the *Lady Dundas.* This was the first of the inter-insular mail-boats that gained Harbour Island new fame. Designed by Lawrence Huntington, the 92 foot *Lady Dundas,* with a two spar rig, was fitted with a Fairbanks-Morse 150 horsepower engine, able to drive her at a speed of 10 knots and carry up to 80 tons of freight.[41] Her Captain, William G. Harris a veteran sailor, had captained both previous Harbour Island mailboats, the *Dart* and the *Endion.*

It was announced in December 1941 that Harbour Island shipbuilders were to be given a contract by the Royal Navy to build 12 small ships.[42] Later the British War Secrecy Act prevented the news media from making announcements giving details that may have been of use to the enemy and so details of these vessels were never published. In 1942, William Higgs built the *Princess Elizabeth,* which was christened by Mrs. G. V. E. Higgs. The *Nassau Tribune* of August 1942 congratulated the Harbour Island ship owners, who had struggled on before the war in competition with subsidized steamship lines but were now operating alone and had become the lifeline of the colony.[43]

George William Kelly Roberts sailed before the mast on the three masted schooner *Bentley* under his father before moving to Nassau at the age of 12. As a self-made man he grew to own the City Lumber Yard and become Leader for the Government in the House of Assembly, was appointed President of the Legislative Council and received a CBE and a knighthood. Sir George was immortalized in Harbour Island by naming the new library, The Sir George Roberts Library and the erection of his statue in the grounds. His other business was the Richard Campbell Ltd. and vessels owned by this company were government subsidized for the Out Island mail service. He named all his ships after his children; the first two, the *Richard Campbell* and *Alice Mabel* were not built in Harbour Island but he forged a connection with his hometown friends Earl and Gerald Johnson. The result was the 70 foot vessel *Gary Roberts,* fitted with a Cooper-Bessemen diesel engine, for the Andros mail service. The Johnson brothers followed this up in 1943 with an addition to the Bahamian Merchant Fleet, the 120 foot *Noel Roberts.* Earl and Gerald built the MV *William Sayle* for Roland T. Symonette, which was launched in 1944. The following year G. W. K. Roberts brought his fleet up to eight vessels with the launching of the MV *Captain Roberts,* named after his father. This was the third boat built for him in four years by Earl and Gerald Johnson. It was 111 feet long, specially designed for shallow waters and equipped with a Fairbanks Morse Diesel Engine.[44] Unfortunately, in October 1945, freakish winds destroyed a number of small boats on Harbour Island and the *Captain Roberts* was wrecked on its maiden voyage.[45]

Shipbuilding in Harbour Island like the *Equator* and her cat is now long gone but remembered with nostalgia. The ring of the shipwright's hammer still echoed in Harbour Island after 1945 as Earl and Gerald Johnson turned their shipbuilding skills to the construction of beautiful homes for Winter residents.

Notes

1. *Nassau Guardian*, 5 September 1857.
2. Major General J. H. LeFroy, *Memorials of the discovery and early settlement of the Bermudas or Somers Islands,* Published by the University of Toronto Press for The Bermuda Historical Society and Bermuda National Trust, 1981, Vol 1, p. 21.
3. William Reyner to John Winthrop, Winthrop Papers, Vol. V, 1645-1649, Mass. Hist. Society 1947, p. 73.
4. 749/CR G-H/16, Shipping Register, Bermuda Records on microfilm at Bahamas Dept. of Archives.
5. From 'The Building of a Ship' by Henry Wadsworth Longfellow.
6. CO 23/23/28 Montford Browne to Earl of Dartford, 6 May 1775.
7. Craton and Saunders, *Islandersin the Stream,* The University of Georgia Press, Athens, Georgia, 1992, Vol 1, p. 174.
8. Xerox of typed copy of 'Letter of Marque' provided by Shirley (Oakes) Butler.
9. Ibid.
10. CO 23/18/7, Governor Shirley's Report, 1768.
11. CO 23/25/351, Governor Powell's Report, 1785.
12. CO 23/35/149 Governor Forbes' Report, 20 February 1797.
13. Customs Shipping Register 1826, Bahamas' Department of Archives.
14. *Royal Gazette*, 19 November 1805.
15. *Royal Gazette*, 18 October 1815.
16. CO 23/43/147, Report of Governor John Halkett, March 1803.
17. CO 23/44/38, Governor John Halkett to My Lord, Secretary of State, August 1803.
18. Governor Rawson's Report for the year 1864, Appendix 26.
19. Report of Wrecking in the Bahamas, chapter 16 by H. D. Grant, Goldsmiths, Pamphlets 1868, Senate Library, London.
20. CO 23/169/121, Letter from J. H. Bethel 9 July 1862.
21. CO 23/169/200, Bayley to Newcastle 30 August 1862.
22. CO 23/201/277, Judgement of *Cespedes (Lilian),* 19 February 1870.
23. *Nassau Guardian*, 1 April 1876.
24. From 'The Building of a Ship' By Henry Wadsworth Longfellow.
25. Resident Justice J. S. Solomon's Report in Votes of the House of Assembly, 1885.
26. Resident Justice J. S. Solomon's Report in Votes of the House of Assembly, 1890.
27. *Nassau Guardian*, 23 October 1891.

28 *Nassau Guardian*, 18 May 1904.
29 *Nassau Guardian*, 2 November 1904.
30 Resident Justice, Dewees Johnson's Report, Votes of House of Assembly 1920.
31 *Nassau Guardian*, 6 October 1925.
32 Paul Albury, *History of a Ship,* Talk to Rotary Club of East Nassau, 9 October 1970.
33 Interview, Jim Lawlor with John L. Saunders, August 1990.
34 Commissioner Dewees Johnson's Report, Votes of House of Assembly, 1923.
35 *The Illustrated London News,* 14 April 1945.
36 *Nassau Guardian*, 1 December 1923.
37 *Nassau Guardian*, 8 November 1936.
38 *Nassau Guardian*, 10 November 1937.
39 Steve Dodge, *Abaco: The History of and out island and its cays,* Decatur, Ill. White Sound, 1983, p. 10.
40 *Nassau Guardian*, 12 July 1938.
41 *Nassau Guardian*, 4 April 1939.
42 *Nassau Daily Tribune*, 3 December 1941.
43 *Nassau Daily Tribune*, 17 August 1942.
44 *Nassau Tribune*, 9 June 1945.
45 *Nassau Guardian* 13 October 1945.

11

'Wrack ashore!'

From the earliest time, the men of Harbour Island had kept an eye on the reef-strewn sea around them. Every family had a boat of some kind, and skill with wind and sail was a point of honour. Knowledge of the intricate channels and passes, the depths, shoals and pinnacles of the danger-fraught sea was a common heritage, passed from father to son; and many womenfolk could handle a boat alongside their men.[1]

The blowing of the conch shell and the excited cries of 'Wrack ashore!' alerted the residents of Dunmore Town to the plight of yet another vessel that had struck the 100-mile-long barrier reef along the windward coast of Eleuthera, or bilged in the raging seas driven by a stiff north-east wind or stranded on a hidden shoal or uncharted bank. A great sense of anticipation pumped adrenaline through the veins of the swarthy mariners, as they hastily prepared to go to the rescue of the floundering vessel. Donning their foul-weather gear and carrying axes and bundles of spare clothing, members of the Harbour Island wrecking fraternity converged from all parts of the township to the beautiful bay on the foreshore, where their home-built fleet of wrecking sloops and schooners lay. There they busied themselves in setting up the rigging and as soon as the full complement of crewmembers was assembled, they expeditiously hoisted their sails and hove up their anchors. The race was to the swiftest, for the first man to 'speak' the wreck became the wreckmaster and was in command of the rescue venture. This sight of 6 to 8 wrecking vessels with 14 to 15 men in each, all pressing canvas to speak the wreck first, was not uncommon in the heyday of the Bahamian wrecking industry.[2]

The islands, cays and rocks of the Bahamas arise from two irregular platforms, $2\frac{1}{2}$ miles above the Atlantic Ocean floor, known as the Little Bahama Bank and the Great Bahama Bank. In and around the islands, the hidden reefs and shoals, the changing sandbanks and the unpredictable winds and currents, especially in the hurricane months, all conspired to make Bahamian waters the terror of navigators and the delight of wreckers. Before settlement, many Spanish galleons succumbed to the treacherous intricacies of Bahamian waters on their return voyage to Europe as observed by George Gardiner: '… amongst the Islands are wrecks of divers of their Ships'.[3]

Just as the entire Bahamas archipelago is strategically located at the gateway to the Gulf of Mexico, the Caribbean Sea and the entire Central American region, so is Harbour Island ideally positioned on the north-east edge of the Great Bahama Bank, at the gateway to the Northeast Providence Channel – the single body of water through which all merchant sailing vessels had to pass to go to New Providence or to access the Florida Gulf for destinations farther south. In the days of sail, the north-east winds and uncertain currents drove many a vessel onto the reefs of Abaco and Eleuthera as they attempted to enter the Northeast Providence Channel; others, once successfully in the channel, were sometimes driven too far south onto Egg Island or the North Eleuthera coast, well known for its extremely dangerous stretch of reef. The lofty hills to the north of the island offer a commanding view of much of this area, so that once a floundering vessel was spotted, the wreckers of Harbour Island were fast to the rescue. Table 11.1 lists reported wrecks in the vicinity of Harbour Island between the years 1804 to 1970.

It is perhaps ironic that the location of the first Puritan settlement, on the north coast of Eleuthera was decided by the fateful shipwreck of Capt. William Sayle on the Devil's Backbone. Even after returning to Bermuda, the entrepreneurial first governor of Eleuthera retained a house and a shallop at Governor's Bay, which the Bermudians used as a base on their woodcutting and wrecking expeditions. The first documented story of a wrecking adventure in the Bahamas is passed on to us by a young Bermudian wrecker, Richard Richardson, who, fired by the tales of the treasure-laden Spanish galleons through the Bahamas, came to Sayle's house at Governor's Bay. There he met the servants of Bermudian Capt. William Jeames who were staying at Sayle's house and had contracted the use of his shallop for wrecking purposes.

On a bright August day in 1657, Richardson and his company manned their shallop and sailed with Jeames' company to a wreck north of Jeames' man Island. There they met with great success and on the first journey recovered £2600 sterling which was placed in £100 bags, and shared at Governor's Bay, according to the agreement of 'share and share alike'; one £100 bag went to Capt. Sayle's shallop and £130 to each wrecker. After a second journey to the same wreck, they returned to 'Spanish well' to make the share, and each wrecker received about £80 sterling plus a share of silver that weighed about 1400 pieces of eight.[4]

The £68,000 troy of silver treasure, raised from the Spanish Galleon *Conception* at Silver Bank, north of the Old Bahama Channel, by Capt. William Phips in 1687, stirred the imagination of every sailor in the region

156   The Harbour Island Story

Table 11.1 List of wrecks in the Harbour Island/Eleuthera area

Year	Name	Captain	Nationality	Sailing From	To	Wrecked at	Cargo/Comments
1804	Elizabeth			Philadelphia	Campeachy	Elson's Reef Hbr I.	Indian meal, brandy, wine, dry goods
1819	Hazard	Crocker			staves	Egg Island Reef	beef, house frames etc
1820	Adeline of Quebec without a soul on board						
1821	Amelia		American	Eleuthera		Egg Island Reef	
1822	Mary	Clarke	American	Boston	Baracoa	Eleuthera	lumber, flour, provisions
1824	Invicible	Biscoe	American	Philadelphia	Nassau	Elison's Reef, Hbr I	flour, corn etc
1824	Aeolus	Dickenson	French	France	Mobile	Pear Rock, Eleuthera	potatos
1824	Live Oak	Brill	American	Gibralta	Havana	nr Harbour Island	wine, raisons, paper, quicksilver
1825	Triad	Flockhart	British	London	Nassau	Egg Island Reef	stores & provisions for troops
1825	hull of a large size schooner					S E of mouth of Hbr I	lumber, flour, provisions
1827	Repid	Rice	American	Portland	Mobile	Egg Island Reef	hay, lime
1831	Margaret	Gisselman	German	Breman	Havana	Harbour Island	
1833	Olive	Slowman	American	New York	Mobile	nr Harbour Island	nails, pots, ovens, soap, candles, champagne
1833	Orbit		American			Egg Island Reef	potatoes, china, books etc
1833	Lorton	Duncan	British	Liverpool	St Domingo	Egg Island Reef	chains, anchors, cables, sails etc
1833	Rose	David	French	Bordeaux	Havana	north side of Eleuthera	
1833	Three Sisters	Gander	American			nr Spanish Wells	53 slaves saved
1837	Slave schooner	A J Bretto	Portugese			Harbour Island	chairs, lumber, shoes, boots, candles etc
1837	Rhine		American	derelict		north side of Eleuthera	
1841	Rinaldo	Parsons	American			Eleuthera	
1842	Stephen Phillips	Farnham	American	Boston	Havana	Egg Island Reef	in a gale
1842	Farmer	Tittle	American	Wilmington	Aux Cages	Reef 5 mile north Hbr I	Lumber
1843	John Hale	American	Havana	St Jago		north side Eleuthera	
1843	Birmingham	Robinson	American	New York	Mobile	Ellison's Reef nr Hbr I	
1844	Francis Stanton	LeFavour	American	Boston	Mobile	Russell Island	
1846	Commerce	Burnham	American	St John	Nassau	nr Harbour Island	Lumber
1846	Boston	Pearson	American		Gulf of Mexico	north side Eleuthera	20 guns sloop of war
1851	Providence	Henry Carr	American	Boston	New Orleans	reef NW of Hbr I	50 bales of hay and 36 barrels of onions
1858	Rolling Wave	Vigues	American	Port au Prince	Philadelphia	off Harbour Island	logwood, mahogoney

Year	Ship	Captain	Nationality	From	To	Location	Cargo
1865	a barge		American	Boston	New Orleans	Devil's Backbone	Train
1865	Conquest	Lewis	British	St Domingo	New York	Man Island nr Hbr I	fish, potatoes, nails, gunny sacks
1865	Orion	Falder	New York	Galveston		North Eleuthera	cotton
1866	Baltic	American	British	Boston	Port au Prince	nr Ridley's Head Eleuthera	housewares
1866	Mogul	Gagnee	British	Boston		Pearce Isl nr Hbr Isl	logwood, coffee
1866	Evelyn	Partridge	American	New York	Key West	nr Harbour Island	salt, potatoes, hams, saw-mill
1869	Lady of the Lake		British			coast of Eleuthera	
1871	Richmond		British			Piere Reef nr Spanish Wells	
1873	Secret					Reef nr Royal Island	
1882	Blenheim	Morrell	British	Nassau	Jamaica	off James Point, Eleuthera	
1895	Cienfuegos	B F Hoyt Jr	American	New York	Cuba	Reef 5 mile north Hbr I	Ward Line Passengers
1899	Adele Ball		New York	Matanzas	Spanish Wells	Coal, lumber, bricks	
1904	James A Wright	Bowson	American	Philadelphia	Havana	nr Ridley's Head Eleuthera	Petroleum
1904	Arthur McArdle	Shepherd	American	Philadelphia	Havana	Egg Island Reef	Crude Oil
1914	Advance		British	Jamaica	Cuba	El Autre Cay north Eleuthera	In ballast
1916	Carnarvon		Welsh			north side Eleuthera	
1916	Margaret M Ford		American	Santa Domingo	New York	Purn Rock north Sp Wells	Lumber
1928	Yungay		American	New York	Port au Prince	Eleuthera	Petroleum products
1954	US Navy Tank Landing Ship		American	Eleuthera			
1970	Arimoroa		Lebanese	South America	Europe	Egg Island Reef	Guano based fertilizer

'to fish for silver'. In 1715, Lord Hamilton, Governor of Jamaica, gave commissions to the captains of 10 ships, including Captains Benjamin Hornigold and Henry Jennings to suppress the pirates, but they used the commissions to 'fish for wracks'.[5] Jennings and a consortium of 2 ships and 3 sloops sailed to the Gulf of Florida, where two years before several Spanish galleons of the Plate Fleet had been cast away. Spanish divers had 'fished up' some millions of pieces of eight and carried them to Havana. But when Jennings arrived at the wreck with 300 men, 350,000 pieces of eight in silver had been taken on shore and were guarded by 60 men. Jennings' men overpowered the guard, took the treasure and made his way to Nassau to enjoy the spoils.[6] When Governor Fitzwilliam arrived in 1733, he remarked on the wrecking exploits of the inhabitants who knew where every Spanish wreck lay except for one on which there were 3 million pieces of eight.[7]

In order to secure wood for their emerging boat building industry, the Harbour Islanders throughout the 1700s resorted to Little Abaco and the offshore cays, rich in cedar, mastic, madeira and pine. The woodcutting expeditions lasted weeks at a time, and while the primary task was the collection of good timber for their fine home-built vessels, these crafty mariners always kept an eye out on the reef-strewn shore for some fortuitous wreck. Many miles of the north-western windward shore of the Abacos were still uncharted as shown on the 1794 Admiralty Chart, which states:

> *This side, which has not been as explored as the others, is said by the wreckers to be the most dangerous on account of the currents.*[8]

Therefore many unsuspecting vessels found themselves in trouble among the reefs and shoals of the Little Bahama Bank, which had become, not surprisingly, a favourite rendezvous of the wreckers.

When the Loyalists arrived in Abaco, Philip Dumaresq, the appointed magistrate of the new settlement, complained bitterly of the difficult life in Abaco, the social isolation and the insults of the 'Abaco blackguards'.[9] Since Abaco was thought to be uninhabited prior to the arrival of the Loyalists, historians have interpreted the 'blackguards' to be the woodcutters and wreckers from Harbour Island, Eleuthera and perhaps Nassau, who resided on the island for short periods of time.[10] Both old inhabitants, even though temporary, and the newcomers probably felt a sense of mutual resentment, similar to the divide between old and new inhabitants that played out in Nassau.

The business of wrecking during the eighteenth century was more guided by the governor's discretion than by legislation. Customary practice was that the wreckers brought their stranded or wrecked goods into Nassau, where they were consigned to an agent, who auctioned them off. After the governor was paid 10 per cent of the proceeds, the balance was given to the wreckmaster, who then shared it among the wrecking crews. The wreckers enjoyed great support from Governor Dunmore who supplied them with wrecking papers and did not require them to store the wrecked goods for 12 months or pay import or export duties as required by law, despite the protests of the Attorney General, Moses Franks. Arbitration of the salvage was only required if the master or crew stayed with the wreck.[11] During Dunmore's tenure, the number of wreckers in the colony increased to 1,400.[12]

The shipping news from the *Bahama Gazette* and the *Royal Gazette* confirm that many of the Harbour island wreckers did indeed follow customary practice in bringing salvaged goods to Nassau for auction. When the *Nymph* of Baltimore went ashore off Abaco, several vessels went to her assistance, and the wrecking sloop *Hazard* of Harbour Island brought her stranded goods to Nassau. In the same entry, the *Thurston* of Charleston, sailing to Havana, was cast away on Walker's Cay, Abaco, and a Harbour Island wrecker brought her crew and a small part of her cargo to Nassau.[13]

Consortship was a negotiated contract among wreckers by which the crew of two or more vessels shared the profits of the salvage. There were two types of consortship: a temporary contract, which the wreckmaster determined at the site of each wreck as he chose which of the attending vessels would actively participate; a permanent contract made by two or more vessels to share the salvage even if one of the vessels was not present at the wreck.[14] A typical example of a consortship involving Harbour Island wreckers is shown in the wreck of the American schooner *Vixen*, cast away on Fish Cay, Abaco:

> Schooner *Vixen*, Captain Samuel Evans, 8 days from Philadelphia to Havanna, cast away on Fish Cay, Abaco, 80 miles north west of Hole-in-the-Wall. Cargo saved by several vessels, which happened to be in that place at that time.
> Schooner   *Venus*, Barnett (built 1814 in Harbour Island)
> Schooner   *Humming Bird*, Pinder
> Sloops: *Mayflower*, Russell
>   *Spinwell*, Albury (built 1812 in Harbour Island)
>   *Eagle*, Johnson (built 1796 in Harbour Island)
>   *Isabella*, Hudson
>   *Eliza*, Petty
>   *Nimble Rake*, Albury
>
> To be sold all the cargo of wrecked schooner: 400 pieces white Russian sheeting, flour, beef, butter, lard, spermacetti, tallow candles, soap, hats, potatoes, apples and hull as she lies on Fish Cay.[15]

Although these wrecking vessels formed a consortship for the wreck of the *Vixen*, they may very well have had private or permanent consortships with vessels that were not at the wreck. The larger the stranded vessel, the more wrecking vessels were required in the salvage, and so tight was the Bahamian fraternity of wreckers, that wreckmasters generally accepted all attending wreckers at the risk of overcrowding the vessel in despair.

The growth of commerce in the 1800s was a great boost to the wrecking industry. American industrial expansion began in the early 1820s, before the time of inter-connecting roads and railways. Farm produce, lumber and livestock from inland states were loaded on flatboats and carried down the rivers and streams to the Mississippi and then south to New Orleans. At that port everything was transferred to coastal sailing vessels, which carried cargoes across the Gulf of Mexico, around Florida and up the coast to the eastern seaboard cities – or even to Europe. On the return voyage large ships sailed east of Abaco, through the Hole-in-the-Wall channel, continued on to Sturrup's Cay then entered the Gulf by the Northwest Providence Channel around Great Isaac's Rock. Smaller ships to Sturrup's Cay could pass over the Great Bahama Bank until they got south of Cat Cays and sometimes Orange Cay, when they entered the Gulf.[16] Some brave or foolhardy American captains, in the interest of time, took the more dangerous route around the north of Walker's Cay, North Abaco and into the Gulf, sometimes stopping for a pilot at Green Turtle Cay. This new growth in commerce across Bahamian waters led to an increase in wrecks at the notably dangerous spots: the windward coasts of North Eleuthera, Harbour Island and Abaco, Great Sturrups Cay, the Gingerbread Grounds, the Bimini Cays and the west end of Grand Bahama. A new rendezvous for the Harbour Island wreckers was established at North Bimini harbour, which commanded an excellent view of the route south through the Gulf of Florida, along the western edge of the Great Bahama Bank. An intelligence network of fishermen, turtlers and lighthouse keepers in the vicinity of the wrecking hot spots reported news of wrecks to the vessels in the harbour.

This increased navigation through the Gulf of Florida also resulted in an increase of wrecks at the Florida Keys and although Bahamians had wrecked, turtled and fished at the cays since 1763, new legislation by the US Government in 1824 made it illegal for these activities to continue; any wrecking ship engaged in the jurisdiction of the US on the Florida Coast was to be seized and forfeited and any wrecked goods salvaged on the Keys belonged to the US.[17]

As the wrecking activity increased in Bahamian waters, the lax control of the wrecking industry in Dunmore's time was replaced by more stringent measures with regard to the claiming, adjudicating and sharing of salvage. Governor Gregory's 1850 report outlined the changes:

> Formerly these 'wreckers' were uncontrolled in their proceedings, and the consequences most discreditable to the general character of the Bahamian population. Latterly the local Legislature has brought them under subjection to order. Each wrecker is now licensed by the Governor, for which the owner pays from 8s. to 40s. a-year, in proportion to his tonnage, and a code of stringent regulations compels these hardy and adventurous mariners, whose power of diving is most extraordinary, to deliver every article they pick up to the proper authorities, and prevent those frightful scenes of pillage and disorder, which tended to demoralize the whole community.[18]

Appendix 12 shows a facsimile of a wrecking licence, the fee structure for wreckers and vessels, the consort share system and estimated licences for several Harbour Island wrecking vessels.

No longer could salvage be fixed by agreement between the wreckers and the master of the stranded vessel or by friendly arbitration. Wreckers were required to declare the salvaged goods at Nassau, which were consigned to an agent, who received a commission from the sale of the goods. Arbitrators were then appointed to represent the relevant parties and determine the salvage awards based on the success of the salvage, the risk to the wrecker, the distance travelled and the value of the cargo. The commission agent then auctioned off the salvaged goods and after deducting the 15 per cent customs duty and his commission, he shared the proceeds based on the decision of the arbitrators. In the case of derelict vessels, the Vice-Admiralty Court adjudicated the salvage. Governor Gregory paints a vivid picture of the sale of salvaged goods:

> A public building called the 'Vendue House' has been erected on the wharf of Nassau, and there are the retail traders to be seen in great numbers almost every day, bidding for cases and packages whose contents are often only guessed at, and which have been thrown upon the Bahamian shores, or picked up by the numerous 'wreckers' that are always ready to start from the various ports of the colony the moment they hear of a disaster.[19]

To prevent the overcrowding of wrecking vessels, legislation also fixed the distribution of shares for each wrecking vessel based on tonnage (see Appendix 12). The owner of the wrecking vessel received one-third of the amount awarded and the other two-thirds was divided between the captain and crew. While the law allowed the master, mate and crew equal shares, customary practice through negotiation with the owner, gave the master two or three shares, the mate from one and a half to two shares and the remainder of the crew one share each.[20]

After Harbour Island became a port of entry in 1836, the wreckers of Harbour Island and the neighbouring settlements had the option of declaring the salvage in Dunmore Town. A customs officer collected the revenue from import taxes on salvaged goods, and the special magistrate, the resident justice, and the elite merchant class provided a pool of residents from which arbitrators were chosen. In the 1860s, the police magistrate J.B. Burnside and acting magistrate T.W. Johnson adjudicated wrecking inquiries and wrecked goods were consigned to William H. Cleare and William H. Sears, the American Consul on the island. The advantage of declaring wrecked goods at Harbour Island was time saved in travel and adjudication. The disadvantage was the problem of finding a market for certain items and disposing of large quantities. The establishment of the marketplace in 1857 and the warehouse port in 1867 not only facilitated the wrecking industry but also contributed to Harbour Island's rising eminence as the second city with a healthy and diverse economy.

By 1846 wrecking was the principal source of income for the majority of the inhabitants of Harbour Island and three-quarters of the male population, approximately 300 men (of a total population of 1745), earned some part of their livelihood as wreckers.[21] These were prosperous times for the island whose boat building industry, pineapple cultivation and merchant shipping, in addition to wrecking, had turned the sleepy eighteenth century village settlement into a thriving, bustling, commercial town. The schooners and sloops built in Harbour Island were engaged year round, apart from the hurricane season, in fishing and turtling, transporting fruit or lumber and wrecking. While the mariners of Harbour Island might go on wrecking excursions to the Abaco Cays, Bimini or the Gulf of Florida for 6 to 8 weeks at a time, many of their wrecking exploits were a welcome diversion on trading voyages.

Most of the wrecking families were the sons and grandsons of the men who assisted Deveaux in the recapture of Nassau from the Spaniards. Prior to emancipation, the owners and shareholders of the wrecking vessels took their 2–3 slaves to crew on their wrecking voyages. And after emancipation, many former slaves had the skills and knowledge to become captains and owners of wrecking vessels, positions denied them before they were freed. Of the 95 slave mariners listed on the 1834 Slave Registers (Table 11.2), 80 are designated as participating in wrecking. Records of these ex-slave mariners are scant until the 1850s and 1860s, when various wrecking documents show that Chatham Albury, Henry Cleare, Peter Cleare, Moses Johnson, Peter Saunders, London Cash and mulatto Isaac Saunders were stalwart members of the Harbour Island wrecking fleet. Although many of the ex-slave mariners may have experienced poverty and would have been victims of the truck system, some fared very well. Governor Matthews in

1846 granted lots in the prestigious Pitt Street area, near to the Farmer's Dock (site of PLP dock), to ex-slave mariners Chatham Albury, Clinton Sawyer, Chatham Roberts, Boston Saunders, his son Boston Saunders and widow Patience Saunders.

Chatham Albury became captain of the 50-ton, 57-foot, 2-masted schooner *Manchester*, built in 1839 by James Kelly and owned by William and John Cleare, both big men in the wrecking trade. When the *Vallonia* was wrecked in 1854, she was salvaged by wreckmaster Stephen Roberts of the 50-ton, Harbour Island built wrecking schooner *Vesper*, owned by Chatham Albury, George, Jeremiah and Matthew Sawyer. The 14 crew-members are listed in Appendix 13.[22]

Another prominent black wrecker was Matthew 'Mott' Lowe, captain of the *Nellie Covert*. He had been a wrecker for 30 years, in 1865, when he assisted Capt. John Buck Saunders of the *Galvanic*, wreckmaster for the brigantine *Ella*. Sailing from St. Johns, New Brunswick to Matanzas, Cuba, with a cargo of lumber, the *Ella* accidentally struck a bank east of the Biminis and grounded hard and fast.[23] The following year 'Mott' Lowe in the *Nellie Covert* became the wreckmaster for the American barque *Evelyn*, stranded on a bar near the northern end of Harbour Island while carrying coal, salt, potatoes, hams and a sawmill from New York to Key West. In the inquiry into the wreck, no evidence of collusion was found by police magistrate J. B. Burnside, who relied on the evidence of Elias Cleare, another coloured man, described as one of the best pilots in Harbour Island.[24]

Capt. Elias Cleare and a crew of 13 men from the *Splendid* assisted wreckmaster Capt. William Alfred Kemp and the 13-member crew of the *Desdomonia* in the wreck of the *Mary Leve* in 1860. In consort were the *Annie Sophia, Star, A. Canale, Galvanic, Lady Bannerman* and *Defiance* also assisting in salving the *Mary Leve*.[25] (See Appendix 13 for details of crew members.) In 1868, Capt. Elias Cleare became wreckmaster for the American brig *C. B. Allen* when it wrecked at Little Sturrup's Cay in a gale. Capt. Johnson of the Harbour Island schooner *Corine*, and the *Excel* assisted him.[26]

The best diver in the Bahamas was reputed to be mulatto Isaac Saunders of Harbour Island. He belonged to that rare breed of men who could dive down 70 feet through two hatchways into the lower holds of a vessel and find their way through a mixture of debris and bilge water to throw a grappling iron round floating packages of valuable cargo. They would rise and spend five minutes gasping for air on deck and return below to strip sheets of copper sheathing from the bottom of the vessel in three minutes. They did this for six hours every working day until the ship was stripped of every saleable commodity.[27] In 1866, Capt. W. H. Stuart, Deputy Inspector of Lighthouses, called upon him to examine the British ship *Rhine* that sank

Table 11.2 Ex-Slaves registered as Mariners in 1834

#	Owner		Occup.	ex Slave	Col.	Loc.	Race	Occupation of ex slave
1	Ann	Albury	Widow	Chatham	Blk	HI	C	34 Mariner, wrecking etc
2	Ann	Albury	Widow	Tom	Blk	HI	C	34 Mariner, wrecking etc
3	Ruth	Albury	Widow	Ishmael	Blk	HI	C	34 Mariner, wrecking, etc
4	Ruth	Albury	Widow	Jerry	Blk	HI	C	34 Mariner, wrecking, etc
5	Ruth	Albury	Widow	Prince	Blk	HI	C	34 Mariner, wrecking, etc
6	William	Albury	Planter	Davy	Blk	HI	C	34 Mariner, wrecking etc
7	William	Albury	Planter	Israel	Blk	HI	C	34 Mariner, wrecking etc
8	Martha El	Cash		Davy	Blk	HI	C	34 Mariner
9	Martha El	Cash		Henry	Blk	HI	C	34 Mariner
10	William	Cash	Planter	Jack	Blk	HI	C	34 Mariner, wrecking etc
11	William	Cash	Planter	London	Blk	HI	C	34 Mariner, wrecking etc
12	William	Cash	Planter	Prince	Blk	HI	C	34 Mariner, wrecking etc
13	William	Cash	Planter	Stephen	Blk	HI	C	34 Mariner, wrecking etc
14	John	Clear	Planter	Tembo	Blk	HI	A	34 Mariner @ HI
15	John	Clear	Planter	Jim	Blk	HI	C	34 Mariner, wrecking etc
16	Ephraim	Cleare	gift to	Davy	Blk	HI	C	34 Mariner, wrecking etc
17	Ephraim	Cleare	children	Peter	Blk	HI	C	34 Mariner, wrecking etc
18	Ephraim	Cleare	1831	Philip	Blk	HI	C	34 Mariner, wrecking etc
19	Patience	Cleare	Widow	Benjamin	Blk	HI	C	34 Mariner, Seized by Customs & freed
20	Patience	Cleare	Widow	Charles	Blk	HI	C	35 Mariner, wrecking, woodcutting etc
21	Patience	Cleare	Widow	Henry	Mul	HI	C	36 Mariner, wrecking, woodcutting etc
22	Ruben	Cleare	Planter	Davy	Blk	HI	C	34 Mariner, wrecking
23	Charity	Cornish	Widow	Morris	Blk	HI	C	34 Mariner, wrecking etc
24	Margaret	Curry	Widow	Bob	Blk	HI	C	34 Mariner, wrecking etc
25	Margaret	Curry	Widow	Charles	Blk	HI	C	34 Mariner, wrecking etc
26	Margaret	Curry	Widow	Dick	Blk	HI	C	34 Mariner, wrecking etc
27	Christopher	Fisher	Planter	Esau	Blk	HI	C	34 Mariner, wrecking etc HI
28	Christopher	Fisher	Planter	Alick	Blk	NP	C	34 Mariner, wrecking, fishing etc @ HI
29	Christopher	Fisher	Planter	Anthony	Blk	El	C	34 Mariner, wrecking, woodcutting etc
30	Christopher	Fisher	Planter	Castletown	Blk	El	C	34 Mariner, wrecking, woodcutting etc
31	William	Harris		Tom	Blk	HI	C	34 Mariner, Fishing
32	Anne	Higgs		Duke	Blk	El	C	34 Mariner, wrecking
33	Anne	Higgs		James	Blk	El	C	34 Mariner, wrecking
34	Henrietta	Higgs	Widow	Joseph	Blk	El/PC	C	34 Mariner @ HI
35	Henrietta	Higgs	Widow	(S)Cotland	Blk	El/PC	C	34 Mariner at sea
36	Henrietta	Higgs	Widow	Glenton	Blk	HI	C	34 Mariner at sea
37	Henrietta	Higgs	Jeremiah	Thomas	Blk	HI	A	34 Mariner at sea
38	Joseph	Higgs	Sam & Jer	Dick	Blk	sea	C	34 Mariner, wrecking, woodcutting etc
39	Sarah	Higgs		Anthony	Blk	HI	C	34 Mariner
40	Thomas	Higgs	Planter	Edward	Mul	HI	C	34 Mariner, wrecking etc
41	John	Ingraham	Planter	Steven	Blk	HI	C	34 Mariner, fishing, woodcutting etc
42	John	Ingraham	deceased	Jack	Blk	HI	C	34 Mariner, wrecking, fishing etc
43	Joseph	Ingraham	Planter	David	Blk	HI	C	34 Mariner, wrecking
44	Joseph	Ingraham	Planter	Sam	Blk	HI	C	34 Mariner, wrecking etc
45	Jane	Johnson	Widow	Ben	Blk	HI	C	34 Mariner wrecking etc
46	Jane	Johnson	Widow	Ebo	Blk	HI	C	34 Mariner, wrecking, woodcutting etc
47	Mary HI	Johnson	widow	Ben	Blk	HI	C	34 Mariner, wrecking, woodcutting etc
48	Mary HI 2	Johnson		Bob	Blk	Sea	C	34 Mariner, wrecking, woodcutting etc

95 mariners belong to 47 owners 80 designated as wreckers belong to 41 owners

#	Owner	Occup.	ex Slave	Col.	Loc.	Race	Occupation of ex slave
49	Mary HI 2	Johnson		Peter	Blk	El	C	34 Mariner, wrecking, woodcutting etc
50	Samuel HI	Johnson	Planter	Chatham	Blk	HI	C	34 Mariner, wrecker etc @ NP
51	Samuel HI	Johnson	Planter	Moses	Blk	El	C	34 Mariner, wrecking etc
52	Mary	Johnson El	Wife Saml	Jacob	Blk	HI	C	34 Mariner, wrecking, fishing etc
53	Mary	Johnson El	Wife Saml	Moses	Blk	HI	C	34 Mariner, wrecking, fishing etc
54	James	Kelly HI	minor Robt	Simon	Blk	sea	C	34 Mariner, wrecking etc
55	William	Kemp		Harry	Blk	HI	A	34 Mariner, wrecking @ Abaco
56	Maria Pat	Mather	by 1828	George	Mul	HI	C	34 Mariner, wrecking, fishing etc
57	Patience	Mather	died 1828	Dick	Blk	HI	C	34 Mariner, wrecking, fishing etc
58	John El	Nix		Bob	Blk	HI	C	34 Mariner, wrecking, woodcutting etc
59	Ridley	Pinder	Planter	Henry	Blk	HI	C	34 Mariner, wrecking etc
60	Ridley	Pinder	Planter	Isaac	Blk	NP	C	34 Mariner, wrecking etc
61	Ridley	Pinder	Planter	Jenkins	Blk	Ab	C	34 Mariner, wrecking etc
62	Ridley	Pinder	Planter	Sam	Blk	HI	C	34 Mariner, wrecking etc
63	Bethia	Roberts	Widow	Chatham	Blk	HI	C	34 Mariner, Wrecking etc
64	Bethia	Roberts	Widow	Thomas	Blk	HI	C	34 Mariner, Wrecking etc
65	George	Roberts	Planter	Manuel	Blk	HI	C	34 Mariner, wrecking etc
66	Joseph	Roberts	Planter	Charles	Blk	HI	A	34 Mariner, wrecking etc
67	Joseph	Roberts	Planter	Isaac	Blk	HI	C	34 Mariner, wrecking etc
68	Joseph	Roberts	Planter	John	Blk	HI	C	34 Mariner, wrecking etc
69	Martha	Roberts	Widow	Nick	Blk	El	C	34 Mariner @ El
70	Mary	Roberts	Widow	Caesar	Blk	HI	C	34 Mariner, wrecking etc
71	Mary	Roberts	Widow	James	Blk	HI	C	34 Mariner, wrecking etc
72	Mary	Roberts	Widow	Thomas	Blk	HI	C	34 Mariner, wrecking etc
73	Sarah	Roberts	Widow	James	Blk	HI	C	34 Mariner, wrecking etc
74	Sarah	Roberts	Widow	Samuel	Blk	HI	C	34 Mariner, wrecking etc
75	Richard	Roberts 1	Planter	David	Blk	HI	C	34 Mariner, wrecking, woodcutting etc
76	Richard	Roberts 1	Planter	George	Blk	HI	A	34 Mariner, wrecking, woodcutting etc
77	Richard	Roberts 1	Planter	Isaac	Blk	HI	C	34 Mariner, wrecking, woodcutting etc
78	Richard	Roberts 1	Planter	James	Blk	HI	C	34 Mariner, wrecking, woodcutting etc
79	Richard	Roberts 1	Planter	Joseph	Blk	HI	C	34 Mariner, wrecking, woodcutting etc
80	Joseph	Saunders	Mariner	Dick	Blk	HI	C	34 Mariner, wrecking etc
81	Kesiah	Saunders	Widow	Boston	Blk	HI	C	34 Mariner, wrecking etc
82	Kesiah	Saunders	also known	Boston	Blk	HI	C	34 Mariner, wrecking etc
83	Thomas	Saunders	Planter	Chatham	Blk	HI	A	34 Mariner, wrecking etc
84	William	Saunders	Planter	Clinton	Mul	HI	C	34 Mariner, wrecking etc
85	William	Saunders	Planter	Isaac	Mul	HI	C	34 Mariner, wrecking etc
86	Benjamin	Saunders 1	Planter	Seivvy	Blk	HI	C	37 Mariner, wrecking, woodcutting etc
87	Benjamin	Saunders 2	Planter	Peter	Blk	sea	C	34 Mariner, wrecking etc
88	Edmund	Sawyer	Mar/Plant	Bonner	Blk	sea	A	34 Mariner, wrecking etc
89	Edmund	Sawyer	Mar/Plant	Isaac	Blk	HI	C	34 Mariner, wrecking etc
90	William	Sawyer	Planter	Robert	Mul	HI	C	34 Mariner
91	Richard	Sweeting	Mariner	Duke	Blk	HI	C	34 mariner wrecking, woodcutting etc
92	Richard	Sweeting	Mariner	Moses	Blk	HI	C	34 mariner wrecking, woodcutting etc
93	William	Thompson	Planter	Joe	Blk	HI	C	34 Mariner, seized by Customs 1832
94	William	Thompson	Planter	Port Royal	Blk	sea	C	34 Mariner, seized by Customs 1832
95	Patience	Tucker	Widow	John	Mul	HI	C	34 Mariner, wrecking etc

under suspicious circumstances west of Memory Rocks, north of West End, Grand Bahama. Saunders found wilful damage to the hull for the purpose of sinking her on the bank. Several holes with jagged outer edges, all rough and newly bored diagonally through the timber below the level of the low-water mark, were proof of there not being receptacles of original fastenings; and further, the ballast was all heaped to one side. All holes were below the low-water mark and all on the starboard side. The ship was lying down on her starboard side, leading off seaward, and her stern in 9 feet of water. Saunders as master of the wrecking vessel *Golden Eagle* had helped wreckmaster, Capt. Lewis Grant Thompson of the wrecking schooner *Brothers* along with the crews of *Lady Bannerman* and *Rambler*[28] unload the cargo and he had seen these holes in the *Rhine* before she was burnt and took Capt. Stuart directly to them. Saunders advised Stuart that in his opinion this was a glaring case of the ship being stranded on purpose. The master of the *Rhine* was implicated in a criminal act and was committed to trial.[29] In the initial hearing he committed perjury but left the island before sufficient evidence could be gathered.[30] Within months Isaac Saunders in the aged wrecking schooner *Vesper* became wreckmaster way down on the Labanderous Shoal, in the Old Rock Channel, where an error of judgement by Master Wilson Stout had run the British Barque *Salween* aground.[31]

An examination of vessels and men licensed to wreck in 1865 seems to show that Harbour Island had a relatively small wrecking fleet of 20 vessels in contrast to Nassau with 113, Inagua with 46 and Abaco with 44 (see Table 11.3). But it is important to note that Bimini was in the Abaco constituency and almost everyone there took out a wrecking licence. Thus the count for Abaco included Bimini's large 'floating population' of wreckers from Harbour Island and Nassau.

The Harbour Island fleet over the years acquired a reputation for their skills and expertise in the salvage business. The Harbour Island licensed

Table 11.3 Vessels and men licensed for wrecking 1865–1868 (Blue Books)

Island	V 1865	V 1866	Ton 1866	Men 1866	V 1867	Ton 1867	Men 1867	V 1868	Ton 1868	Men 1868
New Pro	113	89	2096	927	87	2240	644	65	1438	271
Inagua	46	19	143	142	1	25	43	1	35	14
Abaco	44	30	314	248	15	282	136	18	362	406
Harbr I	20	5*	211	54	14	475	139	-	-	1
Crkd I	5	16	165	126	3	100	85	3	45	101
Eleuth	1	1	39	5	-	-	2	-	-	-
Long Isl	1	1	18	0	-	-	-	-	-	-
Total	230	161	2984	1502	120	3122	1049	87	1880	836

* This figure probably reflects the loss of Harbour Island vessels in the 1866 hurricane.

wrecking schooner *Galvanic* was known as the 'Queen of the Bahamian wrecking fleet' as she was *'always lucky'* and her owner and captain John Buck Saunders Senior, might be called 'King of the Wreckers'. Buck Saunders of Harbour Island, although having to sign his name with an 'X', could 'smell out a wreck', having been a wrecker for 25 years, and was well acquainted with all the reefs, currents and shoals in the waters of the Bahamas and beyond. Many of his wrecking exploits took place on his trading voyages to and from Cuba and the Yucatan. He also owned the *Jane* and was a part owner of the *Golden Eagle* and *Sarah Elizabeth*. Based on the analysis of 23 wreck inquiries involving Harbour Island wrecking vessels, Buck Saunders was involved with 11 cases in the Bimini area, often as wreckmaster, and sometimes all 4 of his vessels assisted in the same wreck (Table 11.4).

One of the most interesting wrecks in which Buck Saunders participated, was the wreck of the *Margaret Ann* in July 1864. In June, the *Margaret Ann*, Capt. Charles Ansell Russell, left New York with a cargo of furniture and provisions. Obviously intending to take the quick but dangerous route south through the Gulf, Capt. Russell pulled into Green Turtle Cay and took on Capt. John Lowe as pilot to take him to the Biminis. Capt. Russell knew Bimini very well and could not resist the temptation to visit his good friend Capt. Joe Buck Saunders, the brother of John Buck Saunders. The Bimini police had to suppress a disturbance caused by a riotous party of revellers that included not only the crew of the *Margaret Ann* but also the crew of the *Galvanic*, which by a strange coincidence had just arrived at Bimini from Cuba with a cargo of sugar for Harbour Island.

The next day, Capt. Russell, with Bimini pilot Capt. William Sweeting, left for the Orange Cays, but the *Margaret Ann* became fixed on the shoe of Cat Cay Bank and in a few hours a swarm of wreckers gathered around her. Although Pilot Sweeting ordered a large anchor to be put out, Capt. Russell only put out a light anchor and refused the services of the 200 wreckers for two days. Witness, James Alpheus Hanna of Bimini, later revealed that there was a whispering among wreckers that nothing could be done until the *Golden Eagle* arrived from Bimini. On the arrival of the *Golden Eagle*, Capt. Buck Saunders and co-owner Richard Watkins went aboard the *Margaret Ann* and the crew of the *Golden Eagle, Galvanic, Gilpin* and *Olive Branch* proceeded to unload the cargo. Capt. Russell stopped them and then invited Buck Saunders to become wreckmaster and imposed certain conditions on the general consortship, which were accepted by the entire force of wreckers. Just one hour before the *Margaret Ann* floated, the *Sarah Elizabeth* arrived and was taken into general consortship. Buck Saunders never claimed salvage for his part in the 'rescue' of the *Margaret Ann*, perhaps because the weight of evidence showed that this was a flagrant act of collusion.[32]

Table 11.4 Location of selected wrecks with Harbour Island salvors

John Buck Saunders and the boats owned by him are shown in bold letters
X# Refers to location on Map of Location of the Selected Wrecks on page opposite

X#	Date / Location	Wreck	Wreck Master	Wreck Sch.	Assisted by: Capt	Wreck Sch.
1	03/04/1857 At Gingerbread Grounds	*Saxon*	Joseph Albury **Also assisted by** *Racer, Arctic, Mary Jane, Emulous, Baltic*		*Agnes*	*Corine*
2	26/12/1863 Not stated	*Jenny Lind*	Jeremiah Curry	*Sun*	**John Saunders**	*Galvanic*
3	24/12/1864 At Shoe of Cat Cay Bank	*Margaret Ann*	**Buck Saunders Sr** **Also assisted by** *Golden Eagle, Gilpin, Olive Branch,* **Sarah Elizabeth**	*Galvanic*	Drudge	*Lynx*
4	25/01/1865 At North of Orange Cay	*R M Demill*	**Buck Saunders Sr**	*Galvanic*	**Also assisted by** *Try, Foreward, Eliza & Catherine, Susan, Goodwill, Elva, Ventrosa, William H Cleare, George Eneas, Equator,* **Jane**	
5	19/03/1865 At Blackwoods Bush Bank	*Carl Emil*	Royley **Also assisted by** *Dandy, Splendid, Sarah Jane, Wesleyan,* **Galvanic**, *Tweed, Lynx*	*John W Pinder*	Roberts	*Ventrosa*
6	04/04/1865 At Great Sturrup's Cay	*J L Gerity*	Joseph Wm Albury	*Bob*		
7	27/05/1865 At Blackwoods Bush Bank	*Rowena*	**Buck Saunders Sr**	*Galvanic*		
8	23/09/1865 At Gingerbread Grounds	*Ella*	Matthew Lowe **Also assisted by** *Nonesuch,* **Sarah Elizabeth**, *Golden Eagle, Edith, William H Cleare, Evelina*	*Nellie Covert*	**Buck Saunders**	*Galvanic*
9	23/10/1865 At North of Sandy Cay, GB	*Panama*	John Bain **Also assisted by** *Proof, Teazer, Adennas, Ellen Francis, Sarah Jane*	*Eclipse*	**Buck Saunders Sr**	*Galvanic*
10	29/11/1865 At Man Island	*Conquest*	James Curry **Also assisted by** *Dart, Goodwill, Mary & Susan, Elyn, George Eneas, Nina, Warley*	*Mary Jane*	Wm H A Roberts	*Ventrosa*
11	27/01/1866 Off Harbour Island	*Evelyn*	Matthew Lowe	*Nellie Covert*		
12	14/05/1866 At Great Sturrup's Cay	*Orion*	Edward Wilkinson	*Georgiana*	Lewis G Thompson	*Brothers*

13	14/02/1866 At Wood Cay west GB	Caroline	Jeremiah Bethel **Also assisted by** *Ellen, Racer, Eclipse*	*Bahamian*	*Mary*
14	15/06/1866 On Labanderous Shoal,	Salween	Isaac Saunders	*Vesper*	*Ellen Ann*
15	15/08/1866 near Bimini	Jane Goodyear **Also assisted by** *Jane, Hutwing, Try, Eliza & Catherine, Lion*	Thomas Lloyd	*Georgiana*	Lewis G Thompson *Brothers*
16	01/10/1866 At Ridley's Head, El.	Baltic			
17	02/01/1867 Off Harbour Island	Mogul	Obadiah Saunders	William Rogers	
18	14/02/1867 At South West Point of Cat Cay	Lady Emily Peel	Gilbert Kelly	*Mary & Susan*	John Carey *Elva*
19	15/02/1867 At Dollar Harbour Reef nr Cat Cay	Henry Nutt	William Sophias	*Superb* **Also assisted by** *Jane*	Eneas *Fleetwing*
20	15/05/1867 On Holmes Rock, west of GB	Fawn	John Martin	*Polar Star*	*Mary*
21	15/06/1867 Not stated	San Nicholas	Thomas Lloyd **Also assisted by** *Isabella, Reform*	*Georgiana*	*Nonesuch*
22	15/10/1867 At Orange Cays	B F Shaw	Roberts *Nonesuch, Excel, Dart, Pearl,* **Golden Eagle***, Cicero, Sunbeam, Brothers, Fleetwing, Reform*	*Azorian*	**Buck Saunders** *Jane* **Also assisted by**
23	12/2/1868 Not stated	Cartbegene	Jeremiah Curry	*Splendid*	*Tweed*
24	16/10/1868 On Blackwoods Bush Bank	Electric	John Murray	*Vanderbilt*	**Buck Saunders** *Jane*
25	00/12/1868 At Little Sturrups Cay	C B Allen	Elias Cleare **Also assisted by** *Corine*	*Emulus*	Johnson *Excel*
26	00/09/1904 Off Harbour Island	James A Wright	William Kemp	*Fearless*	

By the mid-nineteenth century, the wrecking industry of the Bahamas had mushroomed into a thriving business, the chief wrecking centres being at Nassau and Harbour Island.[33] Unfortunately, the criminal actions of the few tarnished the reputation of the many noble wreckers, bringing adverse criticism of the industry. Within the colony, the governors and missionaries worried about the gambling prospects of gain, the spiritual well being of the wreckers and the international reputation of the Bahamas. And outside the colony, the underwriters from New York and Liverpool, the Hanseatic League, and the Board of Trade in London raised concerns about the high risks and loss of vessels in commercial trade, fraudulent practices and collusive wrecking – the practice of wilful wrecking through a prior agreement between a wrecker and a captain of a foreign vessel. While Saunders and Craton suggest that the Out Island wreckers took the high road in contrast to the Nassau merchants, there is evidence that some Harbour Island wreckers were involved in collusive wrecking and did not flinch from 'smuggling' salvaged goods.[34]

As early as 1821, the Methodist missionary John Davis at Harbour Island woefully complained about his fallen flock:

> The Church of God is awfully fallen… the wolf has entered and the sheep scattered. A Spanish ship wrecked in sight of Harbour Island, the people immediately went to her assistance and when they got on board they found her going to pieces; they saved what cargo they could but instead of taking it up to Nassau for salvage as set by the Chamber of Commerce, they secreted a large part of the cargo, and after the captain of the ship had gone to town, they shared the cargo equally between themselves. It is awful to relate, all men, except 2 who professed religion, took a share of the plundered goods. This caused me to use strict discipline according to our rules, these I read before the society present, the evil of their doings and exhorted them to make restoration and pointed out a way for them to do this, allowing them a week to reconsider the evil and to put away this accursed thing. At the expiration of this time I found they did not comply with the proposal, which obliged me to cast them out of the Society. Then I had scarcely any Society at all.

When Governor Grant heard of the stolen goods, he sent a vessel with the chief constable and soldiers to search for the missing flour and merchandise from the Spanish ship *Arrogante*, but when they landed 'the utmost confusion prevailed' and the goods were not found.[35] Although Joseph Curry, William Harris, Joseph Alberry and another Joseph Curry were charged with grand larceny, their trial was adjourned several times and finally dismissed.[36]

Davis' concerns about wrecking as an impediment to spiritual prosperity were echoed 25 years later by another missionary at Harbour Island, John Blackwell, who bemoaned the length of time the wreckers were at sea, '... so that the preacher seldom knows them when he sees them. The wrecking vessels are little more than floating hells, so that if part of the crew have any religious experience when they go to sea, they return seven fold more the children of the wicked one'. Blackwell also condemned the wreckers for smuggling a part of the salvage and complained how they 'come home to riot and trifle for a while and then to sea again'.[37] Quite clearly the missionaries saw wrecking as a nefarious enterprise that diminished the spiritual health of the inhabitants.

Another charge levelled at the wreckers was their efforts 'to decoy strangers into the very dangers from which they subsequently offer to extricate them'.[38] This was the alleged practice of wreckers setting up false navigation lights on the windward shore to lure vessels onto the reefs. There is little documented evidence that Harbour Island wreckers engaged in such unethical conduct. However, the Bahamas Handbook (1965–1966) describes an old wrecking tower on the Atlantic shore of Eleuthera. Made of stone and mortar, it had a chimney of considerable height into which a trimmed pine tree was thrust and lighted.[39] At Bimini, where 25 wrecking vessels rendezvoused in anticipation of a wreck, fires were lit at Alice Town and along the beach in the turtling season to mislead vessels.[40]

Insurance underwriters decried the high rates of salvage awarded to the wreckers by the arbitrators. It was well known that many commission agents and arbitrators in both Nassau and Harbour Island owned wrecking schooners or were connected to wrecking families. This conflict of interest had plagued the justice system in the colony from the days of piracy and privateering. In the case of the wreck of the American brig *Lawrence*, its cargo was consigned to Saunders & Sons even before its arrival in Nassau. H.R. Saunders, the senior partner of Saunders & Sons, appointed Thomas K. Moore and Manuel Menendez as arbitrators, who awarded salvage at 50 per cent. Saunders and Moore owned wrecking vessels and Menendez was known for his favourable judgments towards the wreckers.[41] All three were related through marriage and represented Harbour Island in the House of Assembly. In their arbitration of salvage involving Harbour Island wreckers, their conflict of interest was heightened by political considerations.

An unscrupulous element in the fraternity of the Harbour Island wreckers was revealed when Capt. Fader at the wreck inquiry of the British schooner *Orient*, wrecked off Eleuthera, told Judge Taylor that all along the shore of Harbour Island men shouted out, '*Give up your cotton! We want a wreck*'![42]

The final deliberations of the courts of enquiry more often than not upheld the integrity of the wreckers and praised their acts of courage and daring. E.B.A. Taylor, the presiding judge at the enquiry of the *Panama* wreck commented:

> Signal acts of daring, directed by skill, deserve more than a passing commendation. It may be said that the satisfaction felt on rescuing a fellow creature from a watery grave is its own reward; but I believe that if the humane and spirited wrecker had his efforts publicly noticed by the reward of a medal…it would bring about, and raise the employment of wrecking to a standard which would entitle it to the claim of being noble and useful.[43]

Despite the negative image promoted by foreign officials of the wreckers as unscrupulous and unethical, many within the colony appreciated their humanitarian efforts in saving life and cargo.

A most compassionate effort on the part of the Harbour Island wreckers was evident in the wreck of a Portuguese slaver off Harbour Island. After the abolition of the slave trade in 1807, many slave ships carrying Africans to America and Cuba were wrecked on the coasts of the Bahamas, especially near the entrance to the Northeast Providence Channel. In October 1837, a Portuguese slaver, bound from Cape Verdi Islands to Matanza Islands, Cuba, having aboard upwards of 200 slaves valued at 20,000 pounds, was wrecked about one mile from Dunmore Town. Stipendiary Magistrate, Major Donald McGregor praised the intrepidity and skill of several boatmen navigating their vessels through shoals, reefs and rocks in a violent storm. He assisted Capt. William Cleare in the 50-ton sloop *Rover*, whose crew of 10 men, at great personal risk, took up cutlasses to subdue the ferocious slavers. Only 53 young Africans were saved, as the adults were fettered and drowned. McGregor praised the humane and Christian attitude of the Harbour Island people, who stripped themselves of some of their clothing to cover the naked Africans. The young Africans were given a place of shelter and 2 quarts corn and rice at a cost of $1.00 each, with the intention that they would be sent to Nassau as soon as possible. William Cleare absolutely refused to proceed unless McGregor could guarantee 10 shillings Bahamian currency for the transport of each African to Nassau. As a result, the 53 young liberated Africans remained in the Harbour Island District as apprentices. Of the 53, six were listed as mariners, including Harry aged 12, employed by Capt. William Cleare, who no doubt became a wrecker.[44]

The primary advantage of the wrecking industry in Harbour Island was its more inclusive nature in contrast to the boat building or pineapple industries. In addition to the benefits to wreckers and ship owners, the

Table 11.5 Wrecking income and annual earnings in the Bahamas 1856–1872

Year	Income from wreck licenses £	Licensed Wrecking vessels	Licensed wreckers	Estimated earnings of wrecker £-s
1856		302	2679	18-00
1857				17-10
1858	731			16-02
1859	700			17-03
1860	736			17-03
1861	455			
1862	458			
1863	325			
1864	213			
1865	379	230	1045	10-04
1866*		161	1502	28-13
1867		120	1049	42-04
1868				16-09
1869	165			28-06
1870	355			
1871*	285	37	836	
1872		70	651	

* Hurricane 1866 and severe storm 1871

wrecking industry offered opportunities to shipbuilders, stevedores, shopkeepers, and homebuilders. And further, salvaged goods created a buyer's market so that the people of Dunmore Town and the neighbouring settlements on Eleuthera could purchase necessary household items at reasonable prices. With the majority of the adult males holding a wrecking licence, the quality of life for most people on the island was positively affected by the wrecking industry.

Bacot possibly overstates the rewards of nineteenth century wreckers when he comments: 'A day's luck may prevent all necessity for further labour for a year; and a lucky season enrich a man for life.'[45] Wright estimates that from a single wreck in 1865, the owners of the wrecking vessels received £1826 14s. 4d. and the wrecking crew £17 11s. 5d each; and further that the average wrecker's annual earnings between 1856 to 1869 ranged from £10 4s. to £42 4s.[46] See Table 11.5. For both wrecker and ship owner in Harbour Island, this was more than likely not their only source of income.

The wrecking industry enriched the shipbuilders by creating a demand for more vessels and providing wrecked rigging, barometers, steering wheels, anchors, lumber and other chandlery supplies at good prices. In the heyday of wrecking, between the years 1855 to 1864, Harbour Island shipwrights built 26 vessels, totalling 1,227 tons, some of which were custom built for wrecking.[47]

Stevedore services were in great demand by the wreckers to empty the cargo, take it to customs for assessment, then to the warehouse to await arbitration and finally to the market for auction. The 14 shopkeepers in Harbour Island were able to buy merchandise very cheaply to stock their shops and export the surplus. Cargoes that were broken open sold at a very low price. In the wreckers' philosophy, the furnishings from the bilged or stranded vessels were not a part of the cargo. Many homes in Harbour Island were furnished with salvaged mirrors, clocks, chests of drawers, chairs, tables and even beds from the cabins of the fated vessel. These undeclared items were regarded as trophies of the wrecking adventure.

A day that lived on in the memories of the Harbour Island wrecking community for the remainder of the nineteenth century was the morning of the 26 November 1865. The American ship *Conquest*, Capt. Lewis, left Boston on the 12 November 1865 bound for New Orleans with a cargo of gunny bags, fish, potatoes and nails. After 6 days, light westerly winds forced her to take a more southerly course, and by Saturday noon of the 25th, she was ascertained to be at latitude 25° 32' and longitude 75° 20' 15", but by dead reckoning, as recorded in the log book, the latitude was 25° 39' and the longitude 75° 31' – a difference in longitude of 11 miles and latitude 7 miles. The ship, sailing by the wind, headed West North West, travelling at $3\frac{1}{2}$ to 4 knots, until 1:30 a.m. Sunday morning, when a squall from the North West moved in. Capt. Lewis ordered the crew to tack immediately, but before the mate could reach the deck, the ship had struck a reef and bilged.

Anchored at Current Point (the northern entrance to Harbour Island) at that same time, because of the weather, was Capt. James Curry of the Harbour Island built wrecking schooner *Mary Jane*. Curry had left Harbour Island on Saturday noon of the 25th to collect a cargo of fruit and passengers from the settlement at Bluff and take them to Key West. He spotted the *Conquest* wrecked on Man Island, sailed across, boarded her and Capt. Lewis was relieved to appoint him wreckmaster. In less than half an hour about 400 Harbour Islanders, wreckers and spectators included, arrived in their boats. As wreckmaster, Capt. Curry found that he could not control so large and excited a number, so he gave permission for all to go to work and convey the cargo to the 6 wrecking schooners (Appendix 13 gives details of captains and crews), which had come out from Harbour Island.[48] Although the cargo on the *Conquest* was not of high value, the salvage operation included a large number of wreckers from Dunmore Town and however small the rewards, most of the families benefited.

Harbour Island has been viewed as 'the spawning ground of the wrecking fraternity'[49] as many of its wreckers eventually settled at popular wrecking rendezvous sites to become professional wreckers. In the early

1800s many Harbour Island wreckers moved to Abaco to settle the cays and harvest wrecks on their front doorstep. After US legislation in 1824 prohibited Bahamian wreckers to wreck off the Florida Cays, the American initiatives to attract Bahamian seamen to settle proved irresistible to some, and many Harbour Island and Abaco wreckers settled Key West where salvage earnings were much higher than in the Bahamas. Bimini's location on the reef-strewn eastern edge of 'the narrowest, fastest flowing, and roughest stretch of the Florida Channel' initially became a popular rendezvous site for wreckers as more and more vessels sailed south through the Gulf. By the 1840s, wreckers from Harbour Island, Abaco and Nassau made their permanent homes there.[50]

The wrecking centres in the colony made significant contributions to the Public Treasury through customs duties from the import and export of wrecked goods. While there are no figures available for revenue collected from imports of wrecked goods by island, Table 11.6 shows the fluctuation of these revenues for the colony. In the best year, 1870, the import value of wrecked goods was £153,539, representing 54 per cent of the total imports; in 1865, the worst year before the demise of wrecking, the import value of wrecked goods was £28,017, representing only 2 per cent of the total imports.[51] It must be borne in mind that a considerable number of wrecks and their cargoes were brought into Nassau by boats fitted out and manned by the inhabitants of Abaco, Harbour Island, Grand Bahama and the Biminis.[52] As for exports, more than 66 per cent comprised of wrecked goods during the 1850s.[53]

William C. Church tells the story of a colonial governor who was about to return to England. In his farewell speech he offered to use his good office to procure from the Home Government any favour the colonists might desire. The unanimous reply was as startling as Salome's request for the head of John the Baptist on a platter: 'Tell them to tear down the lighthouses; they are ruining the prosperity of the colony'.[54] The building of lighthouses at the danger spots throughout the archipelago signalled the beginning of the end of wrecking. By the mid-1860s nine lighthouses and seven beacons had been erected much to the dismay of the wreckers. The people of Harbour Island and Abaco were very incensed at the erection of the lighthouse at Elbow Cay and condemned the lighthouse keeper for preventing many wrecks.[55]

Of greater import to the demise of wrecking was the decline in trading vessels passing through Bahamian waters. During the American Civil War, the blockade of the southern ports by the northern navy disrupted trade. And the expansion of the roads, canals and railways from the eastern seaboard ports west provided an alternative means of transportation by land, which was faster and safer. Fewer trading vessels meant fewer wrecks.

Table 11.6 Wrecked imports and salvage for the colony 1850–1903

Year	Total Imports £	Imports from wrecks £	% wreck imports of total imports	Derelict Cases	Salvage Awarded £-s-d	Salvage Cases	Salvage Awarded £-s-d
1850*	92,756	16,768	18.0%				
1852	139,563	46,515	33.3%				
1855				10	3,836-03-09	0	0
1856	189,398	96,304	50.8%	5	3,250-10-09	4	8,742-09-11
1857	211,423	87,573	41.4%	5	253-18-00	7	9,185-01
1858	190,523	64,509	33.9%	5	408-14-10	1	4,994-15-08
1859	213,166	69,811	32.8%	2	159-06-06	3	5,512-01-05
1860	234,029	102,890	44%	6	865-13-04	5	10,429-03-09
1861	274,584	66,519	24.2%	8	252-10-06	2	5,540-12-04
1862	1,250,322	49,178	3.9%	6	135-14-11	4	2,859-11-09
1863	4,295,316	50,666	1.2%	5	1,446-15-04	5	10,592-16-01
1864	5,346,112	51,414	1.0%	7	709-02-07	6	2,102-02-04
1865	1,470,467	28,017	2.0%		No further statistics		
1866*	328,622	107,660	32.8%				
1867	365,316	110,634	30.2%				
1868	231,526	34,404	14.9%				
1869	240,584	46,068	19.7%				
1870	283,970	153,539	54.0%				
1871*	239,190	65,043	27.2%				
1872	201,051						
1873	226,306						
1874	183,993						
1875	165,970	30,353	18.3%				
1876	153,689						
1880	No	25,714					
1885	further	33,913					
1890	statistics	1,870					
1891		9,464					
1896		2,164					
1900		2,637					
1903		94					

* Hurricane 1866 and severe storms 1850 and 1871

The mid-nineteenth century was an era of great technological advancement which revolutionized navigation in a number of ways. The steam ship supplanted the sailing vessel and no longer was the mariner at the mercy of the elements. Not only were the captains of vessels better trained and the reefs and shoals better charted but also a number of navigational aids made travel by steamer more precise. With the advent of the electric telegraph, the captain and crew were better informed about adverse weather conditions. In addition, the steamships from the eastern seaboard could take a more direct route south. They no longer travelled through the Northeast Providence Channel to get to Nassau or the Gulf but went directly south, hugging the eastern US coast. So Harbour Island and Abaco were no longer on the main sea-roads and wrecking opportunities were fewer.

As all these factors conspired to close down the wrecking industry, the Harbour Island wreckers suffered a deadly blow with the extensive damage to their wrecking fleet in the 1866 hurricane. By 1868, it was reported that 'the people of Harbour Island at one time the stronghold of wrecking are all gone for pine cultivation'.[56] The call of the sea drew many Harbour Island sailors to the Eleuthera bank in the 1880s where large sponges of fine quality were plentiful.[57] But well into the twentieth century, they embraced the occasional opportunity to save a floundering ship from the perils of the sea.

Notes

1 Birse Shepard, *Lore of the Wreckers*, (Boston: Beacon Press, 1961), p. 109.
2 MMS, File 1846, Box 27, Box 218,1320/3, J Blackwell to MMS, 24 February 1846.
3 George Gardner, *The General Description of America or The New World*, (U.S. Virgin Islands: Antilles Press, 1993), p. 11.
4 J. H. LeFroy, *Memorials of the Discovery and Early Settlement of the Bermudas or Somers Islands*, (Toronto: University of Toronto Press, 1981), Vol. 2: p. 112.
5 David Cordingly, *Under the Black Flag*, (Orlando: Harcourt Brace & Co., 1995), p. 219; CSP 29/408ii, extract from a letter from Capt. Howard of HMS *Shoreham* to Capt. Burchett, 15 Sept. 1716.
6 Charles Johnson, *A General History of the Pirates*, (London: George Routledge & Sons Ltd., 1926), p. 8.
7 CO 23/14/239, Governor FitzWilliam to My Lord, March 1734.
8 A Chart of The Gulf of Florida, 1794, National Maritime Museum, London, negative D8589.
9 Gardiner – Whipple – Allen Family Papers, vol ll 49, Philip Dumaresq correspondence, March 6 1785.
10 Eric Whittleton 'Family History in The Bahamas', *Genealogist Magazine*, 18, (Dec. 1975), p. 189.
11 CO 23/33/125, Atty General Franks to Hon Henry Dundas, 22 September 1794.
12 CO 23/34/288, Memorial to Governor Dunmore from Wreckers, 1795.
13 *Bahamas Gazette*, Shipping News, 9 March 1796.
14 James M. Wright, *The Wrecking System of The Bahama Islands*, (New York: Ginn & Co., 1943), p. 621.
15 *Royal Gazette*, 18 Oct. 1815.
16 CO 23/77/5, Report of Mr. Demayne of Royal Navy, (Board of Admiralty), 15 Oct. 1827.
17 CO 23/73/105, Enactment of a Bill by USA Congress, 25 March 1824, implemented 1 Oct. 1824.
18 CO 23/135/113, Gov. Gregory's Report, 15 May 1850, p. 4.
19 Ibid.
20 CO 23/155/269, Mr. Tappan (of Liverpool Underwriters) outlines the practice of wrecking, 1857.
21 MMS, File 1846, Box 27, Box 218,1320/3, J Blackwell to MMS, 24 February 1846.
22 Vice Admiralty Records, 30 November 1854.
23 CO 23/181/224 – 230, Report of Wreck Inquiry into the wreck of *Ella*, 29 September 1865.
24 CO 23/184/160 – 166, Report of Wreck Inquiry into the wreck of *Evelyn*, 30 January 1866.
25 Vice Admiralty Records, 13 December 1860.

26　CO 23/191/188, Report of Wreck Inquiry, into wreck of *C B Allen,* January 1868.
27　Merchants Magazine and Commercial Review, vol. 44, Jan–June 1861, 53; Birse Shepard, *Lore of the Wreckers,* (Boston: Beacon Press, 1961), p. 169.
28　CO 23/184/75 – Report of Inquiry into British Ship *Rhine,* January 1866.
29　CO 23/184/136, Rawson to Rt Hon Edward Ardwell MP enclosing report from Capt. W. H. Stuart, Deputy Inspector of lighthouses, 1866.
30　CO 23/184/412, Governor Rawson to Edward Cardwell, 30 May 1866.
31　CO 23/184/584, Report of Wreck Inquiry into the wreck of British Barque *Salween,* June 1866.
32　CO 23/181/58, Report of Wreck Inquiry into the wreck of British Schooner *Margaret Ann,* August 1865.
33　Merchants Magazine and Commercial Review, vol. 44, Jan–June 1861, p. 53.
34　Craton & Saunders, *Islanders in the Stream: A History of the Bahamian People, Vol. Two,* (Athens: Univ. Georgia Press, 1998), p. 142.
35　MMS, File 1846, Box 3, Box 117,145/13, J Davis to MMS, 7 August 1821.
36　*Royal Gazette,* 25 July 1821.
37　MMS, File 1846, Box 27, Box 218,1320/3, J Blackwell to MMS, 24 February 1846.
38　United Service Journal III, October 1834, p. 220.
39　'Lusty Days of the Wreckers', *Bahamas Handbook and Businessman's Annual, 1965–1966,* p. 67.
40　CO23/139/51, Report of W. R. Inglis to Governor Gregory, 25 August 1852.
41　CO23/151/62, Report by John W. Bacon, 7 July 1856.
42　CO 23/184/588-592, Report of Wreck Inquiry into the wreck of British Schooner *Orion,* June 1866.
43　CO 23/183/44-49, Report of Wreck Inquiry into the wreck of American Ship *Panama,* November 1865.
44　CO23/100/237, Report of Major McGregor, 28 Oct. 1837; CO 23/109/45, McGregor's Report on Liberated African Apprentices, 1838.
45　J. T. W. Bacot, *The Bahamas: A Sketch,* (London) 1869.
46　James M. Wright, *The Wrecking System of The Bahama Islands,* (New York: Ginn & Co., 1943), p. 639.
47　CO23/180/387, Governor Rawson's Report on The Bahamas 1864, 4 June 1865.
48　CO 23/183/381, Report of Wreck Inquiry into the wreck of American Ship *Conquest,* November 1865.
49　Birse Shepard, *Lore of the Wreckers,* (Boston: Beacon Press, 1961), p. 109.
50　Craton & Saunders, *Islanders in the Stream: A History of the Bahamian People, Vol. Two,* (Athens: Univ. Georgia Press, 1998), p. 142; Helen Duncombe, 'Bimini's 100th Anniversary', *Nassau Tribune,* 8 April 1940.
51　James M. Wright, *The Wrecking System of The Bahama Islands,* (New York: Ginn & Co., 1943), p. 637.
52　CO 23/185/74, Report of Blue Book 1865.
53　Paul Albury, *The Story of The Bahamas,* (London: Macmillan, 1975), p. 135.
54　William C. Church, *A Mid Winter Resort.* Midwinter Number, The Century Magazine, Vol XXXIII, February 1887, #4, p. 505.
55　CO 23/194/417, Captain Hewith Grant, Royal Navy to Buckingham, 3 August 1868.
56　CO 23/197/36, Government Blue Book Report, 1868.
57　Votes of the House of Assembly, Resident Justice JS Solomon Report, 1886.

12

Cast in the Foundry

> *I was brought to hear the word of God at the Foundry, where the Lord was pleased to lift up the light of his countenance upon me.*[1]

Thus spake the Rev. Richard Moss, the very first missionary to make his home in Harbour Island bringing organized religion to the inhabitants for the first time in over a hundred years of settlement, at the same time presiding over education and justice in the community.

It is likely that the early inhabitants of Harbour Island followed the Puritan religion of the Eleutheran Adventurers rather than the Anglicanism of the more aristocratic Bermudians. But by 1721, when military chaplain Thomas Curphy visited them from Nassau to perform the necessary 'rites of passage', they must have welcomed a man of any cloth. In 1729, the Church of England in the Bahamas was established by law under the Bishop of London, Edmund Gibson[2] and missionaries sent by 'The United Society for the Propagation of the Gospel' (hereafter USPG) continued the yearly round of baptisms, marriages and burials. Over the years, Rev. Guy, Rev. Smith and then Rev. Carter operated from the only Church in Nassau in an Anglican parish that embraced New Providence, Eleuthera and Harbour Island. Recognizing that 'more labourers in the vineyard' were needed, Rev. Carter and Governor Shirley were inspired to write:

> I have often regretted the want of a Catechist or Schoolmaster on Harbour Island and Islathera…. They are both at present in a lamentable state….[3] They may be reckoned among the dark corners of the earth with little hopes of being enlightened as long as they remain in their present state.[4]

The USPG, formed in 1701, answered the call and Harbour Island gained its own minister, Richard Moss, becoming the head of the newly constituted St. John's Parish in the same year, 1767/8. Within two years St. John's Parish had its first Anglican Church, 44 by 24 feet, with stone walls, a wooden floor and a shingled roof.[5] The parish included the whole of Eleuthera and was to become somewhat of a headache for the early missionaries, due to the distance of travel, tropical diseases and the wild nature of the inhabitants.

Moss is an extremely interesting character for several reasons. Some historians have painted him as a bigamist. From his own account he did not appear so and the inhabitants of Harbour Island and New Providence testified to his honour, character and behaviour over the 14 years he spent in the island.[6] Moss said that as a young man he was fond of 'life's diversions' and one afternoon spent some time with his friends in an Ale House, and was waited upon by a young widow, Mary Robinson. She invited him upstairs for a bottle of strong ale and he was surprised to wake up in her bed next morning. Sometime later, she sent some strong-armed 'brothers' to his home to tell him she was 'with child'. He was coerced into marriage but after the wedding the 'so called brothers' told him she was already pregnant before he had his pleasure. He left and went to London. Eleven years later, a clergyman advised that his marriage was no longer valid and Moss married again, had five children, then his wife died. He then married Mrs. Batchelor, who after he left for the Bahamas, wanted to marry someone else and thus charged him with bigamy.[7]

Of greater interest was Moss' conversion to religion by John Wesley in 1740. This rebirth of Moss took place in 'The Foundry', known as 'the womb of Methodism' and owned by the 'midwife', John Wesley.[8] He entered the itinerancy after accompanying Wesley on a preaching tour to Newcastle in 1744 and was later ordained into the Anglican ministry.[9] Hence Moss, who kept up a lifetime correspondence with Charles Wesley, was really a Methodist at the time when Wesleyans were still within the Anglican tradition. Thus, the next missionary, Rev. Thomas Robertson, could say that a dissenting minister, a 'Disciple of Mr. Wesley', had taught and preached his Wesleyan doctrine to the people at Harbour Island.[10]

The USPG gave strict guidelines for the kind of society they thought would establish the Kingdom of Heaven on earth. The Anglican minister had to lead an orderly life, observe all canonical requirements and diligently perform his duties of preaching and catechizing. The church warden was to keep the church fabric in good repair, the pulpit and ornaments clean, and the accounts in order. Moss was also to take on the duties usually performed by an Archdeacon in censoring those members who absented themselves from church, left their pews early, neglected to take communion or broke the Sabbath. As a minister, he was to admonish brawlers and ne'er-do-wells, parents of unbaptized children, married people who lived apart and unmarried people who lived together. He also had to ensure that schoolteachers were licensed, wills were approved and judgments of oath taken of persons protesting innocence. Moss, as constable and justice, dealt with wrongdoing, and as the church pastor he dealt with omission and frailty. In turn the obligations of the citizen were to conduct one's trade in the manner prescribed by common and statuary law, to serve a turn in unpaid parochial office, to clear out ditches and repair roads, to present one's neighbours for their sins, to eat fish on Fridays and during Lent. The hierarchy of command was the King, the Lords Proprietors then the Governor.

The letters and notitia parochial, written by Moss, clearly reflected the USPG guidelines as if he had them on his table as he wrote. Especially humourous was the contrast Moss observed between the inhabitants of Harbour Island and those of Eleuthera. All the communicants in Harbour Island had converted from a disorderly and unchristian course to a life of Christian purity, meekness and charity while the people of Eleuthera stupefied their senses with drinking spirituous liquors to excess and even the magistrates were profane to the highest degree.[11] However Moss worked surely and steadily, built a church, formed a vestry and made provision for the poor.[12] By 1772, he was able to report that Richard Curry, a communicant, had become very useful at reading prayers while he was absent ministering to the people of Eleuthera.[13] In spite of his alleged bigamy, Moss was clearly very successful in establishing religion in Harbour Island and St. John's Parish. In the words of the petition of sixty parishioners, certified by the leader of the militia, Samuel Higgs, JP:

> … his constant and unwearied attention to the duties of his mission has had the best effects on the religion and morals of his parishioners, whilst his regular and upright manner of living has been an excellent lesson for their example.[14]

During the Loyalist period, a 1795 Act of the Legislature divided the Bahamas into parishes.[15] In the new arrangement, St. Patrick's Parish took in the eastern settlements of Eleuthera: Governor's Harbour, Palmetto Point, Savannah Sound, the Bullards, Tarpum Bay and Rock Sound while St. John's Parish comprised the North Eleuthera settlements: Harbour Island, Governor's Bay, the Bogue, the Current and the Bluff. St. John's Parish had four more Anglican missionaries between 1787 and 1806: Thomas Robertson and Philip Dixon, who both died in office, William Gordon, who was removed following a petition from the inhabitants and Henry Jenkins, who transferred to St. Matthew's, Nassau. In 1806, St. John's Parish Church was destroyed by a hurricane and the following year the USPG withdrew from the Bahamas and did not return until after Emancipation.[16]

Towards the end of the eighteenth century, the Bishop of London, Dr. Beilby Porteus, whose portfolio included Anglican work overseas, was instrumental in forming 'The Incorporated Society for the Conversion,

Religious Instruction and Education of the Negroes'. This missionary outreach to the slaves and free blacks was first undertaken by the United Brethren (Moravians) and Methodists. Unfortunately, the first of these new Methodist preachers was not welcomed by the Harbour Island inhabitants, who were attached to the established church and were insulted by his intrusion.

> He had the effrontery to demand the key of the Church from the Church Warden, who refused to do so. None of the settlers took the least bit notice of him and he was left to walk the beach until night. At last one of the inhabitants sent to him saying 'you should have bed and victuals for tonight but you must take yourself off early in the morning on the vessel to Nassau'.[17]

Much more successful was William Turton, who arrived in Nassau in October 1800 and first visited Harbour Island in 1805. He was to become, along with John Rutledge and William Dowson, architect of the Methodist Church in Eleuthera and Harbour Island. The composition of the 703 Bahamian members of the Wesleyan Society in 1813 was, New Providence: 54 white and 267 black; Eleuthera: 232 white and 138 black; Harbour Island: 11 white and 22 black. In one year the Harbour Island membership rose to 54 white and 150 black and by 1820 the membership was 412 comprising of 229 white and 183 black. Turton, writing from Harbour Island to London informs the Methodist Missionary Society:

> The congregation are very rejoicing and lively. Some women are very attentive and deserve praise. Some black people have made progress but they need teachers. Harbour Island is small. There are no large plantations containing slaves but in general the people possess a few slaves, who with their own labours procure them a living.[18]

He found the following to be the most respectable characters: William Mather Esq. the First Magistrate, a friend to our missionaries; Joseph Ingraham Esq; another magistrate, possessing slaves and a member of the Wesleyan Society; Capt. Christopher Fisher, an old sea captain who had resided there many years, sailing among the islands, America and Cuba; Mr. John Saunders, possessing slaves and a little plantation on Harbour Island, who loaned the Society money to build a chapel; Samuel Kemp, possessing slaves and a little plantation.[19]

Turton's statement, *'they need teachers'*, highlighted the growing problem of education in Harbour Island at the beginning of the nineteenth century. The first known attempt at formal education was in 1729, by

Samuel Flavell, 'a sober person, who reads the prayer book daily at Harbour Island to interest children, making it his whole employment with what books he has of his own'.[20] In 1763, Rev. Carter reported that the people of Harbour Island had built a house for a school and place of public worship and Benjamin Russell, who 'writes with a tolerable hand, reads tolerably well, and has some small knowledge of Arithmetick, has by my persuasion been prevailed upon to keep school and teach the children…and he has not less than 40 children….'[21] John Petty, a 'worthless man, who was formerly a surgeon on a privateer', supplanted Russell.[22] The Harbour Island School entered a state of stability with the appointment of William Lewis, which was to last until 1781. Rev. Thomas Robertson, on his arrival at Harbour Island in 1786, found the church bare of furniture and that, although many could read, the education of children was very much neglected. He taught both black and white children until his death in 1792.[23] The schoolroom at that time was on Lot 100, granted by Lord Dunmore, located on the corner of Bay and Church Streets, and presently occupied by Doris' Dry Goods Store and Dunmore Rentals.

The Education Act of 1795 sought to establish schools in several islands and provide duly qualified schoolmasters, who were of good morals and sober life, skilled to teach English, Latin, Writing, Arithmetic and Merchant Accounts. At Harbour Island the Rev. William Gordon applied for the post of schoolmaster as he had Latin, and the regular teacher, John Cook, was employed as his assistant because he had no Latin. Again the school did not last long and too few students were taught. The burgeoning population of children under 14 years of age, the concentration on war and privateering and the withdrawal of the USPG left Harbour Island without adequate instruction. As Rev. Dixon observed of his parishioners:

> To me they are civil, obliging and inoffensive, with each other, they are at constant variance, they appear as proud, as poor, no police, no regulations no power of coercion… the slaves seem more desirous of instruction than their masters are that they should receive it. It takes up too much of their time and will put them above slavery… Schoolmasters we have none.[24]

The third hat worn by the Rev. William Gordon who gloated that 'gentlemen with more than a hundred slaves will have to obey me', was that of Justice of the Peace:

> The Governor (Dunmore) does honour to Anglicans in this respect that he inserts the name of the clergymen in the commission of 'Justices of Peace'.[25]

But Gordon was not up to the wrath of Mr. and Mrs. Joseph (King) Curry as he tried to sentence their valuable slave Prince and 3 others to 39 lashes for sexual misconduct with a female slave. Gordon and Constable Uriah Saunders found that they were ineffectual against the wiles and influence of the leading citizens of Harbour Island as Attorney General Moses Franks overturned the judgment. This apparent miscarriage of justice highlighted another problem, the lack of a suitable judicial system.

Traditionally, the Justice of the Peace was the Harbour Island Representative to the House of Assembly in Nassau. The name of one of the first representatives, Seaborn Pinder, gives us a clue to the occupations of the men chosen to represent Harbour Island – men born to the sea, captains, merchants and privateers. This is particularly true of the late eighteenth century when privateering was big business and most Harbour Island Representatives were privateers themselves and owned or had shares in privateering vessels. Among them were Richard Sweeting, Samuel Higgs, Ridley Pinder, Rush Tucker, John Miller, Robert Bell, Anthony Roxburgh, Robert Rumer, James Kelly, Edward Shearman, Henry Greeneslade and Robert Elliot. Then at the beginning of the nineteenth century, Loyalists such as John Ferguson, Frederick Fine, William Edgecombe, Walter Finlay and James Malcolm took over. These men enjoyed the benefits of Harbour Island but were rarely present to perform their judicial duties. Consequently, in the early 1800s local magistrates were employed. Of particular interest is the first magistrate, the long-serving William Mather, a former schoolmaster, who named one of his slaves Jedburgh after his home-town on the Scottish Border with England. Another long serving magistrate was William Smith, who in the absence of a minister performed most of the rites of passage.

The first two Anglican Dioceses were established in the West Indies in 1824: the Diocese of Jamaica included the Bahamas and the settlements in the Bay of Honduras, and the Diocese of Barbados included the Leeward and Windward Islands, Trinidad and Guiana. This gave a decided impetus to the work of the Church, which set about rectifying the discriminatory practices found in the ministrations of the Church to whites and blacks. At the same time the Methodists in the West Indies were instructed from England to preach the Gospel to the coloured population. In Harbour Island the Methodists were able to comply but the Anglicans would have to wait until the abolition of slavery. At Emancipation the British Government was to provide a Negro Education Grant of 25,000 pounds annually to be used to further missionary work among freed slaves in the West Indies, and this was to be administered largely through Church programmes for education and social welfare. From this grant the 30 by 20 foot Harbour Island Free School received 250 pounds each year.[26]

Liberated Africans in the Bahamas seemed to take full advantage of opportunities offered to them. The small group in Harbour Island regularly attended divine worship and Sunday school.[27] The Liberated Africans at Grants Town, Nassau, had formed a Friendly Society, a self-help organization, designed to help African solidarity and provide benefits for the sick, aged, widows and orphans, and a fitting and stylish burial for each of its members. Governor Colebrooke encouraged all ex-slaves to form Friendly Societies and steadily these societies increased throughout the islands, giving the members a sense of belonging and the opportunity to provide their own leaders. In Harbour Island, the United Friendly Society, The Anglo Burial Society, The Oddfellows and The Good Samaritans not only provided welfare but also took a vibrant part in social events such as Emancipation Day, Queen Victoria's Birthday, Regattas and the visits of the Governor or other dignitaries. These were lively events and in particular the President of the United Friendly Society would march dressed in a red coat and a cocked hat leading a drum corps with other members waving banners.

Special (Stipendiary) Magistrates were sent out from England to see that the provisions of Apprenticeship were enforced. They took on the wider role of assisting the local magistrates and supervising the building of gaols and schools. Stipendiary Magistrate, Thomas Ripley Winder, appointed Constable Benjamin Albury to take circuits and report monthly on the state of Harbour Island, Spanish Wells, The Bluff, Current Settlement and Pitman's Cove.[28] As well as the Harbour Island Free School with 52 scholars, there were 5 Wesleyan Sunday Schools. With a population of 351 children under the age of 14, Winder recommended that the community needed 5 schools and 5 teachers.[29] In 1835, a spirit of co-operation prevailed as Winder assisted Rev. William Strachan in the opening of the new St. John's Parish Church. Mr. Croft, the Methodist missionary, suspended the regular service at the Wesley Chapel, brought along his congregation and assisted with the music.[30] A new era, the halcyon days, was about to begin and Harbour Island was to become a foundry that would cast men and women of strong character.

Rev. William Strachan, the Rector of St. Matthew's Anglican Chuch, Nassau, had trained for the priesthood a young man named William Kelsall Duncombe, whose great grandfather, Nehemiah Duncombe, had been a successful privateer; his grandfather, Thomas, a Representative of the House of Assembly; and his father, Robert, a Representative for Harbour Island and a Police Magistrate. His mother, Eliza, was the daughter of William Bellinger Kelsall, a prominent Loyalist. Rev. W. K. Duncombe married Sarah Anne Albury of Harbour Island and their son, William, became an Anglican priest, and their daughter Elizabeth married Rev. Strombom, who was to become another loving and devoted minister of St. John's Parish in Harbour Island for many years.

Rev. W. K. Duncombe, the first Bahamian priest, worked tirelessly to evangelize the communities of North Eleuthera, first as a catechist from 1834 and then as priest in 1839. He was instrumental, along with Samuel Sears Johnson, in forming the Branch Bible Society and the Temperance Society and he initiated church-sponsored education by building an infant school on Harbour Island. Duncombe seemed to be inspired by the progress made in England by the Oxford Movement, which sought to return from the 'high and dry', pious, sober, austere worship of the 1662 Prayer Book to the catholic doctrines of the early church fathers with apostolic succession and a revival of elaborate ritual and symbolic decoration with crosses, candles, incense and bells to bring colour and emotion to the drab lives of the poor. He was also a subscribing member of the Colonial and Continental Church Society of Newfoundland, which not only was a source of much needed financial aid, but fuelled controversy by emphasizing division between the catholic 'church party' and the simpler 'evangelical party'. These divisions took root and conflicts of 'churchmanship' raged for the rest of the nineteenth century in England and her colonies, including the Bahamas.

Duncombe saw the need for more clerical assistance and a local ministry. He felt that the employment of locals as priests in every large Bahamian settlement would be more economical and that these locals would have fewer health problems than Europeans. The rate at which some ministers, fresh from England, succumbed to tropical diseases was alarming. In the short space of a dozen years, the Methodists had lost seven ministers connected to Harbour Island and several members of their family.[31] He was given leave to establish the first Bahamian Seminary at Harbour Island to train catechists prior to ordination. Due to Duncombe's foresight, the Bahamas produced several prominent priests, notably, Samuel Minns Junior, the first coloured Bahamian priest, William Sweeting, the first black Bahamian priest and Jeremiah J. S. Higgs, who served loyally at San Salvador and built 17 Bahamian Anglican Churches.[32]

Although Rev. Duncombe's efforts to promote Anglicanism were gallant and influential to the Bahamas in general, the Anglican presence in Harbour Island, Eleuthera and Abaco remained inferior to that of the Methodists, which had flourished during the absence of the established church. In 1852, Methodist missionary Thomas Pearson reported that of a population of 1,840 persons in Harbour Island, 'With the exception of a very small number connected with the Episcopal Church, the whole are under our influence and instruction'.[33] St. John's Parish virtually became the Harbour Island District taking in Abaco, Spanish Wells and the Cove. By 1853, Methodist Missionary John Hartwell was able to say:

> I am forced at Harbour Island to look at Methodism in a new light. It is the dominant religion... the system is quite equal to its position and entirely worthy of it... English clergymen have real influences in the Out Islands of the Bahamas...Methodism in these new circumstances is in some dangers from those evils, which usually attend all churches when they obtain such a station.[34]

It would appear that Hartwell must have looked into a crystal ball as future events proved him to be correct.

Governor Bayley spoke of a race of poor, proud and thriftless whites residing in the eastern part of Nassau, in Abaco and in Harbour Island, its origin popularly attributed to buccaneers and pirates. 'They dislike menial agricultural labour and escape extreme poverty by fishing and wrecking, they reject education and although they admit negroes to share in the labours, dangers and prizes of wrecking, it admits them no share in the ordinary communion or social enjoyment of life.'[35] The problems that brought grief to Hartwell in Harbour Island were the demoralizing influence of wrecking, the prejudice of colour, five licensed liquor shops bringing fearful intemperance and the estrangement of nearly all the youth of both sexes from the Church of God. In spite of all these ills, Bayley avers: 'But still all is not gloom; we have on the whole a good society. Our spacious and magnificent Chapel is well attended and we have a good many tokens of good from our Heavenly Father'.[36]

There were white and black men and women in the community, who followed the Methodist tradition influenced by John Calvin. He taught that it was the will of God that all men must work to fashion the Kingdom of Heaven on earth. Men were not to lust after wealth, possessions or easy living but were to reinvest their profits for the glory of God. And not all wreckers were dishonest; many read their Bible whilst at sea waiting for wrecks and many were commended by the Royal Humane Society for heroic action in the saving of lives. As Harbour Islanders grew wealthy from the produce of the land and sea, they contributed willingly to build magnificent churches to the glory of God and others gave of the sweat of their brow.

> At Current and Bluff the chapels have opened. At Harbour Island the 86 foot by 66 foot chapel has commenced. The community have contributed $2000 and 150 persons, male and female are gratuitously employed; some preparing lime in kilns, some hoisting stones out of the quarry and conveying them to the building and others seeking sand and water. It is great work, and takes up much of my time and attention, but with the blessing of God in the work

of our hands, we go on and fear not, trusting for every needful blessing.[37]

The spirit of cooperation did not last once the chapel, with seating for 1,000 people, was completed in 1843 as 'bickering and heartburning' raged between black and white over the situation of purchased pews. The question of colour plagued the Methodist Chapel for many years until eventually in 1873, two 'African' preachers from Key West induced coloured members to form a separate chapel[38] and so, in 1879, Ebenezer Methodist Chapel was built up on the site now occupied by Willie's Tavern and two Methodist ministers, Elijah Sumner and Fred Smith, each conducted a society on Harbour Island.

At the same time, about 60 disillusioned coloured people from the Methodist Society formed a Baptist Church. The leader was a catechist, discharged for drunkenness and infamous acts.[39] From that time the Native Baptists retained a small presence in Harbour Island and the Mount Olivet Baptist Church had a congregation of 30 people in 1927.[40] Table 12.1 shows that the Baptist congregation fell from 37 to just 15 between 1943 and 1953.

Methodist Minister, F. Moon, reported the visit from an agent of Plymouth Brethren to Current, Spanish Wells and Harbour Island.[41] Cecil Cartwright confirmed that this was William Holder, sometimes called 'the crazy preacher', after whom the sect gained the name of Holderites. From 1880, the Holderites held services in private homes and by the Up Yonder Shipyard at Harbour Island until they were able to build their 'Halls'.[42] Nassau merchant Thaddeus George Johnson built the first 'Bible Truth Hall' on Harbour Island and willed it to the Brethren on his death in 1921.[43] Of course the Brethren were disliked by the Methodist Missionaries as they caused division in the Church and George Lester remarked that 'the Brethren were of the darkest description and a score have joined from here and taken a wicked attitude toward the Church'.[44] Cartwright told the story of the Spanish Wells man who said of Holder:

> I wish some hailstones would fall from the sky and split his bald head open. A few nights later some large hailstones did fall. Instead of Holder, the hailstones fell on the head of the man who had wished him evil and injured him so severely that he died.

After this incident the Brethren spread like wildfire through Spanish Wells and North Eleuthera.[45] A small Brethren group remained faithful at Harbour Island as Table 12.1 shows. On Dunmore Street, about 50 yards south of the Wesley Methodist Church, the Bible Truth Hall, under Brethren preacher,

Mr. Knapp in the 1930s, operated until the 1980s, when the lack of members closed it down.

Meanwhile, St. John's Anglican Church was again destroyed in the 1866 hurricane but Major Cumberland of the Royal Engineers, the architect of St. Margaret's, designed the new replacement church with a neat little bell tower. There was general admiration of the strong construction with the best material, neatly finished by the contractor, Mr. Benjamin Wood. The Diocese of Nassau had been founded in 1861 and its Lord Bishop, Rev. Addington Robert Peel Venables, Rural Dean W. K. Duncombe, Rev. Strombom and several other priests celebrated the Holy Sacrament on Ascension Day, 1868, to open the new St. John's Parish Church.

Despite this competition, the Methodist domination continued throughout the nineteenth century and Magistrate L. D. Powles wrote that:

> The Wesleyan Methodists were the wealthiest, the best organised, and perhaps on the whole, the most influential religious body in the Bahamas.[46]

This was certainly true in Harbour Island as the returns for average attendance in 1895 showed that the main Wesley church had 650 souls and Ebenezer 200 souls, while the average attendance at the St. John's Anglican Church was only 80 souls.[47]

Harbour Island schoolteacher, Marion Johnson, baptized a Methodist but a catechist and sacristan in the Anglican Church, after reading Roman Catholic literature, decided she would like to be baptized again as a Roman Catholic. She took the mail boat to Nassau to talk to Father Chrysostum OSB, who told her, 'If you want to be baptized you have to live a Catholic life'.[48] At first he refused as Harbour Island had no Catholic priest but she persisted and the next day he baptized her. There was a long-standing prejudice against the Roman Catholic Church in the Bahamas and Father Chrysostum felt that it would never be removed unless a Roman Catholic mission was established in Harbour Island, the former home of many leading Bahamians. In 1920, Father Bonaventure Hansen OSB, after spending 15 years in North Dakota, arrived in the Bahamas. After Father Bonaventure had been a short time in Nassau, Father Chrysostum asked him the favour of opening a mission in Harbour Island, 'to break the backbone of Protestantism in the islands'.[49] Father Bonaventure held the first mass on Harbour Island, in the home of Marion Johnson and her friend Hattie Thompson, on 7 Feb 1921, later to become the Little Boarding House.

A headline in the *Nassau Daily Tribune* of 8 July 1943 read: *Brilander in Canadian Army Chaplain Service*. 'Rev. Carl Albury has been assigned to the Pacific Command, Combined Operations School. His talented younger sister Carrie Albury is now 3rd in Command of the Sisters of Service and her advancement is remarkable'.[50] The conversion of the whole Albury family had been Father Bonaventure's second success. The vocation of Carrie and Carl and the faith of Marion and Hattie were said to be the two cornerstones of the new Catholic Church on Harbour Island, which very quickly built up a following and within 5 years had 200 conversions.[51]

In November 1921, Father Chrysostom purchased four pieces of property for a church, rectory, convent and school and a century-old, battered shell of a house as a home for the Sisters of Charity. The Sisters, Mary Giovanni, Maria Agatha Sissler, Catherine Maria Snee, Mary Regina Lynch and Maria Rose O'Neill, arrived in Harbour Island in late January 1922 and met bigotry and prejudice against them. But gradually, 'the locals accepted these smiling tenderhearted women as they won over the people by their charity and long suffering patience'.[52] Life was very primitive at the St. Vincent's Convent where rainwater had to be collected in large tubs and heated on a kerosene stove and their only chairs had to be carried from the chapel to the refectory and to their bedrooms at night. On 2 February 1922, the new combined chapel and schoolhouse on Harbour Island was dedicated and Father Bonaventure assumed charge. Three months later the first 4 converts to the Catholic faith were baptized on Harbour Island.[53] As predicted, the Harbour Island mission was an important step, and as Table 12.1 shows, by 1953, Roman Catholicism was the most popular religious denomination on that island.

Pentecostal Churches came to the Bahamas about the year 1910 and The Church of God started in Harbour Island in 1928. At first services were held in private homes and then the Oddfellow's Hall was used for a short period of time. Table 12.1 shows that by 1953 the attendance had grown to 118 and in 1955, the Church of God was built on Chapel Street. About 200

Table 12.1 Religious Affiliation in the Census of 1943 and 1953 in the N. W. Bahamas[54]

Denomination	Harbour Isl. 1943	Harbour Isl. 1953	Spanish Wells 1943	Spanish Wells 1953	Abaco & Cays 1943	Abaco & Cays 1953	Eleuthera 1943	Eleuthera 1953	New Prov. 1943	New Prov. 1953
Anglican	244	223	19	3	541	569	1765	1585	7846	13145
Roman Catholic	177	330	1	8	5	52	232	349	4881	9770
Methodist	204	201	338	365	711	519	2415	2145	3216	4057
Baptist	37	15	0	1	1017	1244	946	828	8359	12185
Brethren	NA	20	NA	289	NA	429	NA	188	NA	1434
Church of God	NA	118	NA	0	NA	296	NA	274	NA	2129
Others	85	25	287	9	921	210	725	564	3246	2158
Not Stated	21	4	11	11	224	39	302	37	1584	665
None	1	4	9	0	22	39	43	40	259	307
Total	769	840	665	636	3461	3407	6430	6070	29391	46125

people presently attend the Church of God and there is a Haitian Church of God on Pitt Street. In the last few years, the Church of God of Prophecy has been established on Duke Street. Some inhabitants of Harbour Island follow the religion of the Seventh Day Adventists and meet in private homes, the Public Library or go over to the Bluff, where there is a larger congregation with a church. And at Kingdom Hall adjoining Arthur's Bakery, a small group of Jehovah's Witnesses worships.

When Turton arrived in the Bahamas, there was a low general standard of literacy, no educational system and a lack of professionalism among teachers.[55] In 1817, Mr. Langley was the master at the Harbour Island Day School but by 1826 the Government discontinued teachers' salaries at Harbour Island, Eleuthera and Abaco. In 1817, Mrs. Wilson, motivated by 'the desire to do a little good', started a Methodist day school for poor children at Harbour Island to supplement the Sunday Schools implemented by Turton. Samuel Kemp, in a letter to the Methodist Missionary Society, praised the work of the Sunday Schools:

> … there is a few blacks that know nothing of the word of God, nor not so much as a letter of the alphabet now are able to see the word of God for themselves.[56]

In 1829, the Harbour Island Day School, taught by Paul Lightbourne, was re-established by the Board of Public Instruction, using the Madras System as the official mode of education. Table 12.2 charts the progress of the school between 1829 and 1940, showing the maximum and minimum attendance for each period of instruction. At first, 'the poverty of the people, subject of caste and the difficulty of finding persons wishing to become teachers to forward the erection of schools and the lack of daily supplies were the main obstacles to education'.[57] The requirement, in 1836, that all scholars were to be taught the liturgy and catechism of the established church was vehemently protested by Rev. Thomas Lofthouse, Chairman of the Methodist Church in the Bahamas.[58] And the Act forming the Board of Education in 1841 was strongly protested by Presbyterian Minister, William McClure and Baptist Minister, Henry Capron on the grounds that it was biased toward the Anglican Church.[59] The 1841 Act was overturned in 1847 by a ruling that both Board members and the school curriculum were to be non-sectarian. These squabbles and a lack of funds prevented the Board of Education from functioning effectively and Governor John Gregory reported in 1850:

> On account of the Board of Education's inability to erect schoolhouses… at Harbour Island they are obliged to hire the best buildings; but these are totally unsuited to the system of instruction

used. The School at Harbour Island is 20 foot long by 14 foot wide and the new desks have had to be shortened from 16 ft to 12 to fit the room.[60]

This schoolhouse was totally inadequate as the population of children on Harbour Island was rapidly expanding. The number of children under 10 before emancipation had been 350 and in 1841 the number rose to 500, whereas Table 12.2 shows that in the 1840s, as few as 57 and no more than 138 attended the Harbour Island Day School.

The 1865 Board of Education Report by Inspector William Job showed Harbour Island Day School as a third-class school in a most wretched state of inefficiency, with order and discipline defective… 'I am afraid that many of our teachers sit down quietly, or retreat before their difficulties, instead of manfully rising and doing battle. I am, however, firmly convinced that a judicious, earnest, efficient teacher, who understands and loves his work, would succeed in spite of the obstacle of bitter class prejudice'.[61] The next year Mr. and Mrs. George Cole arrived in Harbour Island to find that the schoolhouse had been blown down in the hurricane and conditions were worse than ever. In a hired room the Coles succeeded in enrolling 119 boys and were encouraged by the promise of a new Girls School, which opened in 1869. A new schoolroom was built on 'a more central, elevated and salubrious site'. As Table 12.2 shows, enrolment greatly increased and by 1872, the Harbour Island Boys School was considered unquestionably the best under Board direction as 103 boys under Mr. Cole, assisted by pupil teacher Thomas W. Sweeting and several monitors, achieved a satisfactory state of proficiency.[62] As evidence of conscientious and careful teaching, George Cole produced three teachers in the service of the board and T. W. Sweeting was selected as the next Master of the Harbour Island Day School. Mrs. Cole succeeded in keeping 20 intelligent girls between 16 to 18 years old in school and these young ladies in all probability became private school teachers on Harbour Island.

In this Victorian golden age of economic prosperity due to the protestant work ethic, education seemed to blossom. Alongside the success of the public school a number of private schools opened to cater to wealthier families. Attendance reached a peak at the turn of the century but declined during the war and disappeared when the Roman Catholic and Wesleyan Schools opened. (See Table 12.3.)

During the period 1890 to 1916, the Government of the Bahamas did not contribute to secondary schools and only in Nassau was secondary education provided by religious denominations. In 1912, several Harbour Island Methodist laymen, who 'wanted an Englishman to train their children in English ways' signed a guarantee of 120 pounds for four years, and Rev.

Table 12.2 Harbour Island day school: teachers and students' attendance[63]

| Teachers | Years | Maximum Attendance |||| Minimum Attendance ||||
		Yr	Boy	Girl	Tot.	Yr	Boy	Girl	Tot.
Paul Lightbourne	1829–32	1831	35	44	79	1832	28	33	61
Thomas Higgs	1838–47	1844			138	1847			57
Mr & Mrs Munro	1849	1849	67	18	85	1849	67	18	85
Mr Walton	1850–52	1850	89	18	117	1852	121	24	145
John Camplejohn	1853–56	1856			100	1853			70
Mrs Armbrister	1857–58	1857			100	1858			100
J B Hall	1859–66	1859			100	1863			63
George & Mrs Cole	1867–79	1875	127	95	222*	1867	100	50	150
T W & A Sweeting	1880–81	1880	158	120	278	1881	133	195	238
E A Sweeting & Mrs C J Roberts	1882–85	1884	163	164	327	1885	120	158	278**
Unknown	86–1910	1891	143	147	290	1902	62	45	107
Wm E Higgs	1910–20	1912	109	89	198	1921	107	21	128
C W Curry	1921–22	1922	112	76	188	1922	112	76	188
J S Hall	1923–26	1925	92	80	172	1924	50	40	90
J A Hughes	1927	1927	66	50	112	1927	66	50	112
G A Mansfield	1928–29	1928	78	54	132	1929	73	50	123
Unknown	1930–36	1931	47	29	76	1933	57	47	104
Marion C Johnson	1937–40	1937	54	42	96	1940	51	41	92

* 1875, St. John's Anglican Private School, Teacher J. Kemp: 12 boys, 13 girls, Total 25 1876, St. John's Anglican Private School, Teacher J. Kemp: Total 63
** 1884, 5 Private Teachers: Mary E. Albury, Elizabeth Roberts, Dorah Cleare, Julie Saunders, Maria Roberts, 40 boys, 66 girls, 106 Total

Table 12.3 Private schools in Harbour Island[64]

Year	Schls	Boys	Girls	Year	Schls	Boys	Girls	Year	Schls	Boys	Girls
1884	5	40	66	1904	5	37	156	1916*	1	7	6
									3 gia	17	28
1887		28	29	1905	5	21	49	1917	3	19	35
1891	4	34	48	1906	3	9	42	1918	4	21	33
1893	4	34	48	1907	4	27	35	1919	4	23	42
1895	3	11	21	1908	5	23	55	1920	4	27	44
1896	1	18	18	1909	4	24	41	1924	1**	8	12
1898	7	25	45	1910	6	18	72	1925	1	3	11
1899	5	9	44	1911	3	24	50	1926	1	2	8
1900	6	25	77	1912	5	24	50	1927	1	2	11
1901	6	28	78	1913	5	17	44	1928	1	3	8
1902	6	32	58	1914	4	14	8	1929	1	2	8
1903	3	26	33	1915*	1	12	9				
					3 gia	15	27				

* These 3 schools must have been given grant-in-aid due to war conditions
** Both the Roman Catholics and Wesleyans were also operating schools at this time

Frank Poad was appointed as pastor and teacher to Harbour Island High School, which opened that year with 12 white pupils between 8 and 25 years old. The school only lasted four years as the guarantors were unable to fulfill their financial obligations. The school was very successful as 38 out of 39 students passed the College of Preceptors examination. In Scripture, Carl Albury, who later became the first Bahamian priest in the Roman Catholic Church, achieved the top grade in the world, scoring 195 out of 200.[65] In 1922, the Methodist Synod granted aid to the Harbour Island Elementary School, which was connected to the Wesleyan Society. Table 12.4 shows that this school was poorly attended and the Synod withdrew its support when there was a rift in the church and the missionary's wife, a teacher at the school, left.[66]

Before the Sisters of Charity arrived, Marion Johnson had gathered together 16 students, all non-Catholics, for the new St. Vincent's Academy. The students had the additional duty in the afternoon of pushing the desks and chairs to the walls to convert the room to a church and in the morning re-arranging the furniture to start school. Within two years, the Sisters of Charity opened St. Benedict's School and operated them both for many years as free schools until in 1953, St. Vincent's Academy was discontinued and the 26 students were added to the 136 attending St. Benedict's School. Table 12.5 shows the enrolment at the Roman Catholic Schools from 1922 until 1940.

In the years following emancipation, Harbour Island prospered as a port of entry. Its stability in religion and improvement in education were evidence of social progress. But the island became a melting pot, containing

Table 12.4 Enrolment at Harbour Island Methodist Elementary School[67]

Year	Boys	Girls	Total	Male Teachers	Female Teachers	Total Teachers
1923	9	22	31	-	2	2
1924	7	15	22	1	1	2
1925	8	15	23	1	1	2
1926	5	13	18	1	1	2

Table 12.5 Enrolment at the Roman Catholic schools on Harbour Island[68]

Year	Boys	Girls	Total	Year	Boys	Girls	Total
1922			16	1931	45	55	100
1924	30	41	71	1932	31	46	77
1925	24	51	75	1933	15	19	34
1926	22	41	63	1935	44	55	99
1927	34	49	83	1937	61	81	142
1928	32	50	82	1938	57	69	126
1929	19	38	57	1939	41	46	87
1930	26	43	69	1940	43	66	109

on the one hand, wild and intemperate wreckers and on the other, those who sought a more genteel, cultural way of life based on law and order. It was felt that the consolidation of various magistrates, watchmen and parochial constables was outdated and perhaps Robert Peel's idea of a central police force had crossed the Atlantic resulting in the Police Act of 1833 to appoint salaried constables responsible to the Police Magistrate. And the Government sought to collect the revenue from the ports of entry by appointing Tidewaiters, which as the name implies were officials who waited for the ships entering and leaving on the high tide to assess the duty on their cargoes. Additionally, at larger ports, Colonial Receivers were appointed to collect revenue.

At first the Government relied upon the local Justices of the Peace and the Stipendiary Magistrates, who were paid 300 pounds per year. Fatigue, exertion, tropical conditions and the demands of being a guardian to the apprentices caused the overworked Thomas Winder to become ill. In consequence, to assist the Stipendiary Magistrate, local English Special Justices were employed at 100 pounds per year. At Harbour Island, Paul Samuel Lightbourne and Samuel Johnson helped Winder attend to the 471 male and 467 female apprentices. Additionally, in 1837, on the eve of emancipation, Jeremiah Higgs and Benjamin Harris were appointed as additional JPs. Benjamin Albury became the first salaried police constable in Harbour Island and Joseph Albury, the first salaried police jailer under the Act of 1839.

Lack of Government funds during the early 1840s meant that Harbour Island lagged behind Nassau in the area of law and order. Governor Matthews found solutions that greatly upset the inhabitants. First, he appointed ex-police constable, Thomas Conroy, the new husband of Matthew's pregnant mistress, in the dual posts of Tidewaiter and Special Magistrate. The inhabitants were outraged and called the appointment patronage and a disgrace. Then he manipulated the 1846 election to place Government officials as Representatives to the House of Assembly for Eleuthera, Abaco and Harbour Island. The Harbour Island inhabitants sent a petition to the Queen asking for the removal of Matthews and charging that the election of Provost Marshall, William Vesey Munnings and Stipendiary Magistrate F. A. Eve was unconstitutional.[69] Munnings remained for the rest of the term but William H. Pinder replaced Eve.

After many petitions, praying for an efficient police force for the protection of life and property and a safe and secure jail, an 1852 Act was passed for better administration of justice in Harbour Island, Eleuthera and San Salvador. Resident Justices were appointed in these areas and the most notable in Harbour Island were James Francis Armbrister, Julius Stafford Solomon and former teacher, George C. Camplejohn. Colonial Receiver at Harbour Island, Christopher Martenborough, former Inspector of Police, was appointed Police Magistrate at Harbour Island. Up to this point the Harbour Island jail was so small that it was only used for temporary confinement until the offenders could be sent to Nassau for trial. By 1857, a new prison was complete and occupied by prisoners. It was a two-story stone building, 34 foot by 25 foot with a shingled roof. The upper half was used as a police office and barracks and the ground floor was divided into 5 cells of between 805 and 1105 cubic feet. In the 5 years up to 1865, 339 prisoners, 87 of them females, had been confined in these cells, the males employed in weeding and repairing the roads and the females, washing and mending the prison clothes.[70]

The Out Island Commissioners Act 1908 sought to bring government officers in line with those of other colonies. The Resident Justice in each district was replaced by or promoted to Commissioner by appointment of the Governor. Those with local knowledge became First Class Commissioners at a Port of Entry and took on the extra duties of Collector of Revenue and Warehouse Keeper.[71] Such a man was Percy William Duncombe Armbrister, the first Harbour Island Commissioner and a long-serving member of the Legislative Council. Another great inhabitant of Briland, Dewees O. Johnson, son of Dr. T. W. Johnson, followed him.

The post of Family Island Administrator by the Local Government Act 1996 replaced the position of Out Island Commissioner, who automatically became Secretary of the Local Council. Election fever took the Harbour

59 Methodist Church

60 Bible Truth Hall

61 Anglican Church

62 High altar at St. John's Anglican Church

63 Roman Catholic Church

64 Haitian Church of God

65 William Christopher Barnet Johnson. His bust dominates the entrance to the House of Assembly as a testimony to the importance of religion, education, justice and good government

66 George Cole

67 Glass Window

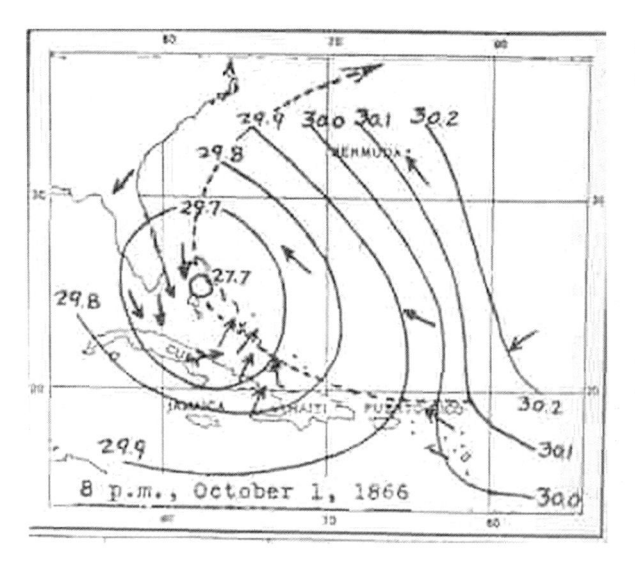

68 Chart of the track of Great Bahaman Hurricane 1866

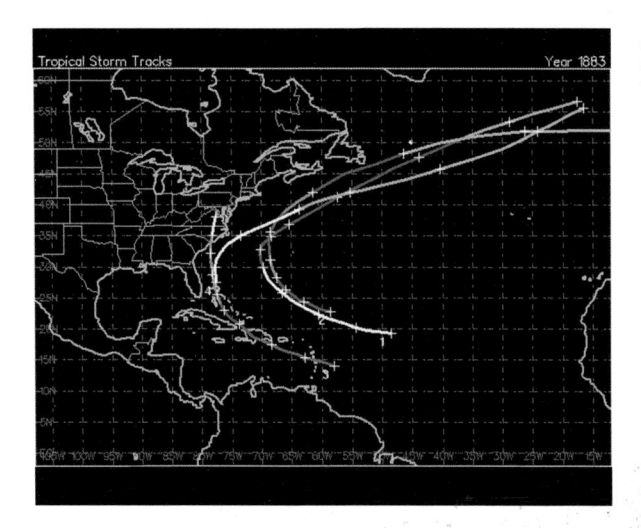

69 Chart of the track of 1883 Hurricane

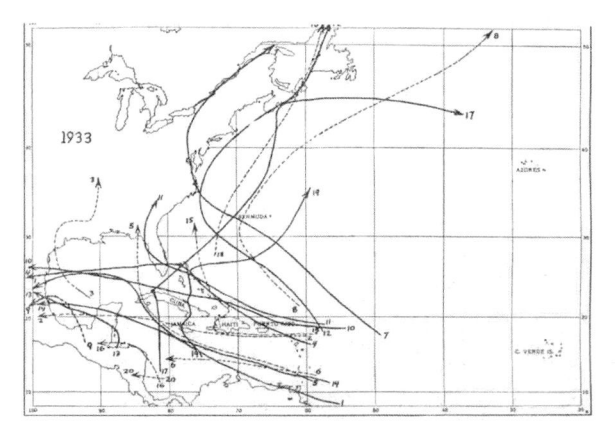

70 Chart of the track of the 1933 Hurricane

71 Cotton Hole, now gone, was a large rock, probably thrown up from the east coast during some distant and fearsome storm

72 Repair of Valentine's Dock 2004

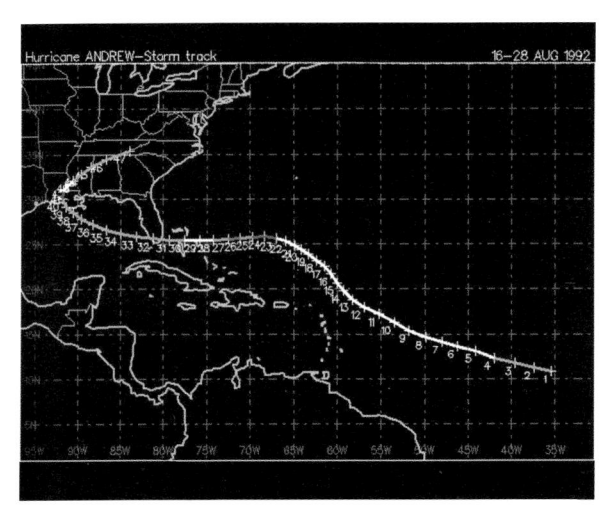

73 The track of Hurricane Andrew

74 Emancipation Day 1890

75 Father Richardson's marching band

76 Africa's Hope

77 Hauling net 1939 belonging to Harry Sweeting

78 The *Endion*

Island community by storm at the first Local Government elections in the summer of 1996. Local Government was looked upon as a blessing and the electors were advised to vote for a contestant regardless of political alliance. Unfortunately, many disregarded this advice and party politics soured many local elections. After a hard-fought contest the Harbour Island Council was made up of Glenroy D. Aranha (Chairman), Byron Bullard, Samuel M. Higgs, Nora P. Albury, Lashay Cleare, Darrel J. Johnson, Elouise D. Knowles and Harvey Roberts, who later became the second Chairman. The Government then gave special training to these officers to take care of the affairs of the island particularly in financial matters.

By the end of the Civil War in America, Harbour Island boasted a Consular Agent to the US, William S. Sears, and had become a prestigious parish and an eligible district, which not only paid higher salaries to officials but served as a stepping-stone to career advancement. More than that though, many of these officials married Harbour Island women, contributed to the local community and helped lay a foundation for progress in religion, education, justice and government for the entire Bahamas.

Just as previous Harbour Island Representatives to the House of Assembly had been connected to the premier industry, privateering, the Representatives of the 1850s were influential in the wrecking and steamship trades. Thomas K. Moore, H. R. Saunders, Manuel Menendez and his young business partner and relative through marriage, Robert H. Sawyer, dominated the House of Assembly for many years and were part of the oligarchy that led the Bahamas Government for the next 100 years. (See Appendix 14.)

In the early part of the nineteenth century, the Anglican and Presbyterian families, acting as a unit, ruled the country, with the Methodists having no influence in government. Denominational differences over the education curriculum, a ban on the use of burial grounds for non-Anglican ministers and the lack of Government funds to rebuild non-Anglican churches after the 1866 hurricane led to a split between the Anglicans and Presbyterians, whereupon the latter formed an alliance with the Methodists.

On Sunday 26 April 1868, prior to the election in Harbour Island, Methodist Minister, F. A. Moon, from the pulpit told the people that the Governor had sent down a number of men but that they were not to be daunted: 'Next week the trial will come…let there be such an outburst of loyalty, not only to Methodism but to yourselves…the Churchmen are here, they must take the consequences…the Policemen have arrived; they have come to eat your Johnny Cakes'. Hearing that over 200 Hercules Clubs had arrived that morning for use on the day of the election, Harbour Island Police Magistrate George C. Camplejohn urged Governor Rawson to send down 50 men from the 2nd WI Regiment to supplement the detachment of Police under G. A. McGregor.[72] After the election, Governor Rawson deplored Moon's actions and reported that 'in the Islands of Abaco, Harbour Island and Eleuthera, in which Methodism chiefly prevails, the members of that body united with the Native Baptists, whose coloured leader used all his influence in their favour, carried away every seat by large majorities in the two islands in which they were opposed, and in Eleuthera without a contest'.[73] The winning candidates on the highly charged Election Day at Harbour Island were Methodists, M. Menendez and S. Higgs, and Presbyterian, G. W. Higgs.

As a result of the 1868 election, the Methodists took control of the Lower House but Presbyterians controlled the Legislative and Executive Council. Robert H. Sawyer, now a Methodist Member of the House of Assembly for the Nassau City District, presented a resolution for the disestablishment and disendowment of the United Churches of England and Ireland within the Bahamas Islands and the Church of St. Andrews. The bill was eventually passed in 1869.[74] The Methodists vowed to take full control and from that time there was considerable intermarrying between the Methodist and Presbyterian groups and they almost became almost one family.

The five daughters of Manuel Menendez were married to T. P. Moore, T. P. Saunders, Dr. J. B. Albury, T. H. C. Lofthouse and T. H. C. Rae, all members of the House of Assembly in the latter part of the nineteenth century. And an anonymous letter to the *Nassau Daily Guardian*, in 1892, showed that Robert H. Sawyer, the leader of the opposition had ten relatives and many business partners in the Government.[75] Another Harbour Island dynasty marrying into the oligarchy controlling the Government of the Bahamas was the Kelly family. Patriarch James Kelly was followed into the House of Assembly by direct descendants, Allan Harcourt Kelly, Charles Gerald Trevor Kelly, Godfrey Kenneth Kelly, Basil Trevor Kelly and by intermarriage, Sir James Patrick Sands, James Patrick Sands II, Arthur Hall Sands, Harry Pickard Sands, Sir Stafford Lofthouse Sands, James Kermit Alexander Kelly, Sir George William Kelly Roberts, Noel Sawyer Roberts, Reginald Farrington and Senator Dr. Paul Albury.

The 1875 elections were again the subject of much controversy. Governor Robinson repeated the Matthew's manoeuvre of putting up two Government officials, H. E. Mosely and J. A. Culbert, who were successful in becoming Harbour Island Representatives. R. H. Sawyer and G. T. R. Kemp and their strong following in the House were antagonistic toward the 'Government Party', a disdain that was to forever remain against English officials.

In the third quarter of the nineteenth century, sponging and pineapples were the dominant industries and it is no surprise that the Harbour Island Representatives were successful in them. Sponge boat owner, J. S. Darling, represented Harbour Island for many years. The pineapple barons were J. S. Johnson and his nephew William Christopher Barnet Johnson, T. H. G. Cleare, Gilbert Alonzo Albury and Sir George H. Johnson, who was also a dentist. Sometimes life presents us with strange bedfellows and the pre-World War II era saw W. C. B. Johnson, who loathed alcohol, representing Harbour Island alongside liquor merchants Roland T. Symonette and Allan H. Kelly. From that time lawyers seem to have dominated the various Houses of the Government.

An obituary appeared in the *Nassau Daily Tribune* 4 February 1946 of J. Goodwin Roberts, 80, 'Mayor of Marsh Harbour' and a Board of Education teacher for many years. He belonged to that golden age of Harbour Island manhood that sent men to Nassau, Miami and Key West and to other places in the hemisphere to make careers for themselves and to give leadership by Brilanders a legendary character.[76] Other educators cast in that foundry were Wilton G. Albury and Professor Roger Johnson, who held the Chair of Mental and Moral Philosophy at Princeton University.

'Briland's Army drove out the Spanish from Nassau and have now come down to run it,' claimed 'a Brilander' in a letter to *The Tribune* in 1941. He listed 19 prominent men and 13 businesses from Briland in Nassau and boasted, 'We might say with gusto that we have raised doctors, lawyers, ministers, commissioners, schoolmasters and we have raised professors'.[77]

The late-1920s was generally a depressed time for the Bahamas, particularly in Nassau, and one lady demonstrated 'service above self' to promote the interests and welfare of ordinary black women. Born of parents from the Harbour Island District, the granddaughter of Police Constable William Durant, Frances Butler (nee Thompson) founded the Mother's Club, originally to relieve hurricane victims but later to help the needy by providing clothing and furniture. 'Mother' Butler was the mother of Sir Milo Butler, the first Bahamian Governor General of the Bahamas and himself a champion of the ordinary people.

Perhaps the greatest Bahamian ever cast in the Harbour Island foundry was their representative William Christopher Barnet Johnson, known as the 'Father of the House of Assembly'. He died at the age of 80 at his home in Union Street after serving 53 years in the House of Assembly, never having lost an election and missing only one session of the House, when he had to go to Miami for medical treatment. He was Deputy Speaker, then Speaker of the House and leader of a political group known as 'The Nor' West Corner Party', who met at his office regularly to discuss measures before the House and to formulate constructive policies. At a time when an appointment to the Executive Council was a great prize, Johnson twice refused it as he saw himself as the leader of the opposition. Sir Bede Clifford recommended him for the OBE without his consent and had difficulty persuading him to attend Government House to receive it.

W. C. B. Johnson was born in Harbour Island but moved to Nassau to manage the Pineapple Canning Factory on Bay Street owned by his uncle J. S. Johnson. At the same time, he managed an extensive sisal farm at the Caves and Cable Beach. When the J. S. Johnson Pineapple Canning Factory closed, W. C. B. parcelled out the company's holdings in lots and laid a foundation for the extensive real estate development in the Cable Beach area, favoured by the British and American winter residents. At the same time he opened his own small canning factory near his home on Union Street and kept the canning industry alive. During both World Wars he collected large sums of money for the Red Cross and made himself a servant in his own canning factory from 4 am until late afternoon for the War Materials Committee.

W. C. B. Johnson could have been the richest man in the country but he had only one use for money and that was to give it to the poor; to help and encourage deserving people who were unable to help themselves. He had one over-riding ambition in life and that was to give and serve to the utmost of his ability and capacity. He died as he lived – quietly.[78] This man showed that he truly believed in the teachings he learned in the Harbour Island foundry, that it was the will of God that all men must work and serve to fashion the Kingdom of Heaven on earth. His bust dominates the entrance to the House of Assembly as a testimony to the importance of religion, education, justice and good government.

Notes

1. Society for Propagation of the Gospel, Reel 1, Rev. Richard Moss to C. Wesley, 11 April 1769.
2. History of the Anglican Diocese of the Bahamas and Turks and Caicos Islands, http://www.bahams.anglican.org/diocese.html. Christ Church Cathedral dates back to 1670.
3. Ibid, Rev. Richard Carter to Rev. Bearcroft, 13 January 1761.
4. Ibid, Governor William Shirley to Rev. Bearcroft, 15 January 1761.
5. Society for Propagation of the Gospel, Reel 1, Rev. Thomas Robertson to Rev. Bearcroft, 17 June 1790.
6. Ibid, Petitions from inhabitants of New Providence and Harbour Island, 24 June 1780.
7. Ibid, Rev. Richard Moss to SPG, 30 June 1780.
8. Colbert Williams, *The Methodist Contribution to Education in the Bahamas*, Alan Sutton Publishing Ltd., 1982, pp. 11, 15.
9. *Methodist Magazine* 1798, pp. 3–8, 53–59.
10. Fulham Papers, Reel 8, Vol 15, folio 86, 17 June 1790.
11. Society for Propagation of the Gospel, Reel 1, Rev. Richard Moss to Rev. Bearcroft, 24 January 1769 and 11 April 1769.
12. Society for Propagation of the Gospel, Reel 1, Rev. Richard Moss to Rev. Bearcroft, 12 December 1769.
13. Society for Propagation of the Gospel, Reel 1, Rev. Richard Moss to Rev. Bearcroft, 10 November 1772.

14 Ibid, Petitions from inhabitants of Harbour Island, 24 June 1780.
15 Colbert Williams, *The Methodist Contribution to Education in the Bahamas,* Alan Sutton Publishing Ltd., 1982, p. 49.
16 Colbert Williams, *The Methodist Contribution to Education in the Bahamas,* Alan Sutton Publishing Ltd., 1982, p. 51.
17 Society for Propagation of the Gospel, Reel 1, Rev. J Richards to USPG, 14 January 1796.
18 MMS, File 1817–1819, Box 2, 41/39, William Turton to MMS, 31 May 1817.
19 Ibid.
20 Colbert Williams, *The Methodist Contribution to Education in the Bahamas,* Alan Sutton Publishing Ltd., 1982, p. 41.
21 Colbert Williams, *The Methodist Contribution to Education in the Bahamas,* Alan Sutton Publishing Ltd., 1982, p. 43.
22 Colbert Williams, *The Methodist Contribution to Education in the Bahamas,* Alan Sutton Publishing Ltd., 1982, p. 45.
23 Colbert Williams, *The Methodist Contribution to Education in the Bahamas,* Alan Sutton Publishing Ltd., 1982, p. 47.
24 Society for Propagation of the Gospel, Reel 2, Rev. Dixon to USPG, 4 April 1794.
25 Society for Propagation of the Gospel, Reel 2, Rev. William Gordon to USPG, 3 October 1792.
26 Schedule A of Copy of Instructions from Sir George Grey to C. J. Latrobe, esq., 5 June 1837.
27 CO 23/103/ Report of Special Justice McGregor, 1 October 1838.
28 CO 23/93/313, Thomas Winder's Report 21 May 1835.
29 CO 23/93/313, Thomas Winder's Report 21 May 1835.
30 CO 23/93/313, Thomas Winder's Report 21 May 1835.
31 John Turtle 1825, John Rutledge 1826, Charles Penny 1833, John Price 1835, Joseph Talbot 1835 and James Sherrocks 1836, Samuel S Johnson 1837.
32 Kirkley C. Sands, *The Anglican Church and Bahamian Cultural Identity, 1784–1900.* Ph.D. University of Edinburgh, 1998. Also interviews and unpublished notes of Father Irwin V McSweeney.
33 MMS, File 1853/54, Box 27, Box 219, 1349/19, Thomas Pearson to MMS, 3 April 1852.
34 MMS, File 1853/54, Box 27, Box 217, 1354/33, John Hartwell to MMS, 9 Nov 1853.
35 CO23/162/264, Governor Bayley to Duke of Newcastle, 25 April 1860.
36 MMS, File 1853/54, Box 27, Box 217, 1354/33, John Hartwell to MMS, 9 Nov 1853.
37 MMS, File 1840/45, Box 27, Box 219, 1312/11, Thomas Pearson to MMS, 8 Aug 1843.
38 MMS, File 1871/3, Box 29, Box 221, 1411/11, H. Bleby to MMS, 12 April 1873.
39 MMS, File 1871/3, Box 29, Box 221, 1411/11, H. Bleby to MMS, 12 April 1873.
40 Blue Book 1927.
41 MMS, File 1880/5, Box 29, Box 221, 1437/23, F. Moon to MMS, 20 June 1882.
42 Interview between Paul Albury and Cecil Cartwright, circa 1984.
43 Brethren Journal, *Field and Work,* 1920–21, p. 110.
44 MMS, File 11903, Box 30, Box 221, 1476/31, G Lester to MMS, 20 March 1903.
45 Interview between Paul Albury and Cecil Cartwright, circa 1984.
46 L. D. Powles, *The Land of the Pink Pearl,* (London, Sampson, Lowe, Searle & Rivington, 1888, p. 305
47 Blue Book returns for 1895.
48 Barry Coleman OSB, *Upon these Rocks, Catholics in the Bahamas,* St. John's Abbey Press, Minnesota, 1973, p. 296.
49 Barry Coleman OSB, *Upon these Rocks, Catholics in the Bahamas,* St. John's Abbey Press, Minnesota, 1973, p. 296.
50 *Nassau Daily Tribune,* 8 July 1943.

51 Barry Coleman OSB, *Upon these Rocks, Catholics in the Bahamas,* St. John's Abbey Press, Minnesota, 1973, p. 299.
52 Barry Coleman OSB, *Upon these Rocks, Catholics in the Bahamas,* St. John's Abbey Press, Minnesota, 1973, p. 300/301.
53 Barry Coleman OSB, *Upon these Rocks, Catholics in the Bahamas,* St. John's Abbey Press, Minnesota, 1973, p. 307.
54 Census Reports of The Bahamas,1943 and 1953 at Department of Archives.
55 Colbert Williams, *The Methodist Contribution to Education in the Bahamas,* Alan Sutton Publishing Ltd., 1982, p. 48.
56 Colbert Williams, *The Methodist Contribution to Education in the Bahamas,* Alan Sutton Publishing Ltd., 1982, p. 133.
57 CO 23/94/445, John Croft to Governor, 26 November 1835.
58 Colbert Williams, *The Methodist Contribution to Education in the Bahamas,* Alan Sutton Publishing Ltd., 1982, p. 152.
59 CO 23/111/296, Petition to Lord John Russell from Ministers of Church of Scotland and Baptists, 1841.
60 CO 23/135/125, Governor John Gregory's Report 15 May 1850.
61 CO 23/184/538, Board of Education Report 1865 by William Job, Inspector of Schools.
62 Votes of House of Assembly, 1872 Resident Justice Report, J. S. Solomon.
63 Compiled from the Blue Books of the years indicated.
64 Compiled from the Blue Books of the years indicated.
65 Colbert Williams, *The Methodist Contribution to Education in the Bahamas,* Alan Sutton Publishing. Ltd., 1982, p. 179.
66 Colbert Williams, *The Methodist Contribution to Education in the Bahamas,* Alan Sutton Publishing Ltd., 1982, p. 166.
67 Ibid.
68 Compiled from the Blue Books of the years indicated.
69 CO 23/131/220, Harbour Island petition to Queen Victoria, September 1848.
70 CO 23/178/326, Police Magistrate, Burnside's Report on Harbour Island Prison, 1865.
71 The Laws of the Bahamas, 1900–1913, p. 113.
72 CO 23/191/575, To Governor Rawson, from Office of Police Magistrate at HI, 26 April 1868.
73 CO 23/191/552, Rawson to Buckingham, 23 May 1968.
74 K. C. Sands, *The Anglican Church and Bahamian Cultural Identity,* Ph.D Thesis 1998, p. 264.
75 CO 23/238/430, anonymous letter to *Nassau Guardian,* 2 Sept 1892.
76 *Nassau Daily Tribune,* 4 February 1946.
77 *Nassau Daily Tribune,* 7 February 1941.
78 *Nassau Daily Tribune,* 9 January 1945.

13

The fury of nature

The tempest arose and worried me so that I knew not where to turn; eyes never beheld the seas so high, angry, and covered with foam... Never did the sky look more terrible. The people were so worn out, that they longed for death to end their terrible suffering.[1]

Columbus' description of the tempest is an experience that people in the Bahamas have faced many times over the centuries. The belief in early times was that the extensive current of wind rushing with great velocity was due to the anger of *Tempestates*, the Roman Goddess of Storms. Similarly, the word 'gale' stems from Norse word *galinn*, which is the furious storm raised up by witches. Hurricane is derived from the Taino and Mayan *Hurakan*, the God of the thunderstorm and whirlwind. The Harbour Island District has suffered greatly at times from the fury of nature, as Table 13.1 shows, through hurricanes, tornadoes, whirlwinds and surges of the sea.

A hurricane is an extremely violent whirling and spiralling tropical cyclone, shaped somewhat like a funnel, that originates in tropical regions of the North Atlantic Ocean, with wind speeds in excess of 74 mph, and, in the northern hemisphere, moves counterclockwise at speeds of 6 to 15 mph. The centre (about 14 miles in diameter) is called the eye and hurricane-force winds can extend 100 miles from the centre. Usually the hurricane season is June through to November but the Bahamas has experienced a hurricane in every month of the year.

In April of 1806, Governor Cameron reported that the Bahamas was in a state of tranquility, the garrison and community in good health.[2] By September both he and more than half of the 99th Regiment were sick and the Bahamas faced four hurricanes within a few weeks – 30 August, 'The Great Coastal Hurricane' of 14 September, 27 September and 5 October.

While recovering from fever at Royal Island with his family, Governor Cameron found himself in great danger. As the storm of 14 September raged, the roof of the house in which they were staying blew off. With great difficulty he removed his family to the cellar of the house, which was full of water. Eighteen people died, the two dwelling houses belonging to Benjamin

Table 13.1 Bahamas hurricanes highlighting Harbour Island damage

OH = Other Hurricanes that hit the Bahamas but no information that Harbour Island was hit or damaged.

Year:	Description of Damage at Harbour Island
OH	3-Oct-1780, 4-Oct-1780
21-Sep-1785	Great damage to crops, buildings and vessels, including 2 sloops of Captain Higgs
in 1789	Dunmore reports that the Anglican Church destroyed in a storm
11-Jul-1792	Severe thunderstorm damages Anglican Church
3-Oct-1796	Lost sloop *Rainbow,* Captain Albury
15-Nov-1796	5 small craft lost and houses blown down by a very severe storm.
OH	5-Sep-1801, 10-Jul-1803, 7-Sep-1804
31-Aug-1806	Church, Barracks, crops, boats and 160 houses destroyed
23-Jul-1813	Tremendous hurricane affected Harbour Island and 3 deaths at Spanish Wells
1-Aug-1813	Bad hurricane, Schooner *Dart* ashore at Current Island/hull for sale
2-Sep-1815	Seized American Schooner sunk in harbour of Harbour Island
OH	17-Oct-1816, 1-Sep-1821
13-Sep-1824	Three quarters of the houses have been destroyed
OH	20-Aug-1827, 27-Oct-1827
13-Aug-1830	All vessels in harbour damaged, many houses blown down, Commonage laid waste
OH	14-Aug-1835
2 Aug 1837	Severe but did little injury, several vessels cutting wood at Andros driven ashore
OH	5-Sep-1838, 2-Aug-1842, 5-Oct-1844, 10-Oct-1846, 22-Aug-1848
5-Apr-1850	All boats swamped, larger vessels driven ashore, a few old homes blown down
12-Sep-1851	Severe thunder storm struck 2 boats in the harbour, 2 men injured
OH	18-Aug-1853
10-Oct-1854	Schooner *J H Johnson* capsized causing death of Dr George Walter Hall
OH	25-Aug-1856, 10-Nov-1857, 16-Oct-1858, 13-Aug-1861, 27-Aug-1862, 23-Oct-1865
6-Oct-1866	St John's Church, Public Buildings, 27 houses levelled, 21 houses, 18 boats damaged
16-Aug-1871	Severe gale in the latitude of Abaco, 23 people killed. Sch. *Corine* wrecked
23-Aug-1871	Great destruction of property, the fruit and produce swept away
14-Dec-1878	Sloop *Intrepid,* Capt. Richard Cleare wrecked at 6 Shillings, *Argo* driven ashore
OH	20-Aug-1880
8-Sep-1883	Walls, fences, trees blown down, 15 houses destroyed, about 100 lives lost
OH	23-Oct-1883
19-Apr-1884	Whirlwind blew clothes away from the washing lines
OH	6-Dec-1887, 17-Sep-1888, 13-Jul-1891
20-Aug-1893	Portion of the wharf washed away
11-Oct-1893	Sea rose and overflowed onto the land
OH	11-Sep-1896, 10-Sep-1899, 2-Jul-1901, 10-Sep-1903
1-Feb-1905	Schooner *Brothers,* Capt. Henry Kelly narrow escape en route to Jacksonville

11-Mar-1905	Destroying and damaging houses of the poor, temporary scarcity of food.
8-Apr-1905	8-Apr-1905, 29-Jul-1908
14-Oct-1908	7 houses, fruit trees blown down, *Beatrice, Hattie Darling* scuttled to save them
OH	9-Jul-1919, 23-Oct-1923
24-Jul-1926	Damage to fields, 2 old houses blown down. Commissioner asks relief for poor
25-Sep-1926	Much damage, Commissioner asks relief for poor by allowing them to clear streets
21-Oct-1926	Damage to boats including *Endion*, Wharf badly damaged, roads swept away
15-Sep-1928	95 houses and public buildings damaged, Wireless Tower destroyed
26-Sep-1928	Damage to 102 houses, Wesleyan Chuch, St John's Schoolroom
25-Sep-1929	Worst hurricane to date
OH	30-Aug-1932, 29-Jul-1933, 27-Oct-1933, 4-Nov-1933
6-Sep-1933	Destroyed Wireless Station, RC & Anglican Churches, Schoolhouse, Jail, many boats
OH	3-Nov-1935, 16-Sep-1944
12-Oct-1945	A number of small boats destroyed
17-Sep-1947	Fruit and trees blown down
OH	Carol, 30-Aug-1955, Edna, 11-Sep-1955, Hazel, 15-Oct-1955
8-Sep-1960	Donna some damage
5-Sep-1965	Betsy some damage
3-Sep-1979	David some damage
23-Aug-1992	Andrew severe damage
15-Sep-1999	Floyd Docks & vessels damaged, flooding, beach severely eroded
5-Nov-2001	Michelle Flooding around some low lying areas
03-Sep-04	Frances Moderate damage mostly to docks in the harbour
26-Sep-04	Jeanne Moderate damage.

Barnett were blown down and his Negro houses received considerable damage. The Government schooner *Nassau* was washed ashore at Royal Island, damaged, the stern post and keel broken.[3]

In that same hurricane, 34 free coloured people at Bogue were drowned and not a house was left standing. The house of Benjamin Claxton at the plantation of George Butler was blown down. Claxton was crushed and Mrs. Claxton severely bruised. The bodies of 20 people were found about a mile from their place of residence. Seventeen people who escaped the fury of the storm were on the peak of a hill, surrounded by water and without provisions or fresh water.[4] (See Table 13.2.)

The gale on 14 September at Royal Island was from West North West and at Harbour Island, a distance of 7 leagues it blew with equal violence from South East to South. During these violent storms at Harbour Island, a total of 160 houses were damaged, of which 121 were destroyed. (See Table 13.3.) The Church and the barracks containing 60 men (a detachment of the 99th Regiment) were blown down, a soldier killed and another taken to hospital.[5] Subscriptions opened in Nassau for the relief of the indigent

Table 13.2 Free coloured people drowned at the Boag in 1806 hurricane

Resident:		plus family	Resident:		plus family
Benson	Rebecca	1 daughter	Martin	W	2 children
Carmichael	Elizabeth	McBeth	Hannah		
Claxton	Benjamin		Middleton	William	1 daughter
Easton	Moses		Middleton	Mrs	
Feston	Mary		Rivers	William	2 children
Frances	Hannah	2 children	Smith	Nancy	2 children
Johnson	Jane	2 children	Wilson	Lucinda	3 children
Kemp	Willet		Wilson	Rose	1 daughter

sufferers and the money given to James Dunshee and William R. Edgecombe, Representatives for the Harbour Island District.[6]

At Exuma the hurricane of 30/31 August continued for five hours and blew down all cotton machines on both Exumas. And on 13/14 September the storm from North and North West lasted 14 hours and caused extensive damage. The Church and nearly all houses in the harbour were blown down. At Little Exuma not a house was left standing. The loss of cotton, corn and salt was immense.[7] Similar damage was reported at Crooked Island, Acklins Island and Long Island. Cameron reported that the Colony faced severe problems: no provisions and few boats to trade with. The food shortage was so acute that Cameron asked permission to import pork, salt beef and butter for a limited period and England granted this request for the ensuing six months.[8]

Although Evangalista Torricelli, a pupil of Galileo, invented the mercury barometer in 1643, it was with the invention of the aneroid barometer in 1843 by Lucien Vidie that the barometer came into common usage. Apparently, the new barometer was used in Harbour Island by 1854 and the following rules for its use were explained by an unnamed observer, an inhabitant of Harbour Island:

1) In hurricane months if the barometer falls with a N or N E wind, it should awake attention, and if it falls below 29.90, it is almost certainly a gale approaching, tho' perhaps a 100 miles off.
2) During the approach, the barometer falls from noon until morning and then rises to noon again; every day falling lower than the previous day.
3) From sunrise to noon, any rise less than .05 is unimportant, but the smallest fall during that period, certainly indicates bad weather.
4) On the contrary, from noon to morning, its fall is not conclusive of bad weather, but its rise certainly indicates improved weather.
5) Though the weather is ever so threatening at sunset, the rise of .05 or upward assures you that there will be no gale before morning.

Table 13.3 Houses destroyed at Harbour Island by the 1806 Hurricane

Owner		Houses	Comment	Owner		Houses	Comment
Albury	Benjamin	1		Roberts	Joseph	1	
Albury	Jemmy	1		Roberts	Joseph	1	
Albury	Joseph	1		Roberts	Joseph	1	
Albury	Joseph	1		Roberts	Joseph	1	
Albury	Joseph	1		Roberts	Joseph Jr	1	
Albury	Sally	1		Roberts	Joseph Sen	1	
Albury	Widow	1		Roberts	Lawrence	1	
Albury	William	1		Roberts	Mott	1	Free Black
Albury	William	1		Roberts	William	1	
Brady	William	1		Russell	Benjamin	2	
Brown	Caesar	1	Free Black	Russell	Joseph	1	
Cash	Widow	1		Russell	Joseph	1	
Cleare	Ephraim	1		Russell	Widow	1	
Cleare	Joseph	1	broken arm	Russell	Widow	1	
Cleare	Reuben	1		Saunders	Benjamin	1	
Cleare	Widow	1		Saunders	Benjamin	1	
Coleman	Widow	1		Saunders	Joseph	1	
Collins	John	1		Saunders	Joseph K	1	
Cox	Dim	1	Free Man	Saunders	Nathaniel	1	
Curry	Benjamin	1		Saunders	Widow	1	
Curry	Benjamin Jr	2		Saunders	William	1	
Curry	Joseph	4		Saunders	William	1	
Curry	Joseph	1		Saunders	William	1	
Curry	Pierson	1		Saunders	William	1	
Curry	Widow	1		Sawyer	Alexander	1	
Evans	Joseph	1	Part down	Sawyer	Edmund	1	
Fisher	Christopher	7		Sawyer	Joseph	1	
George	Sarah	1	Free Woman	Sawyer	William	1	
Harris	Joseph	1		Sawyer	William	1	
Higgs	Jeremiah	2		Sweeting	Benjamin	1	
Higgs	Mrs	5		Sweeting	Benjamin	1	
Holmes	Benjamin	1		Sweeting	Joseph	1	
Ingram	James	1	Free Black	Sweeting	Thomas	2	
Johnson	Polly	1		Sweeting	Thomas	1	
Johnson	Samuel	1		Sweeting	William	1	
Johnson	Thomas	1		Sweeting	William	1	
Kemp	Samuel	1		Tedder	Mrs	1	
Kerr	William	1		Tedder	Mrs	1	
Petty	Martha	1		Tedder	Widow	1	
Pierce	Joseph	5		Thomson	Dick	1	
Pierce	Martha	1		Thomson	John	1	
Pierce	Thomas	1		Thomson	Nathaniel	1	
Pinder	Thomas	1		Thomson	Sarah	1	
Roberts	Benjamin	1		Weatherford	Mrs	1	
Roberts	George	1		Wood	Joseph	1	
Roberts	James	1		Young	Joseph	1	
Roberts	Joseph	4			Adam	1	Free Black
Roberts	Joseph	2			Rachel	1	Black Woman
					Tom	1	Yellow

6) Though the weather be ever so fair in the morning, the fall of .05 before noon, betokens a gale before night (provided its already below 29.90.)[9]

Even though Harbour Island had faced tremendous hurricanes in 1813, 1824 and 1830, (see Table 13.1) it was the severity of 'The Great Bahama Hurricane' of 1866 that lived on in the inhabitants' minds for many years.

The northern shore of Eleuthera, from Harbour Island eastwards, is girdled with precipitous cliffs, against which, even in moderate weather, the waves of the ocean beat incessantly. On 1 October 1866, they were lashed into fury by the north-easter that broke so heavily against that part of the cliff known as the 'Narrow Crossing' ('Glass Window'), west of the 'Cow and Bull', that jets or columns of water like dense columns of smoke, were thrown upward of 200 feet above the cliffs and when the upward force was expended, they were dispersed into a spray like sparks from a fire, glittering in the rays of the sun like burnished silver. These jets were seen at Spanish Wells, distant by 10 miles. The jets were caused by deep indentations in the cliffs, with their sides nearly at right angles to each other. Over the arch and through the aperture of the 'Glass Window' were thrown tons of water and stones of a ton weight were hurled from the heights over a rugged descent into the sea on the south side, distant more than a 100 feet and fish that had been hurled over the cliffs were found there in a mutilated state.

It was the heaviest surge ever witnessed by the oldest inhabitant; and had it continued in its fury another tide, the whole of the low ground of west Eleuthera would have been inundated. The next day when it had in part subsided, the waves were then breaking over the low cliffs and the water was being carried into the low ground by the channels that had been opened the previous day. The northern shore of Harbour Island is guarded by a reef that lies about a quarter of a mile from the shore and is dry and exposed at low water. Over this reef the sea broke in terrific grandeur with white-capped waves.

Distressing accounts of the damage done by the hurricane on Out Islands were received in Nassau. The settlements of Spanish Wells, The Current, Governor's Harbour and other parts of Eleuthera were nearly swept away. At Abaco the destruction was awful: Green Turtle Cay, Hope Town and Marsh Harbour were in ruins. There was said to be no less than ten wrecks at Ship Channel Cays.[10] It was reported as the most alarming hurricane to visit Nassau within the memory of man, worse than the hurricane of 1813, which was dreadful in the extreme.[11] An eyewitness account showed that:

> … the vortex was over Nassau at 8 pm and the barometer read 27.7 inches. The calm lasted from 7.20 to 8.50 pm, from which it was

concluded that the diameter of the vortex was 23 miles. At first the clouds in the zenith seemed to revolve rapidly, then the stars appeared but banks of clouds remained all around the horizon in dense masses. The long black list of wrecks recorded, bears testimony to the devouring energy of the hurricane'.[12]

Police Magistrate Burnside's report on the effect of the hurricane on Harbour Island showed that the St. John's Anglican Church, the schoolhouse and 38 houses at Harbour Island had been levelled. The Police Office, the Prison and 26 dwellings had been destroyed and a further 21 dwellings damaged. The pride of Harbour Island's shipping fleet was severely reduced by the destruction of four schooners and considerable damage to twelve schooners and two sloops. Four Wesleyan Chapels were destroyed or damaged at Spanish Wells, Current and other parts of the Harbour Island District.

The inhabitants sent down to Nassau a deputation consisting of the Wesleyan Missionary and two of the Harbour Island Representatives to the House of Assembly, who approached Burnside for assistance. He told them that Harbour Island was the largest and most opulent settlement after Nassau:

> I urged them the duty and necessity of relying on their own exertions and charitable impulses, and I sanctioned them only a small supply of food for the paupers and others, who could not obtain any.[14]

Just five years later, the fury of nature again struck the inhabitants of Harbour Island with tragic results.

Nature has carved some curious shapes into the limestone of Bahamian sea coasts. One of the most curious is Ridley's Head near Spanish Wells on North Eleuthera. At a certain angle and from some distance this promontory bears a striking resemblance to a man's head. Another interesting design, which is not common, is a large hole right through the rock. Such a hole can be seen today at the south end of Great Abaco. But years ago a similar feature existed on Eleuthera, about four miles from Harbour Island, which was then looked upon as the Harbour Island hinterland. The Abaco people gave their hole in the rock the prosaic name of 'Hole in the Wall'. The Harbour Island people, showing more imagination, called theirs 'The Glass Window'.[15]

Well into the nineteenth century, these distinctive rock formations were both maritime signposts. Hole in the Wall is still there, but the Glass Window is no more. There were two versions as to how it disappeared. Mr. Eddie 'Jinks' Roberts, the man who built the *Marie J. Thompson*, claims to have been the last person to walk over this natural bridge. On his way to Gregory Town one morning he crossed it. In the afternoon on his return he was hoping to repeat the performance. But he found that in the interval the structure had collapsed. Another source claims that it was destroyed by a hurricane in 1893.

While the bridge stood it was considered a thrilling adventure to walk its 60 ft. length and look straight down to 90 feet below, where the green water of the coral reefs meet the deep blue water of the Atlantic Ocean. The daring walk was not performed by men alone, but also by ladies 'of nerve'. A nineteenth-century writer states:

> To lie down on the top of this arch, which was only about three feet wide in the centre, and look over its outer edge down upon the seething, foaming cauldron below, afforded a picture of wild beauty and rugged grandeur not easily matched and never to be forgotten.

Still, people of the area who pass that way by boat or car will point to a place where the rock is scalloped and say 'That is the Glass Window'. The window is gone but the name endures.

When Paul Albury was a boy at Harbour Island, there were two people still living who were survivors of the tragedy of the Glass Window. One was Mary Lowe Saunders, the grandmother of John Saunders, and the other Capt. W. Johnson's son, Alonzo Johnson, who owned and operated a little shop. They were both quite old and quite deaf. It would have been very difficult indeed to get the story of the 'Glass Window' incident from them. Paul thought that he should have tried but didn't – and thereby the opportunity to gain an eye witness account was forever lost. However in a talk to Rotary, he unfolded the story of the Glass Window tragedy gleaned from his research.

> In the early 1870s, Mr. George Cole was headmaster of the Harbour Island Public School for Boys. His wife was headmistress of the girls' school. The Coles had gained some renown and many commendations for their teaching ability. They were admired and respected by all the people of the island. The Christmas holidays began toward the end of 1871 and as they usually did, and still do. And the children were happy to be released from their studies for a few weeks. Mr. and Mrs. Cole had two exciting events planned for their students to enliven the holidays – an entertainment and a picnic.
>
> The entertainment, performed by both pupils and teachers, included the 'Chanting of songs, glees and recitations'. It went off

very well indeed and provided much merriment for all who were present. But the picnic, which lay ahead, was foremost in the minds of the pupils, and was the subject of much discussion. Within an easy distance of Harbour Island there were to be found caves and pleasant coconut groves – all very suitable places for a picnic party of children, and where there was not much likelihood of their getting into any danger; but for some reason or other all these were rejected and it was finally agreed that 'The Glass Window' should be the scene of the anticipated pleasure. This decision was undoubtedly due to the persuasive entreaties of the students. The parents were somewhat apprehensive about the site. That Mr. and Mrs. Cole also felt some anxiety is evidenced by the fact that they strictly stipulated that the picnickers would be comprised only of teachers and pupils of the two upper classes; that is to say boys and girls of 14–16 years of age.

On the morning of 4 January 1872, the group gathered on the recently erected Government Wharf to commence their adventure. There were 22 pupils and probably 4–6 teachers including Mr. and Mrs. Cole. They boarded a boat and set out for Bottom Harbour. The weather was beautiful. In fact the wind was so light that the sail could hardly be kept full and oars had to be employed to speed the progress. After an hour or so they arrived at Bottom Harbour and quickly disembarked with their baskets of food and refreshments. Before them was a rugged walk of four miles to reach The Glass Window. About a mile along the road they came to the famous Bottom Harbour Well, a spring of sweet water, and no doubt they rested there a while and quenched their thirst. A few miles further on the Bottom Harbour road came out to the sea on the western side of Eleuthera at a place called Cotton Hole. Cotton Hole is now gone too, but it was a very large rock probably thrown up from the east coast during some distant and fearsome storm. The rock, weighing some thousands of tons was perforated right through the middle in an east-west direction, forming something like a breezeway. Travellers who went that way were glad to relax in that aperture and cool off and it is likely that the picnic group did the same.

Continuing on from Cotton Hole, it was necessary to navigate one of the worst paths you could ever imagine – a rocky footpath of extreme narrowness and ruggedness. Running right along the edge of the western coast this part of the walk was known as 'Turn Round, Fall Down'. Again you see the imaginative minds of the Brilanders in coining a name like that. After a mile of trudging the

Turn Round Fall Down trail, The Glass Window loomed into view, standing high on the eastern coast, stark and majestic and somewhat forbidding. This window was obviously formed in the distant past when the islands were lower relative to the sea. The waves working continuously against the face of the sea cliff found a soft spot, which they eventually perforated. Later the land became more elevated, the hole in the rock stood out high, stark and clear – and was named The Glass Window. The top of the natural bridge stood 80 or 90 feet above the sea. The rock at the bottom of the window was about 50 or 60 feet high. In that area the water is of great depth – too deep for the coral insect, that persistent builder of reefs, to operate. So that the waves, which come in across the broad Atlantic meet with no obstruction until they are checked by the ironbound coast of Eleuthera.

There was very little wind blowing that day – but even so along the high rocks there was a surge, as there always is, setting up a thunderous roar. The children enjoyed the frolicking among the rocks, a scene of bold and wild grandeur – so different to the surroundings to which they were accustomed. The sun had crossed the meridian when lunch time was announced. Everyone was happy to answer this call for by that time they were all tired, hot and hungry. They took their places in the cool shadow of the great archway over the window. You might say they were sitting on a windowsill.

Laughter and amusing stories went the rounds, hymns were sung, refreshments enjoyed, and all averred that they were having a great time. They thrilled at the sight and sound of the waves assaulting the cliffs far below and exploding into plumes of snow-white foam and spray. But not the slightest danger was apprehended, as not even a particle of spray ascended to the lofty heights on which they were perched. But that was soon to change for far out at sea a tremendous wave of great height and power was moving toward them. No one noticed it. At about 2 pm it struck the coast with terrible violence, washing right through The Glass Window and scattering the picnickers as if they were pieces of drift-wood.

More dangerous still was the efflux or recoil. All those who could do so grasped the rocks and clung to them for dear life as the wave strove to draw them out over the cliff into the fatal arms of the ocean below. The wave receded, leaving behind a melancholy scene. The children, who a moment before were so happy, were now in a state of shock – wet from head to foot – their hands and faces covered with blood flowing from cuts received by being violently dashed against the rocks. Worse than all that, they soon discovered that three of their number were missing. Alonza Johnson, Thomas Kelly and Belinda Harris – all about the age of 15 years. At this realization, shock was transmuted into wild despair. The pupils ran hither and thither, looking into every hole and crevice, wailing and screaming – not wanting to believe their deepest fear.

A few braved the terror of the cliff's edge to look down into the sea. Belinda was seen in the process of sinking beneath the waves. Thomas was never seen at all. It is thought that they had been badly wounded and probably killed or rendered unconscious by their fall down the sharp rocks. There was some alleviation of the party's despair when Alonzo Johnson was seen swimming in the raging surf some sixty yards from the shore. The sea was running high then, for as it transpired, the wave, which caused the havoc was the fore-runner of a rage.

Alonzo was in a perilous state for there was no hope that he might be able to climb up the steep cliffs. Actually, the prolongation of his life depended on his keeping off from the rocks, for there, he would have been dashed to pieces by the raging sea. At this juncture a boat arrived on the south side probably from Gregory Town. An oar from this boat was thrown into the surf and the tide took it within reach of the swimmer. And it was somewhat heartening to see Alonzo resting on the oar and swimming bravely along the shore in the direction of Harbour Island. But all knew he could never make that four mile swim.

In a search of the area for anything that might help to keep the boy afloat, a skiff was found. The skiff was some distance from the site but many willing hands accomplished the laborious task and heaved it over the cliff into the sea. On the way down it struck the rocks and was badly damaged. It filled with water but did not sink, and Alonzo was able to get into it, thereby being better able to rest and to feel some protection from sharks that might be around. By that time he had been in the sea for two hours. It was 4 o'clock and the sun was well advanced in the western sky.

When the news reached Briland the men knew that the only hope of saving Alonzo was to get a boat out there to him. Five or six boats set out, but they all had to turn back – not being able to get out through Harbour's Mouth because of the rage. The sun set and darkness closed in on Alonzo and his fate. But back at Briland six men, John Davis Lowe, Capt. Cornelius Saunders, John Thomas Saunders, Clarence W. Saunders, Isaac A. Saunders and Cubitt

Harris, spurred on by the sheer pathos of the situation, determined to make one last desperate effort to reach the boy before the sea claimed him. Realizing it was useless to try the cut at Harbour's Mouth, they opted for the Narrows where the raging sea was not quite so fierce. Pulling mightily on their oars and keeping a watchful eye on the breaking sea, they made it through the cut and gained the open ocean through dint of muscle and courage. By having to go the Narrows way, the distance to the disaster site was doubled and now 8 miles of turbulent sea lay before them. Another difficulty was that it was very dark – so dark that the rushes, or sea oats, on the eastern hills of Harbour Island were set on fire as a guide to the boatmen.

On reaching the area where Alonzo in his swamped skiff was thought to be, with great joy they heard a voice calling a little way off. Thinking that a boat would come looking for him and knowing it would be difficult to find him in the dark, he had had the presence of mind to keep calling out all night. He was rescued at 10 o'clock no worse for wear, and soon after was returned to his joyous parents. Alonzo reported that when he was carried off by the receding wave he did not hit the rocks but was carried under water to a great depth. On starting his ascent he could see Thomas and Belinda far above him – on the surface, he presumed. On reaching the surface he looked about for them but they had disappeared.

The most visibly distraught of the bereaved parents was the father of Belinda. She was his favourite child. He had tried to dissuade her from going on the picnic but she wanted to be with her friends and her pleas prevailed. The most bitter ingredient of his sorrow was that he would never see her again, even in death. He offered a reward of $1,000 to anyone who would recover the remains of his daughter from the sea. But the search was fruitless. The two survivors of the tragedy who were still alive when Paul Albury was a boy, Alonzo Johnson and Mary Lowe Saunders, were very deaf. And a number of Brilanders told him that many of the other survivors of the tragedy were quite deaf to the end of their days. The cause of their deafness and the cause of the wave were not known.

In June 1883, Jabez Bridges, the Methodist Missionary at Harbour Island was offering special prayers to end the great drought, as the fruit was falling off and the potatoes failing.[16] On 8 September, he was on his knees again as the barometer fell and a severe hurricane approached. The inhabitants battened windows and doors and made the church secure.

I could hear the cries of the captains as they gave the orders for their vessels to be made secure at the moorings. All the smaller vessels hauled up on land long before the hurricane hit us. The North East side of the island stretching to the Atlantic was white with foam and the billows rolled in a terrible manner. The hurricane first blew from the east and gradually shifted to SSE where it blew with tremendous force. It afterwards moved due south where it blew even harder than ever. I should say the hurricane was at its height between 3 pm to 5 pm. About 6 pm the barometer commenced to rise and from then until midnight, with occasional breaks of fury, it gradually subsided, and when Sunday morning came we beheld the sad effects of the storm.

Truly a most distressing picture of ruin presented itself in every direction, walls, fences and trees were blown down and scattered in all directions and about 15 houses of the poor were entirely destroyed. To attempt to describe the misery of the people would be impossible. The loss of property is so great, that nought but starvation is in store for hundreds. So far I hear about 100 lives have been lost. At this place there are 7 new made widows and quite a lot of fatherless children. Throughout this Circuit the distress is incalculable.

From all quarters come details of a most horrid description. I am thankful to God that the lives of my brother missionaries and their families are all preserved, though I believe that Rev. and Mrs. Richardson had a very providential escape. The Episcopal Church mourns the loss of Rev. Jeremiah Higgs and his wife by drowning in the mail schooner Carleton, which became a total wreck. He was on his way to San Salvador. My heart is very sad for the poor sufferers all over the islands and any aid for such a worthy purpose would prove a great blessing. We have lost 2 small chapels and I fear there is no prospect at all owing to the impoverished state of the people to replace them for some time to come. I would not murmur or repine at this heavy stroke, which in the order of this providence inflicted upon us. May He graciously pity the sorrows of His people.

This is my first hurricane and I hope my last.[17]

Indeed it was his last hurricane but a few days later he was prevented from going to Gregory Town by a cyclone. Within weeks he left for England to marry, saying the work in Harbour Island District was too much for one man.

In the early twentieth century, Harbour Island received terrible damage and suffering from fierce hurricanes. Out of season hurricanes in March and April of 1905 brought much destruction. And the Northern Islands sustained devastation in the three hurricanes of 1926, the two hurricanes of 1928 and the hurricane of 1929.

The year 1933 was a great one in the Bahamas for those who enjoy the excitement of hurricane watching. In fact the 21 tropical disturbances reported that year were greater than any other in the known history of the New World. The tenth storm was first reported to the North Eastward of Puerto Rico. On 1 September it was off Turk's Island and had developed winds of 80 mph. During the morning of 3 September, the centre of the storm passed over Harbour Island and there was a calm lasting 30 minutes preceded by hurricane force winds estimated at 140 mph.

Governor Sir Bede Clifford and his technical advisors flew down to Harbour Island to assess the damage. Many of the fields on North Eleuthera were under water and the crops were greatly damaged. In the harbour, the *Endion* rode safely at anchor but all other boats were turned upside down with their spars sticking through holes in their bottoms. The Wireless Station, the Roman Catholic Church, the Methodist Church, the Anglican Church, the Schoolhouse, the Jail and the Government Dock were all ruined. Boats could be seen piled up close along Bay Street, which was flooded with water up to the homes and up South Street. It seemed as though giant hammers and pick axes had been pounding at the dock and road to break them up. Capt. William Harris, the mate of the *Endion*, told Sir Bede:

> In 60 years, I have never known anything like it. We have always prided ourselves on the safety of the harbour, but this time it failed us. The wind came down from the North and piled up the water into the bays. Then when the lull came, and we knew for certain that the centre of the storm had passed over us, the South wind blew the water right onto us. It carried the boats right into the street and left them there. The water came right into the town for nearly 150 feet.

Captain Harris took the assessors to his back window and pointed out:

> Anybody who remembers the town as it used to be will tell you that before you could see nothing but houses from here, now look at it. You can see clear to the Rectory. Every wall in the place has been blown down. The worst damage is at Barracks Hill, where 30 houses have been blown down.

After assessing the damage, His Excellency commented that he was relieved to find no loss of life or injury to persons at Spanish Wells. Dr. Eyres was sent to Bogue, where some injuries were reported. Steps would be taken to repair lost property and sink new wells at Harbour Island, where the damage was more serious.[18]

Tornadoes and hurricanes are both whirling masses of air, spinning in an anti-clockwise direction in this region. And that is perhaps the only similarity between the two monsters. A tornado is comparatively a small thing. The mass of revolving air may be only a few yards wide but it usually destroys everything in its path. A hurricane is hundreds of miles in diameter but not nearly so destructive in a given area. A hurricane is considered to be major hurricane if it reaches a velocity of 150 mph. Tornadoes on the other hand are thought to have wind speeds of 300–500 mph. In considering this, you have to remember that the pressure on a structure is proportional to the square of the windspeed. That is to say that a velocity of 400 miles an hour exerts not twice, but four times the pressure of 200 mph.

There is another characteristic of a tornado that is worth remembering. The whirling is so fast at the centre that the centrifugal force exerted thereby, sets up a small area of low pressure which is almost a vacuum. This creates a sort of suction, which explains the propensity of tornadoes to lift roofs and other objects and carry them through the air for great distances. This low pressure or vacuum also has a peculiar physiological effect on people and animals that leaves them in a severe state of shock. Tornadoes and waterspouts are the very same type of cyclonic storms. The names are different depending on whether they occur over land or sea. The waterspout is so called for obvious reasons. The black cloud, which characterizes it, is shaped like a spout. The broad end, at the top, is an integral part of the cumulus cloud, which generates it. And it descends with an ever-narrowing diameter to the surface of the sea where it causes great turbulence. It looks, for all the world, like a giant spout emptying a water-filled cloud into the sea.

Paul Albury tells the story of a tremendous tornado that hit Harbour Island when he was a boy of 15 years old living in 'The Battery', his family home overlooking the harbour.[19]

> Hadazzah Albury is inextricably linked with the tornado that hit Harbour Island at 2 o'clock of a Wednesday morning 31 March 1937. She was 51 years old at the time of which I speak. A fairly tall, red-faced woman, thin and wiry – she always seemed to be in a hurry. She walked the streets of Dunmore Town with swift long strides. To earn a few shillings, she knitted fishing net and her needle flew so fast the eye could scarcely follow it. She was a widow

with no children and no fixed abode. She slept with different families from time to time and sometimes she slept alone when a vacant house was available.

There was one horror, which intruded on her erratic, if contented, life. And that was a deathly fear of thunder and lightning. Those who knew her well, and who sometimes slept in the same house with her, spoke of her behaviour when the heavens began to flash and crackle. She would go straight to bed, if she was not already there, put her head on a pillow – and cover her head with another pillow. Apparently she felt some security with this flimsy protection from the angry heavens.

Tuesday, 30 March had been a raw and blustery day with a great bank of cloud in the west that threatened a thunderstorm that night. Getting toward sunset, Hadazzah stopped by my Aunt Sue's house with a basket filled with rough-dried clothes. She had washed them at a neighbour's house that day, and said she was going home early so that she could be up early to iron them. I expect another reason she wanted to get home early was the threatening weather – and undoubtedly she quickly got into bed with her two pillows. She slept in a garret or an upstairs in a house belonging to Capt. Charles Pettee who had gone to Nassau to captain the *Ena K.* on the Nassau-Miami run.

Capt. Harold Albury lived Down Yonder on Murray Street. A most competent and careful captain, he took a party fishing on Tuesday afternoon. The weather was too bad for him to venture outside, and so he fished in the channel as the wind blew 40–50 miles an hour from the east-south-east. On getting back from the trip, the captain put his boat, the *Pieces of Eight*, to the moorings and went home to eat dinner and go to bed. But his wife was not feeling well that evening and she felt more comfortable sitting in a chair. He decided to stay up with her as a good husband always does. He drew up a chair next to a western upstairs glass window from which vantage point he could watch the harbour and the threatening dark bank of cloud in the west.

The hours passed and by one o'clock in the morning a fierce squall blew over Briland – this was followed by a hail storm which made a frightful din on the captain's roof. In fact he thought the roof might be broken in. He dressed and went downstairs immediately thereafter to look about. Hailstones, the size of marbles, were still on the ground – but the wind had dropped to a dead calm. He looked toward the harbour and saw there the most frightening sight ever to meet his eyes – a giant waterspout stood there close to Harbour Island and apparently leaning over Dunmore Town. A few moments later he heard somebody yelling from Up Yonder way. He told his wife that something must have happened Up Yonder and started out to investigate.

With my parents I had gone upstairs that night to go to bed at the usual Briland time of 9 o'clock. There were six dormer windows upstairs in our house and we closed most of them because of the inclement weather.

Suddenly I was awakened by a terrific thud on the roof, which sounded as if it had been hit by something solid. At the same instant every window that had been closed and latched blew open and great gusts of wind took possession of the garret. It was like being outdoors in a hurricane. My first thought was to close the shutters. I was 15 years old then and quite tall and strong – and I tugged at one with all my might, but it wouldn't budge. It seemed as if it was nailed in the open position. I persisted and suddenly it closed without resistance – as if whatever devil was holding it open had let go of it.

It probably lasted no more than a minute but that minute is indelibly etched in my mind. While I stood at the open window an awful rattling was going on, on the roof. That couldn't have been the hail that Capt. Harold and others heard, for my hands and arms were outside the window opening and I would have felt the hail against my flesh, and would probably have been bruised by it. In retrospect, I believe the rattling noise was caused by the updraft of the tornado – the ends of the wooden shingles were lifted and they made a loud crack as they fell back into place again.

Mixed with the noise on the roof was the frightening whining and whooshing sound of air moving at a great velocity. And intermingled with it all was the fearful wrenching and splitting of timber. I knew that some awful catastrophe had descended upon us and that not many yards away houses were being smashed and torn apart.

My parents and I dressed quickly and made our way downstairs to determine what had happened. We were greeted by a frantic pounding on the front door accompanied by female cries. I opened the door and there stood an aunt and first cousin. They were in nightgowns, barefooted and soaked to the skin. They were almost speechless with hysteria. Between sobs they told us their house had been blown apart – miraculously they had escaped injury, crawled out of the wreckage and came straight to us.

I walked the few hundred feet to the corner of Bay and South Streets and gazed dumbfounded at the scene of devastation. The waterspout had come ashore at the site of the Up Yonder shipyard at which point I presume it was transmuted into a tornado. A cane syrup mill standing in the shipyard, and built of stone, was totally destroyed. It crossed Bay Street and hit two houses that were very close together, tearing off their roofs. One lost roof belonged to the house where Hadazzah slept that night. The other was the home of Capt. and Mrs. Charles Curry. They, too, had slept upstairs. But they had come down at one o'clock in the morning to knead some dough in preparation for an early morning baking of bread. And they were there when the twister struck their house wrenching off the roof.

On that part of Bay Street there was a house on either side of the two that were wrecked. But these adjacent houses received little damage. Lots in that vicinity were about 30 feet wide. So it seems that the tornado had a diameter of 60 feet or 20 yards. Nearly every house on South Street was destroyed. And men with lanterns spent the dark hours of that fateful morning trying to locate and account for the occupants. All were found except Hadazzah.

Daylight revealed that two vessels in the harbour, the sloop *Mearl* and the schooner *Mayflower* were sunk to the bottom. And with daylight a frantic search for Hadazzah began. Going east, South Street leads to the old burial ground where the Memorial to Sir George Roberts now stands. In those days it was an unweeded and unkempt patch of ground where goats and sheep were put to pasture. There were 25 or 30 creatures there that night, some tied and some loose. The next morning they were all found dead. Further on the body of Hadazzha was discovered at 8 o'clock that same morning.

The day after the tornado, the assistant editor, the Honourable Eugene Dupuch of the *Tribune* flew to Briland to report on the situation. His report appeared in the *Tribune* of Thursday 1 April 1937.

> A beautiful toy village marred only by a streak of scattered blocks and matchlike planks swept away in a destructive curve by the hand of a petulant child – that was what Dunmore Town, Harbour Island, looked like this morning from a Bahamas Airways plane piloted by Capt. Jackson which flew to the island carrying Mr. K. L. Ames.
>
> A *Tribune* representative who made the trip as a guest of Mr. Ames had an opportunity to see the devastation left in the wake of the terrific freak of nature which bore

down on the sleeping town at 2 o'clock yesterday morning and completely wrecked the southern section within the short space of three minutes, carrying away the entire upper storey of the house in which Hadazzah Albury lived, and depositing the torn and mangled body of the 51 year old widow, 700 feet away in a thicket beyond the opposite side of the town.

An old boiler embedded in the roof of a house in the next block, a house split through the centre with the roof of a building two doors away wedged in between, every room of another house laid bare with the roof gone and the four walls fallen outward, a two storey building razed to the ground with only a flat clearing covered with twisted lumber and scattered shingles to mark the site, a dinghy virtually wrapped around an almond tree as though it had been built to fit the contours of the trunk, two periscope-like tips of the sunken *Mayflower's* masts in the middle of the harbour – these were a few of the evidences left in the wake of the disaster.

'I've never seen anything like it in all my born days,' said Mrs. Susan Albury, who was in one of the houses struck by the centre of the tornado. 'I tell you, it was worse than any hurricane while it lasted – and it's a good thing it didn't last long. The house was a-shaking and a-wobbling something terrible and all I could do was pray and try to get out of the window. That wasn't no ordinary storm – it was part of Judgement I tell you.'[20]

Harbour Islanders still call that night the night of the Tornado. And sometimes they refer to it as the night that Hadazzah blew away.

In 1953, the United States' weather services began using female names for tropical storms to avoid confusion when more than one storm threatened in the Atlantic Ocean. In 1978 the names of both men and women began to be used, with the names being recycled every six years. It is interesting to note that a name is 'retired' when that hurricane has caused much damage. *Donna* (1960), *Betsy* (1965), *David* (1979), *Andrew* (1992), *Floyd* (1999) and *Michelle* (2001) all storms that have caused havoc in the Bahamas, have all been retired. Storms were labelled minimal, major, great, severe or extreme but in 1972, the Saffir/Simpson Damage-Potential Scale was conceived with five categories as shown in Table 13.4.

Table 13.4 The Saffir/Simpson Damage-Potential scale

Category	Central Pressure (inches)	Winds Mph	Surge (feet)	Damage
1	28.94 or greater	74–95	4–5	Minimal
2	28.50–28.91	96–110	6–8	Moderate
3	27.91–28.47	111–130	9–12	Extensive
4	27.17–27.88	131–155	13–18	Extreme
5	Less than 27.17	Over 155	Over 18	Catastrophic

Great strides were made in the late twentieth century in early warning and preparation for hurricanes. With the Bahamas Meteorological Department, local radio and television and United States weather channels in combination with maps and advice in the local newspapers, allow tropical storms to be tracked over many days as they leave the coast of Africa.

Although visited by hurricanes during the mid century, Harbour Island escaped quite lightly until 1992, when again it was devastated by Hurricane *Andrew*. Harbour Island sustained some damage by *Floyd* in 1999 and *Michelle* in 2001. The 2004 hurricane season saw many named storms and in particular Hurricanes *Frances* and *Jeanne* devastated Abaco and Grand Bahama, while at Harbour Island there was a moderate amount of damage, mostly to the docks in the harbour. Valentine's Dock was the worst hit and the Eleuthera Construction Company worked feverishly to repair it for the tourist season.

Two great events rocked the Bahamas in late August 1992. One of these was the victory of the Free National Movement under the Honourable Hubert Ingraham in the national elections after 25 years of Government by the Progressive Liberal Party led by Sir Lyndon O. Pindling. A few days later Hurricane *Andrew*, the first hurricane of the season, hit the Northern Bahamas. *Andrew* was described as 'small' and 'fast moving', yet it ranked as a deadly category 4 hurricane, with winds up to 130 mph.[21]

The hurricane warnings had been in effect for several days as Tropical Storm *Andrew* made its way from the coast of Africa across the Atlantic and towards the Northern Bahamas. On 19 August, *Andrew* was a tropical storm, near 19.02° N and 59.05° W, (North East of the Leeward Islands) packing 50-knot winds and moving WNW at 20 knots. The more cautious of the residents of Harbour Island started to take precautions. By 22 August, an eye formed and it was upgraded to hurricane status, moving in the usual WNW direction. ZNS Radio forecast that the edge of the storm would brush the Abacos. Fisherman, knowledgeable about the effects of even a distant hurricane hauled their boats out of the water and battened up their cottages. Suddenly, *Andrew* turned due west, accelerated into a Category 4 hurricane and was still strengthening.

On Sunday 23 August, the people of Harbour Island woke up as usual and dressed for church. By 1 pm that day, *Andrew* was blowing at 145 mph and was located at 25.4° N and 75.0° W. At 4.30 pm it was at 25.5° and 75.3° with maximum sustained winds of 150 mph. It appeared that it was still strengthening but moving a little North. ZNS radio predicted a landfall on Freeport, Grand Bahama Island. By 6 pm, it was back down to 25.4° N latitude and staying there. Advancing at 14 mph with sustained winds of 155 mph, it was just 5 mph away from being upgraded to a Category 5 storm, which is the highest rating for a hurricane. On Miami's *TV-10*, they were predicting the strongest hurricane to make landfall on the US East Coast in 50 years.

The inhabitants of Harbour Island had had many warnings since Hurricane *David* in 1979 and had grown a little complacent in reacting to them as usually the storms deflected into the Gulf of Mexico or up to Bermuda. As this particular Sunday progressed it was realized that Hurricane *Andrew* was threatening the area and the residents began to nail up shutters on their windows, haul boats up to land, shop for food supplies, batteries, nails, plywood, gasoline, kerosene and first-aid equipment.

The warnings on ZNS Radio from the Meteorological Department became more ominous and by 2 pm the sky darkened and the breeze freshened. By 4 pm, everyone knew they were in for an ordeal and prayers went up all through the Northern Bahamas.

About 5 pm, Hurricane *Andrew* came fast and furious. All of a sudden it hit North Eleuthera and Harbour Island, blowing from the North West at 80 knots, with gusts up to 210 mph, while some people cowered in their homes. The anemometer on Harbour Island measured a wind speed of 62 m/s for an unknown period, the maximum that could be measured by the instrument. Some people making late preparations outdoors scattered to find a safe spot. Everything vibrated as gusts got stronger and the pressure built up. A fine mist of seawater and dust swirled with the gusts. Everyone was cold and scared as loud cracking noises emanated from roofs being battered and torn off. Within a half hour all electricity, telephones and running water ceased to function, having been 'knocked out' by severe damage from the ferocious wind.

The wind and rain persisted for two and a half hours and in that time the hurricane had passed west of north east and went on to ravish islands to the west of Eleuthera and on to Florida, where it became the costliest natural disaster in US history, with over $25 billion in damage caused.

Locally, the worst hit was The Current as it experienced a tidal wave 18 feet above the normal flood tide. Fifty-two of the 70 homes were completely demolished and a further 12 were left unsuitable to be lived in. At Lower Bogue, a young mother drowned in eight feet of water in her home as other residents had climbed into their attics to save their lives. A young man was decapitated at the Bluff by a flying piece of plywood, while a woman suffered heart failure in the terror of the moment. Several vessels sank in the harbour of Spanish Wells, several were blown ashore and the roof of every house had light to severe damage. Gregory Town, Hatchet Bay, James Cistern, Berry Islands and Bimini were the scenes of great destruction by the wrath of Hurricane *Andrew*.[22]

When the residents of Harbour Island ventured out of doors utter confusion reigned. The town looked as if a huge bomb had exploded and scattered debris around. Trees were down, thick trunks had snapped like twigs and branches, twigs and leaves were everywhere. Sand, seaweed, roof tiles and water lay on Bay Street and up the side streets, where the sea had washed in huge waves from the harbour. It appeared as if a gigantic mechanical shovel had viciously attacked the eastern side, taking a colossal bite out of the island. About 30 yards of sand, flora, and fauna had been reclaimed by the sea which also snatched walls and stairways, leaving a sheer cliff from the land to the beach on which lay big chunks of concrete, fallen trees, wood and garbage. Utility poles, wires, transformers, railings, parts of roofs and many other objects lay at awkward angles in every area.

Tornadoes within the hurricane blazed two parallel paths across the northern end of the island, laying flat the beautiful cocoanut trees that thrive on that part of the island. Pink Sands Hotel was severely damaged. Most homes stood up remarkably well but many, many roofs were lost – ripped off by the huge tornadoes. Many of the docks in the harbour were damaged; their pilings still stood but the top 2 foot x 6 foot planks were strewn about like matchsticks. Moreover, the pilings of Valentine's Dock were torn up and pushed to the shoreline on The Point, damaging several more docks as they travelled southwards. The new Harbour Island Marina was also destroyed.

The next day, the new government appointed a Hurricane Relief Committee to evaluate the damage and open a relief fund to help the victims of Hurricane *Andrew*. And on that same day, the Harbour Island Hurricane Relief Committee was formed to assist victims and acted as an advisory board to the many outside agencies that rushed into the area to help as the news spread round the world like wildfire.

The British Royal Navy assisted by the Red Cross set up emergency clinics throughout North Eleuthera to treat the wounded. They also set up a 'command caller' and VHF radio system to assist victims to call their next of kin and contact foreign homeowners. Batelco's standby generator was turned on and the telecommunications company ran an 'open house' for calls between 9 am and 9 pm daily. However, most local telephones were 'out of order' for more than a month.

In very little time speedboats arrived with ice, food, clothing, medicine and even building materials. Bacardi Rum Factory donated three 4808-gallon trailer tanks of drinking water and each house was rationed to three gallons of water per day. Both Mosko's Construction Company and Cavalier Construction Company of Nassau generously donated their barges to transport relief supplies to the area and Cavalier also donated their plane for emergency requirements. Aircraft were also provided by Bahamasair, the US government and the Royal Bahamas Defense Force and thus social workers, health professionals, architects, engineers, heavy equipment operators, carpenters and construction workers were able to move on site quickly. Missionary flights out of West Palm Beach delivered more than 10 flights by DC-3 aircraft filled with consumable supplies, generators and building materials.[23]

Once again the Harbour Island District was laid waste, a stark, bare landscape with millions of dollars of damage. But once again as so many times in the past, the residents rebuilt their lives, homes and community with the assistance of many other generous people. The US Army, the Royal Bahamas Defense Force, the Royal Jamaican Defense Force, Bahamas Electricity Corporation, Bahamas Department of Water and Sewage, Bahamas Telecommunications Company, and many, many volunteers brought buildings and infrastructure back. And nature gently reached her healing hand as the flora and fauna slowly regenerated to bring back the enchantment and beauty to Harbour Island.

Notes
1. Columbus Log 1494.
2. CO 23/49/53, Governor Cameron to My Lord, April 1806.
3. CO 23/49/53, Governor Cameron to My Lord, 8 October 1806.
4. *Royal Gazette*, 23 September 1806.
5. CO 23/49/53, Governor Cameron to My Lord, 8 October 1806.
6. *Royal Gazette*, 26 September 1806.
7. *Royal Gazette*, 26 September 1806.
8. CO 23/50/99b, Charles Cameron to England, December 1806.
9. *Nassau Guardian*, 18 October 1854.
10. *Nassau Guardian*, 6 October 1866.
11. *Nassau Guardian*, 3 October 1866.
12. Ivan Ray Tannehill, *Hurricanes, Their Nature and History,* Princeton University Press, 1956, p. 158.
13. Ivan Ray Tannehill, *Hurricanes, Their Nature and History,* Princeton University Press, 1956, p. 158.
14. CO 23/185/436, Police Magistrate Burnside's Report on the hurricane, 20 October 1866.
15. The account of the Tragedy of the Glass Window is adapted from a talk to Rotary Club of East Nassau by Paul Albury, Friday 15 October 1982.
16. MMS, File 1880/5, Box 29, Box 221, 1439/39, J. Bridge from Harbour Island, 5 June 1883.
17. MMS, File 1880/5, Box 29, Box 221,1439/7, J. Bridge from Harbour Island, 8 September 1883.

18 *Nassau Guardian,* 6 September 1933.
19 Talk to East Rotary Club by Paul Albury, 9 October 1981.
20 *Nassau Daily Tribune* of Thursday 1 April 1937.
21 *Nassau Guardian*, Special Hurricane Edition, September 1992.
22 *Nassau Guardian*, Special Hurricane Edition, September 1992.
23 *Nassau Daily Tribune,* 17 September. We are also indebted to Reswell Mather for his article *We survived Hurricane Andrew.*

14

Briland ways

Everyone comes into this world as a helpless infant to the warm bosom of a mother and into the delicate web of community relationships and traditions. The journey to Eleuthera of William Albury, his wife Dorothy and their family on the *William*, with Capt. James Sayle on 24 April 1661[1] took them out of the realm of Bermudian customs and celebrations into a new world. The few families in Harbour Island in 1670 undoubtedly retained some residual folkways of Bermuda but now had the opportunity to forge new ways of life.

On the one hand they remained a covenantal community, grateful to the Lord and sharing a table in the wilderness; on the other, they shared the small island with a 'nest of pirates' and some intermarrying took place. The small island community grew, maintaining within it just, honest men and women but there were others who became thriftless, immoral wreckers. The long slow integration of Negro slaves into the population up to the late eighteenth century allowed the Caucasion language and culture to dominate. But at the turn of the nineteenth century the Negro population swelled with the introduction of slaves from Spanish and French Prizes, the Haitian Revolution and others from Abaco as Loyalists migrated. At this point fear and mistrust seems to have arisen between the coloured and white population of Harbour Island.

The richness of Harbour Island life does not become clear until after 1870 but we see glimpses of the early culture of Harbour Island through the eyes of the missionaries.

'Upon my arrival at Harbour Island,' says Rev. Robertson in 1790, 'the inhabitants were so poor that they were unable to pay fees for marriage, births and burying.'[2] This may have been more due more to custom than to poverty, stemming back from a period when no church was available. Rev. Moss reveals in 1773 that:

> It is customary in these parts for ministers to baptize and marry, not in church but in the people's houses, on any day or any hour of day or night.[3]

In 1817 at Harbour Island, Methodist Missionary Rutledge reports that government magistrates and white owners prevented black people from worshipping because the whites could not abide their dancing, fiddling and songs.[4] Two years later he reports that Harbour Island was miserably fallen because:

> The custom of dancing and rum drinking, had nearly gone away, but now dances are held 2 nights per week and there is carousing till midnight. Some stand fast to the Lord, some leave the church to join the backslider's revels. They need their nightly meetings and songs of praise.[5]

The Methodist missionaries worked very hard in the years before emancipation trying to bring about the Kingdom of Heaven on Harbour Island and they were greatly appreciated by some. John Davis reports a very touching conversation in the street with a free person of colour, who could read tolerably well:

> Davis: 'I hope, Rachel you have received good from these readings'.
> 'Oh, yes Massa', said she, 'me have and me do get good till after day done and all gone to bed, me read times till 12 o clock night, and say Lord teach me, den I pray, go to bed and sleep well, and be good for work tomorrow'.
> She pointed out to me the different tracts she had received from different preachers on the Circuit and said, 'when me see dese me tink of different massas and say Lord bless them for me'.[6]

On the eve of emancipation the Methodist Sunday Schools had 10 white and 18 coloured teachers, all former pupils, and although the slave and free population were 'destitute of opportunity' the children improved in reading, spelling, sewing and Religious Knowledge, despite the strong opposition of their masters.[7] During that time many were dismissed from the society, some for dishonesty in wrecking, others for fornication and some for thieving, to enforce discipline, which was thought to be the bulwark of Methodism.

In 1837, Lord John Russell asked England to pray for the illustrious princess (Victoria), who had just ascended the throne with the purest intentions and the justest desires, that she might see slavery abolished, crime diminished and education improved. He trusted that her people would henceforward derive their strength, their conduct and their loyalty from enlightened religious and moral principles. Almost from that moment

Harbour Island was greatly influenced by the policies of the British Empire in matters of government, education and religion and many of their customs, societies and celebrations grew out of this experience.

The 1 August 1834 was a memorable day in Harbour Island; it passed without excitement. Methodist Missionary Charles Penny supplied liberated black people with the scriptures. More coloured people than he had ever seen before attended the meeting, all with anxious looks and many with tears begging that their names be taken down in order to receive a testament. He reports his exchange with them:

> I said to them, 'Why? You cannot read'.
> They said, No sir, but my little girl goes to Mrs Penny's Sunday School and I am learning at the adult school and before long I will be able to lead too.

Sunday School attendance leapt to nearly 100 white and black children and altogether over 300 diligent and attentive scholars.[8]

Four years later, the Stipendiary Magistrate, Mr. McGregor, organized a special watch-night service for Apprentices and, looking forward to full emancipation, sang:

> Prisoners of hope lift up your hearts
> The Day of Liberty draws near.

Again the white people were as anxious as the coloured people, neither knowing what to expect in the coming months and years but there seemed to be a friendly feeling between apprentices and their masters. McGregor expressed his wish that the late apprentices might celebrate with a dance but Methodist missionary Thomas Lofthouse didn't approve.[9]

Anglican Priest Rev. W. K. Duncombe and Samuel Sears Johnson joined the Methodists in the fight against alcohol and the Sons of Temperance Society was formed. However, drinking of liquor still prevailed at the five taverns in Harbour Island and some wreckers caroused at Gregory Town and Bimini. And the Sons of Temperance split into white and coloured chapters.

The clergy, teachers and government officials sent from Great Britain mostly considered that British ways were superior and that they had a moral imperative to bring British modes of education and religion, 'civilized' customs and other forms of enlightenment to the colonies. In school, the curriculum highlighted religion and British history, geography and culture, especially patriotic songs and loyalty to the Union Jack. Boys were taught cricket, a game that was a British symbol for 'fair-play'. In 1841, Governor Cockburn described Harbour Island as 'a small thriving settlement about 40 miles from Nassau, where the inhabitants have ever been conspicuous for their loyalty and good conduct'.[10] As Harbour Island prospered the social elite became proud of the British traditions and followed a British way of life, especially fund-raising bazaars and other events connected to the Church or Chapel. The rising coloured middle class formed friendly societies or lodges and portrayed their loyalty to Britain in speeches to welcome visiting Governors or on other special occasions.

At the Dunmore Bazaar held on 2–6 January 1850, 'the good collection of articles, useful ornaments and exhibitions of phantasmagoria was the source of much amusement', realizing 38 pounds toward the infant school as part of Anglican Church building purposes.[11] In 1854 the Wesleyan Bazaar was judged to be the very best ever. A large spacious house was selected and admirably fitted up with tables and different flags. Most articles were prepared by the young ladies of the Sabbath School and displayed great taste and originality. The Wesleyan Minister and his lady set up a magnificent refreshment table and visitors did ample justice to the tempting viands. The net proceeds were 60 pounds.[12]

In 1870, the Anniversary of the Emancipation of Slaves was celebrated with great joy. The volunteer companies, headed by bands playing music, carried the British Ensign and other flags bearing the inscriptions 'Freedom' and 'Liberty', through the streets of Dunmore Town and, halting opposite the residence of the Resident Justice, J. S. Solomon, gave cheers to her Majesty the Queen. They entertained their friends and some of the elite of the township over the two days (Monday and Tuesday) with a *dejeurner a la fourchette*. The proceedings were conducted in a very orderly and creditable manner. The volunteers having had arranged that a fine of one pound would be paid if a member was intoxicated and but there was no need to enforce this penalty.[13] Again in 1872, the Volunteers paraded, dinners were given and guns were fired in salute. It was reported that this demonstration broke the usual monotony of Harbour Island.[14] It is possible that the volunteers mentioned were the nucleus of the United Friendly Society, which was formed in 1872.

In England, the Bank Holidays Act of 1871 introduced four Bank Holidays (days when the banks would normally be closed). These were New Year's Day, Easter Monday, Whitsuntide and the first Monday in August and to these were added two national holidays, Good Friday and Christmas Day. This Act came at a time when Harbour Island was experiencing 'hard times'. Many had turned to growing pineapples after the wrecking industry diminished, but the early 1870s was a period of crop failure due to adverse weather and pine-field fires. Many owners refused to give credit and general poverty abounded. The Blue Book of 1874 recorded 38 paupers at Harbour Island, a high figure only surpassed in 1899 and

1912/13.[15] Friendly Societies were formed to assist the poor and they also appropriated the various holidays as gala days and organized events, which transformed the Harbour Island environment.

The Liberated Africans at Grants Town, Nassau, had formed a Friendly Society, a self-help organization, designed to help African solidarity and provide benefits for the sick, the aged, widows and orphans, and a fitting and stylish burial for each of its members. Governor Colebrooke encouraged all ex-slaves to form Friendly Societies and steadily these societies increased throughout the islands, giving the members a sense of belonging and the opportunity to develop their own leaders. The Harbour Island United Friendly Society was formed with about 60 members and quickly made its presence felt in the community as it paraded in the 1875 and 1876 Emancipation celebrations, with bands and banners along with a great crowd of females decked out in all colours of the rainbow.[16]

In 1874, the inauguration of the Independent Order of Good Templars took place with entertainment at the Temperance Hall, which included singing conducted by teacher George Cole and recitations by the Rev. Bleby.[17] In April 1876, a set of coins was laid under the foundation cornerstone of Jordan Lodge #1 as the members wore their regalia, sang songs and Rev. Strombom delivered a prayer and an address.[18]

St. Stephen's Grand United Order of Odd Fellows Lodge 1721 was formed in 1876 under the first President, Peter Ford Saunders. In the old days every member received a casket in which to be buried but nowadays he can receive $2,500 from the Bahamas District Burial Fund. Every member pays $6 for the burial of a member and a Harbour Islander can be flown to a mortuary in Nassau if he so wishes. Presently the Lodge has ten regular members and about another 30 who are 'not financial'. Boxing Day, which is St. Stephen's Day, used to be greatly celebrated by the Odd Fellows, as was the second Sunday in May, which is the anniversary of formation. On this day there was plenty to eat and drink and delegates from other lodges came to join in the celebrations. The sister society, Household of Ruth 99 Grand Order of Odd Fellows were also conspicuous on gala days. The other big celebration was Emancipation Day, when the United Friendly Society invited all societies to parade.

Some of the societies were of fleeting duration. The Dunmore Town Mutual Love Society, 1881, the Star of Victory Lodge 11, the coloured division of the Sons of Temperance, 1882, the Burial Society 1898, the Anglo Burial Society, 1911, briefly took part in gala days and then they were not mentioned again. The Good Samaritan's Society, established in 1894, survived until the Second World War and the United Friendly Society only died out just before Independence.[19] Table 14.1 shows the growth of Friendly Societies and Lodges between 1875 and 1920.

Table 14.1 Growth of Friendly Societies/Lodges in the Harbour Island district[20]

Year	Friendly Societies & Members	The 15 Friendly Societies and Lodges in the Harbour Island District 1915/16	Members
1875	1/60	Bluff Grand Order of Odd Fellows	16
1881	3/205	Harbour Island G O St S Odd Fellows	32
1882	3/312	Lower Bogue United Friendly Society	46
1884	3/166	Lower Bogue Wesleyan Methodists	40
1887	2/165	Harbour Island United Friendly Society	64
1888	2/179	Harbour Island Burial Society	40
1893	2/220	Current Union Friendly Society	40
1895	1/117	Bluff Good Samaritans	50
1896	1/122	Gregory Town Lodge	34
1897	4/222	Hatchet Bay United Burial Society	44
1898	4/263	Gregory Town Household of Faith	30
1899	6/313	Hatchet Bay Friendly Society	36
1901/2	7/288	Gregory Town Yoruba Society	50
1902/3	7/282	Spanish Wells Mutual Aid	70
1903/4	7/290	**Total Members of all Societies 1915/16**	**622**
1905/6	4/187		
1906/7	6/319		
1907/8	7/342		
1908/9	7/371		
1909/10	5/241		
1910/11	7/293		
1911	7/277		
1911/12	7/277		
1912/13	15/613		
1913/14	15/622		
1914/15	15/630		
1915/16	15/576		
1916/17	15/574		
1918	15/573		
1918/19	15/539		
1919/20	15/513		

In 1966, a new lodge was formed and still survives – the Mount Pisgah 96 Lodge, Ancient Free and Accepted Masons under first President Joseph Saunders, each member being the beneficiary of $1500 for burial. Each lodge had its own secret order, unique handshake and signs, which they must guard under pain of death. The secret ceremony for burial involves a church service and a parade, with hand-signs committing the body through the streets similar to the West African practice of visiting the places that were important during the person's lifetime. Many of the characteristics of the Friendly Societies have been incorporated into church groups: the Anglican Church Men, Anglican Church Women, Methodist Men's Fellowship, Methodist Women's Fellowship, Methodist Youth Fellowship all pray for and visit the sick and provide extra-curricular activities for the Church.

The festivities on Emancipation Day expanded as the number of societies grew. In 1878, Governor Robinson visited Harbour Island and was greeted by flags along the main thoroughfare. The Sons of Temperance, the United Friendly Society with past president Peter Saunders in red coat, cocked hat and feathers, the Good Templars, St. Stephen's Odd Fellows, and the Sisters of the Friendly Society decked out in blue ribbons and regalia paraded round the streets. Following the parade a regatta was held in the harbour featuring 40 sailing boats. In the afternoon the town was pretty well cleared as on the Spit Sands a sport was held, which featured a women's egg-and-spoon race, footraces, horse jumping, a tug of war between single and married men and the most popular event of the day, the greasy pole competition.[21] The greasy pole used to be the highlight of Harbour Island gala days: a pole was hung over the water and greased all over to make it very slippery; the opponents hit out at each other with a pillow until one slipped off; the winner of the final round won a prize, usually a ham or a turkey. The day ended with speeches of thanks, expressions of loyalty to the Queen and the singing of the National Anthem, *God save the Queen*.

Emancipation Day celebrations lasted into the 1950s, coming to an end when the old-timers died off. Reswell (Prince) Mather remembers the Parade to church and then round Town, from Dunmore Street as far as Clarence Street, back around Bay Street, and up to the United Friendly Society Hall on Munnings Street, which is now Casey's Snack Bar. At the hall a big party took place with food and drink, tubs of rum sour and flasks of whisky using milkmaid cans as cups. He remembers the sports, races, ladies' egg-and-spoon race and of course the greasy pole. White people also took part and Larry Albury was the greasy pole champion for many years. A dance was held at the end of the evening.

Regard for the royal family had been very low in the reign of King George IV, but over the years, Queen Victoria gained the love and respect of the Harbour Island people and with it grew loyalty and pride in the British Empire. On 24 May 1873, the anniversary of Her Majesty's Birthday, a public holiday was given and a number of Public Officers and others went down to Harbour Island to celebrate it.[22] The celebration of Queen Victoria's Jubilee was a big affair in Harbour Island featuring a regatta, a greasy pole with a fine pig upon it, a tug of war and a torchlight procession. The evening skies were lit up with fireworks and the day concluded with the National Anthem and a Jubilee salute by two cannons on the Public Wharf.[23] The notion of making Queen Victoria's Birthday a celebration of Empire, with patriotic exercises in schools, was initiated in Canada in the late 1890s by a headmistress. Earl Reginald Brabazon championed the idea and by 1905 it was accepted throughout the Empire as Empire Day. Again a society grew up in Harbour Island to cater for Empire Day.

The Imperial Order of the Daughters of the Empire was founded in 1900 at the time of the Boer War by a Montreal woman, Mrs. Margaret Clark Murray, and was designed to be a bond between the women and children of the various parts of the British Empire. The theory behind the IODE in times of peace was to provide patriotic, philanthropic and educational pursuits and during war to collect funds and supplies for the soldiers. By 1903, the Bahamas organized and had five Chapters with 100 women involved. In June 1904, the Lord Dunmore chapter of the IODE was formed with 32 members, with the motto: 'Advance with courage'. The Princess Margaret and Princess Mary of Wales Chapters were added to the Harbour Island IODE by 1906.

The first Empire Day in Harbour Island, 24 May 1906, featured entertainment by the three Chapters of IODE singing *Rule Britannia*, a speech by R. J. Armstrong, and sports at St. John's Schoolroom. Refreshments and entertainment in the evening included musical duets for piano and violin, songs and recitations and the singing of *God Save the King*.[24] Two years later, the Harbour Island Chapters of Daughters and Children of the Empire celebrated Empire Day. St. John's Schoolroom became the scene of a pretty garden party; palm-leaf arbours and bowers were erected and cakes, candies and ices were available at stalls waited upon by Daughters in costumes representing a variety of concepts and personages: 'The Empire', 'Rebecca at the Well', 'Mary, Mary', 'The Gypsies', 'A Grecian Lady', 'Poppy', 'Spring', 'Twilight' and 'Queen of Hearts'. The Junior Chapter, in costume, braided the Maypole and a May Queen was chosen. Evening entertainment, 'The Bachelor's Dream tableau vivant' and Mr. Jarley's waxworks, were a new venture for Dunmore Town. The proceeds went toward a new public well for the township, on behalf of the night patrol organized because of the recent fires.[25] By 1921, Empire Day had expanded to a garden fete in the grounds of the residency and Commissioner E. H. McKinney worked strenuously with the IODE to make the day a huge success. Two years later, Brilanders heard their first Empire Day message by the King and Queen over the new medium of radio. At the opening ceremony, Privates Curry and Higgs of the Bahamas War Contingent were awarded British War and Victory medals.[26]

Empire Day 1930 saw the formation of the 1st Harbour Island Girl Guides Company under Capt. Rossiter, the daughter of the Wesleyan Minister, Rev. H. S. F. Rossiter, who presented them their colours in the presence of the Lord Dunmore and Prince of Wales Chapters of IODE. Rev. Rossiter in his message told the girls that:

> … the flag is a sign and symbol of honour, loyalty, usefulness, friendliness, kindness, obedience, cheerfulness and purity and a

spirit of love and self sacrifice. The Union Jack stands for honour, righteousness and fairplay and the unity of the British Empire to which you belong.[27]

In 1932, House of Assembly Members, Allan H. Kelly and R. T. Symonette, both keen yachtsmen, urged that there was no finer setting than the harbour of Harbour Island to hold an Empire Day Regatta. They persuaded the newly arrived Governor, Bede Clifford, that he must meet the gallant Empire builders, whose ancestors had assisted Deveax to rid Nassau of the Spaniards. Consequently, Harbour Island hosted about 200 visitors who took excursions on the *Ena K, Patricia K, Belize, Sir Charles Orr, Endion* and *Standard J* from Nassau plus many others from the District. The IODE and the Girl Guides arranged arches of palms and evergreens to welcome the visitors. The streets were lined with Union Jacks, bunting and vendors of candies and coconuts. The men wore huge buttonholes, hatbands and belts of red, white and blue and the beach pyjamas of the visiting ladies added a touch of colour and were much admired, even if their appearance in the streets of Dunmore Town gave the staid heads a bit of a jolt at first. The harbour was fuller and livelier than at any time in her history and the white-winged racing yachts, Kelly's *Patsy I* and *Patsy II*, Symonette's *Zelda, Dolphin* and *Feison,* Mr. Lewless' *Falcon,* Stafford Sands' *Arethusa* and others, the *Rosalie, Baby Patsy, Canvas Black, Goldfinch,* all added to the striking view.[28] A few weeks later, motion pictures by Fred Armbrister were shown at the Nassau Theatre and the beauty of the gala weekend shown to a much wider audience.

In 1958, Empire Day was renamed British Commonwealth Day and the date moved to 11 June to coincide with the official birthday of Queen Elizabeth II. It changed again in 1966 to Commonwealth Day and is now celebrated on the second Monday in March. Although Brilanders listen to Queen Elizabeth's speech on Commonwealth Day, the old-timers still remember with fondness the flags, maypole, sports, regattas, the greasy pole and the old song:

> Today's the Queen's Birthday,
> If you don't give us a holiday,
> We'll all run away.

In April 1939, the Empire was about to enter into its darkest days as war threatened Europe. The Hon. Lady Dundas, President of the Bahamas Red Cross Society, entertained the members of the Prince of Wales and Dunmore Chapters of IODE to tea at the Sea View Hotel, Harbour Island.[29] It was a very fortuitous meeting as the two groups would work closely together in

Harbour Island for the next few years. Groups were set up in most Out Islands to teach women to knit for the Red Cross and in Harbour Island under the supervision of two winter residents, Mrs. Gardner and Mrs. Ely. Wool was dispatched from Nassau and all knitted work was sent back free but participants were asked to become members of the Red Cross. By 1941, every house in Harbour Island had a knitter. Forty-three members of the Red Cross led by Mrs. W. R. Roberts, the Commissioner's wife, and Public School scholars under teacher Marion Johnson sent total contributions of £9-17-5d., 45 pairs of socks, 45 sweaters, 18 cap mufflers, 26 plain mufflers, 15 helmets and 1 cap scarf plus £16-6-3d in house-to-house collections. Rev. W. T. Makepeace urged that every one in the Empire should 'do their bit' and the Methodist Church raised £54-1-0d. In addition, Harbour Island was the first island to send a shipment of scrap iron to Nassau for the war effort.[30] For the next three years, Brilanders worked hard to contribute to the war effort, especially with shows and raffles for the Harbour Island Canteen Fund. By 1943 this fund was no longer necessary for British Empire troops so some of the money was sent to the Phillipines to assist the American Forces and some used in Harbour Island to provide a canteen in the Library for British Forces serving in Harbour Island. After the war the Harbour Island Red Cross Chapter provided volunteers for sports games, hotel functions and meals on wheels programmes for the sick and elderly. Unfortunately the Red Cross died out and was not available for the aftermath of Hurricane *Andrew* in 1992.

The Imperial Order of the Daughters of the Empire became involved in another popular event, the Harbour Island Agricultural Exhibition. Exhibitions had become popular in the Empire since Prince Albert had planned the Great Exhibition of Works and Industry in Hyde Park in 1851. In 1876 a Harbour Island Agricultural Society of 60 members had been formed and its Chairman urged more strenuous efforts to develop more generally the resources of the soil.[31] Several Governors promoted agriculture in Harbour Island, none more than Governor Shea, who brought in experts from Kew Gardens. In 1908, the IODE arranged a flower, fruit and shrub social at St. John's schoolroom, which was decorated with rugs, mats, and small tables of embroidery. Prizes were awarded for best exhibits and after refreshments a recitation of *Jackdaw of Rheims* by Mrs. Winifred Sweeting, who praised of the work of the IODE. The evening ended when all joined hands and sang *Auld Lang Syne*.[32] In 1921, Commissioner E. H. McKinney worried that Harbour Island had become a forsaken island and required advertising. Along with the ladies of the IODE an Agricultural Exhibition was organized to attract Nassauvians and Americans to take special excursions there by motor boat.[33]

By February, men had planned and grown their agricultural products and women assiduously worked with their needles. Never before had

Harbour Island welcomed so many visitors at one time. A splendid display met the gaze of the visitor and the standard of excellence was uniform. Opened by Governor and Lady Cordeaux, the exhibition featured drawings and maps of India by schoolchildren in the Art & Craft section, pumpkins from Hatchet Bay, cabbages and palm trees from Bluff, the renowned shellwork of the ladies of Current and needlework so fine that the needlework judges had a difficult task.[34] By 1937, a special wireless report to the *Nassau Guardian* showed that many visitors from Nassau had travelled in perfect weather to Briland in 9 planes and 15 yachts for a gala day at Dunmore Town for the annual Agricultural Exhibition, which had now added a regatta and a dance. Again the inhabitants of the Harbour Island District had worked hard and the display included 50 different kinds of vegetables and fruit, and the beautiful quilts for which the district is famed. Governor Dundas gave an encouraging address, followed by a parade by the band of the Harbour Island Boy Scouts led by Scoutmaster Jaziel Thompson.[35] The Agricultural Exhibition lasted into the war years but gradually diminished and was discontinued until it was revived as part of the Harbour Island District Fair of 14–16 February 1957.

This fair featured exhibits of needlework, art and handicrafts, preserves, cakes, candies, flowers and an agricultural show of produce and animals. The programme over the three days was packed with events; a float parade led by the Bahamas Police Band, sports, band and dance competitions, water sports, including the greasy pole, bicycle races, water skiing and dancing round the Maypole. The Fair, opened by Governor Sir Raynor Arthur was a huge success. This fair continued for a few years but was later discontinued.

In 1989, Donald Cash had the idea of reviving the regatta. He helped form a committee and since then the North Eleuthera Regatta in the harbour of Harbour Island has been a very popular venue for sailors in the Bahamas, attracting up to a dozen 'A', a dozen 'B' Class and a handful of 'C' Class boats. The competition is very keen and attracts thousands of visitors for the Discovery (National Heroes) Day holiday weekend. Bay Street is packed with vendors selling Bahamian delicacies and dancing and partying takes place for the whole weekend. The racing of the Regatta of 2000 was cancelled at the last moment as a whirlwind ran along the Government Dock on the evening before the first race and ran most of the yachts ashore. The following year a Regatta was held at San Salvador on the same weekend, which cut the sailors in the North Eleuthera Regatta down to a mere handful. But the North Eleuthera Regatta bounced back in 2002. The 2003 Regatta provided very exciting racing despite the lack of wind. *The Lady in Red,* in Class B, owned by legendary sailor Eleazor Johnson, blew away the field to win all three races. Skipper Clyde Rolle summed up the true sailor's vocation when he said: 'For me this regatta was more than just winning. It was about using your skills.' In the A Class, the *New Courageous* skipper, Emmit Munroe, held off a strong challenge by *Red Stripe,* skippered by Clyde Rolle to win two out of three races. Again Briland rocked and rolled to music, dancing and partying from Thursday to Tuesday, when the sailors left on the *Captain Moxey,* and the spectators on private boats, the *Daybreak III* and the *BoHengy,* which made two trips a day for the entire weekend.[36]

With two churches and an educational facility to its credit, Methodism was a powerful religious force at Harbour Island during the second half of the nineteenth century. An important part of church activity was support of the Missionary thrust into Africa, then known as the 'Dark Continent'. Missionary boxes were carried around by the faithful throughout the year and pennies, threepences and shillings were collected with zeal.

Unfortunately, there were many who wished to make a contribution but had no money to give. To accommodate these people and thus involve the entire island in the missionary effort it occurred to some of the trustees that a vessel should be built for the collection of farm produce.

The vessel, aptly named *Africa's Hope* but more commonly known as the 'Missionary Boat' was constructed some time prior to 1906. She was built by a father-and-son team of Briland shipwrights, Mr. Albury, nicknamed 'Old Plant', and his son, John T. Albury.

A miniature three-masted schooner, she was destined to make scores of voyages but never to float on water. Fully rigged in the boom and gaff manner, the principal sails were known as spanker, mainsail and foresail. Above these were the mizzen, main and fore-topsails. In addition she carried four headsails: forestaysail, jib, flying jib and outer jib.

Africa's Hope was set on a four-wheeled carrier with ropes attached to the carrier fore and aft. Those at the front (or bow), when manned by teams of boys, provided the motive power, and those at the back (or stern) were for steering. A day of the year was set aside as 'Missionary Day' and, a few days before this, *Africa's Hope* began her annual voyage. For most of her active years, Harry Thompson was the captain – a job he took most seriously. He was not a sea-going man and it was probably because of his captaincy of *Africa's Hope* that he was given the nickname, 'Capt. Leads'.

The Wesley Manse was the port from which *Africa's Hope* set out and to which she returned to discharge her cargoes. It was a great wonderful experience to see and hear this boat rumbling through the rutted streets of Dunmore Town. Pulled along by dozens of enthusiastic boys with their cheerful banter and hearty laughter, she navigated every street that was passable. The Trustees and Reverends of the Methodist Church accompanied it and called at each house for donations. Cash gifts were put in their Missionary boxes, but since cash was sometimes scarce many gave fruit and vegetables from their farms. These gifts were placed in the boat and taken back to the Manse.

Every home was solicited and householders who had nothing to give were few and far between. After a number of voyages extending over two days, the collected cargoes were auctioned off and the cash received was added to that in the boxes.

The meeting on Missionary Night was one of the highlights of the Harbour Island year. The boat was placed in front of the pulpit, under full canvas, with flags flying and illuminated with lighted candles from stem to stern.

The clergy of Harbour Island and from surrounding districts would be in the pulpit for the service. The boat's crew were lined up outside the two doors at the rear of the church, all smartly dressed in full sailor's uniform. They waited in line outside for the congregation inside the church to sing the second hymn of the service. And at the second line of the second verse of the second hymn, 'Capt. Leads' would blow his whistle. At the signal the sailors would all march proudly up the two aisles and take their places around the boat in positions assigned to them by 'Capt. Leads'. It was a magnificent spectacle.

From the pulpit, the financial results of the Missionary year were announced. The log of *Africa's Hope's* voyage was read, spiced with humorous details such as stormy seas encountered around Cape William Pettee and through Broadway Straits. Ministers, especially those who had served in Africa, would tell interesting anecdotes of their experiences. These evenings were, all in all, interesting and joyous affairs.

Capt. Victor Cleare, a venerable son of Briland, reminisced: 'My first trip with *Africa's Hope* was in 1906. Missionary Night was one of the greatest events of the year at Harbour Island, second only to Christmas. My memory of the event, even today, is a very happy one, and the boat was a very lovely one.'

For a number of reasons *Africa's Hope* was removed from active service sometime in the 1930s. She was placed in retirement at the rear of Wesley Church and left to the ravages of termites and decay.

Philip Kemp, another respected son of Briland, discovered her in a deplorable state in 1975 and volunteered to restore the ship to her original condition. With loving care and over a period of three years he accomplished this. And you can see her today, in the Wesley Church, as she looked when first constructed so long ago.

Nowadays, on Missionary Day in March or April, the boat is placed before the chapel in Temperance Square and passersby give gifts of money or produce, then the boat is put back in the evening. The Chapel is decorated with lights and hosts an Ecumenical service with all eight denominations taking part. Missionary Funds are now used in the Bahamas and the contributions from Missionary Day and the yearly boxes from groups within the community, total as much as $10,000.[37]

In mid-December, the Jews celebrated Hannukah, The Feast of Light, which Christians incorporated into the Christmas celebration. In Harbour Island, the St. John's Anglican Church had a candlelight procession a week before Christmas Day and a Bazaar on 23 December, which in 1874 was for the purpose of re-erecting the Parochial Schoolroom. On Christmas Eve the Sons of Temperance Bazaar started and lasted for five days. On St. John's Day, 27 December, the 'Brotherhood' assembled in the Parochial Schoolroom and marched to Church wearing their badge of order on the left breast. On New Year's Eve, after an afternoon service, Sunday-school children, accompanied by teachers, marched in procession displaying bright banners and numerous flags and singing some enlivening hymns, to the Rectory grounds, where they played their usual games and partook of a plentiful supply of cakes and candies. The day's enjoyment ended with a few hymns, *God save the Queen* and three hearty cheers before everyone returned home.[38] A few years later the St. Stephen's Odd Fellows started up the Boxing Day Parade, which regularly featured masqueraders and a torchlight procession with a marching band.

It is a very interesting phenomenon that as the Boxing Day masquerade was dying out in the 1950s the brass band members, Leroy Johnson, King Cleare, Whitfield Higgs, Lambert Roberts and Thomas Sawyer, with children wearing decorated paper costumes, continued to parade to the hotel doors and to Up Yonder private houses. Over the years they gradually split into smaller groups of troubadours going house to house as the number of houses grew. They did this on both Boxing Day and New Year's Eve. By the early 1980s these groups came together again as more formal Junkanoo Parades, influenced by the parades in Nassau but catering much more to the growing tourist trade. In 1993, the Junkanoo parade was shifted from the early morning to the early evening and since then has grown both in content and popularity. The musical content has had a very interesting growth. The Boys Brigade, formed in 1957 with 40 boys under Sydney Albury and Munro Dreher, has now been incorporated into a 100-strong community marching band led by Corporal Howard Pinder of Alice Town, Eleuthera. When the frenzied dancing and the accompanying brass sounds get under way in front of the Harbour Lounge a shudder goes through the crowd, whose feet and bodies move with the rhythm. These two popular Junkanoo Parades are followed by a dance at Sea Grapes Night Club and at midnight the sky lights up with fireworks.

The Jubilee of Queen Victoria's reign marked a 'very British era' in Harbour Island. The very language of the correspondent to the *Nassau Guardian* of 1889 demonstrates the aspirations to gentility:

The inhabitants of Harbour Island felt the true gladness on the return of Christmas accompanied by dear old Santa Claus with his variety of nice things for the little ones and the usual tender and affectionate greetings to old and young. After the St. John's Church Service the 'Victoria Cricket Club', of recent formation, played a very interesting match.

Numerous spectators enjoyed themselves and the correspondent thought that the game of cricket should be encouraged not only for the game itself but for occupying the players in a rational and healthy manner. The game was played in a spirit of rivalry between the Reds and the Blues. The match was followed by a torchlight procession, which was a beautiful spectacle and the following evening a lantern-light procession was held. The report does not give the score of the game but gives us the names of the protagonists:

Blues: G. A. Albury, H. W. F. Sturrup, John T. Albury, T. S. Higgs, G. E. Newton, D. O. Johnson, T. F. Jones, A. Ingraham, Edward Roberts and John T. Harris.

Reds: W. M. Ingraham, W. M. Saunders, James Curry, Samuel Sweeting, Albion Cash, W. Ingraham, T. T. Ingraham, Charles Johnson and John Kemp.[39]

According to old-timers, a fierce rivalry grew in Harbour Island between the cricket teams of 'Up Yonder' and 'Down Yonder'. However the rivals became fervent to defend their honour against teams from Nassau or Spanish Wells. In 1896, the visit of a Nassau team consisting of members of the 'Town Cricket Eleven' and 'United Sports Club' resulted in two victories for the Nassau team. The names of the victors all seemed to have family or other connections in Harbour Island: N. Duncombe, Reginald Farrington, P. G. Thompson, A. de Glanville, R. Duncombe, R. J. Farrington, E. Solomon, J. Bethel, C. Duncombe, G. P. Lester.[40] The following year the Harbour Island Cricket Club paid four shillings for one acre of land near Barracks Hill at Harbour Island, which became known as the Eastern Parade but later was also known as Grant's Oval.[41]

Cricket at Harbour Island was not confined to men only. In 1906, the spectators at Grant's Oval watched a cricket match between Alexandria CC (young ladies) and Dunmore CC (young men), playing left-handed. Marion Johnson and Kate Sturrup made excellent scores for the ladies as did Harry Albury and Howell Saunders for the men.[42] The following Emancipation Day began a gala week in Harbour Island when the *Kate Sturrup* carried cricketers to Harbour Island 'for a jolly good time'. They all stayed at the Sea View Hotel hosted by Mrs. Sweeting and her very charming daughters. It was a week of picnics, sailing, bathing, teas, lunches, dancing and singing with midnight sessions of entertainment and partying. The highlight was to be the Monday cricket match, for which the young people bought ribbons, making bows and rosettes: blue and white for Harbour Island, and crimson and navy for Nassau. Unfortunately, some unpleasantness caused the game to be cancelled. The Alexandria Ladies CC took action as they had leased the only pitch, the Parade at Grant's Oval, which had been used by Dunmore Town CC for many years. Eventually with the aid of barrister Kenneth Solomon the matter was settled and the match proceeded the next day. The following day the Harbour Island Ladies played a cricket match between Reds and Pinks causing great excitement. On Friday the ladies of Nassau beat the boys easily.[43]

The members of the Dunmore Cricket Club were involved in a different kind of match on 24 August 1911, holding banners at a very pretty wedding between one of their players, Harry Sweeting and Mary E. Bethel, daughter of William Bethel. The schooner *Fearless* was gaily decorated for the occasion. Performing the ceremony was the Rev. H. W. Devall of St. John's Anglican Church; maid of honour, the bride's sister Albertha Bethel; bridesmaids, Mollie and Mildred Johnson; flower girl, Emma Roberts; groomsmen, Lewis Thompson and Charles Albury. It was a grand ceremony, Runnard Sweeting gave the bride away and the church was packed with spectators to see the bride in a charming white mull dress. Miss Hilda Higgs presided on the organ and large quantities of rice were thrown at the joyous couple. Afterwards the guests were entertained by Commissioner Mr. Pickwood on the banjo and Stafford Johnson, guitar. At 10 pm the guests went home, while the happy pair proceeded to their home on King Street.[44]

Apparently cricket faded out, perhaps during the First World War, but after a meeting in 1923 to revive the game, cricket fever was at a pitch and there was a practice every Saturday. In March the next year, the Harbour Island Cricket Team visited Nassau but was beaten by a St Patrick's Team. In October that year, they returned to Nassau and gained revenge over St. Patrick's, lost to St. George's and were beaten by an All Nassau Eleven by one run. On the King's birthday celebration of 1932, the 'Cheerio' girls of Harbour Island gave the St. Vincent's Cricket Club a party on the motor boat *Golden Eagle* and a dance at the residence of Robert Bethel with music provided by Honey Boys and Orchestra. The following day, the St. Vincent's Cricket Club played on Eastern Parade watched by a large and enthusiastic crowd of spectators using drums to encourage the contestants. Afterwards a party took place at J. A. Grant's residence on Clarence Street, again featuring the Honey Boys Orchestra. By coincidence it was also the captain's birthday. He was also called 'King George' (Cleare) and as he entered the Dance Hall the National Anthem was played.[45] On New Year's Day 1945,

Spanish Wells had a decisive victory over Harbour Island at cricket at Dunmore Town[46] and maybe Brilanders gave up cricket as according to the old heads, Spanish Wells beat Harbour Island many times. With the advent of television, basketball and baseball became more popular and are now the premium sports in Harbour Island.

Nassau became the new home for many Out Islanders in the early twentieth century and in almost every case they maintained nostalgia for the simplicity of the old ways. Sidney Poitier explains it so very well:

> Unlike Cat Island, Nassau required the selling of one's labour for a price, and using the returns of that labour for food buying and rent paying and clothes buying and the doctor's bills. The new neighbours did not exchange corn for beans, yams for peas, or papayas for sugar apples. Nor did they use the free age old root medicine when sickness came, they bought from a pharmacy the medicine that probably originated from the root that used to be free but was now packaged and refined and cost money.... That place (Nassau) was not good for raising tomatoes or children... the crowded slum conditions led to a steady erosion of Out Island morals and morale.[47]

The displaced Brilander suffered the alienation of no longer belonging to the community, where every afternoon, a 'house of assembly' had met under the fig tree to discuss the affairs of state. Groups of men sat on the bench, whittling and talking, and all matters of great import were argued about if not settled there. On the death of an islander, a woman in white dress, black belt, hat and umbrella would walk from house to house announcing the death and the time of the funeral. If a man and a woman walked as far as the beach together that was tantamount to announcing their engagement. The man had to write to the father for permission to court the daughter. When a new Methodist minister arrived, every young girl was after him.[48] Many ministers and other officials did marry Harbour Island girls. Rev. Thompson in 1825 had an affair with Eliza Margaret Fisher, whom he later married[49] and Rev. Henderson in 1904 married 16-year-old Miss Harris.[50] In 1944, the first Royal Air Force wedding at Harbour Island took place between Lila Mae Curry, daughter of Mr. and Mrs. Richie Curry and Frederick Ross of RAF Marine Section, who was stationed at Harbour Island. The couple walked under an arch of guns and oars decked with flags and royal poincianas at the gate of church.[51]

Away from home the Brilander missed the springtime pursuit of soldier crabs and pigeon plums and in summer picking sea grapes and hauling for jacks. He recalls the sailing ships riding in the harbour, the games of marbles, cricket and rounders, the pink sands, riding the breakers and that aesthetic feeling:

> The lilies in the valleys,
> and the rushes waving fair,
> In the breeze from the Atlantic,
> that would rumple up your hair.[52]

A haul in the harbour is a memorable experience.

Just before dawn the men gathered round the hauling net and stubbed out their last cigarettes as they heard the hum of the Seagull engine at the stern of the *Black Dragon*. Captain and owner Robbie Albury skillfully drew alongside the dock and his heart gladdened to see the 'good crew' of five men, whose combined hauling skills made certain the catch of the big school of jacks he had sighted the previous day.

Robbie had bought the eighteen-foot-long hauling boat from Harry Sweeting in the early 1960s. Previously named the *Cartilla*, she was rechristened *Black Dragon* by her new captain because she was painted black with red trim. The hauling boat was custom built by John T. Albury in the 1880s, with a low gunwale to allow the net to be pulled in with ease and the crew to climb back into the boat with speed. It was built at Harbour Island's renowned shipyard (site of the popular fig tree on the front shore), where John T. Albury also built the *Sainte Marie*, the *Melrose* and the *Lady Shea*. These three schooners were part of the great Harbour Island fleet that carried pineapples to Baltimore and the Eastern Seaboard, dragged lumber from Abaco or Jacksonville to Cuba or were sold to be used in the sponge or sisal industry.

In the early days, Capt. Robbie could count on 800 runners or skip jacks in a single haul but by the turn of the century he knew he would have to be satisfied with 150; and then there were those dreaded days when not once did he spot a school of jacks skipping the water's surface or even 'wet the net'. The 150-foot-long seine net, made today with nylon fibre and plastic corks, was in the old days made of cotton with pond apple roots for floats. The corks kept the top of the net afloat while lead weights at the bottom of the net kept it vertical in the water. Over the years the depth of net grew from 6 feet, when the harbour teemed with fish, to 20 or 30 feet as the fish became scarce.

All hauls were made in the harbour. Some mornings the wily captain might head 'down along' to haul the banks or the rocks at Long Point, but on this morning he was bound 'up along' to Whale Point, where the current from Harbour's Mouth drove many a rich bounty onto the banks of the harbour.

As the *Black Dragon* made its way up the harbour, with its glistening waters smooth as oil and the light of the sun creeping across the land, the crew watched intently for the ripple on the water or the gulls circling. The birds also searched for the fish beating the water as the jacks chased small fry up to the surface. Then comes the much-anticipated cry, 'School ahead!' and the arm pointing in the direction of the skipping fish. The school sighted, Capt. Robbie figures how the tide is flowing in order to set the net so as not to lose the school against the tide. He then skillfully circles the school.

Once in position, the first wingman is ordered overboard with one end of the rope, as the *Black Dragon* slowly encompasses the school. At regular intervals the remaining crew ease themselves over the low gunwale, taking the net with them, until all the net is passed out into the water. The last man, Capt. Robbie, dives over with the other end of the rope and completes the circle. He drags the leads under his feet until the net is ready to pull and then he hurdles over the corks to trap the fish inside the net. He breaks the surface and shouts, 'Pull hard!' With great effort, the net, heavy with fish, is hauled into the boat by the crew, who by now has scrambled back into the boat. If the school is as large as 500, Robbie 'breaks the net', closing the net halfway so as to pull half of the school safely into the boat, leaving the other half trapped to be pulled in later.

Occasionally, the crew will attempt what is known as a 'blind haul'. They choose a favoured shoal and knowing where to throw the net over they usually pull in a mixed catch of yellow tails, yellow jacks, porgies, grunts, snappers, tangs and boxfish. Whatever the catch, they anchor the *Black Dragon* off a convenient beach, pick and thread some palmetto leaves (thatch palm) and tie the fish on the strings ready to be shared or sold. The share system is different in the various settlements but the tradition in Harbour Island is one-third to the person who owns the boat and the net, and the remaining two-thirds is shared among the crew. If the haul is small the share is equal between owner and crew.

In the early days when the hauls were plentiful, the *Black Dragon* approached the ramp at about mid morning and announced its successful catch to potential customers by blowing the conch shell. People converged from all directions to buy a string of 5 or 6 fish for $1.50 (nowadays a string sells for $5). The hot, tired crew would take a welcome shower and breakfast before continuing the day as farmer, carpenter, painter or whatever their primary trade may be.

No one who has been on a haul can ever forget the hard work of dragging the leads or pulling the corks and the exhilaration of bringing the catch in.

There is an old Bahamian expression: *You can take the man out of the island but you can't take the island out of the man.* This is very true of those men and women who for one reason or another left Harbour Island. They remember Briland ways with great fondness. Many expatriate Brilanders return home for August, New Year and long weekends to join the many American, German, British, French and other visitors who love the Briland ways and have homes there or vacation there regularly.

Notes

1. Bermuda Records, microfilm, Bahamas Dept. Archives, 749/CR G-H/24, 24 April 1661.
2. Fulham Papers, Reel 8 Vol 15/86 (40) Letter from Rev. T. Robertson 17 June 1790.
3. SPG Reel 1, Reverend Moss to Rev. Dr. Burton, 27 May 1773.
4. MMS, Box 112, Box 1817, Sheet 41/19, Rutledge to MMS, 3 Jan 1817.
5. MMS, Box 113, Box 1819, Sheet 89/23, Rutledge to MMS, 13 April 1819.
6. MMS, Box 118, Box 1822–3, Sheet 178/175, J. Davies from Harbour Island, 1 Jan 1823.
7. MMS, Box 133, Box 1833, Sheet 477/105, C. Penny from Harbour Island, 30 May 1833 and MMS, Box 135, Box 1834, Sheet 500/17, C. Penny from Nassau, 18 July 1834.
8. MMS, Box 135, Box 1834, Sheet 506/25, C. Penny from Harbour Island, 28 August 1834.
9. MMS, Box 217, WI corr. Bahamas File Box # (FBN) 27, Sheet 1300/19, T. Lofthouse from Harbour Island, 9 Aug 1838.
10. CO23/109/19, Cockburn to Lord Russell, 29 January 1841.
11. *Bahama Herald*, 18 January 1850.
12. *Nassau Guardian*, 2 November 1854.
13. *Nassau Guardian*, 6 August 1870.
14. *Nassau Guardian*, 20 August 1872.
15. Blue Books for the years 1874, 1899 and 1912/13.
16. *Nassau Guardian*, 20 August 1875 and *Nassau Guardian* 12 August 1876.
17. *Nassau Guardian*, 26 September 1874.
18. *Nassau Guardian*, 15 April 1876.
19. Interview with Reswell (Prince) Mather, August 2003.
20. Blue Books for the years stated.
21. *Nassau Guardian*, 17 August 1878.
22. *Nassau Guardian*, 21 May 1873.
23. *Nassau Guardian*, 29 June 1887.
24. *Nassau Guardian*, 6 June 1906.
25. *Nassau Guardian*, 3 June 1908.
26. *Nassau Guardian*, 14 June 1923.
27. *Nassau Guardian*, 28 May 1930.
28. *Nassau Guardian*, 25 May 1932.
29. *Nassau Guardian*, 13 April 1939.
30. *Nassau Guardian*, 21 August 1940.
31. *Nassau Guardian*, 15 April 1876.
32. *Nassau Guardian*, 20 May 1908.
33. *Nassau Guardian*, 5 January 1921.
34. *Nassau Guardian*, 19 February 1921.
35. *Nassau Guardian*, 6 March 1937.
36. *Nassau Tribune*, 14 October 2003.
37. Interview with Reswell (Prince) Mather, August 2003.
38. *Nassau Guardian*, 7 January 1874.
39. *Nassau Guardian*, 19 January 1889.

40 *Nassau Guardian*, 7 October 1896.
41 CO 23/249/59, Blue Book 1897, 27 September 1897.
42 *Nassau Guardian*, 14 March 1906.
43 *Nassau Guardian*, 14 August 1907.
44 *Nassau Tribune*, 31 August 1911.
45 *Nassau Guardian*, 8 June 1932.
46 *NassauTribune*, 4 January 1945.
47 Craton & Saunders, *Islanders in the Stream,* Vol 2, The University of Georgia Press, Athens & London, 1998, p. 285, Sidney Poitier, *This Life,* New York: Ballantine, 1980, pp. 1–4.
48 Memories of Harbour Island by Hilda Higgs, unpublished notes circa 1913.
49 MMS, Box # 6, Box 122–1824, Sheet 226/82, R. H. Moore from Harbour Island, May 1825.
50 MMS, File 1904, Sheet 1494/59, Arthur Robinson from Nassau, 19 June 1904.
51 *Nassau Tribune*, 23 June 1944.
52 From *Memories of Briland* by William E. Albury.

15

The enchantment of Harbour Island

Not all the enchantment of Harbour Island belongs to the land and the sea. There is 'something in the air'. The cool gentle breezes off the Atlantic Ocean are unpolluted by fetid vapours from bog and swamp. Rather, on passing over the island, their fragrance is enhanced. There is a slight taste of salt, a faint awareness of aromatic medicines, a hint of perfume. The appeal is not to the cortex, but to the deeper and older brain. There is the stirring of ancient memories of an elemental association of man with the earth and sea.[1]

The gentle Taino Indian walked her shores. He was the first to love her. And he perhaps appreciated her freshness and her beauty more than all the rest who came later, for he made no effort to change her virgin beauty. He himself lived a life of simplicity and happiness. It was a perfect match, the Taino and the island. This beautiful creature was very, very close to paradise.[2]

By the early eighteenth century, Harbour Island had become a reputed health resort as the pure, serene and healthful air brought sick inhabitants from other islands[3] and ailing refugees from the malarial rice lands of Carolina.[4] At the end of that century, it became Lord Dunmore's summer retreat. And in the early nineteenth century sick troops were sent from Nassau to the newly built barracks at 'the most healthy island in the Bahamas to recover their health'.[5] The inhabitants of Harbour Island at that time 'were a kind hospitable race, and although their buildings might have been covered in thatch, their doors were open to strangers'.[6]

With the rapid improvement of Dunmore Town in the mid-nineteenth century a Joint Stock Company was formed to establish the Dunmore Hotel and the Harbour Island Packet with half the stock taken up in Harbour Island and half in Nassau.[7] This company was dissolved within a few months. In 1868, a similar company was set up and the Harbour Island packet schooner *Mary Jane* carried the mail and passengers from Dunmore Town and Spanish Wells to Nassau.[8] Although briefly replaced in 1892 by the *Kate Sturrup*, the schooner, *Dart*, had the contract to carry the mail, freight and passengers from 1870 until 1922, when the MV *Endion* replaced her.

The *Dart* built up a reputation for reliability, as did the Harbour Island fleet of international and inter-insular sailing vessels with fruit and supplies. Dunmore Town, more than any other Out Island settlement, was becoming accessible to an increasing number of visitors. A report in the *Nassau Guardian* of 1888 tells us that:

> Harbour Island is becoming quite a watering place. Several pleasure parties have visited it during the past few weeks and enjoyed even the slight change it affords in hot July. Delightful walks on shining sands may be had on the wide firm North Beach and excursions to the Glass Window or sailing the fine harbour. We would suggest a well-kept boarding house might add to the attractions and perhaps induce some of the American visitors during the season to give it a trial.[9]

It would appear that many of those early visitors were Brilanders returning home on family reunions, business visits or excursions at holiday celebrations for New Year, Easter and Empire Day. Excursions to Harbour Island gained in popularity. On a moonlit night in early May 1895, the SS *Nassau*, captained by William Ranger, steamed out of Nassau Harbour with 33 pleasure seekers for the round-trip fare of 6 shillings. Some stayed at Albert Ernest Sweeting's house, boarding with meals.[10] Mr. Sweeting died and the following year his wife, Julia, and her daughters opened their house to guests as the Sea View Hotel. The first guest was Commissioner H. E. Grant, who paid 4 shillings a day room and board. Julia ran the Sea View Hotel for 46 years and her daughter Nellie for a further 14 years. The hotel was razed to the ground in 1960.[11]

The number of foreign tourists to Nassau increased steadily in step with improvements in steamship service during the last four decades of the nineteenth century reaching a peak of 750 each winter season.[12] Some of them found their way to Eleuthera, Harbour Island and Abaco. The *Harpers New Monthly Magazine* of 1874 gives a glowing description of a steamship journey to the Bahamas, with an informative background history and suggestions on what to see while there. The writer includes a description of a trip to the North-Western Out Islands, stressing its safety.

> The cruise to Harbour Island and Eleuthera is one of the most interesting within easy reach of Nassau. It can be made in a yacht or in many of the little schooners constantly plying to and fro; keys are always in sight, and a lee can be made at any time; while one can return by way of Abaco …[13]

He further extols the virtues of Harbour Island as 'a very pleasing little place, it is encircled by beautiful cocoanut groves, and dreaming by the green water in an air of solitude and peace is very bewitching to one who is weary of the rush and giddy whirl of the nineteenth century, while the cool trade-winds always moderate the heat'.[14] At that time travellers to Harbour Island could find tolerable accommodations at the house of Mrs. Stirrup, where the cuisine was by no means elaborate, and 'the rooms were not sumptuous but will do for a week or two'.[15] The sea trip from New York to Nassau took 80 hours but by 1896, travelling by rail followed by an overnight passage on the 'Great Ocean Ferry' from Florida took much less time. The number of visitors to the Bahamas increased steadily until America entered the war in 1917 at which time tourism almost came to a halt.

In the early 1920s, E. H. McKinney became Commissioner of the Harbour Island District. Feeling that Harbour Island was a forsaken island that required advertising, he organized an Agricultural Exhibition to attract sufficient Nassauvians and Americans to justify special excursions by motorboat.[16] Governor and Lady Cordeaux attended the first exhibition and never before had Harbour Island welcomed so many visitors at one time.[17]

Commissioner McKinney gave special attention to popularizing Harbour Island as a 'Health Resort'. In his 5-year tenure, the visitors' book at the Commissioner's Office had over 500 signatures and he met with all the visitors personally and provided them with information and postcard views as souvenirs.[18] Moreover, he pushed forward great improvements to infrastructure and services.

The first priority was the purchase of the 103-foot *Endion* with a Fairbanks-Morse crude oil burning engine capable of carrying 18 passengers in her two staterooms, intended for the Nassau–Miami–Harbour Island run. She was brought over from Miami by Capt. E. B. Sweeting and crewmen Gerald Johnson, Roy Sweeting, Percy Bethel, Frank Johnson, Nick Sawyer and Capt. Albert Sweeting, a director of the purchasing company and her captain over the next 20 years. The *Endion* received the contract for passenger and mail service to Harbour Island and Spanish Wells and made her first trip on 17 January 1922. An advertisement in the *Nassau Guardian* showed that every 10 days, for the price of 8 shillings cabin or 5 shillings steerage, tourists and locals could visit historic and picturesque Dunmore Town – the ideal health resort of the Bahamas.[19]

The second priority was to overcome the difficulties of entering the harbour. At the southern entrance at Harbour's Mouth, there was 16 foot of water running well inside the bar but unfortunately there was only a 9-foot clearance in the channel across the sand bank leading to the anchorage of Dunmore Town. The northern entrance from Bridge Point and the dreaded 'Devil's Backbone', was about two fathoms deep but inside the harbour at

Current Point, the 'great shoal bank' was only 7 feet wide. Inside the harbour, the anchorage of three and three-quarters fathoms was used for a considerable fleet of vessels. Baron Bliss, who had become very attached to Harbour Island, needed a safer entrance for his yacht, *Sea King*. For three months in 1923, men up to their waist in the breaking waves and with a tangle of pipes, ropes, wire, dynamite and fuse blasted out the reefs and shoals of the Devil's Backbone, the water churning white and rising 100 feet into the air as tons of rock were smashed off. For a total outlay of 4,000 pounds, the 360-foot-wide 'Bliss Channel', marked by iron beacons, poles and buoys, now allowed the *Sea King*, Capt. Lafayette Roberts, and Roland Symonette's three-masted schooner, *Alma R*, easier access into the harbour.[20] The grateful inhabitants of Harbour Island presented the Baron with a polished turtleshell as a token of their appreciation.[21]

In 1964, explosives from the British frigate *Leander* attempted to blast the coral reefs at 'The Flats'.[22] Two years later, the 338-foot *Traverse County*, belonging to the Atlantic Undersea Test and Evaluation Center (AUTEC) situated on the Commonage at North Eleuthera, with 200 personnel on board, including two teams of demolition experts, laid and dentonated 30 tons of explosives in about 20 feet of water, 500 feet offshore, between Bridge Point and Ridley Head.[23] Except when the wind is out of the North, the sea journey from Spanish Wells to Harbour Island is now much easier and safer than it used to be.

The third priority was to establish a reliable water supply for those who didn't have a rainwater tank on their premises. Harbour Island on its eastern ocean exposure has a rock ridge, which is flanked and paralleled by a wind-blown sand ridge separated by a narrow valley. Into this elevated valley there is an annual rain fall of some 40 to 50 inches, which seeps through sand ridge and furnishes the drinkable well water of the island and explains at the same time why at the end of the dry season well water becomes brackish by the backing-in of salt water. Boring in the stone ridge reveals only salt water. Before the 1920s, the wells on the eastern shore were well excavated with great expense using large amounts of labour and several lives had been lost. The process commenced by removing the sand from a circle of 60 feet or more in diameter until water was found. A barrel was then sunk half its depth in the water and the sand packed around it; another barrel was then placed over the first, and the sand again carefully filled in, and so on in succession until they reached the surface. This generally terminated with the last barrel, each barrel being of a larger size than the lower one and the uppermost one was closed by a lid under a padlock. Females, who by covering their heads and shoulders with a shawl protected themselves from the dripping water, brought the water from these wells into the town. From the wells to the town was a descent of 30 degrees and in some instances a distance of 200 or 300 yards. As in biblical times, the bronze-faced females had the pitchers so fairly balanced on the head that the hand was rarely required.[24]

The water in Harbour Island was often in short supply due to drought or as reported in 1873:

> We are badly off for water here, scarcely any to be procured, 'either for love or money'. The largest cisterns on the island are dry, and many on the north side have been overflowed by a heavy surge.[25]

In 1914, Medical Officer A. T. W. Johnson requested two additional public wells as the supply from the single public well was totally inadequate in times of drought.[26]

In 1924, Harbour Island became the first town in the colony to enjoy a modern water supply system and Commissioner McKinney received high commendation for his forethought and effort. The principal engine was a Fairbanks-Morse 6 hp gasoline engine with a $3\frac{3}{4}$ by 4 inch pump capable of pumping 3,000 gallons of water per hour with a back up 4 hp Hercules gas engine with Bulldozer pump in case of emergency. The engine house was a neat little structure with green painted window cases, very neat and spotlessly clean. The tank, which held the water pumped from wells at the North Beach, was 20 feet high and 15 feet deep with a capacity of 27,589 gallons, situated 60 feet above sea level to give good pressure. Pipes went from tanks to Dunmore Street, branched north as far as Princess Street and South to South Street down Bay Street to King Street and along all the cross streets from Bay to Dunmore Streets, over 13,000 feet of pipe. In the first instance 30 houses, six gardens and two toilets were connected as well as two stand-pipes in the streets at a price of $\frac{1}{2}$d for five gallons. The house meters had a minimum charge of 5 shillings for 1000 gallons plus 6d per 100 gallons above that. The plant gave work for two men: a collector who read the meters and an engineer, Howard Brady. The total cost of the plant was £2,300.[27] The following year six more wells were dug at the North Beach and water piped toward Harbour's Mouth for farming purposes.

During the Blockade years it was said that men used to play push-penny with $20 gold coins[28] and that the streets were paved with the large pebbles that were used as ballast for the Yankee schooners that carried the pineapples to the US.[29] But by 1885, the streets were in a miserable condition. In some places the grass and weeds had been allowed to grow to cover the whole street and in other places dirt and decomposing matter had accumulated and been allowed to stay there for months and as soon as rain fell the earth was carried away leaving holes and stones behind; and no effort was made to remedy this evil.[30] The 1888 appointments to the Board of Works were Resident Justice J. S. Solomon, ex officio Chairman T. W. Johnson, Richard

E. Roberts, John N. Roberts and J. P. Roberts, who was replaced the following year by H. F. Sturrup. The Board was congratulated for the improvements made by T. G. Johnson in 1902:

> Harbour Island is prettier than before. They have removed all the warehouses and blacksmiths shops along the front and made an abutment of stone, which gives Bay Street a very attractive appearance. They have white MacAdamized the well-kept streets and a fine library. I said to a friend of mine it looks prettier now than in our young days when there was plenty of business and money flowing. Pity such a place is not resorted to by many Nassauvians and American visitors.[31]

In 1923, visitors to Dunmore Town commented on the beautifully kept streets of the township, a credit to the Commissioner, an experienced road builder, supervising its public works. The difficulty had been obtaining suitable material for road making, as the local rock had not a sufficient quantity of lime in it, but McKinney successfully experimented with marl, obtained from a creek on the Eleuthera shore, which was found to be a more suitable covering for the cracked stone than quarry soil.[32]

In 1892, radio telegraph cable was laid between Cable Beach, Nassau and Jupiter, Florida but it was not until 1920 that the first Out Island wireless station opened in Governor's Harbour. On 3 November 1921, large crowds gathered on the grounds of the Commissioner's Residence for the official opening of the Harbour Island Radio Station. The Commissioner's Office had been enlarged to house the Post Office and Wireless Office. A gasoline engine drove the dynamo, which in turn charged a battery, which gave an electric current for wireless and lighting. The transmitter had a normal range of 100 miles and the receiving set could receive from up to 1,000 miles, including the Washington Press News.[33] During the following year 385 messages were dispatched and 435 messages received – a boon to the Harbour Island community and its status as a holiday resort.

The greatest boost to Harbour Island tourism also happened during McKinney's time as Commissioner. On 15 March 1922, the seaplane *Columbus* of the Aero Miami Airways Inc. flew from Miami to Nassau with passengers. Shortly after noon the *Columbus* made the very first flight to Harbour Island from Nassau taking as passengers Mr. & Mrs. R. J. A. Farrington, Misses Kate Menendez, Daisy Curry, Olive Moore, Messrs P. H. Burns, O. H. Curry, Newell Kelly and Dudley Gamblin. The party had lunch at Harbour Island, arranged by wireless and returned to Nassau at 4 pm having enjoyed the trip tremendously. The flight back took 37 minutes. The second flight ten days later returned to Nassau two hours late due to engine failure.[34] From this time, the enchantment of Harbour Island was no longer a secret, as travel writers extolled its virtues:

> The ideal way to enjoy the beauties of a land replete with gorgeous panoramas is from the skies looking down upon an expanse of jade and sapphire waters dotted with tiny white caps and sailboats like painted ships upon a painted ocean…Arriving at Harbour Island is an exciting experience. Below one sees Dunmore Town, once the residence of Lord Dunmore, Governor of the Bahamas, resembling a little Cape Cod fishing village with church steeples shining in the sun and tiny white cottages, replicas of fisherman's homes in old New England. Suddenly the plane has soared downward and shiny black native boys scull out to meet us. Thomas Napoleon, tallest and blackest is at the dock formally dressed in a battered gilded straw hat, and extends us good wishes as the unofficial greeter of Harbour Island…While a fish dinner is being prepared we all wander off to the other side of the island, to bathe in the world's only pink beach. For 1/2 mile the faintly pink tinged powdery sands reflect their colour in the feathery clouds above and slope gently into the sea…A fish dinner follows at the Little Boarding House, which is an event. We all sit at long tables and pass things, family style. Great platters of crawfish salad, fried grouper, boiled yellowtail, potatoes and beets are passed around with beer followed by cake and stewed fruits. Coffee is served on the piazza where we have an opportunity to watch the town's main industry for the past 300 years, shipbuilding. A 180 foot boat is under construction practically in the background…Mrs Marion Loveken came to Harbour Island 2 years ago as a sufferer from arthritis, for 2 weeks sunshine, rest and quiet and has been there ever since and her malady is completely cured…Late in the afternoon the party is sculled out to the plane by the black boys and our clipper ship brings us back to Nassau under a sunset sky – a $\frac{1}{2}$ hour of reversing the shifting scenes of the outward cruise.[35]

Harbour Island is a temptress. Once the American visitors found her, they could not let her go. By 1924, Mr. and Mrs. Frank E. Shearman of Jamestown, New York had made their sixth visit to Harbour Island, saying, 'They don't consider their visit to the sunny Bahamas is complete if they don't visit this beauty spot'. Mr. and Mrs. Frank Davis of Colorado Springs, Colarado on their second visit rented the fine residence of James Roberts on Bay Street, commanding a grand view of the harbour. The enchantment of Harbour Island spread through Morristown, New Jersey as Mr. and Mrs. Fred Ford and Mr. and Mrs. James H. McLean heard of the possibility that with extensive advertising, Harbour Island could be developed as a winter resort.[36] The source of the information was Mr. A. Graves Ely, who, in 1926, became the first American to build a winter home on Harbour Island. By 1933, Harbour Island had become the 'ideal pleasure resort', its beauty appealing to lovers of nature. It shortly became an angler's paradise as by this time it had become possible to ship ice from Nassau. Several Americans had homes there with colourful gardens flaming with bougainvillea and hibiscus.[37] By 1964, 60 homes had been built there by Americans and nowadays there are approximately 200 homes owned by people mainly from America but also by others from France, England, Germany and of course Nassau.

In the 1920s, Harbour Island, because of its easy access to Nassau and its previous success as a commercial centre had many advantages over other Out Islands as a tourist resort, for those who desired complete peace in a soothing climate far from the madding crowd. The radio-telegraph afforded in case of emergency quick and constant communication with the outside world. The island boasted an excellent public library with some 2,000 volumes of general literature, beside a regular supply of the best English and American periodicals. It had several churches for worship. On the seafront, it had an excellent boarding house and visitors could always find suitable accommodation. The streets were clean and well lighted and the general life of the community was in keeping with the usual outward orderliness of the township.[38]

Kerosene street lamps had been secured and erected in Harbour Island in 1895 by funds raised by Resident Justice J. C. G. O'Halloran, who, on leaving, begged the inhabitants to keep them in good working order.[39] These lights were removed prior to 1933 and for a while Harbour Island was without street lighting. Harry S. Albury, who supplied a few homes from his own yard in 1927, pioneered electricity in Harbour Island. Within two years, his brother T. Berlin Albury joined him and they bought a 110-volt Westinghouse generator from John S. George & Co. Homeowners quickly had plugs installed for fans, toasters, irons and other appliances. Within a few years, electric street lights lit a small area of Dunmore Town but were switched off at 10 pm every evening.[40]

By the late 1930s, Harbour Island was a popular resort for charters, excursions and visiting yachts and travel to the island had increased tremendously both by sea and by air. As a result, Bahamas Airways Limited inaugurated scheduled Out Island services to Harbour Island and Governor's Harbour bringing the two most beautiful and unspoiled settlements within easy reach of visitor and resident.[41] In 1939, besides the regular mailboat passenger service, Harbour Island received 402 visitors from 36 plane trips and 28 yachts.[42] The number of visitors to the Bahamas fell drastically due to the cessation in the arrival of cruise ships at the commencement of World

War II, but increased again when the Duke and Duchess of Windsor became Governor and Consort in August 1940 and the Sir Harry Oakes Airport opened in December of that year. In February 1941, Bahamas Airways announced a weekly excursion to Harbour Island on Sundays in addition to its Wednesday flights to Governor's Harbour and Harbour Island and ordered a new Drummond airplane to be delivered in the following April.[43] But again tourism vanished when America was forced to enter the war after the Japanese attacked Pearl Harbour in December 1941.

During the war years, the Harbour Island population had fallen to 769, and Table 15.1 shows the spread of occupations at that time of the 354 male and 415 female inhabitants.

Thus tourism in Harbour Island had to be put on hold until after the war and the inhabitants were employed in their usual pursuits of agriculture, fishing, shipbuilding and trading but other new opportunities would later arise.

The 1930s had seen large strides in the development of colour photography. In 1933, an expert American underwater photographer, Mr. Davidson, came to the Bahamas to assist Fred Armbrister in the filming of underwater scenes. Together they sailed to Harbour Island with Capt. Nicholson in the *Doubloon* and made several hundred feet of film on the underwater life at the various sea gardens.[44] In 1939, Mr. Williamson opened the first sea-floor post office off Nassau and visitors loved this new, colourful, underwater experience. In 1941, Harbour Island hosted Sterling Hayden, his future wife, Madeleine Carrol, and 18 crew members on location for the film *Bahama Passage*. The world premier of this Paramount movie was at the Savoy Theatre on 11 December 1941. At a time when labourers in Nassau earned 3 shillings per day, 60 Harbour Islanders were paid 6 shillings per day to sit in the chicken coops and keep the roosters from crowing while the camera crews filmed the action. Part of the film was shot in Salt Cay, Turks and Caicos and the part shot in Harbour Island cost 21,000 pounds. Thus the enchantment of Harbour Island moved to the big screen and the love affair between show business personalities and Briland began.

Table 15.1 Occupations in Harbour Island adapted from the 1943 census

Category:	M	F	Category:	M	F
Agricultural labourers	24	2	Officials	5	2
Farmers & Planters	70	1	Professions	3	13
Business & Trade Employers	16	0	Scholars	89	96
Business & Trade Employees	41	57	Children	49	50
Domestic Servants	13	90	Women at home	–	90
Fishermen & Seamen	27	0	Retired/Independent	7	2
General Labourers	3	0	Unemployed	7	4

Another wartime boost for Harbour Island was the articles of Mortimore H. Cobb, International Game Fishing Commissioner for the Bahamas, Travel Editor for *Cue Magazine*, and author of *Escape to the Bahamas*. Cobbs' 12-page article in *American Mercury* acclaimed the Bahamas as the best fishing grounds in the Caribbean. Cobb bought a plot of land on Harbour Island and built a home there in 1941.[45] He had highlighted the 10-day visit to Bimini of the Duke and Duchess of Windsor in 1941 for the six Annual Metropolitan Miami Fishing Tournament, during which the Duke presented the Duke of Windsor Cup for largest eligible game fish. Most Americans loved the Duke and Duchess and tried to visit the same places at the same time.

The Duke and Duchess had a special regard for Harbour Island and travelled there often. The Duke's first appointments in the New Year's Honours List of 1941 included two men connected with Harbour Island. A Member of the British Empire was awarded to Immigration and Labour Officer, J. A. Hughes, an ex-Harbour Island teacher from England, married to the daughter of ex-Commissioner Dewees O. Johnson. Hughes accompanied the Duke on his early travels and was known as 'the power behind the throne'. This position was soon taken over by A. K. Solomon, born at Dunmore Town, who was awarded Commander of the British Empire.[46] The Duke was also friendly with Howland Spencer, who claimed that he was distantly related to Prime Minister Winston Churchill and President Franklyn D. Roosevelt. Brilanders still chuckle at the story about the Duke's encounter with one of their outstanding 'characters', Uncle Miller Kelly, who was sailing across the harbour toward Cistern Dock on his way to Lower Bogue. The Duke was casually sailing across the harbour dressed in a pair of old shorts and shirt. Uncle Miller asked him if the Duke was coming. 'I am the Duke', was the reply. Uncle Miller bristled and shouted, 'I ain't talking no damn foolishness. I want to know if the Duke is coming.'

By 1943, the peace and quiet of Harbour Island made it a refuge for British and American troops from the base in Nassau and eventually a Royal Air Force Air Sea Rescue team was based in Harbour Island. Some of these men stayed in the Bahamas. In 1944, the first Royal Air Force wedding at Harbour Island took place between Lila Mae Curry, daughter of Mr. and Mrs. Richie Curry and Frederick Ross of RAF Marine Section, stationed at Harbour Island, the couple having to walk under an arch of guns and oars decked with flags and royal poincianas at the gate of church.[47] Fred was a very useful addition to Harbour Island in the repair and maintenance of marine and motor vehicle engines as post-war Harbour Island became mechanized. The RAF, American Troops and workers on the base were a tremendous influence on the economy of the colony and Harbour Island shared in the prosperity their presence engendered.

Another source of income to the Bahamas, initiated by the Duke of Windsor after the 1942 Nassau riot, was the 6,000 farm labourers on the 'Contract' in the US, who remitted quite large sums of money home from their daily earnings.

> A considerable number of them were zoot-suited young fellows excited by the adventure into the new environment. There was a semi-festive atmosphere as they were moved on to the farming centres.[48]

Their arrival relieved much anxiety among fruit and vegetable growers, who were experiencing an acute labour shortage as America entered the war. Table 15.2 shows the names of 31 men and two women, who went on the 'Contract' from Harbour Island.

Frank 'Curly' Johnson and Alfred 'Buller' Albury were in the first contingent of 1,850 men and women from the Bahamas, who set out by boat but were turned back because of German submarine patrols. On 6 May 1943, they left again on Pan American Airlines from Oakes Field. They both started in Hastings, Florida in a camp that contained 1,500 labourers living in tents; many were Bahamians, including 14 men and Retta Albury from Harbour Island. Frank was chosen as a cook because he was the only one able to cook peas and rice. There were three kitchens, each with a Bahamian cook, who prepared typical meals of 100 pounds of grits and 200 pounds of peas cooked on a wood fire. On a typical day they woke at daylight, ended their work just before dark. They received mail twice a week. While Alfred moved on to Norfolk, Virginia, New York and Minnesota, Frank went to pick corn in Minnesota, where he earned $21.20 per day. Frank laboured for five years and Alfred for a total of eight years. Both men had to work hard and missed Briland but gained valuable experience and their

Table 15.2 Harbour Islanders who went on the Contract to the US[49]

Leslie Barry	Clement Higgs	Clyde Major
Joe Tenner Reckley	Anthony Mather*	Lockwood Sweeting
Alfred 'Buller' Albury	Wentworth Grant*	Victor Sweeting
Baby Sweeting	Hillard Davis	Howard Sweeting
Erskine Sawyer	Arnold Sawyer	Frank 'Curly' Johnson
Sam Barry	Grenville Sweeting	Caleb Major
Joe Saunders*	George Wm Sturrup	Percival G Johnson
David Albury	Howard Sawyer	Henrietta Albury
Conrad Sawyer	Run-Jo(seph) Saunders	Joseph Johnson
Carolyn Martin	Jack Nixon	Cyril Cleare
William Roberts	Percy Saunders	Arthur Bain

* indicates those that went post war.

earnings were very much higher than they could have earned at home.[50] The 'Contract' was extended until 1966 and although the total amount of remittances is unknown, fewer than 5,000 Bahamians remitted a quarter of a million pounds from April 1943 to December 1944.[51]

Towards the end of the war, Nassau, with the two best airports in the Caribbean, was potentially seen as the crossroads of world aviation as British Overseas Airways Corporation and Pan American Airlines collaborated on a plan of a BOAC route from London to Bermuda and on to Nassau. PanAm was to take over the routes to the east and west coasts of South America.[52] As soon as the war ended, the House of Assembly pushed tourism plans and voted 5,500 pounds to the Development Board for 15,000 calendars of Bahamian views to be distributed throughout steamship agencies in the US, Canada and Great Britain. A high priority was given to the restoration of hotels and Out Island Development. Harbour Island was looked upon as a valuable asset to the colony and a model for future Out Island development:

> In fact Harbour Island in recent years attained to an enviable place in the economy of the colony as one of the most economically promising centres in the Out Islands. Its magnificent beaches have attracted visitors from abroad and residents in Nassau, many of whom have built homes.[53]

From the 1920s, Americans were buying every available inch of land in New Providence and paying enormous prices for it. As in Nassau, land sales in Harbour Island skyrocketed. As far back as 1925, there had been a real estate boom on Harbour Island with people buying land at extravagant prices, usually to resell at a higher price to an American, who wished to build a winter residence.[54] On the same day the Duke of Windsor was appointed Governor of the Bahamas, Howland Spencer was granted most of the remaining Crown Land in Harbour Island, which had more than a dozen tenants. Governor Dundas proclaimed the 1 June as Howland Spencer Day and Spencer provided the inhabitants with rum, a pig roast and new clothes for the tenants. At that same time Mrs. Edmund Lynch sold her Nassau home to Axel Wenner-Gren and bought the northern tip of Harbour Island[55] and several large houses were built in that area during the war years.

The sale of Crown Land brought protests from the House of Assembly to Governor Dundas, but nothing like the furor in 1944 when Stafford Sands introduced into the House of Assembly a Bill for an Act to provide for the more beneficial use of Lands held in Common and for the disposal thereof under certain circumstances.[56] The Commonage on Eleuthera seemed destined to become a vacation home paradise for the English, escaping the new Labour Government's taxes, and enterprising Americans. After many petitions and meetings the Commoners of Harbour Island and Spanish Wells were successful as the resolution by Roland Symonette that the Members of the House of Assembly had no right to interfere in the affairs of the Crown was carried by a vote of 10 to 8.[57]

By 1947, Out Island tourism was on the rise again. Empire Day and Whitsun saw one of the largest outpourings of visitors over the 3 days holiday to visit several adjacent Out Islands. The greater part of the burden of transport fell on Bahamas Airways' four planes. The *Catalina*, the *Commodore*, the *Grumman Goose* and the *Seabee* began operating on Friday and continued until Monday to convey excursions to and from Harbour Island, Spanish Wells, Governor's Harbour, Rock Sound, Abaco and Grand Bahama. The four planes transported almost 400 passengers over the weekend. The mailboat *Lady Dundas* carried some 90 passengers leaving Nassau Midnight Friday stopping at Spanish Wells and Harbour Island and both these towns were alive with noise. It was said that Harbour Island had seldom in the past received such an influx of visitors.[58] Again Harbour Island received rave reviews from travel writers:

> Due to the advantage of regularly scheduled passenger service from Nassau and two adequate guest-houses, this progressive little island is rapidly developing a tourist trade and becoming a popular resort spot. Fine fishing and splendid sea bathing are available in accessible seclusion.[59]

By 1951, the mailboat *Lady Dundas* was replaced by a former reconditioned Coastguard vessel, the *Air Swift* who lived up to her name making the Harbour Island run in $5\frac{1}{2}$ hours. With her weekly sailing, two regular Bahamas Airways flights, as well as charter flights, Harbour Island was becoming more and more like a suburb of Nassau. More winter homes were built alongside the pink sand beach and rentals increased as more visitors were attracted by the quiet solitude and the fascination of the beautiful dunes bound together by a solid mass of creepers with yellow and purple blossoms and covered with white spider lilies, frangipani and gallardia with the yellow butterflies flitting over them while the breeze from the sea refreshed and soothed. By this time Pink Sands Lodge, opened, as a vacation village in 1949, managed by Allen and Rem Malcolm, was firmly established and by 1958 the beautiful 40 acre estate overlooking the dunes had 22 cottages with electric refrigerators and cooking facilities. Dining under the stars on the open terraces of the Central Lodge, surrounded by tropical foliage, serenaded by the calypso music of the Percentie brothers or Harold Saunder's bands enhanced the enchantment of an evening in the tropics. The energetic could dance the night away at Willie's Tropical Gardens, John

79 Beach picnic

80 Cricket team

81 Regatta

82 Races

83 Blasting

84 Blasting at sea

85 Catch of the day

86 Club and marina

87 Capt. Howard Brady

88 Nurse shark

89 Picarron Cove Club

90 Deep sea fishing

91 BoHengy

92 Pin cushion

93 Eel teeth

94 Diving amongst wrecks

95 Fish

Cash's Briland Arms Club and later at the VicHum Nightclub built by the Percentie brothers in 1956.

In the early 1950s, Bahamas Airways operated a Grumman Goose seaplane belonging to Royal Mail Airline, a subsidiary of BOAC, flying from Miami Airport direct to Harbour Island, the pilot thrilling the passengers with an aerial tour of the island before landing in the harbour. Small locally built, pink wooden ferry boats with outboard motors picked the passengers up from this plane and from charter flights and took them to the Government Dock. Bahamas Airway's Seaplanes from Nassau taxied up the newly built ramp at the Up Yonder Shipyard. The passengers were met by young men with wheelbarrows, who carried their luggage to the boarding house of their choice. Some passengers preferred to take a horse-and-surrey ride, taking in the local sights on the way. Guests of the Pink Sands Lodge were met on the dockside by the pink cars of Rem, with her beautiful platinum hair and trim, feminine clothes and Allen in his gayest shirt. A young, handsome Venetian, Garstone, met the newly opened Picaroon Cove Club guests in a royal-blue station wagon. Garstone, on loan from Harry's Bar, Venice, an expert at mixing Gibsons, acted as both bartender and chauffeur, happily driving along with loads of laundry or food. Two other Venetians, on loan from Dorian's Café in Piazza San Marco, played the violin and accordion to entertain the diners. The Picaroon Cove Club, owned by Mr. Bruce Hunter had three main buildings overlooking the harbour, comprising 28 double rooms all with private bath and five outlying cottages. On the beach, Hunter maintained the Dunes Club for the use of Picaroon guests. By the late 1950s, the Sea View Hotel had fallen into disuse and visitors had the choice of the 12-room Little Boarding House, Willie Mather's Sunset Inn, opened in 1958 alongside Willie's Tavern, opened in 1948, and the Up Yonder guest house managed by Mrs. Maud Patterson.

An amazing change had occurred in less than two decades. Harbour Island had grown from a quiet little fishing village, a tiny speck on the map, to a 'fountain of youth', one of the finest pleasure resorts that could put the visitor into a peaceful state of mind free from the clamour of city life. It seemed incredible that one could breakfast in New York and dine at Harbour Island or fly there from Miami between breakfast and lunch. The visitors were enchanted by the remnants of colonial habitations and fortresses, game fishing, bone fishing, trolling for yellowtail and grouper, and swimming in the harbour or at the beach. The delicious pink conch could be found in abundance along this beach and even an amateur swimmer with a glass mask could bring a conch up dive after dive. Some visitors even attempted SCUBA diving off the beach. Simplicity itself was the answer to the question of what to wear. It was quite correct to stroll the beach or the harbour-front wearing shorts, for both men and women, and for afternoon teas, for the pre-dinner gatherings and the sweet starry evenings too, gay cottons and little silk frocks were the choice. Men blossomed in the maddest shirts and anyone who wore a hat at all, man or woman, sported a native one, made to individual order,[60] usually by Sarah, the straw worker with a lively wit.

The magnificent harbour, once so important for defence, security and the building of finely crafted one, two, three and four-masted trading schooners, remained just as busy but as the beautiful backdrop of an island pleasure resort. Mail boats, seaplanes, charters and excursions brought the visitors and the harbour was filled with locally built single-sail fishing boats and small motor boats but now it became alive with speed boats and skiing enthusiasts led by Dick Malcolm, Socks Curry and the younger tourists, who rented skis and boat by the hour. Fishing competitions were held on a very regular basis at the fishing grounds at Harbour's Mouth, the Northwest Banks or Dutch Bars to the southwest. Capt. Kenneth Johnson with fishing parties in the MV *Harrouch* brought in a lot of fish, some as large as a 43 lbs amber fish, 30 lbs rock fish; mutton fish, grouper and barracuda all on the heavy side. The ocean near Harbour Island teemed with wahoo; the *Lisandra,* captained by Kenneth Albury and the *Sora* caught wahoo as big as 42 lbs but not as big as the record by Snake Ames of 133.5 lbs in 1943.[61] Mr. Stanley Babson of the Loyalist Cottage and Bonefish Joe Cleare led the search for the beloved bonefish, a Harbour Island delicacy. Both Pink Sands and the Picaroon Club owned a fleet of brightly painted bonefishing boats for the use of their guests. At certain times the harbour was full of yachts, whose owners loved Harbour Island. Most did not remain long as they were generally on a cruise through the islands. The Japanese-built MV *Suriago,* belonging to Admiral Berky visited every season for fishing and in 1960 Harbour Island hosted the yawl *Heloise,* sister ship to Carlton Mitchell's famous racing yacht *Finesterre* and a fast sloop *Flying Scot* both designed by Sandy Douglas, a famous yacht designer of that period.[62] While the fishing guide cleaned the fish, the sunburnt fishermen and yachtsmen retired to the newly refurbished Pink Sands Front Row Lounge to embellish their fishing yarns over cocktails.

On Washington's Birthday in 1956 yachts blocked the Government Dock, making it very difficult for late fishermen to tie up. Bahamas Airways was running into traffic problems owing to the number of 'snowbirds' flocking down from the North to Harbour Island; nearly all the passengers had fishing gear in their luggage having heard of the big catches there. Something needed to be done and both Government and the Board of Works started to think of improvements to the Dock, a marina for private yachts and a land airstrip to enable more passengers to come in by air.

Although a stone wharf had been contemplated since the time of Governor Francis Cockburn, the first course of rock was only laid in 1849 and the dock completed in 1866. A sketch of Harbour Island in 1921 described 'a good sized jetty of wood and stone that runs a little distance into the harbour from the main street'.[63] A portion of the dock was rebuilt in 1922. In 1959, Sir Roland Symonette was given the contract to remove the existing wooden portion and build a new dock from the existing concrete abutment and extending approximately 300 feet from the shore. The new dock would be 100 feet long and 60 feet wide.[64] The new Government Dock was planned to be completed at the same time as the North Eleuthera Airstrip, the dredging and building of the ferry dock at Three Islands and the interconnecting roadways on North Eleuthera, but it took almost four years to complete. The Government Dock was always a focal point of the community; inhabitants and visitors alike gathered there to greet or see off passengers and freight, catch ferries and generally catch the local gossip.

The first time a land plane landed on Harbour Island the inhabitants received quite a scare. In 1940, pilot Louis McClure of Tampa, Florida, flew his Taylor Cub, 2-seater land plane from Nassau to Harbour Island, accompanied by Harold Chipman, and landed on the beach. The locals were alarmed as they thought it was a German plane.[65] On 19 December 1959, passengers gasped as Capt. Eddie Ballard and co-pilot Capt. Johnnie Whitehead flew the first 30-passenger, Bahamas Airways DC-3, through a magnificent rainbow to land at the newly built, 5,280 foot North Eleuthera Airstrip after a 30-minute flight. As the land transport bus had not yet arrived, veteran Harry Albury shuttled passengers in bus and truck to Three Islands. There they were transported to Harbour Island in Carlyle Albury's new boat driven by Dick Malcolm assisted by young 'hot rod' Socks Curry, who collected the fares.[66] By 1961, Mackey Airlines started service three times per week from Miami to Fort Lauderdale via Bimini.[67] The new airport provided employment for taxi drivers and ferries. One of the most notable ferry captains was Anthony Mather, a former monk, who looked like a bearded buccaneer. Anthony made about 20 round trips a day, ferrying many famous personalities such as Governor Nelson Rockefeller and actor Raymond Burr, who played Perry Mason on television.[68]

By 1968, Island Flying Service's President and Chief Pilot Gil Hensler had been for ten years providing amphibious charter flights to Harbour Island. Hensler leased a strip of land on Harbour Island and built a very short runway, 1,000 feet, just long enough to accommodate their 19-passenger, *DH Twin Otter* STOL (short takeoff and landing) aircraft, in order to attract passengers away from Bahamas Airways Ltd, which went into voluntary liquidation in 1970. By this time the lease on the land was running out and the landlord demanded a huge increase in rent and the company then known as Out Island Airways moved to North Eleuthera Airport.[69] The Harbour Island airstrip was used by private pilots but quickly fell into disrepair and was then only used for practice by learner car drivers.

For a good number of years, American Ben Morris acquired land in Harbour Island and his major development was 'La Dava Landing' on a section of land bounded by South Street, Bay Street, Clarence Street and Dunmore Street. Morris owned most of the land within this area. On the waterfront close to the ramp Ben Morris built a private dock with blue neon lights, where yachts could tap in for light and water, a boathouse and a spectacular New Guinea house with slanting white roofs and black walls. Ben Morris was a lavish and generous host and constantly planted candies everywhere for the children. In 1961 he sold the La Dava Landing[70] and the new owners developed it into the Briland Yacht Club, using the dock to cater for visiting yachts. For four years, McPherson and Brown of Nassau, developed both the New Dunmore Estates at New Jews Hill and Trianna Shores (the old Sassoon property) contracting Sir Roland Symonette to build, near the ocean entrance, the Harbour Island Yacht Club and Marina able to accommodate 12 yachts of medium size. Both yacht clubs failed and the Harbour Island Yacht Club and Marina fell derelict. In 1975, Jack Valentine, a retired American Hospital Administrator and his wife Gloria bought the Briland Yacht Club, upgraded it and renamed it Valentine's Yacht Club and Inn. The new building had 21 tastefully furnished rooms, a 170 foot dock, a conference room and facilities for watersports, diving and tennis.[71] Jack and Gloria made a huge success of the property and improved it year by year. Unfortunately their son Jim went missing in a small aircraft and was never seen again. Heartbroken, the Valentines sold the property, which still bears their name but is now in the hands of its second set of owners since they left the Bahamas. In 2003, John Nichols and Tom Murphy Jr., architect and builder, respectively, avid boaters and fishermen, pooled their money and dreams and bought Valentine's Resort & Marina where they plan to build a 46-unit condo-hotel.[72] The Harbour Island Yacht Club and Marina, under new management, was rebuilt in 1999 and caters to many luxury yachts. Alongside, Hammerhead's Restaurant and Bar provides for yachtsmen, visitors and locals.

The new accessibility of Harbour Island in the early 1960s was bringing more visitors than the 90 hotel rooms could accommodate and the island saw a boom in construction of both visitor and rental houses and new hotels. In 1961, Runaway Hill and Up Yonder Bar, Mrs. Maud Patterson's new guest house on the ocean side, capable of accommodating ten guests, opened in time for the winter season.[73] The following year, Basil Albury, a chef of great repute, Sidney Albury and John C. Litt opened the Dunmore Beach and Manor Club, a cottage colony on the beach with its own dining and club facilities.[74] Later in 1962, Harbour Island had another new resort on the ocean side, Poinciana Inn and Bar which had grown from the old 'Pink Elephant' property owned by Bertell W. King, long-time winter resident.[75]

By 1965, the Coral Sands Hotel, adjacent to Pink Sands Lodge, was under construction by 'Buzz' King.[76]

In the late 1960s, Roy Schmidt from Long Island, New York, fell in love with Harbour Island and with Moyra, a tall, nubile Scottish blonde amid the fragrant oleander, jasmine and other tropical blooms that decorate this sapphire-sea-girt island and married her. They developed Romora Bay Hotel (a combination of their names and the name of a local fish) on a 7-acre citrus plantation that slopes gently down to the crystal-clear iridescent sea that washes the harbour side of the island. The couple invested all their savings to create a major marine sports and SCUBA diving centre. The hotel, which opened in 1969, comprised the main house, built in the 1940s, a cottage and 24 room guest rooms with views of both the ocean and the harbour.[77] The Schmidts worked hard, long hours to make the hotel successful, Roy often flying his own plane from the Harbour Island Airstrip to Nassau for urgent supplies.

Although fishing remained popular in Harbour Island, a wave of enthusiasm internationally, in the 1970s, brought SCUBA-diving fanatics to the Bahamas and the Turks and Caicos Islands. Both Romora Bay and Valentine's Yacht Club and Inn employed qualified instructors and staff to train and guide those who wanted to view and photograph under the sea. There is great visibility at The Grotto off the north-east corner of Harbour Island and most divers eagerly bound off the stern of the boat into the jewel-coloured, clear sea, descending in awe, peering more than 100 feet in every direction. Diving down to the sandy bottom at about 70 feet, the diver passes mountains of colourful coral formations surrounded by hordes of reef fish. Hundreds of yellow-tailed snappers can be seen swimming right up and staring into the masks of the divers and armies of tiny fish and shrimps gliding across the body, into the mouth and through the gills of a docile grouper. Nearing a dark cavern and looking into a labyrinth of caverns and ocean holes, shafts of light form blue-dappled patterns on the sand. On another dive in another sea garden area a small hawksbill turtle swims past and in the pink-tinged sandy bottom could be seen the tiny red bits that give the pink sands their name. Divers of every level of experience can dive more than 30 dive sites.[78]

Alongside the construction throughout the 1960s, Harbour Island wrestled with its four perennial problems – electricity, water, roads and garbage disposal. In 1954, Harry Albury sold his Direct Current plant to Stafford Sands and Bobbie Symonette and they built the first Power House at the north end of Bay Street and formed the Harbour Island Power and Light Company, introducing Alternating Current Electricity. Subsequently, Sands and Symonette sold out to another group, the Bahamas Power and Light Company, formed by Colonel Neave, Harold Johnson, Harold

Albury, Mr. Noulder, William Johnson and Earle Johnson. Eventually by 1959, William Johnson became the sole owner of the Bahamas Power and Light Company and purchased new equipment including a 140 KW and a 125 KW generator, which supplied the town and also 60 creosote light poles to supply electricity to the Narrows, a distance of a mile and a half. At that same time, The Harbour Island Waterworks on Eleuthera had five engines and five windmills on Eleuthera pumping and supplying water to Harbour Island, with a sixth engine that had needed parts for the previous two years. Even though the water was piped from Eleuthera, the demand was too great and both electricity and water were turned off several times a week for several hours a day. Children of those who did not have piped water were sent to carry buckets full of free water to their homes from faucets, which tapped the water from the wells on the beach.[79] In 1963, five new wells were dug on Eleuthera and new pipes were laid along Bay Street to replace the old corroded pipes but still the residents faced frustration with the electricity and water situation.

The plight of the utilities was again in the news in the late 1970s, as a series of fires shocked the residents of Harbour Island. In January 1977, Willie Walker was burned to death in his home when there was no water available to extinguish the blaze.[80] Two years later, after a series of water shortages, the inhabitants petitioned the Government as visitors could not shower in the hotels and many Brilanders were infected with a skin disease.[81] And in September 1979, the Harbour Island Power Plant burnt to the ground, while the fire engine was in Nassau for repair, leaving Harbour Island without electricity or water.[82] The problem was further compounded by the fact that the Government had only given the Bahamas Power and Light Company a 3-month franchise to supply electricity and Capt. W. H. Johnson claimed it was not economically feasible to rebuild the Power Plant unless granted a 10-year franchise. By late November electricity was restored and the Eleuthera Power and Light Company took over the supply of electricity for a few years until Bahamas Electricity Corporation took control of all Family Island electricity supplies in the 1980s. In 1981, 21 people died and 21 were rendered homeless in a fire, the second in four days. The electricity and water supplies were both shut down at the time and so the fire engine could not pump water into the blaze.[83] Again in 1984, the services in Harbour Island were in a poor state as roads were nothing more than potholes, as it was a long time since they were last repaired and the water pipes had nothing more than thin air coming out of them.[84]

Garbage disposal has been a problem in Harbour Island for many years. The Board of Works made the unpopular move in 1952 to use the Parade as a dumping ground. The locals were outraged that the hallowed ground where 'once long ago sounded the tramp of armed men and not long ago rang out with cheers of the spectators of contesting cricket teams from Barracks Hill' should be used as a garbage dump.[85] By 1996, the 'Dump' at the Parade was much too small an area to contain the refuse of the modern community and had become an eyesore. The decision was made to take the garbage to an area of the Commonage on Eleuthera by barge and return the Parade to use by the public as a playground park. The park now features basketball and tennis courts. A channel was dredged for the barge, and after initial difficulties in contract negotiations with the barge and trucking owners, the garbage is now taken over to Eleuthera. Unfortunately, due to the volume of material and the small holding capacity of the barge, garbage disposal in Harbour Island remains a problem.

Fortunately, the enchantment, beauty and peace of Briland allow both visitor and resident to shake their heads and carry on as best they can despite potholes, water and power shortages and overflowing dumpsters near Girl's Bank.

In 1961 the Bahamas Telecommunication Department, using Haitian labour, erected Briland's 'Eiffel Tower', a 225-foot-high antenna, consisting of 18 sections of 12.5 feet each. Telephone calls could now go direct to Nassau instead of through Governor's Harbour.[86] At that same time the Johnson and Curry Service Station opened on Princess Street, operated by Kenneth Johnson and David 'Socks' Curry and they supplied gas on the Government Dock. Ex-Commissioner Pickwood, who retired to Harbour Island in the 1950s, wrote that 'Brilanders from away would hardly know Harbour Island with its cars, trucks, planes, bikes, motor boats, skiing, streets well lit, beautiful residences and our new clinic with running water. A big difference to 1911 when we had a "donkey shay" (a light open carriage often with a hood), property of Commissioner and Mr. Armstrong – today cars and trucks are increasing at such a fast rate we'll soon have to have a traffic cop'.[87] With the advent of Inspection and Licensing of vehicles in 1959, when Howard Brady registered car 1, there were then on Harbour Island, seven trucks, 15 cars, four jeeps, six station wagons and four scooters, a total: 36 vehicles.[88] This is a far cry from the hundreds of golf carts and trucks on Harbour Island roads today.

The transition of Harbour Island from a commercial trading centre into a pleasure resort for tourists was a slow, gradual process but quickened in the early 1930s when her sailing vessels were no longer suited to foreign trade.[89] Many migrated to Nassau to obtain work on Bay Street or in the growing tourist trade and thus the pattern of life for those remaining in Harbour Island slowly changed from a lifestyle dictated by seafaring to one which became moulded by tourism. At first the tourist season was confined to the period from early January until mid-April for American tourists, who liked nothing better than to be able to say that they had been to the Out Islands. A favourite trip was the short flight from Nassau to Harbour Island, 52 miles to the North

East, a half hour trip by plane.[90] By 1948 the season extended into the 'summer siesta' as more visitors continued to pour in until early May.

> Harbour Island has been unusually popular with the tourists this year and a greater number of them have paid this unique little island a visit, they have all been captivated by the delightful and untouched charms of the place and most have announced their intentions to return next winter.[91]

By the early 1950s, the winter season opened in early November, with workers employed in September and October painting and overhauling for the next bumper season. The winter residences were painted in many hues and the beautiful gardens were transforming the island into an artist's dream. In the mid-1950s, Harbour Island had a foreign and a local season. From October to April visitors flocked down from the North, while the summer months, June to August, attracted Brilanders who came back to have a look at the old rock.[92] The Harbour Islanders called Nassauvians 'Gullies' as summer is the time when seagulls cry and the sound of 'nightfeeders' is heard in the gardens.[93] In the summer of 1955, Harbour Island was full of 'Nassau Brilanders': chartered planes brought those who could not get seats on the regular planes and others came up on the *Air Swift* and some came in small motor boats. George Johnson, Jenkins Roberts and son, Mr. & Mrs. Polly Johnson, Alex Maillis, Doreen Albury and Violet Johnson were some of the Nassau Brilanders who came 'home' that summer.[94] The following year Pink Sands Lodge re-opened in June for the summer and from then the seasons blended into year long tourism with peaks in the winter and quiet times in the autumn. Briland now buzzes year round and the inhabitants of Harbour Island have become almost totally immersed directly or indirectly in tourism. Nowadays, instead of 200 Brilanders sailing to Eleuthera each morning, about 200 workers from all over Eleuthera, some from as far south as Green Castle, travel to Harbour Island to work in the construction of winter residences and other tourist projects.

Each week the *Yokomika* brings lumber and supplies from Miami, the *Eleuthera Express* and *Daybreak III* bring passengers and freight from Nassau and an oil tanker regularly brings gasoline to Harbour Island. In the 1950s rival business czars were former shipbuilders, Harry Albury and Earle Johnson, who were the agents for the airlines and boats respectively and they and their sons built houses and owned stores and boats. Miss Mae Stirrup's grocery store with her daily fresh flowers in the window and beautiful paintings of cats and flowers was a great attraction for tourists buying postcards, stamps and other necessities. Old grocery stores like Tip Top, owned by Sidney Albury, and Piggly Wiggly, which passed from owner

Earle Johnson to Doreen Albury have now been supplemented by Johnson's and Sawyer's Grocery Stores and others, to supply food and necessities to the burgeoning population of locals and tourists. Chacara Lumber, a clever use of the owner's name, *Cha*rles *Ca*rlyle *A*lbury and Higgs Construction supply the building industry. Many new businesses have opened up to cater to every need of the visitor to Harbour Island, even a cyber café at Arthur's Bakery. In the 1980s Tingum Village & Ma Rubie's Restaurant were opened by the Percenties and the Royal Palm Hotel by Jack Grant and both have earned a high reputation for good, inexpensive accommodation. Many more Brilanders share the tourism pie, small boats ferry passengers from Three Islands, trucks deliver freight from the dock, several companies rent golf carts and some run taxi services. Cabbie Reggie Major and his blue van are in great demand both as a pick up and a knowledgeable tour guide. The Vick-Hum still operates as a late-night club and has been joined by Gusty's, famous for its pool and karaoke and Seagrapes for late-night dancing and entertainment. Many other small restaurants and bars offer sustenance to locals and visitors. The latest is the Sip Sip restaurant, overlooking the pink sands beach, which has quickly become a favourite of the rich and famous.

Perhaps the greatest boost to Harbour Island tourism has been the *BoHengy*, a comfortable 177-passenger, 2-deck high-speed ferry boat which leaves Nassau every morning at 8.00 am, briefly stops in Spanish Wells and arrives in Harbour Island at 10.15 am, returning to Nassau in the late afternoon, making two trips on Fridays and Public Holidays. The Bahamas Fast Ferries Service Limited formed in 1999, was named the *BoHengy* after Brother Henry (Bo Hengy) Sawyer, a community leader, church leader, farmer, seaman and boatbuilder, born in Harbour Island in 1856.[95] Bahamians use the *BoHengy* for convenient travel to Spanish Wells and Harbour Island, some business persons travelling back and forth once or twice per week. Reminiscent of the Seaplane outings in the early days, the *BoHengy* has built up a regular day trip for tourists to Harbour Island, which includes an historical tour of the island, a swim at the pink sands beach and lunch either at the Coral Sands Beach Deck or the Front Row Lounge.

The new millennium has seen Harbour Island riding a wave of prosperity. Briland is a hot spot for tourists and land prices have soared to an astronomical level. Celebrities love the easy, laid-back atmosphere in a community where the golf cart is the main mode of transport. People go around in bare feet and bathing suits; they talk, play dominoes, just shoot the breeze and nobody bothers them. Nobody cares who they are. Famous, not-famous, rich, poor, black, white – it makes no difference. Many famous personalities have visited Harbour Island and some have built homes there. In the 1980s top photographer Gilles Bensimon, inspired by the island's turquoise waters and rose-sand beaches, started bringing *Elle* magazine models and *Victoria's Secret*, *Sports Illustrated* and *Glamour* magazines soon followed. Fashion model, Elle McPherson, regularly walks the pink sands beach and Tyra Banks and Christie Brinkley love Harbour Island. Sean Connery, the first James Bond, Harrison Ford, Daryl Hall of Hall and Oates, Elijah Blue (Cher's son), Diane Sawyer, David Copperfield, Jimmy Buffett, Bill Gates, Mick Jagger, and Calvin Klein have all enjoyed the pink sand between their toes and Julia Roberts shared a birthday in Briland with 50 friends. After Hurricane *Andrew's* devastation in 1992, record mogul turned hotelier, Chris Blackwell, invested in the Pink Sands Lodge saying, 'You take one look at the beach and how could you not want to be here? It is simply one of the most beautiful beaches on the planet'.[96] Local people are no less thankful. 'I am very blessed,' says straw vendor, Jacqueline Percentie. 'I was born on Harbour Island, raised on Harbour Island and have lived on Harbour Island for 78 years'.[97]

As far back as the early days of World War II, tourists regretted leaving the enchantment of Harbour Island behind:

> This pleasant island faded into the horizon all too soon, but in leaving, we carried fond memories of a peaceful way of life in these troubled times.[98]

Even today, 'if you should hear a stranger express the desire to burn his identity and his clothes, it is just another way of saying that he would like never to leave. And if in the evening, when the gentle breeze rustles the palms, and the magic sound of the breakers delights the ear, you should see him standing on the hills overlooking the beach and the ocean, watching a full moon rise out of the sea – and if you should suddenly note that there are tears in his eyes – move away my friend; leave him alone. For at that moment, he too, like the ancient Taino, is close to Paradise'.[99]

Notes
1. Paul Albury, *Harbour Island*, Unpublished Talk at Rotary or elsewhere circa 1975.
2. Paul Albury, *Harbour Island*, Unpublished Talk at Rotary or elsewhere circa 1975.
3. CO 23 2 part I/77 Carrington to Council of Trade & Plantations; CSP 33/127, 4 May 1722.
4. George Frederick Frick & Raymond Phineas Stearns, *Mark Catesby, The Colonial Audubon*, University of Illinois, 1961, p. 33.
5. CO 23/43/139, March 1803, Gov. Halkett to Secretary of State.
6. *Nassau Guardian* 10 March 1866, Extract from Correspondent.
7. *Nassau Guardian*, 3 March 1849, Advertisement: Harbour Island Packet Company.
8. *Nassau Herald*, 8 August 1868.
9. *Nassau Guardian*, 1 August 1888.
10. *Nassau Guardian*, 8 May 1895.
11. *Nassau Daily Tribune*, 25 March 1960, Harbour Island Nowadays by K. L. Snake Ames.

12. Craton & Saunders, *Islanders in the Stream,* Vol 2, The University of Georgia Press, Athens & London, 1998, p. 77.
13. *Harper's New Monthly Magazine,* #CCXCIV- November, 1874 – Vol XLIX, The Bahamas, p. 770.
14. Ibid, p. 771.
15. Ibid, p. 771.
16. *Nassau Guardian,* 5 January 1921.
17. *Nassau Guardian,* 7 February 1921 and 19 February 1921.
18. *Nassau Guardian,* 4 June 1925.
19. *Nassau Guardian,* 26 January 1922, Advertisement.
20. *Nassau Guardian,* 19 July 1923.
21. *Nassau Guardian,* 13 November 1924.
22. *Nassau Daily Tribune,* 3 April 1964.
23. *Nassau Daily Tribune* 13 March 1966.
24. *Nassau Guardian,* 10 March 1866, Extract from Correspondent.
25. *Nassau Guardian,* 27 August 1873.
26. Votes Of the House of Asembly, Commissioner P. W. D. Ambrister's Report for 1914.
27. *Nassau Guardian,* 5 August 1924.
28. *Nassau Daily Tribune,* 23 Feb 1962, Harbour Island Nowadays by K. L. Snake Ames.
29. *Nassau Daily Tribune,* 7 Nov 1962, Harbour Island Nowadays by K. L. Snake Ames.
30. *Nassau Guardian,* 12 September 1885, Letter to Editor by 'Fair Play'.
31. *Nassau Guardian,* 20 September 1902, Letter to editor from T. G. Johnson.
32. *Nassau Guardian,* 25 January 1923, Harbour Island Correspondent.
33. *Nassau Guardian,* 3 November 1921, Opening of Harbour Island Radio Station.
34. *Nassau Guardian,* 16 March 1922, To Harbour Island by Air.
35. *Nassau Guardian,* 8 March 1938, A Flight to Harbour Island by Sally Broomwell.
36. *Nassau Guardian,* 14 February 1924.
37. *Nassau Guardian,* 27 May 1933, The Ideal Pleasure Resort.
38. *Nassau Guardian,* 23 February 1924, Harbour Island: The Ideal Health resort of the Bahamas.
39. *Nassau Guardian,* 18 September 1895.
40. Interview John L. Saunders, 1983; *Nassau Guardian,* 12 June 1929, Electric Plant for Harbour Island.
41. *Nassau Guardian,* 7 January 1939.
42. Votes of the House of Assembly, Commissioner W. E. Robert's Report, 1940.
43. *Nassau Daily Tribune,* 13 February 1941.
44. *Nassau Tribune,* 27 May 1933.
45. *Nassau Daily Tribune,* 2 January 1941.
46. *Nassau Daily Tribune,* 2 January 1941.
47. *Nassau Tribune,* 23 June 1944.
48. CO 23/760/39, Report Labour Attache, Mr. A. D. Gordon, British Embassy, Washington, 7 July 1943.
49. Interviews conducted by Godfrey Kelly, 1999.
50. Interviews conducted by Godfrey Kelly, 1999.
51. *Nassau Daily Tribune,* 30 December 1944.
52. *Nassau Guardian,* 20 September 1944, Nassau seen as key spot in Aviation.
53. *Nassau Guardian,* 16 July 1947, Editorial.
54. *Nassau Guardian,* 5 September 1925, Letter to Editor: Real Estate Boom.
55. *Nassau Daily Tribune,* 13 November 1940.
56. *Nassau Daily Tribune,* 14 March 1944, Political Backchat by Vitriol.
57. *Nassau Daily Tribune,* 13 June 1944 – Agenda for House of Assembly.

58 *Nassau Guardian*, 27 May 1947.
59 Egbert T Smith, *Travelogue of the Bahama Islands*, 1950, p. 26.
60 *Nassau Magazine*, Winter 1951–52, Picaroon Cove at Harbour Island.
61 *Nassau Daily Tribune*, 14 March 1959, Harbour Island Nowadays by K. L. Snake Ames.
62 *Nassau Daily Tribune*, 2 January 1960, Scenic Christmas at Harbour Island by Betty Field.
63 *Nassau Guardian*, 5 January 1921, A sketch of Harbour Island.
64 *Nassau Daily Tribune*, 14 Nov 1959, Harbour Island Nowadays by K. L. Snake Ames.
65 *Nassau Guardian*, 1 May 1940.
66 *Nassau Daily Tribune*, 2 January 1960, Scenic Christmas at Harbour Island by Betty Field.
67 *Nassau Daily Tribune*, 29 March 1961, Harbour Island Nowadays by K. L. Snake Ames.
68 *Nassau Daily Tribune*, 16 March 1969, Former monk now ferries the famous.
69 *Nassau Daily Tribune*, 12 March 1968; Information by Paul Aranha, 2003.
70 *Nassau Daily Tribune*, 10 October 1961, Harbour Island Nowadays by K. L. Snake Ames.
71 *Nassau Daily Tribune*, 11 July 1975.
72 *Miami Herald*, 12 February 2003, New Owners For Valentine's Yacht Club.
73 *Nassau Daily Tribune*, 10 October 1961 – Harbour Island Nowadays by K. L. Snake Ames.
74 *Nassau Daily Tribune*, 28 August 1962, Harbour Island Nowadays by K. L. Snake Ames.
75 *Nassau Daily Tribune*, 10 April 1962, Harbour Island Nowadays by K. L. Snake Ames.
76 *Nassau Daily Tribune*, 22 April 1965, Harbour Island Nowadays by K. L. Snake Ames.
77 *Nassau Daily Tribune*, 20 September 1969, Romora Bay Club.
78 *Junkanoo Magazine March 2000*, Harbour Island Dive Sites by Connie Crowther.
79 *Nassau Daily Tribune*, 9 January 1960.
80 *Nassau Daily Tribune*, 29 January 1977, Island fire death.
81 *Nassau Daily Tribune*, 5 March 1979, Petitions from Harbour Island for improved fresh water supply.
82 *Nassau Daily Tribune*, 21 September 1979, Harbour Island loses electricity.
83 *Nassau Daily Tribune*, 5 May 1981.
84 *Nassau Daily Tribune*, 27 July 1984.
85 *Nassau Guardian*, 21 June 1952.
86 *Nassau Daily Tribune*, 27 July 1984.
87 *Nassau Tribune*, 4 January 1958, News From Harbour Island H. F. Pickwoad.
88 *Nassau Daily Tribune*, 30 Dec 1959, Harbour Island Nowadays by K. L. Snake Ames.
89 *Nassau Guardian*, 12 September 1933, Commissioner A. T. D. Whitfield's report.
90 *Nassau Guardian*, 8 March 1938.
91 *Nassau Guardian*, 1 May 1948.
92 *Nassau Tribune*, 16 June 1956 – Harbour Island Notes H. F. Pickwoad.
93 *Nassau Daily Tribune*, 23 May 1959 – Harbour Island Nowadays by K. L. Snake Ames.
94 *Nassau Tribune*, 8 August 1955, Harbour Island Notes H. F. Pickwoad.
95 http: //www.bahamasferries.com/hengy.htlm1, Bahamas Fast Ferries, The legend of Bo Hengy.
96 *Nassau Daily Tribune*, 28 June 1999, Harbour Island a hot spot for the world's rich.
97 http://www.miami.com/mld/miamiherald/living/travel/Harbour Island by Shari Myeck.
98 *Nassau Magazine*, March 1941, Harbour Island by George E. Merkel.
99 Paul Albury, *Harbour Island*, Unpublished Talk at Rotary circa 1975.

Appendix 1

An account of the population of the Bahamas in the early years

Year	New Providence	Harbour Island	Eleuthera	Scattered throughout Bahamas	Reference
1656			60 people		Miller p41
1668	250 inhabitants				CSP 7/916
1670	500+ inhabitants			10 families HI, El & Island east of El	Eg MSS 2395/472
1672	500 inhabitants				CSP 7/916
1684	400 men, 200 women & children				CSP 11/1590
1685	100 men, 200 women & children				Eg MSS 3984/302
1687				300 people	CSP 12/1212
1696	160 houses	20 houses	fewer than 20 houses	2 or 3 families on other islands	Oldmixen p. 18/19
1697	re read reference			600 or 700 thro' islands or N.P.?	CO 23/12/46 J. Graves
1701	250 white, 250 blacks, mulat.& mustees				CSP 19/208 E. Randolph
1701	300 families & houses				CSP 19/655 Gov. Haskett
1703	400 people				CSP 23/277 John Graves
1704	20 men	60 people		Exuma = 90, Cat I = 120people	CSP 23/277 John Graves
1704	27 families			400 or 500 people in all islands	CSP 23/277 John Graves
1706				400 or 500 people in all islands	CO 23/12/80
1707				600 among all islands	CSP 23/1128 Capt Chadwell
1709	12 families				CSP 24/340
1710	30 families	12 families		32 families east most part Eleuthera	CSP 25/421 i Capt Smith
1714				200 families NP, HI & El	CSP 27/651 Gov Pulleine
1715	12 families scattered				CO 23/12/84
1717		30 families & several pirates			CSP 29/635/ M Musson
1718		70 families	60 families		Oldmixen p24 & 26
1718		60 families (80 men)	50 families (70 men)		CO 23/1/20 W Rogers
1719	400 inhabitants				CO 23/1/93 W Rogers
1722	470 w 233 blk	124 w 5 blk	150 w 34 blk	Cat I = 12 w 3 blk	CO 23/1/103/pt2 Phenney
1722	85 families			70 plus families on HI, El & Cat I	CSP 33/127/Carrington
1723	500 w 250 blk	130 w 20 blk	200 w 40 blk		CSP 33/801/Phenney
1724		20 to 30 families			CO 23/13/144/Barker
1728	500 w 250 blk	120 w 20 blk	200 w 40 blk		CO 23/2pt2/7
1731	633 white 409 black	160 white 9 black	73 white 21 black		CO 23/3/5/W Rogers
1731	120 families	40 families	40 families		C F Pascoe _Rev Guy
1734	461 white 463 blk	151 white 10 blk	198 white 38 blk		CO 23/3/129/FitzWilliam

NB In some cases a population count is given for New Providence only.

273

Appendix 2
Harbour Island inhabitants in the 1720s

SOURCES: C.O. 23/2 part 2/29 and CO 23/13/480–81
Lists of Marriage, baptisms & deaths
Notes: c = Communicant at Baptism of Joseph and Anna Force 1723
s = Subscriber at Baptism of Joseph and Anna Force 1723
1 = Petition of 1726
2 = Militia of 1727

Baptised:	FirstName:	Surname	Father	Mother	
	John	Allbury [2]			
	Miriam	Allbury [c]		wife of John ?	
	John	Cash			
	Elizabeth	Cash			
7 Feb 1722	James	Cash	John	Elizabeth	
7 Feb 1722	William	Cash	John	Elizabeth	
23 Jun 1726	Joseph	Cash	John	Elizabeth	born 31 March 1726
	Joseph	Cash [1 & 2]			
	Elizabeth	Cash			
19 Oct 1724	Elizabeth	Cash	Joseph	Elizabeth	born 30 Sept 1723
	William	Cash [1 & 2]			
	Thomas	Cash [1]			
	Nathaniel	Coverly Jnr [1 & 2]			
	Martha	Coverly		nee Thompson married Nathaniel 21 May 1728	
	William	Coverly [1 & 2]			
	Thomas	Cox [1]			
	Thomas	Crawlin			
	?	Crawlin			
7 Feb 1722	Elizabeth	Crawlin	Thomas	?	
	John	Curry 2			
	?	Curry 2			
7 Feb 1722	James	Curry 2	John	?	
7 Feb 1722	Joseph	Curry 2	John	?	
7 Feb 1722	Richard	Curry 2	John	?	
	Thomas	Curry [2]			
	John	Curry [s & 1]			
	Koziah	Curry			
7 Feb 1722	Rowland	Curry	John	Koziah	
7 Feb 1722	Sarah	Curry	John	Koziah	
19 Oct 1724	Catherine	Curry	John	Koziah	born 23 Apr 1724
2 Nov 1726	Elizabeth	Curry	John	Koziah	born 16 Oct 1726
7 Feb 1722	Elizabeth	Davis	Evan	?	
	George	Dorset [1]			
	Bridget	Dorset			
19 Oct 1724	George	Dorset	George	Bridget	born 21 Aug 1722
23 Jun 1726	Elizabeth	Dorset	George	Bridget	born 27 July 1725
	Nathaniel	Force [1]	negro		
	Sarah	Force	mulatto		

Appendix 275

20 Oct 1724	Joseph	Force	Nathaniel	Sarah	about 19 yrs, negro	
20 Oct 1724	Anna	Force	Nathaniel	Sarah	aged 20 yrs, negro	
	Boyer	Gething [1 & 2]	died 15 Nov 1728			
	Mary	Gething	nee Thompson married 17 Jun 1725			
14 Dec 1727	Thomas	Gething	Boyer	Marie		
	Edward	Griffin [1]				
	John	Griffin [1]				
	Miriam	Griffin				
7 Feb 1722	Elizabeth	Griffin	John	Miriam		
7 Feb 1722	John	Griffin	John	Miriam		
19 Oct 1724	Mary	Griffin	John	Miriam	John above?	
	William	Griffin [1]				
	Hannah	Griffin	nee Hotham married 4 Oct 1723			
19 Oct 1724	William	Griffin	William	Hannah		
2 Nov 1726	George	Griffin	William	Hannah	born 25 June 1726	
	William	Hale [c,s & 1]				
	Elizabeth	Hale [c]				
20 Jun 1725	Elizabeth	Hale	William	Elizabeth	born 13 May 1725	
	Elizabeth	Hotham [c & s]				
	Thomas	Johnson				
	Catherine	Johnson				
19 Oct 1724	Sarah	Johnson	Thomas	Catherine	born 14 Feb 1723	
2 Nov 1726	Mary	Johnson	Thomas	Catherine	born 18 Aug 1726	
	James	Kimbling [1 & 2]				
	Mary	Kimbling				
7 Feb 1722	Anna	Kimbling	James	Mary		
19 Oct 1724	James	Kimbling	James	Mary	born 13 April 1722	
20 Jun 1725	Elizabeth	Kimbling	James	Mary	born 1 Nov 1724	
7 Feb 1722	George	Maycock	George	?		
	Abednego	Morton				
	Sarah	Morton				
20 Jun 1725	Sarah	Morton	Abednego	Sarah	born 36 May 1725	
	Joseph	Pearce				
	?	Pearce				
7 Feb 1722	Joseph	Pearce	Joseph	?		
	Seaborn	Pindar [s]				
	Mary	Pindar				
7 Feb 1722	Mary	Pindar	Seaborn	Mary		
7 Feb 1722	Sarah	Pindar	Seaborn	Mary		
18 Oct 1724	Catherine	Pindar	Seaborn	Mary	born 29 May 1723	
18 Oct 1724	Martha	Pindar	Seaborn	Mary	born 10 Aug 1724	
23 Jun 1726	William	Pindar	Seaborn	Mary		
	James	Pye [s]				
	Ann	Paddock				
19 Oct 1724	Jacob	Pye	Jacob	Ann Paddock	20 Jan 1723	
	James	Roberts				
	?	Roberts				
7 Feb 1722	James	Roberts	James	?		
	John	Roberts 1 [1]				
	Martha	Roberts				
7 Feb 1722	Benjamin	Roberts	John	Martha		
7 Feb 1722	Marjery	Roberts	John	Martha		
	John	Roberts 2 [2]				
	Mary	Roberts				

19 Oct 1724	Miriam	Roberts	John	Mary	born 23 Oct 1723
	John	Roberts 3			
	Catherine	Roberts			
20 Jun 1725	Benjamin	Roberts	John	Catherine	born 26 Feb 1725
23 Jun 1726	Mussey	Roberts	John	Martha	born 23 April 1726
	Robert	Roberts [2]			
	Daniel	Saunders			died 25 Nov 1725
	Jane	Saunders			
7 Feb 1722	James	Saunders	Daniel	Jane	
7 Feb 1722	Joseph	Saunders	Daniel	Jane	
19 Oct 1724	Catherine	Saunders	Daniel	Jane	born 25 Dec 1723
23 Jun 1726	Mary	Saunders	Daniel	Jane	born 30 Dec 1725
	John	Saunders [1]			
	Martha	Saunders			
18 Oct 1724	Martha	Saunders	John	Martha	
19 Oct 1724	Mary	Saunders	John	Martha	born 17 Feb 1722
23 Jun 1726	John	Saunders	John	Martha	born 1 June 1726
	Thomas	Saunders [s]			
	Ruth	Saunders [c]			
19 Oct 1724	Elizabeth	Saunders	Thomas	Ruth	born 21 March 1723
	Samuel	Saunders [c & s]			
	Benjamin	Sweeting [1 & 2]			
	Martha	Sweeting			
7 Feb 1722	Mary	Sweeting	Benjamin	Martha	
7 Feb 1722	William	Sweeting	Benjamin	Martha	
21 Jun 1725	Samuel	Sweeting	Benjamin	Martha	born 10 May 1725
	Thomas	Sweeting [1]			
	Sarah	Sweeting			
7 Feb 1722	Benjamin	Sweeting	Thomas	Sarah	
7 Feb 1722	Thomas	Sweeting	Thomas	Sarah	
19 Oct 1724	Sarah	Sweeting	Thomas	Sarah	
23 Jun 1726	Nathaniel	Sweeting	Thomas	Sarah	born 1 Dec 1725
	John	Sweeting [s & 1]			
	William	Sweeting [2]			
	John	Tedder			
	Mary	Tedder			
7 Feb 1722	Thomas	Tedder	John	Mary	
20 Jun 1725	Joseph	Tedder	John	Mary	
	John	Thompson 1 [s]			
	Miriam	Thompson [c,s & 1]			
7 Feb 1722	Richard	Thompson	John	Miriam	
19 Oct 1724	Joseph	Thompson	John	Miriam	
2 Nov 1726	Catherine	Thompson	John	Miriam	born 1 Oct 1726
	John	Thompson 2 [1]			
	Martha	Thompson			
19 Oct 1724	Martha	Thompson	John	Martha	born 13 Feb 1722
19 Oct 1724	Mary	Thompson	John	Martha	born 15 Nov 1723
	Joseph	Thompson [s]			
	Ann	Thompson			
19 Oct 1724	William	Thompson	Joseph	Ann	
20 Jun 1725	Sarah	Thompson	Joseph	Ann	born 4 Feb 1725
6 Nov 1726	Joseph	Thompson	Joseph	Ann	born 6 Nov 1726
	William	Thompson Snr [s]			
	William	Thompson Jnr [s]			
	Mary	Thompson			

7 Feb 1722	Joseph	Thompson	William	Mary		
7 Feb 1722	Wiliam	Thompson	William	Mary		
19 Oct 1724	Elizabeth	Thompson	William	Mary	born 7 July 1723	
20 Jun 1725	Catherine	Thompson	William	Mary	born 1 March 1725	
	Richard	Thompson [c & s]	Capt			
	Katherine	Thompson [c]				
	George	Watkins [1]				
	Miriam?Martha	Watkins				
7 Feb 1722	Miriam	Watkins	George	Miriam		
7 Feb 1722	Sarah	Watkins	George	Miriam		
19 Oct 1724	Martha	Watkins	George	Martha	born 26 Aug 1724	
	Henry	White	Capt			
	Sarah	White				
	Sarah	White	Henry	Sarah		

20 Oct 1724	9 negroes			
31 children baptised into 19 families			app 69 people	
55 white children to approx 31 families			Plus negroes: 4 Force + 9 negroes	
			app 130 in 1724	
23 Dec 1723	married			Elizabeth Johnson m Benjamin Kemp
17 Jun 1725	married	Gething	Boyer	Mary Thompson
				Boyer died 15 Nov 1728
21 May 1728	married	Coverly	Nathl Jnr	Martha Thompson

Appendix 3

List of Harbour Island inhabitants in 1731 and 1734

Census of 1731 source CO23/3/8							Surname	First Name	Census of 1734 source 23/3/132					
White			Negroes						White			Slaves		
Men	Wom.	Child.	Able		Child.				Men	Wom.	Child.	Men	Wom.	Child.
Not listed in 1731							Albury	Benjamin	1	1	1			
Not listed in 1731							Albury	John	1	1	1			
Not listed in 1731							Cash	James	1	0	0			
Not listed in 1731							Cash	James	1	0	0			
1	0	6	0		0		Cash	John Snr	1	0	3			
0	1	2	0		0		Cash	Mary	Not listed in 1734					
1	0	0	0		0		Cash	John Jnr.	1	0	0			
nee Lettice Coverly?							Cash	Lettice	0	1	0			
1	1	6	0		0		Clare	John	Not listed in 1734					
0	1	0	0		0		Conners	Mary	Not listed in 1734					
1	0	0	0		0		Conners	?	Not listed in 1734					
0	1	2	0		0		Coverly	Lettuce	Not listed in 1734					
Not listed in 1731							Coverly	Elizabeth	0	1	0			
1	0	0	0		0		Coverly	Thomas	1	0	0			
1	1	0	0		0		Coverly	Nathaniel	Not listed in 1734					
Not listed in 1731							Crewland	Elizabeth	0	1	1			
1	1	6	0		0		Curry	John	1	1	3			
Not listed in 1731							Curry	John Jnr	1	0	0			
Not listed in 1731							Curry	Richard	1	0	0			
Not listed in 1731							Curry	Rowland	1	0	0			
Not listed in 1731							Gibbons	Mary	0	1	0			
Not listed in 1731							Gibbons	Samuel	1	0	0			
1	1	0	0		0		Griffin	Nathaniel	Not listed in 1734					
1	1	5	0		0		Griffin	John	Not listed in 1734					
1	1	4	0		0		Griffin	William	Not listed in 1734					

Appendix   279

				Surname	Forename			
Not listed in 1731			0	Griffin	Hannah	0	1	3
1	0	0	1	Flavelle	Samuel	Not listed 1734		
Not listed in 1731				Force	Nathan	Not listed 1734		
Not listed in 1731				Hatham	Elizabeth	0	0	0
Not listed in 1731				Johnson	Alice	0	0	0
1			7	Johnson	Catherine	1	1	4
1				Johnson	Thomas	0	0	0
0	1		2	Kimbling	John	1	1	5
Not listed in 1731				Maycock	Martha	Not listed in 1734		
Not listed in 1731				Maycock	George	1	1	0
Not listed in 1731				Pye	James	1	0	2
1	1		8	Roberts	Benjamin Jnr	0	1	0
1	0		0	Roberts	John 1	1	1	5
1	1		7	Roberts	John 2	0	0	0
Not listed in 1731				Roberts	John 3	1	1	4
Not listed in 1731				Roberts	John Jnr	1	0	0
Not listed in 1731				Roberts	John Jnr.	0	0	0
Not listed in 1731				Roberts	Joseph	1	0	0
Not listed in 1731				Roberts	Michael	1	0	0
0			0	Russel	Benjamin	1	0	0
1	0		4	Russel	Daniel	1	0	0
0			0	Russel	Elizabeth	0	1	0
1				Saunders	Daniel	1	0	0
Not listed in 1731			3	Saunders	Hannah	0	1	0
1	1			Saunders	John	Not listed in 1734		
Not listed in 1731				Saunders	Martha	0	1	2
0	0		0	Saunders	Ruth	1	0	0
1	0		0	Saunders	Samuel	0	0	0
1	0		7	Saunders	Thomas	1	1	0
0	1		0	Sweeting	Mary	1	1	5
1	1		6	Sweeting	Benj Snr	0	1	0	2
1	0		0	Sweeting	Benj Jnr	1	1	4
1	0		0	Sweeting	John Sn	Not listed in 1734		

Census of 1731 source CO23/3/8 | | | Census of 1734 source 23/3/132 | | |

Census of 1731 White			Negroes			Surname	First Name	Census of 1734 White			Slaves		
Men	Wom.	Child.	Able	Child.				Men	Wom.	Child.	Men	Wom.	Child.
1	0	0	0	0		Sweeting	John Jnr	1	0	0			
1	1	6	0	0		Sweeting	Thomas	1	1	4			
Not listed in 1731						Sweeting	Thomas Jnr.	1	0	0			
Not listed in 1731						Sweeting	William	1	0	0			
Not listed in 1731						Symmons	Anne	0	1	0			
Not listed in 1731						Symmons	Nathaniel	1	1	0			
1	1	5				Tedder	Joseph	1	1	4			
1	1	7	0	0		Thompson	John	1	1	5	3		
1	1	5	2	0		Thompson	Joseph	1	1	6			
Not listed in 1731			0	0		Thompson	Richard	1	0	0			
Not listed in 1731						Thompson	Sarah	0	1	0			
Not listed in 1731						Thompson	William	1	1	4			
1	1	9	0	0		Thompson	William Jnr	1	0	6			
Not listed in 1731						Thompson	William	1	0	0			
1	0	0	2	1		Thompson	William Snr.	1	0	0	1	1	3
Not listed in 1731						Watkins	John	1	1	1			
Not listed in 1731						Watkins	Sarah	0	1	0			
31	27	102	8	1		< Totals >		45	33	73	4	1	5

NB: 1) Many names not listed in 1731 are Harbour Island children who became adults in 1734, especially those single male or female with no children

2) Names not listed in 1734 may have died, left the colony or are at sea.

Appendix 4

Pirates pardoned by Capt. Vincent Pearse 1717

The names of such pirates as surrendered themselves at New Providence to Capt. Vincent Pearse, Commander of His Majesty' ship, Phenix and accepted His most gracious pardon and had certificates from this said Commander to carry them to some Government.   Note those that are marked * are gone out pirating again.
[Authors have added # to mark Bahamian residents]

Packor	Robert	Adams	William	John	Rouse	John	Mitchell * #
Arthur	Henry	Allen #	Joseph	Edward	Clapp #	Edward	Rogers *
James	Robert	Coates	Peter	Michael	Goudet * #	Michael	Rogers #
John	James	Dalrymple #	Mark	John	Holmes	John	Kemp #
Benjamin	Richard	Hornigold #	**Daniel**	Othenias	**Stilwell #**	John	Sipkins
Josiah	Thomas	Burgess #	John	William	Edwards #	Othenias	Davis #
James	Robert	Lesley	Charles	Pearse	Garrison	William	Pinfold
Thomas	Daniel	**Nichols**	Joseph	Jacob	Pearse #	Pearse	Wright #
Paligrave	John	Williams #	William	William	Graham #	Jacob	Roberts #
John	George	Lewis #	Alexander	Edward	Campbell #	William	Williams #
Richard	John	Nowland #	James	**John**	Neville	Edward	Wells
John	Thomas	Martin #	James	Joseph	Fasset ?	**John**	**Cockram #**
William	William	Conner *	Edward	George	Berry	Joseph	Fryers
Thomas	John	Graham *	John	John	Andrews	George	Rounseville #
Thomas	William	Terril #	David	William	Nearne *	John	Creugh #
John	Thomas ?	Ealing	Garret	Matthew	Peterson	William	Roberts
Robert	Griffith	Wishart #	Richard	Joseph	Develty	Matthew	Revere
James	Edward	Gratricks	**Charles**	Robert	**Veine ***	Joseph	Micklebro
Edward	John	Stacey	Reginald	James	Houghson	Robert	Bass
John	Richard	Tennet	Robert	Edward	Valentine	James	Kerr #
John	Henry	Hunt	Samuel	Thomas	Boyce	Edward	Kerr #
John	David	Pearse	Richard	Thomas	Leggat #	Thomas	Williamson *
James	John	Bryan	Richard		Rawlings	Thomas	Chandler *

281

Henry Berry	William Willis	Darby	Samuel Moodey *
Thomas Lamb	Tristram Wilson	Arthur Von Pelt	William Spencer
John Allen #	Daniel Jones	John Richards	William Hunt
Martin Carril	Philip Calverly	Samuel Beach	Nathaniel Hudson
Thomas Cleis	James Brown	William Peters	William Smith #
John Hipperson	John Sutton	John Smith	Doonijah Stornburg
John Charlton	George Raddon #	George Sinclair	Edward Bead
Thomas Charnock *	Adam Forbes	William Hasselton	Edward Parmyter
David Merredith *	Cornelius Manon *	William Barry	Thomas Stoneham *
Edward Nowland *	Thomas Pearse	William Chow	John Crew *
James Goodsir *	David Ross	Abra Adams	William Edmundson
Denis McCarthy #	Jacob Johnson *	Joseph Thompson #	Richard Hawkes
Rowland Harbin	William Bridges #	James Peterson	Andrew Davis
George Gater	Robert Brown	Peter Mallet	Thomas Pearse
George Mann	Robert Muggeridge	William Titso	Richard Ward
Richard Richards	Henry Shipton #	John Arterile #	Henry Glenn
Anthony Jacobs	John Cullimore #	John Mounsey *	Leigh Ashworth
Nabel Clarke	Peter Johnson *	John Johnson	Dominick Dwoouly
Henry Hawkins	Charles Morgan *	John Bley #	George Chipsem
Daniel White #	**John Auger #**	John Furrow	David Turner
Edward Savory	William South	Samuel Adey	Clois Derickson
Peter Marshall	Marmad LeGee	John Magness	Thomas Bradley #
Archibald Murray *	James Mowat	Thomas Trouton	Thomas Emily
Daniel Hill #	Benjamin Turner	Edward Miller	Nicholas Woodall #
William Savory	John Mutlow	Daniel Swoord	Edward Hays
Richard Taylor	John Stout	Richard Earle #	Christopher Peters
Martin Townsend	Thomas Reynolds #	Anthony Kemp #	John Jackson #
Michael Swainston *	James Wheeler	John Carye #	Charles Whitehead #
Samuel Richardson #	Alexander Lyetts	Robert Shoar #	Edward Arrowsmith
			John Perrin #

Appendix 5
Harbour Island inhabitants participating in Deveaux' Raid

#	First	Last		Count	Surname
1	John	Albray			
2	John	Albray			
3	Joseph	Albray			
4	Joseph	Albray			
5	Joseph Jnr	Albray			
6	William	Albray	6	Albray	
7	Ephraim	Cleare			
8	John	Cleare			
9	Ruben	Cleare			
10	Thomas	Cleare	4	Cleare	
11	John	Currey			
12	John Jnr	Currey			
13	John Snr	Currey			
14	Joseph	Currey			
15	Richard	Currey			
16	Richard	Currey			
17	Thompson	Currey	7	Currey	
18	Samuel	Higgs	1	Higgs	
19	Nathaniel	Johnson			
20	Thomas	Johnson	2	Johnson	
21	Benjamin	Kemp	1	Kemp	
22	John	Kimblin	1	Kimblin	
23	Gideon	Lowe	1	Lowe	
24	George	Parks	1	Parks	
25	Joseph	Pearce	1	Pearce	
26	Thomas	Pierce	1	Pierce	
27	John	Pinder	1	Pinder	
28	Benjamin	Roberts			
29	Benjamin	Roberts			
30	Benjamin Jnr	Roberts			
31	George	Roberts			
32	James	Roberts			
33	James	Roberts			
34	John	Roberts			
35	John	Roberts			
36	John	Roberts			
37	John	Roberts			
38	John	Roberts			
39	Joseph	Roberts			
40	Joseph	Roberts			
41	Richard Jnr	Roberts			
42	Richard Snr	Roberts			
43	William	Roberts	16	Roberts	
44	Benjamin Jnr	Russell			
45	Daniel	Russell			
46	Joseph	Russell			
47	Nathaniel	Russell			
48	Thomas	Russell			
49	William	Russell	6	Russell	
50	Benjamin	Sands	1	Sands	
51	Benjamin	Saunders			
52	Benjamin Jnr	Saunders			
53	John	Saunders			
54	John	Saunders			
55	Joseph	Saunders			
56	Nathaniel Jnr	Saunders			
57	Nathaniel Snr	Saunders			
58	Thomas	Saunders			
59	William Jnr	Saunders	9	Saunders	
60	Admun Jnr	Sawyer			
61	Admun Snr	Sawyer			
62	Richard	Sawyer			
63	Richard	Sawyer			
64	William	Sawyer	5	Sawyer	
65	Thomas	Sweeting			
66	William	Sweeting	2	Sweeting	
67	John	Tedder			
68	Joseph Jnr	Tedder			
69	Joseph Snr	Tedder	3	Tedder	
70	Nathaniel	Thompson			
71	Thomas	Thompson	2	Thompson	
			71	**Total**	

Appendix 6
1842 Grant of Land (Commonage)

Benjamin	Albury 1	OI	London	Cash	XS	John	Hall	NI	Thomas	Johnson 1	OI	David	Roberts 1	XS	George	Saunders 1	OI	Duke	Sweeting 2	XS
Benjamin	Albury 2	OI	Prince	Cash	XS	Tony	Hamilton	NI	Thomas	Johnson 2	OI	David	Roberts 2	XS	George	Saunders 2	XS	Frederick	Sweeting	OI
Benjamin	Albury 3	XS	Richard	Cash	OI	Samuel	Hardy	NI	Thomas	Johnson 3	OI	Duke	Roberts 1	XS	James	Saunders	OI	Ganum	Sweeting	XS
Benjamin	Albury 4	OI	Robert	Cash	OI	Benjamin	Harris	OI	Thomas F	Johnson 4	OI	Duke	Roberts 2	XS	John	Saunders	OI	John	Sweeting	OI
Benjamin G	Albury	OI	Thomas	Cash 1	OI	John S	Harris	OI	William	Johnson 1	OI	George	Roberts 1	OI	Joseph	Saunders	OI	London	Sweeting	XS
Chatham	Albury 2	XS	Thomas	Cash 2	OI	Roger	Harris	OI	William	Johnson 2	OI	George	Roberts 2	XS	Lewis	Saunders	OI	Marshall	Sweeting	XS
Chatham	Albury 2	XS	William	Cash 1	OI	William	Higgs	XS	William	Johnson 3	OI	Henry	Roberts 1	XS	Peter	Saunders	XS	Stephen	Sweeting	OI
David	Albury	OI	Clinton	Cash 2	OI	George	Higgs 1	OI	George	Kelly	OI	Henry	Roberts 2	XS	Pomp	Saunders	XS	Thomas	Sweeting 1	OI
Gilbert	Albury	OI	John	Clarke	NI	David	Higgs 2	OI	James	Kelly 1	XS	Isaac	Roberts 1	OI	Richard	Saunders 1	OI	Thomas W	Sweeting 2	OI
Ishmael	Albury	XS	Benjamin	Cleare 1	XS	David	Higgs	XS	James	Kelly 2	XS	Isaac	Roberts 2	XS	Richard	Saunders 2	OI	William	Sweeting 1	OI
Israel	Albury	XS	Benjamin	Cleare 2	OI	George	Higgs	XS	Jane	Kelly	XS	Isaac	Roberts 3	XS	Samuel	Saunders	OI	William	Sweeting 2	OI
J A	Albury 1	OI	Charlotte	Cleare	XS	Jacob	Higgs	XS	Benjamin	Kemp	OI	Jacob	Roberts 4	XS	Stephen	Saunders	OI	Job	Tedder	OI
John	Albury 2	OI	Freeman	Cleare	XS	James	Higgs	XS	William	Kemp 1	OI	Jacob	Roberts	XS	Thomas	Saunders 1	OI	Cato	Thompson	XS
John	Albury 3	OI	James	Cleare 1	XS	Jane	Higgs	XS	William	Kemp 2	OI	James	Roberts 1	OI	Thomas	Saunders 2	XS	Edward	Thompson	OI
John	Albury 4	OI	James	Cleare 2	OI	Jeremiah	Higgs	OI	William	Lewis	SCH	James	Roberts 2	XS	Violet	Saunders 1	XS	Henry	Thompson	OI
John	Albury 5	OI	John	Cleare	XS	Joseph	Higgs	XS	Joseph	Lofthouse	REV	John	Roberts 3	XS	William	Saunders 1	OI	Ishmael	Thompson	XS
John	Albury 6	OI	Patience	Cleare	OI	Richard	Higgs	XS	Thomas	Lowe 1	OI	John	Roberts 1	OI	William	Saunders 2	OI	James	Thompson	OI
John	Albury 7	OI	Peter	Cleare	XS	Samuel	Higgs	OI	Benjamin	Lowe 2	OI	John	Roberts 2	OI	Bonner	Sawyer	XS	Jeremiah	Thompson	OI
Joseph	Albury 1	OI	Prince	Cleare	OI	Thomas	Higgs	XS	Benjamin	Lowe	XS	John	Roberts 3	OI	Clinton	Sawyer 1	XS	John	Thompson 1	OI
Joseph	Albury 2	OI	William	Cleare	OI	Barry	Hunter	OI	Joseph	Lowe	XS	John	Roberts 4	OI	Clinton	Sawyer 2	OI	John	Thompson 2	OI
Joseph	Albury 3	OI	Prince	Coleman	NI	Benjamin W	Ingraham	OI	Matthew	Lowe	OI	John	Roberts 5	OI	Edward	Sawyer	OI	John	Thompson 3	OI
Peter	Albury	OI	Morris	Cornish	XS	David	Ingraham	XS	Thomas	Manuel	NI	John	Roberts 6	OI	Henry	Sawyer	OI	John G	Thompson	OI
Richard	Albury 1	XS	Sancho	Cornish	OI	John	Ingraham 1	OI	Maurice	Mather	XS	John	Roberts 7	XS	Isaac	Sawyer	XS	Margaret	Thompson	OI
Richard	Albury 2	OI	Thomas	Cox	NI	Joseph	Ingraham 1	OI	Richard	Mather	XS	John D	Roberts	OI	John	Sawyer	OI	Robert	Thompson	OI
Richardson	Albury	OI	Charles	Curry	XS	Joseph	Ingraham 2	OI	Robert	Mather	XS	Joseph	Roberts 1	XS	Joseph	Sawyer 1	OI	Thomas	Thompson 1	OI
Samuel	Albury	OI	Jacob	Curry	OI	Benjamin	Johnson	XS	John	McKenzie	JP	Joseph	Roberts 2	XS	Joseph	Sawyer 2	XS	Thomas	Thompson 2	OI
Sharper	Albury	XS	John	Curry	OI	Deborah	Johnson	OI	Mosa	Moss	NI	Joseph	Roberts 3	OI	Joseph	Sawyer 3	OI	William	Thompson	OI
William	Albury 1	OI	Richard H	Curry	OI	Frederick	Johnson	OI	Francisco	Nabour	NI	Joseph	Roberts 4	XS	Mary	Sawyer 1	OI	Jacob	Tynes	NI
William	Albury 2	OI	Robert	Curry	XS	Frederick R	Johnson	OI	Thomas	Neely	NI	Middy	Roberts	XS	Mary	Sawyer 2	OI	Joseph	Williams	NI
William	Albury 3	OI	William	Curry	OI	George	Johnson 1	OI	David	Nix	NI	Pleasant	Roberts	XS	Peter	Sawyer	XS			
William	Albury 4	OI	Joseph	Demeritt	NI	George	Johnson 2	OI	Robert	Nix	NI	Richard	Roberts 1	OI	Richard	Sawyer	OI			
Rebecca	Barnett	?	Thomas	Dorsett	NI	Henry	Johnson 1	OI	James	Palmer	OI	Richard	Roberts 2	OI	Thomas	Sawyer 1	OI			
Benjamin	Bethell	OI	Andrew	Driggs 1	NI	Henry	Johnson 2	OI	Jacob	Parks	OI	Richard	Roberts 3	OI	Thomas	Sawyer 2	XS			
John	Bethell 1	OI	Andrew	Driggs 2	NI	Henry	Johnson 3	OI	George	Pearce	OI	Robert	Roberts	OI	William	Sawyer 1	OI			
John	Bethell 2	OI	William K	Duncome	REV	Jacob	Johnson	XS	William	Petty	OI	Ruth	Roberts	XS	William	Sawyer 2	OI			

284

Appendix

Noah	Bethell	OI	Dundee	XS	John	Johnson 1	OI James Pierce	OI Uriah Roberts	XS William Sawyer 3	OI
Richard	Bethell	OI	William Durant	NI	John	Johnson 2	OI John Pierce	OI William Roberts 1	OI William H Sears	NI
William	Bethell	OI	Anthony Eneas	NI	John H	Johnson	OI Esau Pinder	NI William Roberts 2	OI Richard Simons	NI
Winer	Bethell	OI	Alexander Fisher 1	XS	Judy	Johnson	XS Stephen Pinder	NI William Roberts 3	OI Samuel Simons	NI
George	Bill	NI	Alexander Fisher 2	XS	Louis	Johnson	OI William Prudden	NI Alice Russell	OI Joseph Skelton	NI
Jeremiah	Blatch	NI	Anthony Fisher	XS	Lucy	Johnson	XS John Ranger	NI George Russell	OI Matthew Skelton	NI
Isaac	Brady	XS	Devonshire Fisher	XS	Moses	Johnson	XS William Ranger 1	NI Sampson Russell	OI Ann Smith	NI
Joseph	Brady	NI	Jane Fisher	XS	Nathaniel	Johnson	OI William Ranger 2	NI Thomas Russell	OI John Smith	NI
William	Brady	NI	Limerick Fisher	XS	Quintus	Johnson	OI Richard Richardson	NI Simon Ryner	NI Samuel Smith	NI
William	Burton	NI	Paul Fisher	XS	Robert	Johnson	OI Alexander Roberts	OI Anthony Saunders	XS William Smith	NI
Henry	Cash	OI	David Galaspie	NI	Samuel	Johnson 1	OI B Roberts	XS Boston Saunders	XS Benjamin Sweeting 1	OI
John	Cash 1	OI	John B Galpin	NI	Samuel	Johnson 2	OI Benjamin Roberts	XS Chatham Saunders 1	XS Benjamin Sweeting 2	OI
John	Cash 2	OI	John Gay	NI	Samuel	Johnson 3	OI Charles Roberts	XS Chatham Saunders 2	XS Caesar Sweeting	XS
John	Cash 3	OI	Thomas Gibbons	NI	Scotland	Johnson	OI Cuffy Roberts	XS David Saunders	XS Duke Sweeting 1	XS

Key: OI = Old Inhabitant REV = Minister of religion
     XS = Ex-slave   SCH = Schoolteacher
     NI = New inhabitant

Appendix 7
Early migration of the inhabitants of Harbour Islanders to neighbouring islands

Inter marriage between Hope Town and Harbour Island

Reference: The Bahama Island's study by The Baltimore Geographical Society and St John's Parish Baptism records 1795 to 1822

Descendents of:

Wyannie Malone		married			From
Malone	Ephraim	to	Elizabeth	Tedder	HI
Malone	Wyannie	to	Jacob	Adams	HI
Malone	David	to	Patience	not named	HI

Descendents of Ephraim, David and daughter Wyannie

Malone	Benjamin	to	Jane	Thompson	HI
Malone	Ephraim	to	Jane	Roberts	HI
Malone	Anne	to	Edward	Russell	HI
Malone	Eliza	to	Charles	Sands	Ch Snd (ex HI)
Malone	Wyannie	to	Thomas	Russell	Abaco (ex HI)
Adams	Elizabeth	to	Thomas	Russell	HI
Adams	Peggy	to	William	Thompson	HI
Adams	Susan	to	John	Tedder	HI
Adams	Jacob	to	Charlotte	Sawyer	HI
Adams	Sarah	to	Benjamin	Bethel	HI
Malone	Susan	to	John	Rutherford	USA
Malone	Elijah	to	Miss	Roberts	HI
Malone	Benjamin	to	Elizabeth	Bethel	Abaco (ex HI)
Malone	Samuel	to	Effie	Albury	Abaco (ex HI)
Malone	Augustus	to	Mahalie	Albury	HI
Sands	William	to	Frances	Albury	Ch Snd (ex HI)
Sands	Romelda	to	Octavius H	Dorsett	Nassau
Sands	Elizabeth A	to	Adin	Roberts	Abaco (ex HI)
Tedder	Susan	to	John	Roberts	HI
Tedder	Elizabeth	to	William	Albury	Abaco (ex HI)
Malone	Richard	to	Susannah	Tedder	HI
Rutherford	Susan	to	Joseph	Russell	Abaco (ex HI)
Malone	Anne	to	Wyner	Bethel	Abaco (ex HI)
Malone	William	to	Effie	Albury	Abaco (ex HI)
Roberts	Nancy	to	John	Albury	Abaco (ex HI)
Malone	Joshua	to	Adelaide	Russell	Abaco (ex HI)
Russell	Martha	to	William	Albury	Abaco (ex HI)
Russell	Mary Anne	to	Richard	Albury	Abaco (ex HI)
Russell	Elizabeth	to	John	Thompson	HI
Russell	David	to	Caroline	Roberts	HI
Russell	Randall	to	Sarah Jane	Albury	Abaco (ex HI)

Russell	George	to	Isabella	Russel	Abaco (ex HI)
Russell	John Wilson	to	Charlotte	Roberts	Abaco (ex HI)
Albury	William	to	Elizabeth	Tedder	Abaco (ex HI)
Russell	Elizabeth	to	Richard	Pinder	Ch Snd (ex HI)
Russell	Thomas	to	Charlotte A	Albury	Abaco (ex HI)
Russell	David	to	Susan M	Roberts	Abaco (ex HI)
Russell	Wyannie	to	John	Malone	Abaco (ex HI)
Key	Nathan	to	Martha	Roberts	HI (Key from Britain)
Key	William	to	Sarah	Thompson 2	HI
Key	Nathan	to	Charlotte	Russell	Abaco (ex HI)
Key	Edward	to	Mary	Russell	Abaco (ex HI)
Albury	John	to	Sarah	Saunders	HI both
Bethel	Melissa	to	Wm Alonzo	Russell	Abaco (ex HI)
Key	Matilda	to	John	Roberts	Abaco (ex HI)
Key	Nathaniel	to	Sarah A	Albury	Abaco (ex HI)
Albury	John	to	not named		Abaco (ex HI)
Albury	Robert	to	Sarah	Pinder	Span Wells
Albury	John	to	Martha	Russell	Abaco (ex HI)
Albury	Emily	to	Nathaniel	Sawyer	Abaco (ex HI)

Inter marriage between Man o' War Cay and Harbour Island

Reference: Man-o-War, My Island Home by Haziel L Albury
and St John's Parish Baptism records 1795 to 1822

Benjamin Archer to Elizabeth Pinder in HI 1798
Their daughter Eleanor (Nellie) married Benjamin Albury of HI circa 1820
Marriages of their children:

Betsy	Albury	to	Richard	Sawyer	of HI
Henry	Albury	to	Mattia	Key	of Hope Town
Benjamin	Albury	to	Eliza	Weatherford	
William	Albury	to	Lydia	Thompson	of HI
Samuel	Albury	to	Susan	Weatherford	
John	Albury	to	Laura	Weatherford	
Mary	Albury	to	William	Thompson	of HI

Migration and inter marriage between HI and Green Turtle Cay

Reference: Sandra Riley and St John's Parish Records 195 to 1822

Richard	Curry	and	Mercy (nee Albury)	before 1800
Gideon	Lowe	and	Nancy (nee Saunders)	early 1800s
Benjamin	Curry	and	Deborah	early 1800s
Benjamin	Saunders	and	Elizabeth	early 1800s
Benjamin	Roberts	and	Martha	early 1800s
Matthew	Lowe			early 1800s
John Hancock	Kelly			early 1800s
William	Russell			early 1800s
William	Saunders			early 1800s
Nathaniel	Saunders			early 1800s
Thompson	Curry	and	Mary	early 1800s
Uriah	Saunders	and	Sarah	early 1800s

Migration and inter marriage between HI and Cherokee Sound

Reference: St John's Parish Records 195 to 1822

The following couples are listed in the Baptism Records of 1818:

John and Elizabeth Sweeting, Noah and Jemimah Bethel
Joseph and Ruth Pinder   Benjamin and Fanny Albury
Benjamin and Mary Russell

Early inhabitants of Spanish Wells
Compiled from the Records of Christ Church, St John's Parish Church and Bahamas Gazette.

Marriages :

Lowe (El)	Benjamin	to	Mary Sweeting from HI	at SpW	1760
Albury	William	to	Ruth Curry	in HI	1800
Albury	William	to	Sarah Russell	in HI	1802
Bethel	Noah	to	Jemima Sands	in HI	1802
Weatherford	Charles	to	Sarah Roberts	of HI	1803
Stirrop	James	to	Mary Pinder	in HI	1805

Noah & Jemimah Bethel seemed to have migrated later to Cherokee Sound

Baptismal records (1792–1822) indicate migration of 4 more couples:
John & Love Roberts   Joseph & Sarah Russell
William & Sarah Albury   John & Francis Albury

Appendix 8

Population of Harbour Island, Eleuthera and New Providence from 1773–1900

Year	Settlement	Families	White	Slave	Free Col	Total
1731[1]	Harbour Island		160	9		169
	Eleuthera		73	21		94
	New Providence		633	409		1042
1773[2]	Harbour Island		410	90		500
	Eleuthera		509	237		746
	New Providence		1024	1800		2824
1776[3]	Harbour Island	64	375	162	0	537
	Eleuthera	112	508	230	–	738
	New Providence					

1782: Wilson's Report giving population before Conquest[4]

Island	White	Taxables: Free Mul	Manmit	Slaves	Total	Not Tax Total	Total inhabs	Spanish Report[5] Total
H.I.	97	2	–	80	179	321	500	611
El	102	25	–	23	150	300	450	602
N.P.	229	75	15	642	961	1789	2750	1755

Year	Settlement	White	Slave	Free Col & B	Total
1788[6]	Harbour Island	472	197	15	684
	Eleuthera	584	299	28	911
	New Providence				
1790[7]	Harbour Island	600	250		850
	Eleuthera	658	300		958
1794[8]	Harbour Island	560	212	8	800
1805[9]	Harbour Island		272	13	1200 (1804)
	Eleuthera		1108	117	
	New Providence		3047	999	
1812[10]	Harbour Island	661	539	52	1252
	Eleuthera	582	1058	143	1783
1810	New Providence	1720	3190	1074	6084
1834[11]	Harbour Island	760	578 *	68	1406
	Eleuthera	1138	1303	187	2628
	New Providence	1418	2881	2955	7254

* Gail Saunders, *Slavery in the Bahamas*, gives a slave total of 511 (from Slave Registers 1834)

1851[12]

Settlement	White	Black	Coloured	Total
Harbour Island	973	658	229	1840
Eleuthera	1211	2873	526	4610
New Prov	1534	5377	1248	8159

• This is the last racial breakdown until the census of 1943

Population Totals from Blue Book Reports:

Settlement	1838	1839	1841	1851	1861	1871	1881	1891	1901
Harbour Island	1633	1655	1745	1840	1994	2,172	1970	1472	1232
Eleuthera	2633	2638	3445	4610	5209	6058	7010	7358	8733
Spanish Wells			267		331	395	440	414	534
New Providence	9505	9638	8385	8159	11,503	11,410	11,653	10,914	12,534

Endnotes for Appendix 8

[1] SPG Reel 1
[2] SPG Reel 1
[3] SPG Reel 1
[4] Report of LT John Wilson on the Bahamas Islands, 1783.
[5] Report of Governor, Don Claraco, 1782
[6] SPG Reel 1, This report differs from Whylly's Report of 1788. Compare table below:

State of Bahama Islands, June 1788, from Whylly's Report

Island Category >	White Male Head of Family			Slaves		
	Old	New	Total	Old	New	Total
Harbour Island	94	0	94	142	0	142
Eleuthera	119	0	119	310	0	310
New Providence	131	165	296	1024	1264	2288

[7] SPG Reel 1
[8] SPG Reel 2
[9] 1804 The seemingly high total of 1200 inhabitant's statistic is from SPG Reel 2
    1805 Statistic is from the CO 23/48/44 Report of Mr Dyer to My Lord
[10] CO 23/59/37, An Account of the Population of the Bahama Islands, June 1812.
    An Account of the population of New Providence, 13th December, 1810
[11] Blue Book Reports, 1834.
[12] Blue Book Reports, 1851

Appendix 9

Slave registers 1821–1834   Selected Harbour Island slave units

#	Owner	Occuptn	Slave	Age		Sex	Col	PE	A/C	Yr	Yr	Yr	Yr	Yr & Occupation	Slave marriage and baptism records
An example of a slave family with father, mother and children
	Christopher	Fisher	Planter	Nicholas	17	M	Blk	HI	C	22	25	28	31	34 Mariner, wrecking etc @ HI	father of Nicholas with Flora
1	Joseph	Curry		Flora	22	F	Blk	HI	C				31	34 Domestic on owner's land	surname Fisher
2	Joseph	Curry		Mary Anne	2	F	Blk	HI	C				31	34 Nil NE	
3	Joseph	Curry		Matilda	3	F	Blk	HI	C					34 Nil NE	
4	Joseph	Curry		Nicholas	1	M	Blk	HI	C					34 Nil NE	son of Nicholas & Flora Fisher
An example of a mulatto slave family with father, mother and children, which mirrors the close knit white family
1	Martha	Saunders	Widow	Hannah	44	F	Mul	HI	C	22	25	28	31	Manumitted 1832	
2	Martha	Saunders		Peter	25	M	Mul	HI	C	22	25	28	31	Forfeited to Crown 1832	fthr of Easter Ann w Eleanor m 1834
1	William	Saunders	Planter	Sarah	70	F	Blk	HI	C	22	25	28	31	34 Field labourer on owner's land	
2	William	Saunders	*William*	Clinton	38	M	Mul	HI	C	22	25	28	31	34 Mariner, wrecking etc	mthr of Clinton
3	William	Saunders	*died 1825*	Eleanor	21	F	Mul	HI	C	22	25	28	31	34 Field labourer on owner's land	son of Sarah
															mthr of Easter Ann w Peter S m 1834
4	William	Saunders	Widow	Isaac	12	M	Mul	HI	C	22	25	28	31	34 Mariner, wrecking etc	
5	William	Saunders	*Sarah*	Melinda	1	F	Mul	HI	C		25	28	31	34 Domestic @ HI	
6	William	Saunders		Satyra	2	F	Mul	HI	C				31	34 Nil NE @ HI	
7	William	Saunders		Easter Ann	3	F	Mul	HI	C					34 Nil NE @ HI	dtr of Peter & Eleanor Saunders
8	William	Saunders		Elena Jane	1	F	Mul	HI	C					34 Nil NE @ HI	

292   *The Harbour Island Story*

An example of a family with no adult male.

#				Age	Sex	Race	Loc	St	'22	'25	'28	'31	'34	Notes
1	Ruth	Albury	Widow	Bash	55	F	Blk	HI	C	22	25	28	31	34 Domestic @ HI	
2	Ruth	Albury		Sibel	30	F	Blk	HI	C	22	25	28	31	34 Field labourer	
3	Ruth	Albury		Patience	25	F	Blk	HI	C	22	25	28	31	34 Field labourer	dtr of Bash Albury
4	Ruth	Albury		Rachel	3	F	Blk	HI	C	22	25	28	31	34 Domestic @ HI	dtr of Bash Albury
5	Ruth	Albury		Harriott	2	F	Blk	HI	C	22	25	28	31	34 Domestic @ HI	
6	Ruth	Albury		Ishmael	1	M	Blk	HI	C	22	25	28	31	34 Mariner, wrecking, etc	
7	Ruth	Albury		Prince	1	M	Blk	HI	C	22	25	28	31	34 Mariner, wrecking, etc	
8	Ruth	Albury		Jerry	2	M	Blk	HI	C	22	25	28	31	34 Mariner, wrecking, etc	
9	Ruth	Albury		Robert	1	M	Blk	HI	C	22	25	28	31	34 Field labourer @ HI	
#	Ruth	Albury		Clarinda	2	F	Blk	HI	C		25	28	31	34 Domestic @ HI	
#	Ruth	Albury		Sary	1	F	Blk	HI	C		25	28	31	34 Domestic @ HI	
#	Ruth	Albury		Caroline	1	F	Blk	HI	C			28	31	34 Domestic @ HI	
#	Ruth	Albury		Rebecca	3	F	Blk	HI	C				31	34 Domestic @ HI	
#	Ruth	Albury		Patience	1	F	Blk	HI	C				31	34 Nil NE @ HI	

An example of a 'working unit'

#				Age	Sex	Race	Loc	St	'22	'25	'28	'31	Notes
1	Susannah	Albury	Widow	Lewis	29	M	Blk	HI	C	22	25	28	31	Mariner
2	Susannah	Albury		Sharper	26	M	Blk	HI	C	22	25	28	31	Mariner/Forfeited 1832
3	Susannah	Albury		Chatham	28	M	Blk	HI	C	22	25	28	31	Mariner/Forfeited 1832
4	Susannah	Albury		Dick	20	M	Blk	HI	C	22	25	28	31	Mariner at New Providence
5	Susannah	Albury		Secunda	15	M	Blk	HI	C	22	25	28		sold to Henshel Stubbs
6	Susannah	Albury		Rose	31	F	Blk	HI	C	22	25	died		

Appendix 10
Liberated African apprentices at Harbour Island District

CO23/109/folio45 Major McGregor's Report of African Labourers (Apprentices) Harbour Island 1838

Employer	Labourer	Residence	Age	Sex	Employed	Remarks
Rev K Duncombe	Simon	Dunmore	12	M	Domestic	Well treated
Rev K Duncombe	Jane	Dunmore	14	F	Domestic	Well treated
William Smith esq	Charles	Dunmore	11	M	Mariner	Well treated
William Smith esq	Sarah	Dunmore	14	F	Domestic	Well treated
Jeremiah Higgs esq	Toby	Dunmore	12	M	Domestic	Well treated
James Minors	Sam	Dunmore	13	M	Domestic	Well treated
James Minors	no name	Dunmore	?	M	Domestic	Well treated
James Kelly	Robert	Dunmore	14	M	Carpenter	Well treated
John Albury	John	Dunmore	12	M	Domestic	Well treated
John Albury	Sarah	Dunmore	14	F	Domestic	Well treated
Prince Coleman	Tom	Dunmore	11	M	Domestic	Well treated
William A Smith	Colly	Dunmore	14	F	Domestic	Well treated
John Albury Jun	Juno	Dunmore	15	F	Domestic	Well treated
Elizabeth Sweeting	John	Dunmore	13	M	Domestic	Well treated
Elizabeth Sweeting	Susan	Dunmore	12	F	Domestic	Well treated
Matilda Clear	Uisiclt	Dunmore	14	M	Mariner	Well treated
Matilda Clear	Jacob	Dunmore	13	M	Domestic	Well treated
Capt William Clear	Harry	Dunmore	12	M	Mariner	Well treated
George Roberts	Joseph	Dunmore	13	M	Mariner	Well treated
Thomas Sweeting	George	Dunmore	9	M	Domestic	Well treated
Samuel Johnson	John	Dunmore	13	M	Domestic	Well treated
Thomas Sweeting	Nathan	Dunmore	14	M	Domestic	Well treated
Benjamin Albury	Billy	Dunmore	13	M	Domestic	Well treated
Joseph Clear esq	Adolphus	Dunmore	12	M	Domestic	Well treated
H Sears	Mary	Dunmore	12	F	Domestic	Well treated
John Clear	Bethel	Dunmore	13	M	Domestic	Well treated
Robert Kelly	Nancy	Dunmore	12	F	Domestic	Well treated
James Sawyer	John	Dunmore	9	M	Mariner	Well treated
Mary Saunders	Jane	Dunmore	13	F	Domestic	Well treated
Miss Mary Roberts	Binah	Dunmore	8	F	Domestic	Well treated
Joseph Ingraham	Paul	Dunmore	15	M	Domestic	Well treated
Benjamin Albury	Dundee	Dunmore	12	M	Domestic	Well treated
Robert Thompson	Peggy	Dunmore	14	F	Domestic	Well treated
W Johnson	George	Dunmore	13	M	Domestic	Well treated
Mary Johnson	Margaret	Dunmore	8	F	Domestic	Well treated
Mary Johnson	George	Dunmore	13	M	Domestic	Well treated
John Cash	Boston	Dunmore	14	M	Domestic	Well treated
George Johnson	Jacob	Dunmore	14	M	Field	Well treated
Matthew J Lowe	Barry	Current	12	M	Field	Well treated
Matthew H Lowe	Gay	Current	17	M	Field	Well treated

Joseph Hall Sen	Frederick	Current	17	M	Field	Well treated
Benjamin Griffin	Toby	Current	12	M	Domestic	Well treated
Joseph Hall Jun	Philip	Current	14	M	Field	Well treated
Joseph Hall Jun	Jim	Current	12	M	Field	Well treated
Henry Hall	Collins	Current	13	M	Field	Well treated
John Hall	Joseph	Current	13	M	Field	Well treated
John Hall	Fanny	Current	15	F	Field	Well treated
John Sweeting	Cato	Cove	?	M	Field	Well treated
William Sawyer	Mike	Bluff	13	M	Mariner	Well treated
Mrs Sawyer	Mary	Bluff	12	F	Domestic	Well treated
Mrs Sawyer	John	Bluff	13	M	Domestic	Well treated
Richard Saunders	Courio/David	HI	25	M	Deceased	

landed from *Invincible* 12th Dec 1837 died Jan 1838

Appendix 11

Ships entering and clearing Harbour Island and Eleuthera 1855–1901

Abbreviations: wc = with cargo; b = in ballast   Halcyon Years **bold**

Year	Entered HI British wc	b	Foreign wc	b	Tot	Cleared HI British wc	b	Foreign wc	b	Tot	Entered Eleuthera British wc	b	Foreign wc	b	Tot	Cleared Eleuthera British wc	b	Foreign wc	b	Tot
1855	27	7	3	1	38	28	0	2	0	30	Not recorded									
1856	30	0	0	0	30	29	0	2	0	31	Not recorded									
1857	23	6	0	4	33	13	6	7	0	33	18	0	0	0	18	Not recorded				
1858	22	4	2	2	32	30	3	5	0	38	17	2	1	3	23	16	9	3	0	19
1859	Not recorded																			
1860	27	8	0	7	42	31	14	7	0	52	14	4	1	4	22	18	0	22	0	40
1861	29	7	3	0	39	33	9	1	0	43	13	1	1	2	17	22	0	1	0	23
1862	**26**	**12**	**2**	**0**	**40**	**47**	**6**	**0**	**0**	**53**	**9**	**0**	**2**	**0**	**11**	**15**	**0**	**3**	**0**	**18**
1863	**31**	**11**	**4**	**0**	**46**	**44**	**0**	**9**	**0**	**53**	**24**	**0**	**5**	**0**	**29**	**12**	**0**	**4**	**0**	**16**
1864	**20**	**11**	**3**	**0**	**34**	**45**	**0**	**2**	**0**	**52**	**10**	**0**	**3**	**0**	**13**	**19**	**0**	**4**	**0**	**23**
1865	**44**	**7**	**7**	**1**	**59**	**46**	**7**	**6**	**1**	**60**	**1**	**6**	**8**	**1**	**16**	**20**	**0**	**8**	**0**	**28**
1866	**37**	**21**	**4**	**3**	**65**	**50**	**6**	**6**	**0**	**62**	**10**	**6**	**16**	**4**	**36**	**19**	**0**	**7**	**0**	**26**
1867	30	3	3	1	37	33	8	3	0	44	7	9	5	1	22	9	0	7	0	16
1868	21	0	2	0	23	20	4	2	0	26	12	4	6	2	24	17	1	11	0	29
1869	30	2	13	5	50	33	0	23	1	57	11	4	8	2	25	15	0	10	0	25
1870	12	2	14	17	45	24	0	18	1	43	7	6	9	7	29	16	0	17	0	33
1871	16	1	13	15	45	12	2	31	1	46	4	6	12	13	35	16	0	25	0	41
1872	Not recorded																			
1873	Not recorded																			
1874	18	1	12	10	39	23	0	19	0	42	1	8	26	24	59	8	0	54	0	62
1875	20	0	11	12	43	15	1	22	0	38	2	5	12	16	35	21	0	31	1	53
1876	15	3	9	5	32	19	2	15	0	36	6	8	12	9	35	19	0	23	1	43

295

Year	Entered HI British wc	b	Foreign wc	b	Tot	Cleared HI British wc	b	Foreign wc	b	Tot	Entered Eleuthera British wc	b	Foreign wc	b	Tot	Cleared Eleuthera British wc	b	Foreign wc	b	Tot
1877	18	2	5	4	29	17	0	10	0	27	3	7	15	10	35	13	0	26	0	39
1878	23	0	7	1	31	25	0	6	0	31	4	6	15	12	37	15	0	30	0	45
1879	18	1	8	2	29	15	0	18	0	33	4	7	18	10	39	11	1	28	0	40
1880	19	0	2	0	21	19	0	2	0	21	6	7	17	16	46	14	1	31	0	46
1881	12	0	2	0	14	13	2	1	0	16	2	4	18	23	47	9	0	42	0	51
1882	16	0	3	1	20	16	0	0	0	16	2	6	17	18	43	12	1	48	0	61
1883	12	1	2	0	15	16	2	2	0	20	4	6	17	21	48	12	2	45	0	59
1884	11	0	1	0	12	12	2	2	0	16	8	5	7	17	37	11	1	29	1	42
1885	12	1	1	0	14	13	0	0	0	13	6	7	13	21	47	15	0	26	1	42
1886	No Blue Book listed																			
1887	12	2	6	3	23	6	2	5	0	13	5	4	12	29	50	9	0	34	0	43
1888	No Blue Book listed																			
1889	9	0	2	0	11	8	1	1	0	10	11	5	5	19	40	15	0	23	0	38
1890	8	1	0	0	9	6	0	2	0	8	7	2	12	22	43	16	0	47	0	63
1891	8	0	2	0	10	8	1	1	0	10	8	2	12	44	66	5	1	61	0	67
1892	No Blue Book listed																			
1893	2	0	3	1	6	1	3	3	0	7	6	5	14	21	46	16	0	37	0	53
1894	5	1	1	1	8	4	2	1	1	8	8	5	15	34	62	19	0	53	0	72
1895	10	2	0	0	12	7	1	0	0	8	9	4	10	24	47	22	0	46	0	68
1896	7	1	10	0	18	4	0	1	0	5	9	0	25	26	60	15	0	61	0	76
1897	9	1	1	0	11	6	3	0	0	9	7	1	35	30	73	17	0	71	1	89
1898	5	2	0	0	7	3	3	0	0	6	13	5	19	24	61	26	0	41	0	67
1899	6	2	0	0	8	2	16	0	0	18	8	0	17	18	43	11	0	42	0	53
1900	4	0	0	0	4	8	14	0	0	22	10	0	11	25	46	11	0	44	0	55
1901/2	6	0	0	0	6	6	11	0	0	17	17	0	21	32	70	17	0	57	0	74
1902/3	6	1	0	0	7	4	10	0	0	14	10	0	20	23	53	17	0	51	0	68
1903/4	2	3	0	0	5	6	4	0	0	10	12	0	12	13	37	19	0	34	3	56
1904/5	2	3	0	0	5	6	5	0	0	14*	7	1	9	13	29	13	0	27	1	41
1905/6	None recorded for HI					6	4	0	0	10	7	0	7	6	21	9	0	1	22	31
1906/7	2	1	0	0	3	3	3	0	0	6	5	0	16	3	24	8	0	24	0	32

Appendix 297

Year																		
1907/8	0	0	2	2	3	5	2	0	10	2	5	2	9	1	0	9	0	10
1908/9	None recorded for HI				3	4	0	0	7	1	8	0	10	1	0	14	0	15
1909/10	None recorded for HI				3	5	0	0	8	1	5	1	7	1	0	9	0	10
1910/11	0	4	0	4	2	1	0	0	3	1	1	0	4	0	0	1	0	1
1911	2	5	0	7	2	0	0	0	2	1	0	0	1	1	0	1	0	1
1911/12	2	5	0	7	2	0	0	0	2	1	0	0	1	1	0	0	0	1
1912/13	4	3	0	7	2	2	0	0	4	Not recorded	0	0	0	0	0	0	0
1913/14	0	3	0	3	1	1	0	0	2	0	2	0	2	0	1	2	1	2
1914/15	1	4	0	5	0	1	0	0	1	Not recorded	Not recorded	Not recorded	0	0	0	0
1915/16	2	4	0	6	0	2	0	0	2	Not recorded	Not recorded	Not recorded	0	0	0	0
1916/17	2	2	0	4	0	2	0	0	2	1	0	0	1	Not recorded	0	0	0
1918	2	2	0	4	2	2	0	0	4	1	0	0	1	Not recorded	0	0	0
1918/19	1	2	0	3	0	5	0	0	5	2	0	0	2	Not recorded	Not recorded	0	0
1919/20	1	3	1	6	0	2	0	1	3	Not recorded	Not recorded	Not recorded	2	0	0
1920/21	2	3	1	7	3	1	0	0	1	Not recorded	Not recorded	Not recorded	0	1	0
1921/22	0	3	0	3	2	0	0	0	3	Not recorded	Not recorded	Not recorded	2	0	0	0
1923/24	0	4	0	4	2	7	0	0	9	Not recorded	Not recorded	Not recorded	Not recorded	0	0	2

Appendix 12
Wrecking licence, fees and consort shares

Facsimile of a Wrecking Licence:

> Wrecking Licence
>
> By
> These are to licence the British _____
> Of and belonging to the Port of _____
> Whereof _____ To sail and be
> employed as a wrecking vessel within the limits of the Bahama Islands, under the authority of the Act of the general Assembly, passed in the 11th year of Her Majesty's reign entitled *An Act for the government of vessels, boats, and Persons employed in rendering assistance and saving ships, persons and goods, stranded or in peril within these islands*, as amended per 16 Vic cap 1
>
> Given under my hand and Seal-at-Arms, at Nassau, New Providence, this _____ Day of _____ 18
>
> By His Excellency's command.   (CO23/153/358 Wrecking Licence 1856)

Fees

Estimated amount of licences paid for Harbour Island and other Wrecking Vessels 1860 (Based on the share system outlined in the 1855 Act).

Vessels	Crew inc Master	Estimated Tonnage	Licence Fee
Vesper	14	50 to 55 (actual 49.5)	£7-12-0d
Desdomonia	14	50 to 55	£7-12-0d
Splendid	14	50 to 55	£7-12-0d
Lady Bannerman	17	65 to 70	£8-16-0d
Defiance	13	45 to 50	£7-4-0d
Magnet	10	Actual 33	£4-12-d
Clyde	15	55 to 60	£8-0-0d
Mary Elizabeth	9	25 to 30	£4-7-0d
Mary Jane	9	25 to 30	£4-7-0d
Ventrosa	23	95 to 100	£11-4-0d
Dart	23	95 to 100	£11-4-0d
Mary & Susan	28	120 to 125	£13-4-0d
Elyn	10	30 to 35	£4-12-0d

Schedule of licence fees

Licence of persons: taxed at 8 shillings for each licence issued

Licence of boats: Open or decked boat not exceeding 5 tons burthen, 8 shillings
A vessel larger than 5 tons but not exceeding 20 tons burthen, 12 shillings
A vessel larger than 20 tons but not exceeding 40 tons burthen, 25 shillings
A vessel larger than 40 tons burthen, 40 shillings

Consort share system:

That in cases of consortship the shares allotted..shall be as follows:
To every vessel or boat (carrying a crew including the Master and officers of able men)

under 10 tons 5 able men – 5 shares.
10 tons or upwards but under 15 tons, 6 able men – 6 shares.
15 tons or upwards but under 20 tons, 7 able men – 7 shares.
20 tons or upwards but under 25 tons, 8 able men – 8 shares.
25 tons or upwards but under 30 tons, 9 able men – 9 shares.
30 tons or upwards but under 35 tons, 10 able men – 10 shares.
35 tons or upwards but under 40 tons, 11 able men – 11 shares.
40 tons or upwards but under 45 tons, 12 able men – 12 shares.
45 tons or upwards but under 50 tons, 13 able men – 13 shares.
50 tons or upwards but under 55 tons, 14 able men – 14 shares.
55 tons or upwards but under 60 tons, 15 able men – 15 shares.
60 tons or upwards but under 65 tons, 16 able men – 16 shares.
65 tons or upwards but under 70 tons, 17 able men – 17 shares.
70 tons or upwards but under 75 tons, 18 able men – 18 shares.

And 1 additional share for every 5 tons over 75 tons, providing 1 additional man is carried for each such additional 5 tons.

CO 23/153/313 – A Bill (1855)

Appendix 13
Harbour Island wrecking vessels and crews

Wreck of the *Vallonia* (Vice Admiralty Records 30 November 1854)

Wreck Master: Stephen Roberts of *Vesper* of Harbour Island.
Owners: George Sawyer, Chatham Albury, Jeremiah Sawyer, Matthew Sawyer.
Crew: Jacob Thompson, Geautier Collie, Charles Thompson, Samuel Micklewhyte, Richard Poitier, William Sands, Michael Culmer, Peter Mingo, Hezekiah Saunders Joseph Nesbitt, Joseph Davis, Thomas Wilson, George Hall, Dennis Swain.

Wreck of the *Mary Leve* (Vice Admiralty Records 13 December 1860)

Wreck Master: Captain William Alfred Kemp and 13 crew of the *Desdomonia*, of Harbour Island. **And**
Captain: Elias Cleare and 13 crew of the *Splendid* of Harbour Island
Captain: William Adams of the *Annie Sophia*, (owned by H H Saunders)
Captain: John McFleming of the *Star*,
Captain: Henry Sweeting of the *A Canale* of Harbour Island.
Captain: Azaiah Curry of the *Galvanic* of Harbour Island.
Captain: John Thomas Roberts and 16 crew of the *Lady Bannerman* cleared Green Turtle Cay.
Captain: John Tedder and 13 crew of *Defiance* of Harbour Island

Wreck of the *Charles Coker* (Vice Admiralty Records 14 December 1860)

Wreck Master: Captain William Henry Sweeting of *Magnet* of Harbour Island. **And**
Captain: Joseph Saunders and 15 crew of the *Clyde* of Harbour Island
Captain: Robert Henry Saunders and 9 crew of the *Mary Elizabeth* cleared Green Turtle Cay
Captain: Thomas Evans of the *C J Marshall*

Wreck of the *Conquest* (Vice Admiralty Records 13 December 1865)

Wreck Master: Captain James Curry of the *Mary Jane* of Harbour Island. **Owner:** John Clear.
Crew: John T Albury (Mate), Nicholas Sweeting, William Roberts, John Kemp, Joseph Brady, John Tedder, Joseph Thompson, Joseph Cash,
Extra Crew: John Watkins, Samuel Johnson, Benjamin Thompson, Thomas Palmer, Thomas Cleare, Joseph Kemp, Thomas Kemp. **And**
Captain: William H A Roberts of the *Ventrosa* of Harbour Island. **Owner:** James Roberts
Crew: Frederick Higgs (Cook), James A Roberts, Joseph H Roberts, William Ranger, Amos Sweeting, Thomas Sweeting, John Kemp, John H Bethel, George Sweeting, George Saunders, John Ranger, John Thompson, Robert H Cleare, William A Kemp, Thomas S J Higgs, Henry Cleare, Peter Cleare, Thomas Albury, George A Kelly, Albert Albury. **And**

Captain and owner: George Henry Pearce and 22 crew of *Dart* of Harbour Island. **And**
Captain: Richard E Roberts of *Goodwill,* of Harbour Island. **Owner:** Samuel Johnson.
Captain: William Albury of *Mary & Susan* of Harbour Island **Owner:** William Henry Cleare.
Crew: Jacob Parks, John Adams, Peter Dixon, Wens Cambridge, Henry Johnson, Robert Culbert, George Ingraham, Jeremiah Black, William Albury, Robert Cash, John Cash, Joseph A Roberts, Samuel Johnson, Alexander Saunders, Benjamin Sweeting, Joseph Saunders, Jeremiah Johnson, John Pinder, John Sands, Moses Johnson, Jacob Butler, John T Thompson, Thomas Higgs, Timothy Wood, William Brown, Daniel Hudson, William Sego. **And**
Captain: Henry E Kelly of the *Elyn,* of Harbour Island.
Crew: Peter Saunders, London Cash, David Albury, Daniel Sawyer, Stephen Saunders, Missick Cleare, Richard Roberts, Benjamin Johnson, Abraham Thompson. **And**
Captain: Charles P Johnson of the *George Eneas,* of Harbour Island.
Captain: William J Munro of the *Nina* of Harbour Island
Captain: George Lightbourne of the *Warley,* of Harbour Island.

Appendix 14

House of Assembley Representatives for Harbour Island and Eleuthera

Year	Harbour Island	Eleuthera
1729	John Thompson Sr, John Thompson Jr, John Roberts, Seaborn Pinder,	
Pre 1734	Sam Flavell, Robert Archibald (deceased)	
1734	John Collemore, William Spatches	
1741	Benjamin Saunders	Nicholas Rowland, Richard Thompson
1762	Thomas Wilson, Ebenezer Love, Nathaniel Harrison, Richard Sweeting	
1766	Clement Hudson, James Sturrup, William Beake, Richard Sweeting	Ebenezer Love, Daniel Sturrup, John Kemp Sr, Charles Walker
1767	Ebenezer Love, William Beake, James Sturrup, Daniel Sturrup	Nathaniel Harrison, Richard Lake, John Kemp Sr, Downham Newton
1768	Nathaniel Harrison, Abraham Pratt, John Kemp Sr, Joseph Evans Sr	Downham Newton, Joseph Thompson, Edward Turner, Richard Sweeting
1770	Nathaniel Harrison, Abraham Pratt, John Kemp Sr, Thomas Wilson	Joseph Thompson, Richard Sweeting, Joseph Gordon, William Farr
1773	Abraham Pratt, Daniel Sturrup, James Sturrup, James Gould	Ridley Pinder, Rush Tucker, John Harrod, Joseph Thompson
1779	Samuel Higgs, Rush Tucker, Ridley Pinder, William Farr	William Spatches, John Kemp, Richard Sweeting, Joseph Saunders
1780	Samuel Higgs, Ridley Pinder, John Miller, Robert Bell	William Spatches, John Kemp, Joseph Saunders, George Dorsett
1784	Thomas Johnson, Samuel Higgs, Robt Thompson Henzell	Ridley Pinder, William Farr Sr, Robert Bell, John Petty
1785	Samuel Higgs, Robert Rumer, John Christie	John Kemp, John Petty, Robert Bell
1787	Samuel Higgs, Robert Rumer, Robert Thompson Henzell	
1789		John Petty (seat vacated), John Kemp (deceased) Alex Muray, James Brisbane, Michael Grant
1794	Robert Rumer, Anthony Roxburgh, Thomas Darrell	John O'Halloran, James Kelly, Samuel Mackey
1795	John Ferguson, John Carmichael, Richard Sweeting > Thomas Thompson 98,	John O'Halloran, James Kelly, Samuel Mackey
1796	George Gray	Henry Tucker
1801	John Ferguson, Thomas Thompson, Robert Duncombe	Samuel Mackey, James Kelly, Henry Tucker
1801	Edward Shearman, James Armbrister, Frederick Fine	Tidderman Carr, Henry Wood, Freeman Johnson
1802	Robert Duncombe, James Kelly, Edward Shearman,	Freeman Johnson, Tidderman Carr;Sam Williams
1803	Robert Duncombe > Wm Robt Edgecombe, Edward Shearman > Richard Meeres,	
1804	William Edgecombe, James Kelly, James Dunshee	Freeman Johnson, Tidderman Carr, Brisbane Williams
1805	William Edgecombe, Richard Curry, James Dunshee	Thomas Johnson, Tidderman Carr, Brisbane Williams
1807	Richard Curry, Christopher Fisher	

302

1808	Wm Robt Edgecombe, John Bootle, George Butler > Charles Russell 1810	
1813	George Saunders, Charles Russell (deceased)	
1814	George Hawkins, Walter Finlay, James Armbrister > Elias J Solomon	
1815	George Hawkins, John Bootle	
1817	George Hawkins > Henry Greenslade, Robert Butler, Robert W Elliot	
1819	Joseph Thompson, Robert Elliot, Robert Butler	
1832	Henry Greenslade, John Saunders > Wm R B Sands, Henry Adderley	
1836	Henry Greenslade, Wm R B Sands, James Malcolm	
1837	Henry Greenslade, James Malcolm, John E Meadows = Speaker of House	
1838	Henry Greenslade, James Malcolm, John E Meadows = Speaker of House	
1839	Joseph Cleare, Wm Weech, Lionel Fitzgerald	
1843	John Saunders, Wm Weech, Lionel Fitzgerald	
1848	Vesey Munnings, Francis Eve, Anthony Eneas	
1849	Vesey Munnings, Anthony Eneas, Wn H Sands	
1853	Henry R Saunders, Robert H Whitehead	
1855	Thomas Moore, HR Saunders, RH Whitehead	Tidderman Carr
1861	Robert H Sawyer, Bruce L Burnside, Manuel Menendez	
1868	George W Higgs, M Menendez, James A Higgs	
1875	J S Darling, J S Culbert, H E Moseley	Wm I P Johnson,Joseph Thompson
1882	John S Darling, Joseph S Johnson, T N G Cleare	Wm I P Johnson
1889	Joseph S Johnson, Gilbert A Albury > T N G Cleare 1895, John S Darling	Wm A C Johnson, Wm Wayde Rigby
1896	W C B Johnson, O F Pritchard, W W Lightbourne	William I P Johnson, Samuel Mackey, Joseph S Johnson
1903	W C B Johnson, E P L Solomon, G H Johnson	Wm Farrington
1910	W C B Johnson, E P L Solomon, G H Johnson	Wm R B Sands, Conrad Duncome, M Stuart
1921	W C B Johnson, T A V Munro > R T Symonette 1925, G H Johnson	Wm R B Sands, Wm Stuart, Donald MacIntyre
1928	W C B Johnson, R T Symonette, G H Johnson > Allan H Kelly 1931	Copeland Adderley, Thomas Winder, John I Burnside
1936	W C B Johnson, H N Chipman, R R Farrington	not stated
1942	R R Farrington, A R Braynen, Harry P Sands	
		J D Harris, J J R Kemp, Abraham J Holmes
		O D Malcolm, L T Sands, James W Culmer
		O D Malcolm, L T Sands, James W Culmer
		O D Malcolm, C J Sands, James W Culmer
		W C B Johnson, O D Malcolm, James W Culmer
		O D Malcolm, James W Culmer, H C F Sturrup
		James W Culmer, H G Malcolm, H C F Sturrup
		James W Culmer, H G Malcolm, J J Culmer
		R W Sawyer, Bruce S Bethel, E H Burnside
		R W Sawyer, O H Curry, A H Pritchard
		R W Sawyer, O H Curry > A H Pritchard 1939, G W K Roberts
		R W Sawyer, G W K Roberts, Asa H Pritchard

Index

1806 hurricane 76, 203, 206, 207

Abaco 5, 75–6, 158
Africans *see* liberated Africans
Africa's Hope 238–40
agriculture 64–6, 123 *see also* exports; Harbour Island Agricultural Exhibition
air travel 253–4, 260, 261, 263
Albury, Chatham 163
Albury, Hadazzah 217–18, 220
Albury, W. E. 7
amelioration reforms 100
America *see* United States
American Revolutionary War 58, 69–71
Anglicanism 10–11, 179–82, 184, 185–6
apprenticeship system 101–2, 103–4, 142
army 82–3, 257

Bahamas
 colonisation 9–12
 defences 78
 navigation difficulties 1–2, 43, 154–5
 parish system 181
 population 273
Bahamas Airways 260, 261
baptism 38, 100
Baptists 188
Barracks Hill 82–3
bazaars 230
Beatrice (ship) 125–6, 145–7

Bermuda 10, 18–19
blacks 18–19, 66, 162–3 *see also* slaves
Blanco, Augustin 36–7, 45, 49
Board of Education Act (1841) 191
boat building 34, 124, 132–6, 137–41, 143–9
 decline 150–2
 mail-boats 151
 motor boats 149–50
 and wrecking 158
Briland *see* Harbour Island
Briland dialect 6
British influence 229–30
Butler, Captain 13, 14, 21
Butler, Frances 199

canning industry 121–2
Catholics 189–90
celebrities 269–70
Charles Coker (ship) 300
Charles Town 26, 27
children 38, 99
Christmas celebrations 240
Church of England in the Bahamas 179 *see also* Anglicanism
Church of God 190–1
Civil War *see* English Civil War
Claraco y Sanz, Antonio 55–8, 60, 62
Cleare, Elias 163
climate 3, 82–3
Cobb, Mortimore H. 257
Cockram, John 1–2, 29, 30, 34-5, 47, 52, 281
Colebrooke, governor 103, 185

colonisation 9–16, 25 *see also* settlements
commonage 4–5, 64–7, 259–60, 284–5
Commonwealth Day 235
Company of Adventurers for the Plantation of the Islands of Eleutheria *see* Eleutheran Adventurers
Conquest (ship) 174, 300–1
Consolidated Slave Act (1797) 93
consortships 159–60, 299
contract labour 258–9
corruption 77, 170-3, 183–4, 196
cotton industry 93
cricket 241–3
criminals 18, 170–3
Current 21, 36

Dart (ship) 248–9
Deveaux, Andrew 55–8, 60–1, 63, 64
dialect, Briland 6
discrimination 102, 105-6, 184, 188
divers 163, 166
domestic slaves 96–7
Duncombe, William Kelsall 185–6
Dunmore, John Murray, earl of 73–5, 77–80
Dunmore Town 2, 24–5, 74–5, 102–3, 162, 251–2
Dunmore Town Sugar Company 119, 121

economy 60, 172–3, 175, 176
education 182–3, 184–5, 191–4
Education Act (1795) 183
elections 196–8
electricity 265–6
Eleuthera
   links with Bermuda 18–19
   links with Harbour Island 4–5
   pineapple cultivation 2
   slaves 93–4, 95
   Spanish occupation 59–60
Eleutheran Adventurers 9, 12–16
   articles and orders 12

factions 13–14
first landfall 14–16
emancipation 77–8, 101–2, 184, 228
Emancipation Day 103–4, 229, 230, 233
Empire Day 233–5
Endion (ship) 149, 248, 250
English Civil War, effect on colonies 10–11, 16
Equator (ship) 132, 144
exports 76, 110, 113–14, 115–17, 119–21

families 20, 38–9, 95–6
field slaves 97–8
firefighting 266
fishing 124–5, 244–5, 257, 262
France, attacks on Bahamas 28–9
free blacks *see* blacks
freedom 12, 13 *see also* blacks; emancipation; slaves
Friendly Societies 185, 231–2

Gallows Bay 15
garbage disposal 266–77
Glass Window Incident (1872) 209–14
Gordon, William, Rev. 181, 183–4
government
   corruption 77, 78, 196
   Eleutheran Adventurers 12
   Loyalists 72–3
   and piracy 43
   Proprietary Governors 25–6
   resistance to 30–1
Government Dock 261–2
Governor's Bay 15–16, 26
Great Bahama Hurricane (1866) 208–9
Green Turtle Cay 76–7

Harbour Island
   climate 82–3
   culture 227–46
   defences 35, 36, 47, 74, 88
   geographical features 1–3

Harbour Island (*continued*)
  improvements to harbour 250–1
  links with Abaco 5
  links with Eleuthera 4–5
  Loyalists 72, 75–6
  population 274–80
  and recapture of Nassau 55, 56, 283
  relations with pirates 47–8
  schools 184, 190–1, 194, 195
  slaves 93–7, 98–9, 100–2
  Spanish occupation 59–60
  tourism 248–57, 259–62, 264–70
  trade 5–6, 109–17, 295–7
Harbour Island Agricultural
  Exhibition 236–7, 250
Harbour Island Commonage
  Development Association 66
Harbour Island Preserving Company
  121
'haul in the harbour' 244–5
health 82–3, 99, 248
Holderites *see* Plymouth Brethren
holidays 230
Hornigold, Benjamin 48–9, 52, 281
Hurricane Andrew 222–5
hurricanes 203–9, 214–17, 221–5
  economic effects 76
  prediction 206, 208

Incorporated Society for the
  Conversion, Religious
  Instruction and Education of the
  Negroes 181–2

Johnson, Alonzo 213–14
Johnson, Joseph S. 121–2
Johnson, William Christopher Barnet
  199–200
Junkanoo parade 240
justice 18, 77, 183-4, 195–6
  King George's pardon 46, 51

Key West, immigration 111

land prices 259

land tenure 25, 73, 74, 78
  commonage 4–5, 64–7, 259–60,
    284–5
Larco, Juan de 26
launching 143–4, 147–8
legislation 64–6, 100–1, 161, 196–7
liberated Africans 104, 172, 185, 231,
    293–4 *see also* slaves
lighthouses 175
Local Government Act (1996) 196
Lowe, Matthew 'Mott' 163
Loyalists 71–3, 75–6, 84
lumber trade 125–6

mail service 151, 248
maps 1-2, 3–4, 24
Margaret Ann (ship) 167
mariner slaves 93, 98, 162–3
marriage 100–1, 227–8
Mary Beatrice (ship) 148
Mary Leve (ship) 300
McKinney, E. H. 250–2, 253
Melrose (ship) 145
Memories of Briland 7
Methodists 182, 186–8, 189, 228,
    238–40
  political influence 197–8
  and segregation 105–6
  and slave marriage 100–1
Midas (ship) 86, 87–90
migrants 111, 127, 258–9, 286–8
militia 35
missionaries 179–82, 227–8
and slave marriage 100–1
Missionary Day 238–40
Moss, Richard 183–5
Mother's Club 199
motor boats 149–50
Mount Olivet Baptist Church 188

names 20, 38
Nassau
  Loyalists 71
  piracy 27–8, 49–50

recapture 55–8, 60–4
  salvage auctions 158–9
  Spanish invasion 36, 58–60
navigation routes 1–2, 9
Negro Education Grant 184
New Providence 82–3, 93, 94–5
Northeast Providence Channel 85–6, 88, 155

Orient (ship) 144
Out Islands Commissioners Act (1908) 196

parish system 181
patriotism 228, 229–30
Phenney, governor 30–1
pineapple industry 2, 4–5, 112–14, 115–17, 121–2
piracy 42–53
  ethos 44–5
  Golden Age 42
  Harbour Island 47–8, 50
  King George's pardon 46, 51, 281–2
  Nassau 27–8, 49–50
  Queen Anne's War 45
  Red Sea men 43
  and relations with Spain 46
  suppression 29–30, 50–3
Plymouth Brethren 188–9
politics 196–200
population 273, 289–90
  decline 126–7
  early settlers 18, 22
  effect of Spanish attacks 37–9
  Harbour Island 274–80
  Loyalist migrants 71–3, 75–6
  racial composition 37, 71, 92–4
ports of entry 112
poverty 118–19, 230–1
Preacher's Cave 15, 16
priests, training of 186
privateers 44–5, 63, 84–6, 87–90, 136
Prohibition 126
Proprietary Government 25–6

Providence 25, 27
punishment 98–9
Puritan settlements, location 15–16
Puritanism 10–11, 17–18, 179

Queen Anne's War 45

race
  master-apprentice relations 104
  and population 37, 71, 92–4
  segregation 102, 105–6, 188
raids 26–9, 36–7
Ranger, R. H. 125
Red Cross 236
Red Sea men 43
regattas 235, 237–8
religion 179–82, 184–91
  effect on colonies 10–11
  freedom of worship 12
  and politics 197–8
Rhine (ship) 163, 166
Richardson, Richard 155
Roberts, Eddie Jinks 143, 144, 149
Roberts, G. W. K. 151–2
Roberts, Sonny Jenks 143, 144
Rogers, Woodes 29–30, 36, 51–3
Roman Catholics 189–90
Royal Air Force 257–8
Royal Island 87
Royalists 16 see also Loyalists
Rumer, Robert 57–8, 60, 61, 62–3

sailing ships 1–2, 132–6, 137–41, 143–9
salvage auctions 158–9, 171 see also wrecking
Saunders, Isaac 163, 166
Savannah Island see Windermere Island
Savannah Sound 21
Sawyer, Henry 'BoHengy' 143, 149
Sayle, William 11, 13–14, 18, 19
schools 185, 191–4
schooners 125–6, 137, 141
scuba diving 265

sealing 32
segregation 102, 105–6, 188
settlements *see also* colonisation
   Puritan 15–16
   spread of 20–1, 34, 75–6
   support of 17–18
shipbuilding *see* boat building
sisal cultivation 122
Sisters of Charity 190
slaves 37, 39, 71, 92–106, 291–2 *see also* race
   emancipation 77–8
   fertility 99
   occupation 93, 96–8
   punishment 98–9
   socio-economic conditions 94
sloops 137
smack boats 124–5
smuggling 70–1, 110–11, 126, 141–2
Spain
   attacks on Bahamas 26–9, 36–7, 53
   attitudes to piracy 46
   invasion of Nassau 58–60
Spanish Wells 21–2
St Benedict's School 194
St John's Church 189, 209
St John's Parish 179–80, 181
St Patrick's Parish 181
St Vincent's Academy 194
St Vincent's Convent 190
Stillwell, Daniel 46
street lighting 255
Stroude, Elizabeth 28
sugar industry 119, 121

telecommunications 253, 267
Thompson, Alexander 86, 87–90
timber industry 34, 158
tornadoes 217–21
tourism 6, 149, 248–57, 259–62, 264–70
trade 34–5, 110, 125–6, 175 *see also* exports
   effects of war 69–71, 85–6
   Eleuthera 295–7

growth 160
Harbour Island 5–6, 109–17, 295–7
Trott, Nicholas, governor 43
truck-and-credit system 118–19
turtling 32–4
Turton, William 182

United Society for the Propagation of the Gospel *see* USPG
United States, attacks on Bahamas 36, 58–60, 85–90
USPG 179–80
utilities 251–2, 265–6

Vallonia (ship) 300
Vane, Charles 52, 281
Versailles, Treaty of (1783) 63, 71
Victoria, Queen 233

Walker, Thomas, judge 28
War of 1812 83–90
wars *see also* raids
   American Revolution 58, 69–71
   English Civil War 10–11, 16
   Queen Anne's War 45
   War of 1812 83–90
   World War II 235–6
water supply 251–2, 266
whaling 32
William (ship) 13, 19
Winder, Thomas Ripley 102
Windermere Island 14
Windsor, Duke and Duchess 256, 257
women's cricket 241–2
World War II 235–6
wrecking 79, 141, 142, 154–77, 300–1
   consortships 159–60, 299
   criminal activities 170–3
   economic effect 172–3, 175, 176
   Harbour Island 31–2
   licences 161, 298–9
   rescues 104, 172
   salvage auctions 158–9
   treasure 155, 158
wreckmasters 154